# Managing Organizations in a Global Economy
## An Intercultural Perspective

**John Saee**
*IÉSEG School of Management*
*Lille, France*

**THOMSON**

**SOUTH-WESTERN**

Australia · Canada · Mexico · Singapore · Spain · United Kingdom · United States

**Managing Organizations in a Global Economy: An Intercultural Perspective**

John Saee

| | | |
|---|---|---|
| **VP/Editorial Director:**<br>Jack W. Calhoun | **Marketing Manager:**<br>Jacquelyn Carrillo | **Design Project Manager:**<br>Justin Klefeker |
| **VP/Editor-in-Chief:**<br>Michael P. Roche | **Production Editor:**<br>Starratt E. Alexander | **Production House:**<br>Electro-Publishing, Inc. |
| **Publisher:**<br>Melissa S. Acuña | **Manufacturing Coordinator:**<br>Rhonda Utley | **Cover and Internal Designer:**<br>Justin Klefeker |
| **Executive Editor:**<br>John Szilagyi | **Media Developmental Editor:**<br>Kristen Meere | **Cover Images:**<br>© The Stock Illustration Source - Bob Commander, Illustrator |
| **Developmental Editor:**<br>Monica Ohlinger,<br>Ohlinger Publishing Services | **Media Production Editor:**<br>Karen L. Schaffer | **Printer:**<br>Thomson-West<br>Eagan, Minnesota |

# Dedication

This book is dedicated to my parents with love.

# Preface

At the dawn of the third millennium, the most persistent theme that is dramatically transforming national economies and social relations around the world with far-reaching implications for contemporary organizations is the notion of globalization. As a consequence, managers operating within the global economy face formidable challenges. These challenges emanate from differing political, social, legal, technological, economic, and more importantly, cross-cultural dimensions within which business activities worldwide are inherently predicated.

Throughout an academic career in Australia and Europe, I have found a pronounced need for a textbook that would comprehensively address wide-ranging contemporary issues and challenges confronting modern management of enterprises in the global economy. This need was also corroborated by widespread feedback based on surveys that I received from students in both undergraduate and MBA classes over the years. Therefore, I was strongly motivated to write a textbook capable of illuminating contemporary managerial issues and challenges in a systematic manner while providing the stimulus for critical debates and practical applications by academic and professional business communities.

In recognition of the growing importance of cultural diversity in most modern organizations around the world in terms of clientele, human resources, and ownership, this book is designed to:

- Provide a comprehensive theme throughout for the development of effective intercultural communication, which has been exalted in many academic and professional communities as the key indicator of managerial competence within the global economy.

- Provide the latest conceptual tools and practical applications on aspects of management of cross-cultural dimensions and hence international organizational behavior.

- Draw on a spectrum of interdisciplinary fields of study that are essential for a meaningful understanding of management of contemporary organizations within the global economy including cultural anthropology, economics, psychology, sociology, philosophy, social psychology, management, and communication.

- Integrate the wide-ranging themes of cross-cultural dimensions in a comprehensive manner that is designed to equip both existing managers and aspiring managers (such as business students) with a contemporary cross-cultural knowledge of management coupled with intercultural competence needed to be effective in managing enterprises in the 21st century.

- Enrich students' knowledge with theoretical discussions of wide-ranging themes in a balanced fashion followed by real-life examples based on the latest research with implications for managerial functions and strategies.

- Provide critical discussion questions and experiential applications as well as Internet applications, a vital knowledge for managers in a global economy.

- Provide additional pedagogical tools throughout the text including exhibits and examples designed to further clarify the issues raised.

- Cater to the intellectual and professional needs of postgraduate students including MBAs and Master of International Business, as well as undergraduate business students who may be interested in furthering their knowledge in academic areas such as international management, comparative and cross-cultural management, and international organizational behavior.

- Be of interest to executives of modern organizations who may want to deepen their knowledge of world-cultures and a global mindset, which are essential indicators for managerial competence within the contemporary global economy.

The book discusses the key themes of cross-cultural and global management within 15 chapters. Each chapter begins with a set of learning objectives that foretell issues under discussion and guide the reader. Each chapter also addresses practical applications of the theories and issues raised for management.

Chapter 1, *Globalization*, critically examines the issues of globalization of trade and national economies and their impact on business practices around the world. The merits and drawbacks of globalization, which have considerable implications for management of enterprises in the 21st century, are provided. Managers operating within the global economy face the major challenge of a systematic understanding of cross-cultural dimensions within which business activities worldwide are inherently predicated. To succeed strategically, these international managers need to develop a high-level understanding of cross-cultural dimensions so that they can formulate appropriate business strategies based on these understandings.

Chapter 2, *Understanding Cross-Cultural Management Dimensions*, discusses the notion that contemporary management principles and theories mainly developed in the west cannot be universally applied across all nations. This chapter focuses on many research findings that justify the notion that contemporary managers should integrate and synthesize differences arising from cross-cultural dimensions as part of their viable managerial strategy.

Chapter 3, *Worldview and Religion*, discusses world views representing different religions and socio-cultural systems that have considerable implications for effective management and business strategy throughout the world.

Given the fact that communication is central to human life in terms of sharing ideas and feelings, Chapter 4, *Communication and Culture*, examines the inextricable link between communication and culture with important implications for managerial communications across cultures in terms of managerial intercultural communication competence.

Chapter 5, *Nonverbal Communication across Cultures*, provides a detailed discussion on various aspects of nonverbal communication across cultural frontiers. It further provides practical knowledge on how to read and understand nonverbal communication across cultures deemed as critical competency in day-to-day intercultural interactions including international business negotiations and managing cultural diversity.

Chapter 6, *Theoretical Perspectives on Intercultural Communication*, explores in some detail, sophisticated theories of intercultural communication originally pioneered by scholars in fields of study including communication; psychology; and sociology that have much wider philosophical and educational values for leaders and management overall involved in intercultural encounters at all levels.

Chapter 7, *Organizational Culture*, defines organizational culture and further deals with the relationship between culture and the success of an organization. An international perspective on how culture influences organizational performance is provided.

Chapter 8, *Leadership across Cultures*, deals with different strategies and styles of leadership that prevail across cultures and have important implications for international management.

Chapter 9, *Motivating across Cultures*, discusses different theories of motivation and guidelines for diagnosing and inspiring motivation within members of international organizations.

Chapter 10, *Negotiating across Cultural Frontiers*, describes different types and styles of negotiations prevalent across the world. It further provides general guidelines on how to successfully carry out international negotiations.

Chapter 11, *Conflict and Conflict Resolution across Cultural Frontiers*, provides a systematic explanation and analysis of conflict and conflict resolution techniques within an organizational setting involving cultural diversity.

In Chapter 12, *Ethics across Cultures*, ethical dimensions present in different cultures are examined. The chapter also delves into philosophical schools of thought on ethics with particular reference to international business.

Chapter 13, *International Human Resource Management*, examines different strategies and practices associated with international human resource management.

Chapter 14, *International Project Management*, explains the dynamics of international project management and further identifies key factors that are crucial in the context of effective international project management.

Chapter 15, *Managerial Excellence in Global Management*, provides managerial best practice based on a synthesis of research studies conducted internationally. Practicing managers will in turn derive considerable benefits through effective implementation within their organizational dimensions.

## Supplements

The book is supported by a Web site: http://saee.swlearning.com. The site includes a complete set of PowerPoint slides for each chapter that may be downloaded from the site and Internet activities.

## Acknowledgements

I would like to record my deep appreciation and thanks to numerous people for rendering assistance and support during the compilation of this book including Olga Muzychenko, John Szilagyi, Monica Ohlinger, Diane Durkee, James Reidel, Starratt Alexander, Shirley Saunders, Michael Kaye, Willem A. Hamel, Bruce Roberts, Dennis Ottley, James Liberty, Henri Jolles, Heinz Klandt, Jean-Philippe Ammeux, Daniel Buyl and Jacques Doutté.

Furthermore, I am grateful to my academic colleagues from around the world whose scholarly writings and ideas have greatly enriched my life over the years.

Finally, I am grateful to my numerous students from around the world who have provided major intellectual stimuli and challenges throughout my academic career by actively participating in the critical discussions of major organizational issues of national and international significance in my postgraduate and undergraduate classes including, MBA, MIB, and BBA held in Australia, Asia, the United States, and Europe, including United Kingdom, Romania, Germany, and France.

*John Saee*

# About the Author

John Saee is currently the Chair Professor of International Business, Corporate Strategy and Management and the Academic Director of the M.B.A. and M.I.B. post graduate degree programs at Institut Economie Scientifique et de Gestion (IESEG School of Management, Lille, France).

Dr. Saee received a Ph.D. from the University of Technology, Sydney, a Master of Commerce from the University of New South Wales, and a B.A. from Flinders University, South Australia. He is an Associate Fellow of the Australian Institute of Management and a member of the Academy of International Business, Australian and New Zealand Academy of Management, International Management Development Association, and Association of Management and International Association of Management.

Dr. Saee has authored more than ninety publications and refereed international conference proceedings in Australia, Europe, Asia, and the United States. He was appointed Chairperson of Global Divisions, Association of Management and International Association of Management, and Editor-in-Chief of the International Association of Management Journal. Dr. Saee recently received an excellence award from the Romanian American University, Bucharest, for outstanding contributions related to scientific knowledge and the internationalization of education and culture.

# Brief Contents

# Contents

# Chapter 1

## *Globalization*

---

*After reading this chapter, you should be able to:*

- *Understand the phenomenon of globalization.*

- *Understand the historical dimensions of globalization.*

- *Describe theories of international trade.*

- *Understand the motivations behind a firm's globalization strategy.*

- *Understand the main catalysts for globalization.*

- *Understand advantages and disadvantages of globalization.*

- *Understand the implications of globalization for contemporary managers.*

*There is a tide [. . .] which, taken at the flood, leads on to fortune. On such a sea we are afloat. And we must take the current when it serves or lose our venture.*

—William Shakespeare. Julius Caesar

*When the world was big, we could think small. Now that the world is small, we have to think "big."*

—Modern proverb

# GLOBALIZATION: AN OVERVIEW

There has been a sea of change in the world economy with far-reaching consequences for all aspects of human civilization—and especially for managers whose companies and corporations already are or plan to be involved in business ventures that interact beyond their domestic environment. The phenomenon of globalization largely precipitated this dramatic transformation. In other words, we are moving progressively further from a world in which national economies are relatively isolated from each other because of distance and the different time zones, languages, cultures, government regulations, business systems, and other similar barriers to cross-border trade and investment. We are moving toward a world in which national economies are merging into an interdependent global economic system, commonly referred to as globalization (Hill 2000, 4).

The transformation now taking place in the global economy is unprecedented. The increasing availability of global capital, coupled with advances in computing and communications technology, is serving to speed up the processes of globalization. Concurrently, the barriers to globalization are increasingly disappearing in most countries of the world (Cullen 1999). Globalization has accelerated the process of increasing interconnectedness between societies. More than ever, events in one part of the world have a direct effect on peoples and societies far away. A globalized world is one in which political, economic, cultural, and social events become more and more interconnected, and also one in which they have a wider impact (Baylis & Smith 1997).

This chapter provides a conceptual analysis of globalization from both a historical and contemporary perspective. At the same time, however, differing theoretical paradigms underlying globalization are critically discussed, including Mercantilism; Absolute Advantage Theory; Theory of Comparative Advantage; Factors Proportions Trade Theory; International Investment and Product Life Cycle Theory; Porter's Competitive Advantage of Nations; and Theory of International Investment. An explanation of why firms are motivated to go global is also given as well as the main catalysts for globalization at a macro level of analysis. Finally, the advantages and disadvantages of globalization are critically examined, with implications for national economies and organizations intent upon internationalizing their products, services, and operations.

But what do we mean by *globalization*? In the following sections, we learn the ways in which globalization is defined.

# GLOBALIZATION DEFINED

The phenomenon of globalization means different things to different people. A review of literature suggests differing ways of looking at this phenomenon. For example, viewed purely from an economic standpoint, globalization is conceived as a process of increasing involvement in international business operations (Welch & Luostan 1999). Thus, globalization is a worldwide business trend for expanding beyond domestic boundaries. This, in turn, creates an interconnected world economy in which companies do their business and compete with each other anywhere in the world, regardless of national boundaries (Cullen 1999). Within this economic interpretation of globalization, nations and their home firms elect to trade with each other in their attempts to increase wealth and economic prosperity for their nations, firms, and ultimately their citizens.

The sociological view of globalization defines it as a more pervasive force throughout the world. That is, globalization occurs when *the constraints of geography on social and cultural arrangements recede as people around the world become increasingly aware that they are receding* (Waters 1995)

Underlying these definitions is the belief that technological innovations in areas such as communications and transport have been the driving force behind the breaking down of national and international barriers, including vast geographical distances and the presence of myriad linguistic and cultural groupings across the world. In other words, the world increasingly becomes a "Global Village."

A more critical view of globalization, based on Marxist philosophy, argues that globalization is what people in the Third World have already experienced for several centuries. It is called *colonization.* Proponents of this school of thought maintain that capitalist Western countries exploit raw materials and cheap labor found in the Third World countries at the enormous expense of the peoples of the Third World countries (Banarjee and Linstead 2001). Such a point of view begs the question: Is globalization of businesses a recent development in human history?

## HISTORICAL ORIGINS OF GLOBALIZATION

Broadly speaking, there is a common misconception in various academic and professional circles that globalization, which is rapidly transforming the landscape of the world economy, is a "new" phenomenon. However, this claim of globalization being a "new" phenomenon in human history is not justified in the light of historical evidence. Even before there was the colonialism that Karl Marx and his followers addressed, human societies have always traded among themselves for thousands of years.

Phoenician, Persian, Egyptian, Greek, and Roman civilizations were evidently involved in trade and commerce, though in a different scale in terms of reach and marketplaces. Throughout history, and particularly since the establishment of agriculture as a mode of production in human civilization, local marketplaces emerged in which farming communities traded their surplus produce in exchange for products and services in kind without the medium of money. This type of commercial activity was referred to as the *barter system.*

The growth of population and formation of cities gave rise to new social classes of petty bourgeois and mercantile classes who set out on a voyage across national and then international frontiers in their attempts to maximize the rate of return for their commercial activities. Archaeological evidence supports the notion that human society has always traded goods across great distances. A famous example for international trade are the ruins of cities that still mark the *Silk Road,* on which merchant caravans traversed from China through Afghanistan to the Middle East and Europe for the purpose of trading commodities.

Throughout history governments of many powerful countries often saw tremendous benefits in accessing strategically important raw materials for their growing kingdoms. Instead of conducting trade with the rulers of country in which these materials were found, however, in the contemporary mode of transaction then in practice, these governments chose large-scale violence in conquering other countries to access these vital raw materials. In many respects, it was a brutal form of international trade, which, from the vantage point of our own modern sensibilities, would be condemned as sheer exploitation and oppression.

A large-scale transactional form of international trade between producers, middlemen, and purchasers emerged in different marketplaces, both national and international, in the 18th century. This trend was observed in the 1780s by the English philosopher Jeremy Bentham, who coined the term "international" to describe the emerging reality of his day, namely, the rise of nation states and the cross-border transactions taking place between them (Baylis and Smith 1997).

# THE BEGINNING OF THE MODERN CONCEPT OF GLOBALIZATION

Globalization today describes a far more pervasive and deep phenomenon than has never existed before. Thousands of goods, services, and even ideas are produced globally, creating complex interconnections between states. A book, for example, can be written in Sydney, copyedited in the United States, typeset in India, printed in China, and then distributed globally via an international company like Amazon.com. The Internet has made global supply chain management, including manufacturing, distribution, and communication, simple and cheap.

According to some writers, the onset of interpreting what modern globalization is really begins in the mid-nineteenth century. Baylis and Smith (1997) discuss several precursors to the modern concept. First, it is argued that globalization has many features in common with the Theory of Modernization. Increasing industrialization brought into existence a whole new set of contacts between societies that changed the political, economic, and social processes that characterized the preindustrialized world. Thus, modernization is part of globalization (Modelski 1972).

Second, the Economic Growth Theory, originally developed by Rostow, advocated that economic growth followed a pattern in all economies as they went through industrialization. This implies that for any national economy to grow around the world, it has to adopt a free market economy, and it has to, like western developed economies, undergo different stages of economic development before it can reach its full potential namely, the status of a developed economy. What this has in common with globalization is that Rostow saw a clear pattern to economic development, one marked by stages that all economies would follow as they adopted capitalism (Baylis & Smith 1997).

Third, there have been notable similarities in the picture of the world painted by globalization theorists that have been drawn or influenced by the world portrayed in Marshall McLuhan's concept of the "global village." According to McLuhan (1989), advances in electronic communications resulted in a world in which we could see in real time events that were occurring in distant parts of the world. For McLuhan, the main effect of this development was that time and space became compressed to such an extent that everything loses its traditional "isolated" identity.

Fourth, globalization theory has several points in common with the controversial argument of Francis Fukuyama about the "end of history." Fukuyama's main claim was that the power of the economic market is resulting in liberal democracy replacing all other types of government (Fukuyama 1992).

Contemporary world globalization has led to the creation of large multinational enterprises. (This is another crucial dissimilarity between our notion of early or *proto*globalization and the modern concept of globalization. In the ancient world, large companies did not exist that could wield enormous political and economic powers.) Furthermore, these large enterprises have increasingly become powerful across different nations in terms of economic and political dimensions. Current statistics reveal that close to 52 percent of world resources are controlled and owned by multinational companies. At the same time, there are 63,000 multinational corporations with around 700,000 foreign affiliates in the world today (UNCTAD 2000). Furthermore, *Fortune* magazine provides a list of the "Global 500," companies that have enormous sales turnover and assets. For example, less than 30 countries in the world have a GDP that exceeds total annual revenues of *General Motors* (Ball & McCulloch, 1996). For the purpose of illustration, Exhibit 1-1 provides a listing of the world's top 25 multinational companies ranked in terms of their revenues globally.

| Exhibit 1-1 | The World's Top 25 Multinational Companies Ranked by Revenues, 2002 | |
|---|---|---|
| **Global 500 Rank** | **Company** | **Revenues (USD in millions)** |
| 1 | Wal-Mart Stores | $219,812.0 |
| 2 | Exxon Mobil | $191,581.0 |
| 3 | General Motors | $177,260.0 |
| 4 | BP | $174,218.0 |
| 5 | Ford Motor | $162,412.0 |
| 6 | Enron | $138,718.0 |
| 7 | Daimler Chrysler | $136,897.3 |
| 8 | Royal Dutch/Shell Group | $135,211.0 |
| 9 | General Electric | $125,913.0 |
| 10 | Toyota Motor | $120,814.4 |
| 11 | CitiGroup | $112,022.0 |
| 12 | Mitsubishi | $105,813.9 |
| 13 | Mitsui | $101,205.6 |
| 14 | Chevron Texaco | $99,699.0 |
| 15 | Total Fina Elf | $94,311.9 |
| 16 | Nippon Telegraph & Telephone | $93,424.8 |
| 17 | Itochu | $91,176.6 |
| 18 | Allianz | $85,929.2 |
| 19 | IBM | $85,866.0 |
| 20 | ING GROUP | $82,999.1 |
| 21 | Volkswagen | $79,287.3 |
| 22 | Siemens | $77,358.9 |
| 23 | Sumitomo | $77,140.1 |
| 24 | Philip Morris | $72,944.0 |
| 25 | Marubeni | $71,756.6 |

Given that globalization, or trade between nations, always existed and has since accelerated with each wave of technological advancement, the question arises: "Why do nations trade with each other in the first place?" The answer lies in a discussion of theories of international trade that explain the background and even a rationale for globalization in the modern sense.

# INTERNATIONAL TRADE THEORIES

There are a number of perspectives on why globalization of trade and investment occurs around the world. These perspectives are advanced to explain why nations and firms trade with each other.

*Mercantilism* is the term used by early economists to explain the justifying principle of a nation state's policy of international trade that existed from approximately 1550 to 1800. The central ideas behind mercantilism were predicated on the following characteristics:

- A country's wealth is measured by its holding of gold.
- Countries having no gold resources could accumulate gold by exporting more goods than they import.
- Governments should control foreign trade because individuals might trade gold for imports. The government was in a monopoly position to assure that only local products were purchased. In order to export more, governments established monopolies over their countries' trade, for example, by imposing trade restrictions on imports.

A mercantilist nation traded with other nations under the principle that it should encourage exports while discouraging imports. Only in this way, it was argued, could the nation increase its wealth in the form of gold. This economic doctrine was predicated on the premise of a zero-sum game, in which a gain by one nation entailed an equivalent loss by another. Although this doctrine was later discredited, it still remains an appealing international trade policy, even today, by the governments of such countries as South Korea, Taiwan, and China in terms of their strong emphasis on export-led national economies.

From the mercantilists, other sophisticated theoretical paradigms were developed over the years to provide alternative modes of conducting international trade and investment based on more cooperative modes of international trade that have given rise to globalization. An overview of the theories of international trade and investment can be categorized into five broad classifications dating from the end of the Age of Mercantilism (Czinkota & Ronkainen 1998).

## Classical Trade Theories

In the late eighteenth and early nineteenth centuries, the classical theories of international trade were postulated in the works of two important economists, that of Absolute Advantage in Adam Smith's *The Wealth of Nations* (1776) and Comparative Advantage in David Ricardo's *On the Principles of Political Economy and Taxation* (1819).

### Theory of Absolute Advantage

Contrary to the mercantilists' doctrine, Adam Smith argued that it is not accumulation of gold reserves by a nation that renders it rich or economically powerful and secure. Instead, a country can only be considered rich when its citizens are able to enjoy good income levels. Thus, the idea of per capita income level was engendered due to Smith. Moreover, Smith was highly critical of mercantilism for its shortsightedness in terms of creating winning and losing nations; one at the expense of the other. As a *proto*globalist, Smith argued for free, unregulated trade and a free market economy between trading nations. A nation, ideally, should specialize and trade only those goods in which it was seen to have the absolute advantage—that is, for being the most efficient. The surplus, for example, English coal, could be traded to obtain the products that England could not produce advantageously, pine tar, for example. Due to specialization, different countries can produce some goods more efficiently than others; and through this free market economy and free competition, each country achieves an economic efficiency that mutually benefits its trading partners and itself as it increases the output of the goods it is best suited to produce and sell. Consumers are the other winners in that they will be better off if they can buy foreign-made products that are priced more cheaply than domestic ones.

Smith also believed that a country's absolute advantage would either be natural or acquired. A *natural advantage* is the natural resources that a nation is endowed with in terms of absolute advantage. An example would be Australia, a country that is endowed with a relatively large land mass that could be cultivated for agricultural purposes. *Acquired advantage* is a nation's absolute advantage in terms of building a unique technology and/or having workers with a particular skill.

Since Adam Smith published *The Wealth of Nations,* the question has been asked, would it be advantageous for a nation to trade if it were not as efficient as any other in the production of a product? The answer to that important question still remains contentious and polemical among economists, academics, businesspeople, bureaucrats, labor leaders, and the like who base their economic worldview on ideological grounds ranging from conservative to liberal to Marxist.

### Theory of Comparative Advantage

In 1819, David Ricardo published *On the Principles of Political Economy and Taxation* in which he set forth his theory of Comparative Advantage. Ricardo argued that if a nation were less efficient in the production of two products, it could still gain from international trade. To do so, that nation had to specialize in the production of one of those products in which it enjoyed a comparative advantage over other countries.

One of the main limitations of Smith's and Ricardo's theories was that these early economists could only consider labor the only crucial variable in calculating the efficiency of production cost. As a result, no consideration was accorded to the possibility of producing the same goods with different combinations of factors such as capital and technology. In 1933, the Heckscher-Ohlin Theory, also referred to it as the Factor Proportions Trade Theory, which took these variables into account.

## Factor Proportions Trade Theory

The Heckscher-Ohlin theory postulated that trade between countries is caused by a difference in the endowments of their production factors such as land, labor, and capital. Factors in relative abundance are cheaper than factors in relative scarcity. Thus, each country should concentrate on producing the goods that require a large amount of the most abundant factor. For example, given differing endowment factors present in China,

Australia, and Germany, each nation should focus its production differently. Due to the abundance of labor, China should focus on labor-intensive goods; Australia should, in view of its large landmass, specialize in agriculture, and Germany should develop more capital-intensive goods.

Wassily Leontief, an economist, found in a landmark study that the United States, one of the most capital-intensive countries in the world, exported labor-intensive products. This is referred to in the literature as the *Leontief's paradox*. Economists explained that the paradox occurred because the United States exports technology-intensive products produced by highly skilled labor requiring a large capital investment to educate the workers and imports goods made with mature technology requiring capital-intensive mass production processes operated by unskilled labor.

There are exceptions to the Heckscher-Ohlin theory given the reality of production and markets. The theory failed to take account of transportation costs and consumers' varied taste preferences. Furthermore, the theory assumed that the same technology is available to all nations, when in fact the combination of factors used to produce the same product may vary across the nations.

## International Investment and Product Life-Cycle Theory

Raymond Vernon pioneered this theory in the 1960s. Its main idea is that production location for many products moves from one country to another depending on the stage in the product's life cycle. The product's life-cycle undergoes three distinct stages outlined in the following sections.

### Stage 1: New product

A firm develops and introduces an innovative product in response to a perceived need in the domestic market. Most outputs are sold in the domestic market, and thus exports are limited. However, demand for the new product begins to surface in other advanced countries. It is worth noting that the introduction of most innovative products has historically originated from the industrial countries. This pattern of innovation, however, has in recent decades changed as more new products are developed in the newly industrializing countries of Asia.

### Stage 2: Maturing Product

Demand for the product increases both domestically and internationally in a considerable way. The innovating company increases outputs to satisfy domestic and foreign demands.

Meanwhile, as more competition occurs due to rising market demands, competitors then enter the markets. Simultaneously, as demand grows in foreign markets, it requires the startup of foreign production.

### Stage 3: Standardized Product Stage

The market for the product stabilizes. Firms are pressured to reduce their manufacturing costs by shifting production facilities to the countries with low labor costs. As the competition intensifies in the global markets, innovating firms begin to standardize their products due to cost efficiency so that their products still remain price competitive.

The International Product Life-Cycle Theory states that products initially produced in industrial nations such as the United States and Western Europe are subsequently produced in less developed countries for local consumption and in time become the exports of these less-developed countries back to the countries where development and production of these products first originated. Current indications suggest that new product development is also "learned" in this relationship. For that reason, increasingly innovative products are now being developed in and marketed from Asia, Japan and South Korea being the most conspicuous examples.

## Porter's Competitive Advantage of Nations

Porter (1990) studied 100 firms in ten countries to learn that a nation's world prominence in an industry can be explained better than with the older economic theories of comparative advantage and factor endowment.

Porter's findings suggested that there were four major conditions, referred to as Porter's "diamond," that are the determinants of a company's—and, thereby, a nation's—competitive advantage. These are the firm's strategy, structure and rivalry; factor endowments; related and supporting industries; and demand conditions:

- *Strategy, Structure, and Rivalry.* These are the conditions governing the way companies are created, organized, and managed, and the nature of the domestic rivalry that impacts the firm's competitiveness. A firm that faces strong domestic competition is better able to face international competitors.

- *Factor Endowments.* A nation's position in factors of production such as skilled labor or infrastructure necessary to compete in a given industry are critical. These factors are either basic (natural resources, climate, location) or advanced (skilled labor, infrastructure, technological know-how). While both factor sets are important, having more of the advanced factors likely leads to a competitive advantage.

- *Relating and Supporting Industries.* The presence of supplier industries and related industries that are internationally competitive can spill over and contribute to other industries within a nation. Successful industries tend to be clustered in countries. Having world class manufacturers of semiconductor processing equipment within a nation's borders can lead to (and be a result of having) an internal, national competitive semiconductor industry.

- *Demand Conditions.* The nature of home demand for the industries' product or service influences the development of capabilities. Sophisticated and demanding customers pressure firms to be competitive.

Porter's work is considered a synthesis of earlier theories (Hill 2000, 13). However, it can be argued that there are still two major shortcomings inherent within the Porter's diamond and its postulates. First, it lacks an emphasis on culture, one which particularly supports a free enterprise spirit among its rising entrepreneurs; and secondly, it fails to mention the exigency for a stable government in order for a nation to be internationally competitive.

## Theory of International Investment

Dunning (1988) developed the Theory of International Investment by assuming that firms make decisions to enter markets across borders and seek direct involvement in international markets when the following three conditions are met:

- *Location advantage*, meaning that having business operations in a specific foreign location are more profitable for the firm.
- *Ownership advantage,* which suggests that a firm owns valuable tangible and/or intangible assets, such as a superior technology, a well known brand name, or economies of scale that create a domestic monopolistic advantage. The firm can use that advantage to penetrate foreign markets through foreign direct investment (Mahoney, et al., 1998).
- *Internalization advantage*, which means that by retaining information knowledge within the firm, while establishing multinational operations, a firm can internalize its capabilities and further minimize the risk of losing its technology.

A research study (Marquardt 1999) identified further sources of motivations that are in line with Dunning's theory—motivations that are behind the globalization by firms:

1. The ability to reduce costs via the economies of scope and scale that cross-border operations entail.
2. The ability to provide higher quality because of economies of scale and scope.
3. Enhanced customer awareness and loyalty due to the interaction of three forces: global availability, serviceability, and recognition.
4. Increased competitive leverage over competitors by global companies bringing resources of the worldwide network to bear on the competitive situation in individual countries.
5. Greater access to human skills and knowledge, because global companies can access the best people in the world, irrespective of nationality.
6. Increased access to financial resources and capital, including more frequent access to a variety of world stock exchanges.
7. Increased availability of information resources is often *the* competitive edge.
8. Longer and more diversified use of equipment and technology, which includes flexible manufacturing using Computer Assisted Design and Manufacturing (CAD/CAM). Communication technology is initially expensive, but has little or no maintenance costs after installation.
9. Broader customer base, so global companies do not rely too heavily on one market, such as the original domestic market.
10. Geographic flexibility gives choices regarding market and factory sites.
11. Bargaining power becomes enhanced because of the ability to switch production between a variety of manufacturing sites.

12. Cultural synergies mean that cultural diversity is seen as a major source of innovative ideas.

13. Enhanced image and reputation comes from public perception that global companies "must have" better products and services.

14. Opportunities for alliances and partnerships occur because greater choices are available.

15. Power as a global learning organization is closely tied in with the business goals of the company.

## MAIN CATALYSTS FOR GLOBALIZATION: A MACROLEVEL OF ANALYSIS

A number of catalysts stimulated globalization. Trade liberalization, that is, the historic sequence of deregulation in the world economy, came first. It led to an unprecedented expansion of international trade between 1950 and 1970. The liberalization of regimes for foreign direct investment (FDI) came next, which resulted in a surge of international investment that began in the late 1960s. The scale of regulatory changes in investment regimes in the 1990s is illustrated in Exhibit 1-2.

According to the recent statistics, over the period 1991 to 1994, 94 percent of the 1,035 changes worldwide in the laws governing foreign direct investment created a more favorable framework for FDI as shown in the Exhibit 1-2. Complementing the more welcoming national FDI regimes, the number of bilateral investment treaties—also concluded increasingly between developing countries—has risen from 181 at the end of 1980 to 1,856 at the end of 1999. Furthermore, double-taxation treaties have also increased from 719 in 1980 to 1982 at the end of 1990 (UNCTAD, 2000).

Financial liberalization came last, starting in the early 1980s. This had two dimensions: the deregulation of the domestic financial sector in the industrialized countries, and the introduction of convertibility on capital account in the balance of payments. The latter was not simultaneous. The United States, Canada, Germany, and Switzerland removed restrictions on capital movements in 1973, Britain in 1979, Japan in 1980. France and Italy made the transition as late as 1990. The globalization of finance, moving forward at a scorching pace since the mid-1980s, is not unrelated to the dismantling of regulations and controls.

The technological revolution in transport, communications, and production has been a crucial catalyst behind globalization. The second half of the twentieth century has witnessed the advent of jet aircraft,

| Exhibit 1-2 | National Regulatory Changes, 1991–1999 | | | | | | | | |
|---|---|---|---|---|---|---|---|---|---|
| | **1991** | **1992** | **1993** | **1994** | **1995** | **1996** | **1997** | **1998** | **1999** |
| Number of countries that introduced changes in their investment regimes | 35 | 43 | 57 | 49 | 64 | 65 | 76 | 60 | 63 |
| Number of regulatory changes | 82 | 79 | 102 | 110 | 112 | 114 | 151 | 145 | 140 |
| More favorable to FDI | 80 | 79 | 101 | 108 | 106 | 98 | 135 | 136 | 131 |
| Less favorable to FDI | 2 | - | 1 | 2 | 6 | 16 | 16 | 9 | 9 |

Source: Adapted from Cross-Border Mergers and Acquisitions and Development, The World Investment Report, © 2000, which was part of the United Nations Conference on Trade and Development (UNCTAD), Table 1.3, pg. 4 (National Regulatory Changes, 1991-1999).

computers, and satellites. The synthesis of communications technology, which is concerned with the transmission of information, and computer technology, which is concerned with the processing of information, has created information technology, which is remarkable in both reach and speed. Linkages have also become intense at the individual level. The number of Internet hosts has grown from 9 million in 1993 to 72 million in 2000. A total of 304 million people were estimated to be online in 2000 with explosive growth expected from new, and increasingly more afford-able computer and telecommunication technologies (Czinkota & Ronkainen 1998; 2001). These technological developments have had a dramatic impact on reducing geographical barriers. The time needed to travel—and communicate—abroad is a tiny fraction of what it was.

New forms of industrial organization have played a role in making globalization possible. The emerging flexible production system, shaped by the nature of technical progress, the changing output mix and the organizational characteristics (based on Japanese management systems) are forcing firms to constantly choose between trade, investment, and strategic alliances in their drive to expand activities across borders (Hill 2000).

Other trends driving globalization have also been identified (Yip 1995; Hill 2000):

- An emerging trend towards globalization of markets in terms converging consumer tastes and preferences in different parts of the world. For example, products such as Coca-Cola, Levi's jeans, the Sony Walkman, and McDonalds fast food have increasingly gained acceptance with consumers in nearly every country around the world.

- The internationalization of production, based on consideration of costs, procurement of best supplies globally, and proximity to markets in order to remain globally competitive in terms of price and quality.

A major worldview legitimizing globalization has been provided by neoliberal economists who argue that governments are incapable of inter-vening efficiently and propose the following economic policies as an alternative:

- Government should be rolled back wherever possible so that it approximates to the ideal of a minimalist state.

- The market is not only a substitute for the state but also the preferred alternative because it performs better.

- Resource allocation and resource utilization must be based on market prices, which should conform as closely as possible to international prices.

- National political objectives, domestic economic concerns, or even national boundaries should not act as constraints.

It is suggested that such policies would provide the foundations for a global economic system characterized by free trade, unrestricted capital mobility, open markets, and harmonized institutions. Furthermore, neoliberal economists—also sometimes called the Chicago School—and their adherents in politics and business believe that such "globalization" promises economic prosperity for the countries that participate in such a limited government system—and economic deprivation for countries that do not (Sachs 1998).

Recent decades have witnessed the most remarkable institutional harmonization and economic integration among nations in the world history. While economic integration was increasing throughout the 1970s and 1980s, the extent of integration has come sharply into focus only since the collapse of the Soviet Union and other communist states beginning in 1989. By 1995, one dominant global economic system was emerging. The common set of institutions is exemplified by the new World Trade Organization (WTO), which was established by agreement of more than 120 economies—with many other countries eager to join as rapidly as possible. Part of the new trade agreement involves a codification of basic principles governing trade in goods and services. Similarly, the International Monetary Fund (IMF) now boasts nearly universal membership, with member countries pledged to basic principles of currency convertibility (Sachs & Warner 1995).

As can be evidenced, most programs of economic reform now underway in the developing world and in the post-communist world have as their strategic aim the integration of the national economy with the world economy. Integration means not only increased market-based trade and financial flows, but also institutional harmonization with regard to trade policy, legal codes, tax systems, ownership patterns, and other regulatory arrangements. In each of these areas, international norms play a large and often decisive role in defining the terms of the reform policy. In recent years, China made commitments on international property rights and trade policy with the view toward membership of the WTO—which happened when China was admitted as a member of the WTO in December, 2001. Russian economic reforms are similarly guided by the overall aim of reestablishing the country's place within the world market system. In several sections of its April 1995 Agreement with the IMF, the Russian government committed to abide by WTO principles in advance of membership.

# GLOBALIZATION: FACTS AND FIGURES

Recent decades saw global trade rising exponentially from a figure of $250 billion[1] in 1965 to a current level of over $7.4 trillion dollars (World Trade Organization 2002).

Exhibit 1-3 illustrates the magnitude of world merchandise trade, by region, from 1999 to 2001.

In recent decades, there has also been increasing trade within regional trade blocs. Exhibit 1-4 provides a breakdown of merchandise trade of selected regional integration arrangements from 1991 to 2001.

World trade in goods and services has since World War 2, expanded at nearly double the pace of world real gross domestic production (GDP). As a result the volume of world trade in goods and services (the sum of both exports and imports) rose from barely one-tenth of world GDP in 1950 to about one-third of world GDP in 2000 (Mussa 2000).

Similarly, cross-border capital flows rose from $536 billion in 1991 to $1,258 billion four years later, while the world's stock of liquid financial assets grew from $10.7 trillion in 1980 to $41.7 trillion in 1994 and was then forecasted to exceed $80 trillion by the year 2000 (Czinkota & Ronkainen (2001).

---

[1] All dollar amounts are given in U.S. dollars unless noted otherwise.

| Exhibit 1-3 | Network of Merchandise Trade by Region, 1999–2001 | | |
|---|---|---|---|
| **Destination** | **U.S. Dollars (in billions)** | | |
| | **1999** | **2000** | **2001** |
| World | $5,548 | $6,251 | $5,984 |
| North America | $931.58 | $1058.08 | $990.98 |
| Latin America | $298.82 | $359.29 | $347.23 |
| Western Europe | $2,409.45 | $2,503.46 | $2,485.11 |
| European Union (15) | $2,236.25 | $2,312.26 | $2,291.43 |
| C./E. Europe/Baltic States/CIS | $215.01 | $271.36 | $285.62 |
| Central and Eastern Europe | $101.66 | $116.06 | $129.42 |
| Russian Fed. | $75.7 | $105.5 | $103.1 |
| Africa | $116.58 | $148.5 | $141.19 |
| Middle East | $184.64 | $261.4 | $236.76 |
| Asia | $1,391.82 | $1,648.85 | $1,497.36 |
| Japan | $419.37 | $479.25 | $403.5 |
| Australia and New Zealand | $68.54 | $77.14 | $77.11 |
| Other Asia | $903.92 | $1,092.47 | $1,016.75 |

Source: Adapted from Network of merchandise trade by region, 1991-2001, © 2002, World Trade Organization. Reprinted with permission of the World Trade Organization.

| Exhibit 1-4 | Merchandise Trade of Selected Regional Integration Arrangements, 1991-2001 | | | | | | | | | | |
|---|---|---|---|---|---|---|---|---|---|---|---|
| | **1991** | **1992** | **1993** | **1994** | **1995** | **1996** | **1997** | **1998** | **1999** | **2000** | **2001** |
| **APEC (21)** | | | | | | | | | | | |
| Total exports (USD in billions) | 1,426 | 1,535 | 1,636 | 1,865 | 2,189 | 2,284 | 2,444 | 2,345 | 2,494 | 2,930 | 2,700 |
| Total imports (USD in billions) | 1,450 | 1,560 | 1,694 | 1,955 | 2,281 | 2,441 | 2,577 | 2,396 | 2,627 | 3,180 | 2,969 |
| **EU (15)** | | | | | | | | | | | |
| Total exports (USD in billions) | 1493 | 1584 | 1489 | 1703 | 2084 | 2155 | 2141 | 2233 | 2236 | 2312 | 2291 |
| Total imports (USD in billions) | 1579 | 1654 | 1488 | 1691 | 2051 | 2101 | 2090 | 2212 | 2261 | 2401 | 2334 |
| **NAFTA (3)** | | | | | | | | | | | |
| Total exports (USD in billions) | 592 | 629 | 662 | 739 | 856 | 923 | 1014 | 1014 | 1068 | 1224 | 1149 |
| Total imports (USD in billions) | 676 | 738 | 800 | 917 | 1008 | 1082 | 1208 | 1271 | 1421 | 1682 | 1578 |
| **ASEAN (10)** | | | | | | | | | | | |
| Total exports (USD in billions) | 165 | 186 | 212 | 262 | 321 | 340 | 353 | 329 | 359 | 427 | 385 |
| Total imports (USD in billions) | 184 | 201 | 232 | 281 | 354 | 375 | 372 | 278 | 300 | 367 | 336 |

| Exhibit 1-4 | Merchandise Trade of Selected Regional Integration Arrangements, 1991-2001 (continued) | | | | | | | | | | |
|---|---|---|---|---|---|---|---|---|---|---|---|
| | **1991** | **1992** | **1993** | **1994** | **1995** | **1996** | **1997** | **1998** | **1999** | **2000** | **2001** |
| **MERCOSUR (4)** | | | | | | | | | | | |
| Total exports (percent) | 46 | 50 | 54 | 62 | 70 | 75 | 83 | 81 | 74 | 85 | 88 |
| Total imports (percent) | 34 | 41 | 49 | 63 | 80 | 87 | 103 | 99 | 82 | 89 | 84 |
| **ANDEAN (5)** | | | | | | | | | | | |
| Total exports (percent) | 29 | 28 | 28 | 34 | 40 | 46 | 46 | 39 | 43 | 58 | 53 |
| Total imports (percent) | 22 | 27 | 29 | 30 | 38 | 36 | 44 | 45 | 36 | 39 | 44 |

*Note:* The number in parentheses indicates the number of member states.

Source: Adapted from Merchandise trade of selected regional integration arrangements, 1991-01, © 2002 World Trade Organization. Reprinted with permission of the World Trade Organization.

Evidence on the expansion of international production over the past two decades abounds. Gross product associated with international production and foreign affiliate sales worldwide, two measures of international production, increased faster than global GDP and global exports respectively (UNCTAD 2000). Exhibit 1-5 provides a clear picture in terms of the dynamics of foreign direct investment (FDI) in selected country groups.

FDI flowing into developed countries in 2001 rose to over $503 billion, while FDI flowing to developing countries climbed to $204 billion. Worldwide annual sales of the foreign affiliate of MNCs in 1999 reached $14 trillion compared to $3 trillion in 1980, almost doubled the volume of global exports (UNCTAD 2000). It is also illustrative to note that most nations that have participated in international trade prospered. Exhibits

| Exhibit 1-5 | Foreign Direct Investment Inflows, in Country Groups | | | |
|---|---|---|---|---|
| | **USD (in millions)** | | | |
| **Group** | **1998** | **1999** | **2000** | **2001** |
| TOTAL WORLD | $694,457.30 | $1,088,263.00 | $1,491,934.00 | $735,145.70 |
| Developed Countries | $484,239.00 | $837,760.70 | $1,227,476.00 | $503,144.00 |
| Western Europe | $274,738.80 | $507,221.70 | $832,067.40 | $336,210.00 |
| North America | $197,243.30 | $307,811.30 | $367,529.30 | $151,899.90 |
| Least developed countries (LDCs) | $3,947.60 | $5,428.30 | $3,704.30 | $3,837.60 |
| Oil-exporting Countries | $14,441.90 | $5,461.40 | $3,510.00 | $6,557.10 |
| Developing countries | $187,610.60 | $225,140.00 | $237,894.40 | $204,801.30 |
| Africa | $9,020.90 | $12,821.20 | $8,694.00 | $17,164.50 |
| Latin America and the Caribbean | $82,203.30 | $109,310.80 | $95,405.40 | $85,372.60 |
| South America | $51,885.60 | $70,879.60 | $56,837.10 | $40,111.40 |
| Asia and the Pacific | $96,386.50 | $103,008.00 | $133,795.00 | $102,264.20 |
| All developing countries minus China | $143,859.60 | $184,821.00 | $197,122.40 | $157,955.30 |

Source: Adapted from Statistics: Foreign Direct Investment Inflows in Country Groups, United Nations Conference on Trade and Development (UNCTAD), © 2002.

1-6 and 1-7 provide data for 25 leading exporters and importers in world merchandise and commercial services respectively. These statistics show that globalization is highly pervasive and is growing exponentially worldwide. What we learn in the next section are the benefits and disadvantages of globalization.

# ADVANTAGES AND DISADVANTAGES OF GLOBALIZATION

Several influential commentators and researchers (Mahoney, et al. 1998; Hill 2000) argue that globalization has brought great benefits. Increased trade and capital flows have generated gains in productivity and efficiency that have spurred growth and created millions of jobs in the

| Exhibit 1-6 | Twenty-five Leading Exporters and Importers In World Merchandise | | | | | | |
|---|---|---|---|---|---|---|---|
| Rank | Exporters | Value (USD in billions) | Share (%) | Rank | Importers | Value (USD in billions) | Share (%) |
| 1 | United States | 730.8 | 11.9 | 1 | United States | 1180.2 | 18.3 |
| 2 | Germany | 570.8 | 9.3 | 2 | Germany | 492.8 | 7.7 |
| 3 | Japan | 403.5 | 6.6 | 3 | Japan | 349.1 | 5.4 |
| 4 | France | 321.8 | 5.2 | 4 | United Kingdom | 331.8 | 5.2 |
| 5 | United Kingdom | 273.1 | 4.4 | 5 | France | 325.8 | 5.1 |
| 6 | China | 266.2 | 4.3 | 6 | China | 243.6 | 3.8 |
| 7 | Canada | 259.9 | 4.2 | 7 | Italy | 232.9 | 3.6 |
| 8 | Italy | 241.1 | 3.9 | 8 | Canada | 227.2 | 3.5 |
| 9 | Netherlands | 229.5 | 3.7 | 9 | Netherlands | 207.3 | 3.2 |
| 10 | Hong Kong, China | 191.1 | 3.1 | 10 | Hong Kong, China | 202.0 | 3.1 |
| | Domestic exports | 20.3 | 0.3 | | Retained imports | 31.2 | 0.5 |
| | Re-exports | 170.8 | 2.8 | 11 | Mexico | 176.2 | 2.7 |
| 11 | Belgium | 179.7 | 1.8 | 12 | Belgium | 168.7 | 2.6 |
| 12 | Mexico | 158.5 | 1.6 | 13 | Korea, Rep. Of | 141.1 | 2.2 |
| 13 | Korea, Rep. of | 150.4 | 1.5 | 14 | Spain | 142.7 | 2.2 |
| 14 | Taipei, Chinese | 122.5 | 1.3 | 15 | Singapore | 116.0 | 1.8 |
| 15 | Singapore | 121.8 | 1.2 | | Retained imports | 60.4 | 0.9 |
| | Domestic exports | 66.1 | 1.1 | 16 | Taipei, Chinese | 107.3 | 1.7 |
| | Re-exports | 55.6 | 0.9 | 17 | Switzerland | 84.1 | 1.3 |
| 16 | Spain | 109.7 | 1.8 | 18 | Austria | 74.4 | 1.2 |
| 17 | Russian Fed. | 103.1 | 1.7 | 19 | Malaysia | 74.1 | 1.2 |
| 18 | Malaysia | 87.9 | 1.4 | 20 | Australia | 63.9 | 1.0 |
| 19 | Ireland | 82.8 | 1.3 | 21 | Sweden | 62.6 | 1.0 |
| 20 | Switzerland | 82.1 | 1.3 | 22 | Thailand | 62.1 | 1.0 |
| 21 | Sweden | 75.3 | 1.2 | 23 | Brazil | 58.3 | 0.9 |
| 22 | Austria | 70.3 | 1.1 | 24 | Russian Fed. | 53.9 | 0.8 |
| 23 | Saudi Arabia | 68.2 | 1.1 | 25 | Ireland | 50.7 | 0.8 |
| 24 | Thailand | 65.1 | 1.1 | | | | |
| 25 | Australia | 63.4 | 1.0 | | | | |

Source: Adapted from Leading Exporters and importers in world merchandise, © 2002 World Trade Organization. Reprinted with permission of the World Trade Organization.

| Exhibit 1-7 | Leading Exporters and Importers in World Trade in Commercial Services, 2001 |
|---|---|

| Rank | Exporters | Value (USD in billions) | Share (%) | % Annual Change | Rank | Importers | Value (USD in billions) | Share (%) | % Annual Change |
|---|---|---|---|---|---|---|---|---|---|
| 1 | United States | 263.4 | 18.1 | –3 | 1 | United States | 187.7 | 13.0 | –7 |
| 2 | United Kingdom | 108.4 | 7.4 | –6 | 2 | Germany | 132.6 | 9.2 | 0 |
| 3 | France | 79.8 | 5.5 | –2 | 3 | Japan | 107.0 | 7.4 | –7 |
| 4 | Germany | 79.7 | 5.5 | –1 | 4 | United Kingdom | 91.6 | 6.3 | –4 |
| 5 | Japan | 63.7 | 4.4 | –7 | 5 | France | 61.6 | 4.3 | 0 |
| 6 | Spain | 57.4 | 3.9 | 8 | 6 | Italy | 55.7 | 3.9 | 2 |
| 7 | Italy | 57.0 | 3.9 | 2 | 7 | Netherlands | 52.9 | 3.7 | 2 |
| 8 | Netherlands | 51.7 | 3.5 | 0 | 8 | Canada | 41.5 | 2.9 | –3 |
| 9 | Belgium–Luxembourg | 42.6 | 2.9 | –1 | 9 | Belgium–Luxembourg | 39.3 | 2.7 | 2 |
| 10 | Hong Kong, China | 42.4 | 2.9 | 2 | 10 | China | 39.0 | 2.7 | 9 |
| 11 | Canada | 35.6 | 2.4 | –5 | 11 | Ireland | 34.8 | 2.4 | 21 |
| 12 | China | 32.9 | 2.3 | 9 | 12 | Spain | 33.2 | 2.3 | 7 |
| 13 | Austria | 32.5 | 2.2 | 5 | 13 | Korea, Rep. of | 33.1 | 2.3 | 0 |
| 14 | Korea, Rep. of | 29.6 | 2.0 | 0 | 14 | Austria | 31.5 | 2.2 | 6 |
| 15 | Denmark | 26.9 | 1.8 | 10 | 15 | Hong Kong, China | 25.1 | 1.7 | –2 |
| 16 | Singapore | 26.4 | 1.8 | –2 | 16 | Taipei, Chinese | 23.7 | 1.6 | –8 |
| 17 | Switzerland | 25.2 | 1.7 | –4 | 17 | Denmark | 23.5 | 1.6 | 6 |
| 18 | Sweden | 21.8 | 1.5 | 9 | 18 | India | 23.4 | 1.6 | 19 |
| 19 | India | 20.4 | 1.4 | 15 | 19 | Sweden | 22.9 | 1.6 | –2 |
| 20 | Taipei, Chinese | 20.3 | 1.4 | 2 | 20 | Russian Fed. | 21.1 | 1.5 | 20 |
| 21 | Ireland | 20.0 | 1.4 | 20 | 21 | Singapore | 20.0 | 1.4 | –6 |
| 22 | Greece | 19.4 | 1.3 | 1 | 22 | Malaysia | 16.5 | 1.1 | 0 |
| 23 | Norway | 16.7 | 1.1 | 12 | 23 | Mexico | 16.5 | 1.1 | –1 |
| 24 | Turkey | 15.9 | 1.1 | –17 | 24 | Australia | 16.4 | 1.1 | –8 |
| 25 | Australia | 15.7 | 1.1 | –12 | 25 | Brazil | 15.8 | 1.1 | 0 |
| 26 | Malaysia | 14.0 | 1.0 | 3 | 26 | Norway | 15.3 | 1.1 | 6 |
| 27 | Thailand | 12.9 | 0.9 | –6 | 27 | Switzerland | 14.9 | 1.0 | –3 |
| 28 | Mexico | 12.5 | 0.9 | –7 | 28 | Thailand | 14.5 | 1.0 | –6 |
| 29 | Poland | 11.9 | 0.8 | 14 | 29 | Indonesiaª | 14.5 | 1.0 | |
| 30 | Israel | 11.3 | 0.8 | –21 | 30 | Israel | 12.3 | 0.9 | 1 |
| 31 | Russian Fed. | 10.9 | 0.7 | 9 | 31 | Greece | 11.2 | 0.8 | 2 |
| 32 | Egypt | 8.8 | 0.6 | –9 | 32 | United Arab Emirates | 10.5 | 0.7 | |
| 33 | Brazil | 8.7 | 0.6 | –1 | 33 | Poland | 8.7 | 0.6 | –2 |
| 34 | Portugal | 8.7 | 0.6 | 4 | 34 | Finland | 8.1 | 0.6 | –3 |
| 35 | Hungary | 7.6 | 0.5 | 23 | 35 | Argentina | 7.9 | 0.5 | –8 |
| 36 | Czech Rep. | 6.9 | 0.5 | 4 | 36 | Saudi Arabia | 7.2 | 0.5 | –35 |
| 37 | Finland | 5.7 | 0.4 | –6 | 37 | Egypt | 6.5 | 0.4 | –10 |
| 38 | Saudi Arabia | 5.2 | 0.4 | 8 | 38 | Turkey | 6.4 | 0.4 | –16 |

| Exhibit 1-7 | Leading Exporters and Importers in World Trade in Commercial Services, 2001 (continued) | | | | | | | |
|---|---|---|---|---|---|---|---|---|
| Rank | Exporters | Value (USD in billions) | Share (%) | % Annual Change | Rank | Importers | Value (USD in billions) | Share (%) | % Annual Change |
| 39 | Indonesia[a] | 5.2 | 0.4 | | 39 | Portugal | 6.0 | 0.4 | –5 |
| 40 | Croatia | 4.8 | 0.3 | 18 | 40 | Czech Rep. | 5.5 | 0.4 | 3 |
| | Total of above | 1340.0 | 91.9 | –1 | | Total of above | 1315.0 | 91.1 | –1 |
| | World | 1460.0 | 100.0 | 0 | | World | 1445.0 | 100.0 | –1 |

[a]Secretariat estimate.

*Note:* Figures for a number of countries and territories have been estimated by the Secretariat. Annual percentage changes and rankings are affected by continuity breaks in the series for a large number of economies, and by limitations in cross–country comparability.

Source: Adapted from Leading exporters and importers in world trade in commercial services, 2001, © 2002, World Trade Organization. Reprinted with permission of the World Trade Organization.

advanced industrial countries, the emerging economies, and even many of the world's low-income countries. Globalization has raised the incomes of consumers as well as the quality of their material life in terms of increased product choices.

Critics of globalization maintain that globalization is polarizing the world. Developing countries with about 80 percent of world's population have little representation and influence in global institutions and multinational corporations as well as the decision-making processes that take place within them. Global governance is highly centralized; and there is hardly any possibility of breaking the monopoly of the rich countries in this context. These critics argue that integration of poor countries in world trade works to their disadvantage. Conversely, when rich countries are "integrated" in world trade, it works to their advantage. What is true of countries is also true of individuals and groups. For unskilled workers, national frontiers have become rigid and higher; for highly skilled workers, they are flexible and lower. This means that the economics of globalization favor the strong. This is because globalization, as a project undertaken by policymakers, businesspeople, and the like, is driven by market institutions that are wedded to promoting economic efficiency, generating growth, and yielding profits—goals that in themselves do not solve and may even engender inequality, injustice, and insecurity. Meanwhile, in developed countries, labor leaders lament the loss of good paying jobs to low-wage countries (Batra 1993; Barlett & Steele 1996; Goldsmith 1996; Hoogvelt 1997).

In response, proponents of globalization point out that it holds the most promise for developing countries with respect to economic growth, poverty reduction, and the reversal of global inequality. Globalization helps developing countries to replicate the experience that Western countries went through, beginning around 1820, when they broke with the historical norm of low growth and initiated dramatic advances in material well being. Living standard tripled in Western Europe and quadrupled in the United States in the nineteenth century (Vasques 2002). (This does not entail repeating the experience of the Industrial Revolution per se, but rather economic strategies that reap like social and economic benefits.) These proponents also cite empirical studies that show poverty almost always declined in countries that experienced growth due to globalization and increased in countries that experienced economic contractions due to their nonglobalizing economies (Dollar & Kraay 2001). They also cite additional research in which the poverty level was shown to drop decade by decade from 59 percent of the population of developing countries in 1950 to 9 percent in 2000. World inequality, based on people rather than countries, has also declined especially in the last two decades—the period that falls under the aegis of our concept of modern globalization (Bhalla 2002).

One major criticism leveled against the process of globalization is environmental degradation. Environmentalist critics argue that world trade has become the primary—and unseen—force behind much of the uncontrolled environmental problems the world faces; and the increasing integration of the world's economies is rapidly making a bad situation even worse. The continual expansion of world trade—in ways that are not shaped by any real understanding of their environmental impacts—is causing a range of ecological problems. For example, under more or less natural conditions, the arrival of an entirely new organism into a region's ecosystem was a rare event. Today it can happen any time a ship comes into port or an airplane lands. The real problem, in other words, does not lie with exotic species themselves, but with the economic system that is continually showering them over the Earth's surface. Bioinvasion has become a kind of globalization disease (Bright 1999, 51). Developing nations, whose elites believe they have a right to their natural resources, are not the least reticent about allowing firms, escaping the stringent regulations of their own countries, to set up factories that pollute the air and water. Falling trade barriers allow such firms to move—*outsource*—their manufacturing activities offshore to countries where, in addition to lax or no environmental laws, the wage rates are much lower.

Supporters of globalization argue, however, that there are political and economic pressures on firms not to exploit labor or the environment in overseas operations as at least one check and balance. Western firms have been the subject of consumer boycotts when it has been revealed that they, or their independent suppliers, operate at standards below those in developed countries (Hill 2000). "Good" companies have begun to appear, such as the supermarket chain Wild Oats, that offer products that have not harmed the environment or have not been produced by exploited workers.

Hill (2000) maintains that with the development of the WTO and other multilateral organizations such as the European Union (E.U.) and NAFTA in North America, countries and localities are willing to cede authority over their actions. This has given rise to another key criticism of globalization in that national sovereignty is then undermined as economic power is increasingly shifting away from national governments and toward supranational organizations such as the World Trade Organization, the International Monetary Fund, and Transnational companies. Critics also charge that globalization largely benefits advanced societies—or first-world economies—creating new forms of colonial control in the so-called postcolonial world. Thus, globalization becomes increasingly the new global colonialism, based on the capitalist historical materialism. This, in turn, creates a global culture that is essentially a culture of consumption for the greater economic benefit of bourgeoisie in capitalist societies (Banarjee and Linstead 2001).

Given the complex nature of globalization, James D. Wolfensohn, President of the World Bank, makes an eloquent contention by observing:

> *There is no simple answer to dealing with globalization. Instead, the insights are rooted in pragmatic judgments about how the existing conditions of society will affect which policy choices make sense, or how one sequence of policies is preferable to another, or how certain policies can complement and sustain each other. The commitments and actions of the national government remain central to any workable development strategy (Wolfensohn 2000).*

He further notes that:

> *Globalization is not likely to disappear or even to diminish in intensity.... As globalization brings distant parts of the world functionally closer together [. . .] it may well be that successful development policies will achieve results more quickly, while failed policies will have their consequences exposed more quickly and painfully as well. In such a world, exploring the institutional responses to globalization and [. . .] and disseminating the insights broadly, offers enormous potential for advances in development strategy—advances that can be of great and lasting benefit to the poorest people of the world (Wolfensohn 2000).*

On balance, supporters of globalization would argue that benefits associated with globalization far outweigh these perceived drawbacks. Generally speaking globalization has been beneficial to nearly all countries around the world. Data released by the IMF show that "over the past five decades, real GDP in developing countries (as a group) growing in per capita terms at about the same pace as the industrial countries. The result has been that real living standards, as measured by per capita GDP, have improved on average about the three-fold in just half a century" (Mussa 2000, 8).

Globalization is an inescapable reality that no nation can afford to ignore, since it can be beneficial to nations involved in increased international trade. Nations that have pursued closed economies of self-sufficiency, such as Albania under communism and North Korea with its Juche philosophy, at the expense of free trade with other countries have remained economically backward as compared to other nations in the same regions that actively pursue international trade and have thereby become economically and socially secure. Albania still suffers from its catastrophic economy as thousands of its citizens—*economic refugees*—flee to Italy and other prosperous European countries. North Korea endures, but with famine and the inability to light its cities at night while its neighbor, South Korea, is one of the Asian Tiger economies.

# CHALLENGES OF MANAGING INTERNATIONAL BUSINESS ENTERPRISES

Increasing globalization of national economies presents numerous challenges for managers. For example, international managers operating in foreign countries are faced with different cultural, political, legal, economic, and technological systems, which may be yet again different from international managers' home country. Further complexities, arising from an international political and business environments, entail understanding and accommodating differing worldviews, employees' attitudes to work, and varied consumers' needs and preferences among other variables. This, of course, means that international managers in order to succeed in the global marketplace have to develop high level intercultural communication and intercultural management competencies. International managers would also need to make appropriate adjustments to their business management practices so as to adapt and suit a particular international environment.

## *Summary*

This chapter examined the phenomenon of globalization that is rapidly transforming the world economy. As noted earlier, globalization is exalted in many circles as the greatest producer of wealth and prosperity that the world has ever known. However, at the same time, globalization according to its critics is seen as a profoundly destructive force too. It is because globalization destroys unique cultural values and identities so as to exploit labor and natural resources of the developing nations while destroying the natural environment world over for the pursuit of profit maximization. On balance, it was established that benefits arising from globalization of trade can far outweigh disadvantages attributed to globalization.

In this chapter, a conceptual analysis of globalization, discussing both historical and contemporary perspectives, was provided. At the same time, differing theoretical paradigms underlying globalization were critically discussed, including Mercantilism; Absolute Advantage Theory; Theory of Comparative Advantage; Factors Proportions Trade Theory; International Investment and Product Life-cycle Theory; Porter's Competitive Advantage of Nations; and the Theory of International Investment. An explanation was also provided in terms of why firms are motivated to go global. The main catalysts for globalization at a macrolevel of analysis were similarly given. Finally, advantages and disadvantages of globalization were critically examined, which have considerable implications for the national economies and organizations intent upon internationalizing their products and services as well as their operations.

## Critical Discussion Questions

1. In what ways has globalization affected business practices of a nation participating in globalization?

2. Critically discuss the notion that globalization in its present form is only beneficial to big multinational companies.

3. Should the process of globalization be regulated? If so, in what ways?

4. How relevant are Adam Smith's and David Ricardo's theories of international trade in today's knowledge-based global economy?

5. Critically discuss the advantages and disadvantages of globalization for the nations involved in globalization.

6. To what extent has Internet affected globalization?

7. Critically discuss the notion that globalization is a new form of colonization of the developing nations.

## Applications

### Experiential

1. Find a local company, which is going global, and interview an owner or manager about the firm's decision and what globalization means for its operations. Do you think that the firm activities have been good or bad for the countries in which it has dealings?

2. Find a multinational firm in your local area and research its effects on the local community.

3. Identify a major government body or a business association in your country facilitating international trade for businesses and interview the manager or a member of the research staff in terms of the contributions and challenges globalization presents to your country.

### Internet

**Is a Critique of Capitalism Justified?**

**Step 1:** Navigate your Web browser to the following Web site, which has links to classical Marxist texts, http://www.anu.edu.au/polsci/marx/.

**Step 2:** Read *The Communist Manifesto.*

**Step 3:** Analyze Karl Marx and Frederich Engels' critique of 19th-century capitalism in terms of its relevance and applicability to contemporary globalization, as an extension of capitalist ideology, in terms of its impact on capital, labor, markets, production, business ethics, demographic shifts, and the pursuit of profit maximization.

## References

Albrow, M. (1990). Introduction. In M. Albrow & E. King (Eds.)., *Globalization, knowledge and society.* London: Sage.

Ball, D., & McCulloch, W. Jr. (1996). *International business: The challenge of global competition.* Chicago: Irwin.

Banarjee, S.B., & Linstead, S. (2001). Globalization, Multiculturalism and other fictions: Colonialism for the new millennium. *Organization, 8,* 683.

Barlett, D.L., & Steele, J.B. (1996, September, 9). America: Who stole the dream? *Philadelphia Inquire.*

Batra, R. (1993). *The myth of free trade.* New York: Touchstone Books.

Baylis, J., & Smith, S. (1997). *The globalization of world politics: An introduction to international relations.* New York: Oxford University Press.

Bhalla, S.S. (2002). *Poverty, inequality, and growth in the era of globalization.* Washington: Institute of Economics for International Economics.

Bright, C. (1999). Invasive species: Pathogens of globalization. *Foreign Policy, Fall pp.50-64*

Bull, H. (1977). *The anarchical society. A study of order in world politics.* London: Macmillan.

Burton, J. (1972). *World society.* Cambridge: Cambridge University Press

Cullen, J.B. (1999). *Multinational management: A strategic approach.* Cincinnati, OH: South-Western College Publishing.

Czinkota, M.R. & Ronkainen, I.A. (1998). *International marketing* (5th ed.). Orlando, FL: Harcourt Brace & Company.

Czinkota, M.R., & Ronkainen, I.A. (2001). *Best practices in international business* Orlando, FL: Harcourt College Publishers.

Dollar D., & Kraay A. (2001). Trade, growth, and poverty. Working paper. New York: World Bank.

Dunning, J. (1988). *Explaining international production.* London: Unwin Hyman.

Fortune (2002, July 22). The 2002 Global 500: The World's Largest Corporations. *Fortune,* pp. F–12+.

Fraser, J., & Oppenheim, J. (2001). What's New About Globalization? In M.R. Czinkota & I.A. Ronkainen (Eds.), *Best practices in international business.* Orlando, FL: Harcourt College Publishers.

Fukuyama, F. (1992). *The end of history and the Last Man.* New York: Free Press.

Goldsmith, J. (1996). 'The winners and the losers'. In J. Mander & J. Goldsmith, *The case against the global economy.* San Francisco: The Sierra Book Club.

Hill, C. (2000). *International business: Competing in the global marketplace* (3rd ed.) Boston: McGraw-Hill Higher Education.

Hoogvelt, A. (1997). *Globalisation and postcolonial world.* London: MacMillan.

Koslow, L.E., & Scarlett, R.H. (1999). *Global business.* Houston, TX: Cashman Dudley.

Mahoney, D., Trigg, M., Griffin, R., & Pustay, M. (1998). *International business: A managerial perspective.* Melbourne: Addison Wesley Longman.

McLuhan, M. (1989). *The global village: Transformation in world life and media in the 21$^{st}$ century.* NY: Oxford Press

Modelski, G. (1972). *Multinational corporations and world order.* Beverly Hills, CA: Sage.

Mussa, M. (2000, August 25). Factors driving global economic integration. Paper presented at Jackson Hole, Wyoming for a symposium sponsored by the Federal Reserve Bank of Kansas City on "Global opportunities and challenges."

Porter, M.E. (1990). *The competitive advantage of nations.* New York: Free Press.

Sachs, J. (1998). International economics: Unlocking the mysteries of globalization. *Foreign Policy,* (1), 97–109.

Sachs, J., & Warner, A. (1995). Economic reform and the process of global integration. *Brookings Papers on Economic Activity, 1,* 1–2.

United Nations Conference on Trade and Development (UNCTAD) (2000). *World Investment Report 2000: Cross-border mergers and acquisitions and development.* New York: United Nations.

United Nations Conference on Trade and Development (UNCTAD) (2002). *Statistics: Foreign Direct Investment Inflows in Country Groups.* New York: United Nations.

Vasques I. (2002). Globalization and the poor. *Independent Review, 7* (2), 197–207

Waters, M. (1995). *Globalisation.* London, Routledge.

Welch, L.S., & Luostarinen, R. (1999). Internationalization: Evolution of a concept. In P.J. Buckley & P.N. Ghauri (Eds.), *The internationalization of the firm: A reader* (2nd ed.) London: International Thomson Business Press.

Wolfensohn, J. (2000). *Entering the 21st century: World development report.* Washington, DC: World Bank.

World Trade Organization (2002). *Trade Statistics 2002.* Geneva: World Trade Organization.

Yip, G.S. (1995). *Total global strategy: Managing for worldwide competitive advantage.* Englewood Cliffs, NJ: Prentice Hall.

Zakaria, F. (2000, March 6). SILICON Valley, Swedish Style. *Newsweek Special Edition,.* 8-9.

# Chapter 2

*Understanding Cross-Cultural Management Dimensions*

**LEARNING OBJECTIVES**

*After reading this chapter, you should be able to:*
- *Understand the influence of culture on management.*
- *Understand why a management philosophy, based on parochialism and ethnocentrism, is a hindrance to effective management of an enterprise operating in a global economy.*
- *Understand the major theoretical perspectives underlying cross-cultural dimensions.*
- *Understand the benefits of cultural diversity for an organization operating in an international environment.*
- *Describe specific managerial strategies designed for effective management of cultural diversity in both a national and international setting.*

*Human beings draw close to one another by their common nature, but habits and customs keep them apart.*

*—Confucian proverb*

## OVERVIEW

The spread of global trade, cross-border investment, mass migration, and large-scale tourism, coupled with industries adopting ever-more efficient and sophisticated information technology have transformed the world into the "global village." As a consequence, cultural diversity has become a fact of organizational life in many nations around the globe. Most obvious of these are nations with more than one native culture that is not exclusively dominant in population. The frequently discussed differences between French and Flemish Belgians; Francophone and Anglophone Canadians; Ibo, Hausa, and Yoruba Nigerians; Chinese, Malays, and Indians in Malaysia, and the 16 government-recognized cultural and linguistic groups in India are a few of the most notable examples. Similarly, the large-scale immigration of former colonials especially to Netherlands and Great Britain, the tremendous influx of Soviet Jews to Israel, and classic immigration to the United States, Australia, and Canada have created domestic multicultural work environments in these countries (Limaye & Victor 1995). To succeed, firms need to recognize the importance of different cultures in formulating their business plans and strategies. Enterprises that fail to do so can suffer strategic losses and function poorly in a globalized business environment. For example, empirical research showed that there is a high failure rate of cross-national mergers due to lack of understanding of cultural differences. As a result, it is estimated that somewhere between 50 and 75 percent of such mergers end in failure (Frank 1990).

Another related theme in managing cultural diversity, found mainly in American management literature (Child 1981; Child & Tayeb 1983; Form 1979; Hickson, et al. 1974), is that modern management concepts and principles can be uniformly applied to all employees across the globe. Underlying this management thesis is the belief that there are universal human needs, which can provide a common motivational basis for behavior. Management, as such, should not concern itself with any variations that may be found within a multicultural workforce. However, as we will learn, such an "efficiency-minded" viewpoint is not realistic or even workable.

In this chapter, an analysis is provided of cross-cultural dimensions and their influences on management practices around the world. We learn that management practices across the globe are largely influenced by cultural dimensions (Saee 1997). Theoretical perspectives underlying cross-cultural dimensions are also given. Benefits and disadvantages of cultural diversity are outlined and, finally, specific managerial strategies are recommended that enhance the performance of organizations operating in multicultural and international business environments.

## GLOBAL MANAGEMENT: A CROSS-CULTURAL PERSPECTIVE

The growing importance of world trade has created a demand for managers to develop cross-cultural management skills. These are needed to manage employees and interact with clients of culturally different backgrounds. A skill, in this case, is defined in the classic management sense as "the ability to demonstrate a sequence of behavior that is functionally related to attaining performance goal" (Torrington 1994). For the global manager, such performance goals are specific and required, that is, he or she should:

- Understand the nature of culture and how it influences behavior in the workplace.
- Learn about specific cultures and one's own culture. Cross-cultural management should always entail learning one's own values, without which no comparisons are possible.
- Recognize differences between cultures.
- Recognize which—and how—cultural factors influence the expressions of business structures, systems, and priorities.
- Implement the structures of the other culture.
- Recognize how far the structures of one's own culture can be implemented within the other culture and vice versa—and then make the implementation (Mead 1998).

Cross-cultural management relies on understanding the cultural behavior and differences of people working in organizations that operate internationally and making them perform with him or her and together. Similarly, such management must also understand and work with the client populations of different cultures. As a discipline, cross-cultural management describes organizational behavior within countries and cultures. It compares organizational behavior across countries and cultures and seeks to understand how to improve the interaction of coworkers, managers, executives, clients, suppliers, and alliance partners from around the world. Cross-cultural management thus expands the scope of domestic management to encompass international and domestic dynamics. Rather than global management being a subset of traditional domestic management approaches, it is clear that single-culture, domestic management has become a limited subset of global, cross-cultural management (Adler 1997, 10).

# CULTURE AND MANAGEMENT

To understand the differences between domestic and global management, it is necessary to understand the primary ways that cultures vary. Doing so can make the difference in breaking down norms that, when it comes to managing a culturally diverse organization, limits a manager's efficacy.

## Parochialism and Ethnocentrism

Managers who believe in parochialism view the world and their management practices exclusively from their own cultural perspective, and thus they adamantly maintain that: "My way is the only way." With their *mono*cultural perspective, they fail to recognize other people's different ways of living and working. Ethnocentric managers may acknowledge cultural differences, but they may consciously—or more often subconsciously—believe in the superiority of their culture and value system to such an extent that they are inclined to think that their way of doing things is the best, the norm, and indeed, the world norm.

To some extent all people are parochial and ethnocentric. In certain cultures this is stronger than in others (Adler 1997). We learn this from anthropology, which has profound implications for managers, since management practices across the globe are largely influenced by cultural dimensions (Saee 1997). Perhaps, cultural dimensions can explain different degrees of parochialism in different countries. There is a proclivity for collectivist cultures to be more parochial and ethnocentric than individualist cultures. As a result, unlike, individualist cultures, collectivist cultures are strongly biased towards their in-group members.

Naturally, managers working in a cross-cultural business environment cannot afford to think in terms of being parochialistic and ethnocentric in their business practices if they want to succeed in a globalized economy strategically. Such a failure to recognize and appreciate cultural diversity would invite adverse conditions that lead to organizational dysfunction and intraorganizational conflict. Thus, in what way should a manager let culture influence her or his managerial practices? First, understand cultural orientations of human society, as culture will have considerable impact on the way an organization is managed in that society.

# MODALITIES OF CROSS-CULTURAL DIMENSIONS

Cultural orientations and dimensions largely influence management practices across the globe. This is evident in the cultural orientation of any society where it reflects the complex interaction of values, attitudes, and behaviors displayed by its members. Individuals express culture and its normative qualities through the values that they hold about life and the world around them. These values in turn affect their attitudes about the form of behavior considered more appropriate and effective in a given situation, and this includes work behavior (Adler 1997).

Over the years, a number of authoritative modalities of cross-cultural dimensions were developed by the scholars (Kluckhohn & Strodtbeck 1961; Hofstede 1980; Trompenaars 1994; and Ronen & Schenker 1985), which are worthy of discussion here.

## Kluckhohn and Strodtbeck's Modality of Cross-Cultural Dimensions

As shown in Exhibit 2-1, five basic dimensions describe the cultural orientation of societies: people's qualities as individuals, their relationship to nature and the world, their relationship to other people, their primary type of activity, and their orientation in space and time (Kluckhohn & Strodtbeck 1961). The five dimensions answer questions, which have considerable implications for global management.

- Who am I?
- How do I see the world?
- How do I relate to other people?
- What do I do?
- How do I use space and time?

### How People See Themselves

There is a great deal of difference in the way different cultures conceptualize human nature. Americans, for example, in a culture whose members view people as a mixture of good and evil—as in the case of the culture shared by many Americans—who are capable of changing from one to the other. Effecting change in the workplace, then, by managers who view people in this way is possible through offering a choice of changing from one state to another, from not good, that is, not trained or skilled, to good, that is, trained and skilled, hence the reason for ongoing staff training and development. In contrast, there are cultures that view people as intrinsically good or bad and thereby not capable of going from one

| Exhibit 2-1 | Values Orientation Dimensions | | |
|---|---|---|---|
| **Perception of Individual** | **Good** | **Dimensions** **Good and evil** | **Evil** |
| World | Dominant | Harmony | Subjugation |
| Human Relations | Individual | Laterally extended groups | Hierarchical groups |
| Activity | Doing | Controlling | Being |
| Time | Future | Present | Past |
| Space | Private | Mixed | Public |

Source: Lane, H.W. & diStefano, J.J., *Values and Orientation Dimensions, International Management Behavior: From Policy to Practice*, 4e, © 2000, Blackwell Publishing. (Based on Kluckhohn and Stodbeck, adapted by Lane and diStefano)

to the other state. In this context, it is actually harder to bring about change within an organization. Managers in these cultures seek to employ the right people for the right job as they do not believe that employees could change once employed.

### People's Relationship to the World

Western cultures, in particular North Americans, generally regard themselves to be dominant over nature, and they are popularly known as a "can do" culture. Guided by this self-regard, they make every attempt to change the natural environment to suit their particular needs. Based on this belief, progress is made possible in many facets of Western civilization including organizational life. In Islamic cultures, however, individuals see themselves as dependent on God's grace and therefore they are readily willing to submit themselves to the will of God. As such, the Moslem's attitude of *En Shah Allah* ("God's willing") reflects his or her harmony and submission to God. In these cultures, the material world is not valued very highly in respect to Paradise, and this has considerable impact on the efficiency of working life. Still, there are other cultures that view themselves to be entirely at the mercy of Mother Nature, and, as such, they believe that they are subjugated by it. Native Americans and Australian Aborigines, who believe that whatever happens in the natural environment is beyond their control and, therefore, "it can't be helped."

### Human Relationships: Individualism or Collectivism

Western cultures value individual freedom, and they are focused on achieving individual goals and aspirations through hard work. They are optimistic about their future, believing that they are the sole designers of their destiny. They tend to plan their future. They do not feel that their future depends on other peoples' efforts and therefore they are less inclined to build long-term relationships with each other, as is generally evident in their business practices. Managers operating in such a cultural environment need to develop management policies capable of meeting individual needs and career aspirations in terms of promotion, individual responsibility and recognition, and interesting projects for individual high achievers.

In stark contrast, there are other cultures, characterized by collectivism, that are deeply observant of their customs and community values even at an enormous cost to their own individual rights. It can be argued that in these types of societies, individual rights are subordinated to societal rights and greater common goods. In a collectivist society, a sound management practice for high-level productivity calls for group-based incentives, including financial incentives and group decision-making processes at the workplace.

### Activity: Doing or Being

For Americans the dominant behavior is *doing* or action or controlling. As a result, they are focused on achieving outcomes that they can measure by objective criteria. South Americans, however, belong to *being* cultures, they are not entirely focused on achieving outcomes, as is the case with Americans. South Americans are more inclined to live in harmony with the natural environment. This is why they express their value of inaction through the term *Manana*, meaning "tomorrow." In other words, "Leave everything till tomorrow." Doing cultures are more motivated to work harder and are more time conscious, as they may anticipate greater financial rewards and promotional prospects to commensurate with their high level of performance. Being cultures are less time conscious, which is symptomatic of their cultural orientation, and they are not entirely driven by a hard work ethic.

### Time: Present, Past, and Future

Some cultures, such as the Vietnamese, are focused on their past and therefore are more respectful of their history, traditions, customs, and the collective wisdom of their ancient society. They feel that they can learn a lot from past history and ancestral knowledge. They pay greater respect to age. As part of cultural orientation, Vietnamese believe in worshipping their ancestors. In this type of culture, development of a systematic management policy, at least historically, has not been evident, as they mainly focused on the past rather than being concerned with the future direction of a firm (Saee 1998).

Other cultures are present conscious. It can be argued that Australians, for example, are present conscious in that they view work as a means to live in the present time more comfortably. North Americans, however, are more oriented toward the future. Change, including organizational change, is welcome providing that it brings future economic benefits.

### Space

There are differing cultural perspectives about space. For example, Middle Easterners and Asians generally view that space is more public and activities conducted in private are suspect. German culture values privacy highly and tend to work in their offices with doors closed.

## Hofstede's Cultural Dimensions

Hofstede (1980) demonstrated how the underlying values of cultures across the world affected relationships, work, and social values. In his comprehensive study on worldwide sociocultural factors influencing management, Hofstede compared work-related attitudes across a range of cultures. From his survey of 116,000 employees in 62 countries, Hofstede isolated four major dimensions, which were congruent with different cultural values of specific countries. These sociocultural dimensions were:

1. Collectivism versus Individualism.
2. Small versus Large Power Distance.
3. Weak versus Strong Uncertainty Avoidance.
4. Femininity versus Masculinity.

### Collectivism versus Individualism

The individualism–collectivism dimension refers to the extent to which people define themselves as autonomous individuals or through membership of groups. Societies, which are based on individualism, tend to emphasize individual initiative and individual achievement. In contrast, group-oriented societies focus on an individual's commitment and loyalty to a group. In essence, people in individualist societies are primarily concerned with looking after themselves and their immediate family. In collectivist societies people belong to groups or collectives, which look after them in exchange for loyalty (Hofstede & Bond 1984; Irwin & More 1994).

In most collectivist cultures, direct confrontation of another person is considered rude and undesirable. The word "no" is seldom used, because saying no is a confrontation. Instead, some variation of "You may be right" or "We will think about it" are said as polite ways of turning down a request. By contrast, in individualist cultures, speaking one's mind is a virtue. Telling the truth about how one feels is the characteristic of a sincere and honest person (Hofstede 1991; 58).

An important cultural difference is that in some collectivist cultures, such as Japan, classmates, neighbors, and fellow countrymen constitute important in-groups to a greater extent than in more individualistic cultures, such as Australia. An indication of this difference is provided by a study (Mann & Kanagawa 1985) that asked children in Japan and Australia to divide chocolates between their own and another group formed by their own classmates. The Japanese divided their chocolates equally between the two groups, while the Australians did not.

Japanese society provides a striking illustration of the typical nature of collectivist societies with special reference to management practices. The collectivist nature of Japanese society is a major reason why Japanese companies, unlike those in Australia or in any other individualist societies, place extreme emphasis on groups, rather than individuals. According to Atsumi (1979), ostracism from their work groups for failing to adhere to the norms that produce speed, efficiency, quality output, and long hours of work is much more serious for Japanese workers than it is to their counterparts elsewhere. Japanese society penalizes the "loss of face." The extreme kinds of atonement for bringing dishonor, including *hara-kiri* (ritual suicide), cannot be easily understood by the non-Japanese mind (Kahn 1991).

Another related feature of Japanese collectivist society is the belief in consensual management practice. Unlike the United States or Australia, few managers in Japan have offices, and with very few exceptions everyone works together in open spaces without separating walls (Cole 1991; Marsh & Mannari 1976). It is from this arrangement that most Japanese managers spend the majority of their time communicating on the shop floor with their employees. Subordinates are able to provide ideas and suggestions to managers on how to improve specific aspects of work. This concern for involving employees and seeking their advice is part of the overall Japanese concern for consensus building throughout society (Schonberger 1982; Mushashi 1982).

Similarly, to a much greater extent than their American and Australian counterparts, Japanese managers are prepared to put a lot of effort into gathering ideas and expressing them in a way that is at least minimally acceptable to all (Takezawa & Whitehill 1981). The consensus seeking that occurs in Japanese companies, known as the *ringi* system, reflects cultural and social norms that emphasize that all persons are involved in the decision making before it is accepted. This is a unique procedure, whereby ideas are first tested with colleagues and peers until there is a broad agreement before being formally submitted to one's superior for approval (Mushashi 1982; Ouchi 1981). The decision is not a discrete and individual action that is common in Western companies, but something that evolves collectively from the group (Clark 1979).

Other related differences in management practices between collectivist and individualist societies include:

- Motivation, where collectivist values are more discouraging of individual rewards and praise.
- Collectivist, familylike relationships such as those that typify Japan. This is exhibited in the way Japanese employees put in a lot of time and effort to their work, including voluntary overtime. The "Thank goodness it's Friday" mentality is negligible in these collectivist cultures compared to the individualist societies (Khan 1991).
- Conflict management favors the suppression of conflict in collectivist society rather than resolution strategies commonly employed in an individualist society.

African cultures, similar to the Asian and Latin cultures, display cultural patterns that are representative of collectivist cultures. For example, a strong sense of belongingness to a group—such as a tribe—is of overriding importance to an individual African. As such, the average African feels more comfortable when he or she is in a group rather than when he or she is alone (Ahiauzu 1989).

There is a long tradition which places values at the interface between the individual and the set of social group of which they are a member (Zavalloni 1980). African individuals largely conform to their in-group norms, and in return they find their identities in terms of their own group (or tribe) as well as emotional support group.

In organizational life, most Africans favor strict obedience to authorities. In Africa, authority is linked to formal status rather than knowledge and specialized skills. There are sharp distinctions and status between managers and workers. Management has the power, the control, the authority, and regulates rewards and punishment mechanisms. Workers are expected to obey strictly management's directives. The resulting organizations are hierarchical, tall, highly bureaucratic, and mechanistic; and communication is mainly one way, from top to bottom.

Other related collectivist features of African culture include respect for elders and the importance of the extended family.

Arising from the collectivist nature of their societies and the desire to maintain the status quo, Africans often resist change and innovation in the way their social—and, in some cases, business institutions are organized. They perceive that any change that could potentially undermine their collectivist orientation is not only undesirable, but should be avoided. (Beugre and Ofodile 2001)

With these examples in mind, which are, admittedly, generalizations, the major differences between collectivist and individualist cultures are compared in Exhibit 2-2.

| Exhibit 2-2 | The Individualism Dimension |
| --- | --- |

| **Collectivist** | **Individualist** |
| --- | --- |
| In society, people are born into extended families or clans who protect them in exchange for loyalty. | In society, everybody is supposed to take care of himself/herself and his/her immediate family. |
| "We" consciousness prevails. | "I" consciousness prevails. |
| Identity is predicated on the social system, namely, one's in-group. | Identity is predicated in the individual. |
| There is emotional dependence of the individual on organizations and one's in-group. | There is emotional independence of the individual from organizations or institutions. |
| Private life is encroached upon by organizations and clans to which one belongs; opinions are predetermined. | Everybody has the right to a private life and opinion. |
| Harmony within one's group/society is of utmost importance. | Conflict is the vehicle of progress, and management of conflict in a constructive manner can lead to better outcomes. |
| Friendships are predetermined by stable social relationships, but there is need for prestige within the relationships. | The need is for specific friendships. |
| Belief is placed in in-group decisions. | Belief is placed in individual decisions. |
| Value standards differ for in-groups and out-groups (particularism). | Value standards should apply to all (universalism). |

Source: Adapted from The Individual Dimension, *Culture's Consequences: International Differences in Work Related Values*, G. Hofstede, © 1991. Reprinted with permission.

## Small versus Large Power Distance

Managers who must perform in a global business environment and who are cognizant of the need to recognize the cultural diversity inherent in that environment must also understand the importance of "power distance." Power distance is the extent to which a society accepts that power in society's institutions and organizations is distributed unequally. *Small power distance* represents the condition in which people want power to be equally shared and require justification of any differences (Mukhi, et al. 1988). *Large power distance* is represented by a greater acceptance of unequal power, that is, hierarchies in organizations. Large power distance occurs in Japan where paternalism is rife. But Australian workers, for the most part, would not accept this type of rigid hierarchical structure. Exhibit 2-3 outlines major differences that exist in cultures that are typified by small and large power distance in their business environments.

## Weak versus Strong Uncertainty Avoidance

Another important contributing factor to the effective management of cultural diversity is an awareness of "uncertainty avoidance." Uncertainty avoidance refers to people's conscious avoidance of ambiguous and uncertain situations, which appear threatening. In societies characterized by high uncertainty avoidance, behaviors and ideas that deviate from the norm are not tolerated, belief is placed in "experts" and their knowledge, and it is believed that situations should be covered by formal rules and regulations (Dunford 1992). The contrasts between weak and strong uncertainty avoidance cultures are listed in Exhibit 2-4.

| Exhibit 2-3 | The Power Distance Dimension |
|---|---|

| Small Power Distance | Large Power Distance |
|---|---|
| Inequality in society should be minimized. | There should be an order of inequality in this world in which everybody has a rightful place; high and low are protected by this order. |
| All people should enjoy personal independence. | A few people should be independent; most should be dependent. |
| Hierarchy means inequality of the roles, established for convenience. | Hierarchy means existential inequality. |
| Superiors consider subordinates to be "people like me." | Superiors consider subordinates to be a different kind of people. |
| Superiors are accessible. | Superiors are inaccessible. |
| The use of power should be legitimate and is subject to the judgment as to whether it is good or evil. | Power is a basic fact of society that antedates good or evil. Its legitimacy is irrelevant. |
| All should enjoy equal rights. | Power-holders are entitled to privileges. |
| Those in power should try to appear less powerful than they are. | Those in power should try to appear as powerful as possible. |
| The system is to blame. | The underdog is to blame. |
| The way to change a social system is to redistribute power. | The way to change a social system is to remove those in power. |
| People at various power levels feel less threatened and more prepared to trust people. | Other people are a potential threat to one's power and can rarely be trusted. |
| Cooperation among the powerless can be based on solidarity. | Cooperation among the powerless is difficult to attain because of their low-faith-in-people norm. |

Source: Adapted from The Power of Distance Dimension, *Culture's Consequences: International Differences in Work Related Values*, G. Hofstede, © 1991. Reprinted with permission.

### Femininity versus Masculinity.

Femininity versus masculinity is another concept that managers need to understand in addressing issues of cultural diversity and showing competence in intercultural communication. Masculinity connotes dominant social values of aggressiveness, acquisition of money and material possessions, and not caring for others. A masculine society is one in which these values are strongly represented and where gender-based roles are clearly differentiated. By contrast, in a feminine society, nurturing is valued over the pursuit of wealth, human relationships are more important than the acquisition of material goods, and sympathy for the disadvantaged is an important value. The characteristics of feminine and masculine cultures are compared in Exhibit 2-5.

### Hofstede's Cultural Dimensions: An Illustration

Hofstede (1980) characterized forty countries in terms of these four factors. Exhibit 2-6 demonstrates the rating of Australia, Hong Kong, Japan, the Philippines, Singapore, Sweden, and the United States in terms of these factors. Hofstede ranked each country on each dimension, but the dichotomous treatment (high or low) in the following table is enough to illustrate the considerable variations.

| Exhibit 2-4 | The Uncertainty Avoidance Dimension |
|---|---|

| **Weak Uncertainty Avoidance** | **Strong Uncertainty Avoidance** |
|---|---|
| The uncertainty inherent in life is more easily accepted and each day is taken as it comes. | The uncertainty inherent in life is perceived as a continuous threat that must be fought. |
| Ease and lower stress are experienced. | Higher anxiety and stress are experienced. |
| Hard work, as such, is not a virtue. | There is an inner urge to work hard. |
| Aggressive behavior is frowned upon. | Aggressive behavior of self and others is accepted. |
| Less showing of emotions is preferred. | More showing of emotions is preferred. |
| Conflict and competition can be contained on the level of fair play and can be used constructively. | Conflict and competition can unleash aggression and should therefore be avoided. |
| More acceptance of dissent is entailed. | A strong need for consensus is involved. |
| Deviation is not considered threatening; greater tolerance is shown. | Deviant persons and ideas are dangerous; intolerance holds sway. |
| More positive feelings toward younger people are seen. | Younger people are suspect. |
| There is more willingness to take risks in life. | There is great concern with security in life. |
| The accent is on relativism, empiricism. | The search is for ultimate, absolute truths and values. |
| There should be as few rules as possible. | There is a need for written rules and regulations. |
| If rules cannot be kept, we should change them. | If rules cannot be kept, we are sinners and should repent. |
| Belief is placed in generalists and common sense. | Belief is placed in experts and their knowledge. |
| The authorities are there to serve the citizens. | Ordinary citizens are incompetent compared with the authorities. |

Source: Adapted from The Uncertainty Avoidance Dimension, *Culture's Consequences: International Differences in Work Related Values*, G. Hofstede, © 1991. Reprinted with permission.

| Exhibit 2-5 | The Masculine Dimension |
|---|---|

| **Feminine** | **Masculine** |
|---|---|
| Men need not be assertive, but can also assume nurturing roles. | Men should be assertive. Women should be nurturing. |
| Sex roles in society are more fluid. | Sex roles in society are clearly differentiated. |
| There should be equality between the sexes. | Men should dominate in society. |
| Quality of life is important. | Performance is what counts. |
| You work in order to live. | You live in order to work. |
| People and environment are important. | Money and things are important. |
| One sympathizes with the unfortunate. | One admires the successful achiever. |
| Small and slow are beautiful. | Big and fast are beautiful. |
| Unisex and androgyny are ideal. | Ostentatious manliness ("machismo") is appreciated. |

Source: Adapted from The Masculine Dimension, *Culture's Consequences: International Differences in Work Related Values*, G. Hofstede, © 1991. Reprinted with permission.

| Exhibit 2-6 | National Culture in Four Dimensions | | | |
|---|---|---|---|---|
| **Country** | **Power** | **Uncertainty** | **Individualism** | **Masculinity** |
| Australia | Low | Low | High | High |
| Hong Kong | High | Low | Low | High |
| Japan | High | High | Low | High |
| Philippine | High | Low | Low | High |
| Singapore | High | Low | Low | Low |
| Sweden | Low | Low | High | Low |
| USA | Low | Low | High | High |

Source: Adapted from National Culture in Four Dimensions, *Culture's Consequences: International Differences in Work Related Values*, G. Hofstede, © 1991. Reprinted with permission.

### Confucian Dynamism: The Fifth Cultural Dimension

Subsequent to his study on the four cultural dimensions involving power distance, individualism, masculinity, and uncertainty avoidance, Hofstede, in collaboration with Bond, identified an additional cultural dimension by which nations can be classified: Confucian Dynamism or Long Term versus Short Term Orientation (Hofstede & Bond 1984).

Confucian Dynamism was identified through a questionnaire (labeled the *Chinese Value Survey*) and was developed on the basis of traditional Confucian values that are believed to influence East Asian countries, including the People's Republic of China, South Korea, Hong Kong, Singapore, and even Japan. Confucianism is not a religion, but rather a system of practical ethics. It is based on a set of pragmatic rules for daily life derived from experience. As a moral system, Confucianism focuses on the relationship between man and man, which is defined in terms of five virtues; humanity and benevolence (*ren*), righteousness (*yi*), propriety (*li*), wisdom (*zhi*), and trustworthiness (*xin*) (Fan Ying 2001).

Another focus of Confucianism is the unequal relationships between people that creates stability in society. The five basic unequal relationships are ruler–subject, father–son, older brother–younger brother, husband–wife, and older friend–younger friend. The junior owes the senior respect, and the senior owes the junior protection and consideration. The prototype for all social institutions is the family. A person is mainly a member of a family, as opposed to being just an individual.

*Harmony* in the family must be preserved, and harmony is the maintenance of one's *face*, that is, one's dignity, self-respect, and prestige. Treating others as one would like to be treated oneself is virtuous behavior. Virtue with respect to one's tasks consists of attempting to obtain skills and education, working hard, not spending more than necessary, being patient, and persevering. It should be noted that individuals may have inner thoughts that differ from the group's norms and values; however, individuals may not act on those thoughts, because group harmony and not shaming the group is of paramount importance.

## Trompenaars' cultural dimensions

Trompenaars, a Dutch researcher, conducted a major multinational study of cross-cultural dimensions. Tompenaars' work was the most recent attempt to separate and categorize cultural dimensions. The scale of his empirical research entailed 15,000 respondents, largely made up of managers from 28 countries with at least 500 respondents from each nation. Seven relationship orientations have been derived, along with attitudinal dimension towards time and the environment that have considerable implications for managers participating in the global economy (Trompenaars 1994; Trompenaars & Hampden-Turner 1997). For convenience and reference, brief descriptions of each attitudinal dimension and examples are provided in Exhibit 2-7.

As can be seen from the following table, people around the world differ in their value orientations. These in turn affect their work behavior in organizations. As such, this has considerable implications for international management in the managing of culturally diverse workforces, requiring them to be mindful of cultural difference while integrating these cultural differences into their main stream management policies and practices.

## COUNTRY CLUSTERS

Ronen and Shenker (1985) attempted to classify world cultures in terms of nine clusters, predicated on previous studies that looked at variables in the following specific four categories: (1) the importance of work goals; (2) need deficiency, fulfillment, and job satisfaction; (3) managerial and organizational variables; and (4) work role and interpersonal relationships.

As a consequence, these clusters embody Anglo, Germanic, Latin European, Nordic, Latin American, Near Eastern, Far Eastern, Arab—and independent to include countries that did not quite fit in the eight clusters.

According to the Country Clusters Model, individual countries in each cluster appear to enjoy a considerable degree of commonality of cultural values and, therefore, international managers operating in countries within a specific cluster will find significant similarity in the way business is conducted in that cluster. For example, an international manager dealing with two countries such as Australia and the United States being representative of the Anglo cluster, will need to make only minor adjustments in order to operate in these two countries.

On the other hand, with countries that fall within two distinct clusters, an international manager will experience varying degrees of dissimilarity. As a consequence for international managers, to remain effective in their international operations, it would be necessary for international managers to make major cultural adjustments based on differences arising from these clusters.

## CULTURAL DIMENSIONS AND MANAGEMENT PRACTICES

As can be seen from the cross-cultural dimensions discussed in the previous sections, they have a major influence on the way organizations are managed in different nations across the globe. This is in stark contrast with management theories developed mainly by scholars in Anglo culture, in particular the United States, that advocate the universal applicability of modern management theories (Clark, R. 1979; Form 1979; Hickson, et al. 1974; Cole 1991). For example, research found major differences between American management practice and Japanese management practice, even though they have much in common as modern industrial societies.

| Exhibit 2-7 | Trompenaars' Cross-Cultural Dimensions |
|---|---|

**Universalism**

Beliefs and ideas can be applied everywhere without alteration.

Example: The focus is on written management policies and high degree of adherence to the due process of law.

**Particularism**

Circumstances dictate how ideas and practices should be applied.

Example: The focus is on building personal and business relationships. Trust is more valued than written contract.

**Individualism**

People perceive themselves primarily as individuals.

Example: Management's human resource policy is based on individual career aspirations.

**Communitarism**

People in communitarist society view themselves as part of a group.

Example: Human resource managers develop policies that are designed to address group needs and aspirations.

**Neutral culture**

There is a high degree of control by individuals in their expressions of their emotions in a neutral society such as in Japan and/or United Kingdom that are considered to be neutral cultures.

Example: Management's conduct of business is more rationally based.

**Affective culture**

Emotions are expressed openly and naturally.

Example: Management's conduct of business is more emotionally based.

**Specific culture**

Individuals have a large public space that they readily share with others, and a small private space they keep that they are willing to share with only close friends and family members.

Example: Management is less concerned with titles and status.

**Diffuse culture**

Both public and private spaces represent nearly the same size and individuals guard their public space, as entry into it affords them entry into private space, too.

Example: Management is more status conscious.

**Achievement culture**

People are given status based on their high performance.

Example: High recognition and reward are given by management for high performers.

**Ascription culture**

Status is attributed based on who or what a person is.

Example: Business and family ties are valued and rewarded by management accordingly.

**Sequential Time Orientation**

Time is seen as a series of passing events.

Example: The issues are addressed one at a time.

**Synchronic Time Orientation**

Past, present, and future are interrelated and influence the present actions.

Example: People are comfortable in dealing with a variety of issues all at once.

**Inner-directed culture**

People believe in controlling outcomes of their activity and the environment.

Example: Management should develop individualized incentive programs at work.

**Outer-directed culture**

People let things take their own course.

Example: Management should be flexible, but have a strategic focus on outcome.

Source: Adapted from Trompenaars' Cross Cultural Dimensions adapted from Trompenaars, F. and Hampden-Turner, C., *Riding the Wave of Culture: Understanding Cultural Diversity in Business*, © 1997, McGraw-Hill.

American organizations represented the following managerial features:

- Short-term employment
- Individual decision making
- Individual responsibility
- Rapid evaluation and promotion
- Explicit, formalized control
- Specialized career paths
- Segmented concern (Ouchi & Jaeger 1974)

Japanese organizations, on the other hand, displayed the following management characteristics (Ouchi & Jaeger 1974; Hatvany & Pucik 1981; Sheldon & Kleiner 1990; Harris & Moran 1991):

- Long-term employment
- Long-term planning
- Consensual decision making
- Collective responsibility
- Slow evaluation and promotion
- Implicit, formal control
- Nonspecialized careers path
- Holistic concern

A number of empirical studies have since been conducted worldwide that support the notion that cultural dimensions affect the way organizations are managed internationally. Andre Laurent studied the philosophies and behavior of managers in nine Western European countries, the United States, and three Asian countries: Indonesia, Japan, and the People's Republic of China. He found the distinct behavior patterns for managers in each of these countries (Laurent 1983).

## Attitude to Hierarchy within Organization

Laurent (1983) found that cultures that value hierarchical structuring as a means of social cohesion impose severe restrictions on communication flow. This value orientation affected what information was communicated, how it was communicated, and to whom. Laurent canvassed managers for their views about the statement: "In order to have efficient work relationships it is often necessary to bypass the hierarchical line." As outlined in Exhibit 2-8, Swedish managers did not view bypassing as a problem as long as the job is being carried out efficiently. In contrast, Italian managers saw bypassing the boss as an act of disrespect and insubordination.

In Laurent's study, managers also differed in their response to the statement: "The main reason for a hierarchical structure is so that everybody knows who has authority over whom." Managers from Southern Europe, Asia, Latin America, and the Middle East tended to strongly agree, whereas managers from the United States, Germany, Sweden, the Netherlands, and Great Britain disagreed for the most part. Again, differences in their management philosophies are indicative of their cultural orientations. A comparison of their agreement rate across countries is given in Exhibit 2-9.

| Exhibit 2-8 | Bypassing the Hierarchical Line |
|---|---|

**Disagreement Rate Across Countries:**
**In order to have efficient work relationships, it is often necessary to bypass the hierarchical line.**

| Sweden | U.S. | Great Britain | France | Netherlands | Germany | Indonesia | Italy | P.R.C. | Spain |
|---|---|---|---|---|---|---|---|---|---|
| 26% | 32% | 35% | 43% | 44% | 45% | 51% | 56% | 59% | 74% |

Source: Adapted from Disagreement Rates Across Countries from Laurent, A. *The Cultural Diversity of Western Conceptions of Management* in International Studies of Management and Organization, Vol. 13, No. 1-1, Spring/Summer, 1983. © 1983 by M.E. Sharpe, Inc. Reprinted with permission.

| Exhibit 2-9 | Hierarchical Structure and Authority |
|---|---|

**Agreement Rate Across Countries:**
**The main reasons for a hierarchical structure is so that everybody knows who has authority over whom.**

| U.S. | Germany | Sweden | Netherlands | Great Britain | Spain | Italy | France | Japan | P.R.C. | Indonesia |
|---|---|---|---|---|---|---|---|---|---|---|
| 17% | 26% | 30% | 31% | 34% | 34% | 42% | 43% | 50% | 70% | 83% |

Source: Adapted from Agreement Rates Across Countries from Laurent, A: *The Cultural Diversity of Western Conceptions of Management and Organization*, Vol 13, No. 1-1, Spring/Summer, 1983. © 1983 by M.E. Sharpe, Inc. Reprinted with permission.

## Managers: Experts or Problem Solvers?

Laurent (1983) also asked managers to respond to the statement: "It is important for a manager to have at hand precise answers to most of the questions that his subordinates may raise about their work." He discovered little agreement among managers in their different countries. For example, more than four times as many Japanese and Indonesian managers as American managers concurred with the statement. According to Asian Pacific managers, the manager who cannot answer subordinates' questions loses status. Most American managers regarded the role of the manager as a problem solver and believed that managers should help employees find better ways of solving problems rather than simply addressing their questions directly.

Laurent concluded that the cultural and national origins of European, North American, and Asian managers considerably influenced their views on how effective managers should carry out their roles and functions. In addition, the extent to which managers viewed organizations as political, authoritarian, role-formalizing, or hierarchical-relationship systems differed according to their country of origin and cultural differences.

Additional overseas research involving managers from 13 countries showed that managers have displayed differing attitudes towards the following statement: "It is important for a manager to have at hand precise answers to most of the questions that his subordinates may raise about work." Percentages in agreement by these managers are provided in Exhibit 2-10.

| Exhibit 2-10 | Agreement by Managers |
| --- | --- |
| **Country** | **Percentage in Agreement** |
| Japan | 78% |
| People's Republic of China | 74% |
| Indonesia | 73% |
| Italy | 66% |
| France | 53% |
| Germany | 46% |
| Belgium | 44% |
| Switzerland | 38% |
| United Kingdom | 27% |
| Denmark | 23% |
| United States | 18% |
| Netherlands | 17% |
| Sweden | 10% |

Adapted from *International Studies of Management and Organization*, vol. 13, no. 1-1 (Spring/Summer 1983). © 1983 by M.E. Sharpe, Inc. Reprinted with permission.

### Cultural Variations in Performance Appraisal

In another study of management performance appraisals, this time in the United States, Saudi Arabia, and Japan, conducted by Harris and Moran (1991), it was revealed that performance appraisal differed significantly across cultures. In Exhibit 2-11, a comparison is given of the differences in the conduct of performance appraisal in the sample countries.

From Exhibit 2-11, it can be seen that significant differences exist in the conduct of performance appraisal by managers across three different countries and cultures.

## MANAGEMENT OF CULTURAL DIVERSITY

The studies reviewed in the previous sections confirm that management practices differ across cultures. These findings have important implications for management in regard to accommodating cultural diversity and achieving management performance in the global business environment.

### Workforce Diversity Defined

Workforce diversity refers to the mix of people from various backgrounds in the labor force. Within an organization, there is a full mix of cultures and subcultures to which members belong. These subcultures are based on religion, education, ethnicity, marital and family status, sexual orientation, and other unifying life experiences, which provide extreme variation on how to go about achieving day-to-day goals (Adler 1997).

Demographic trends in many countries around the world indicate that the composition of the workforce is increasingly changing. Also, there is

| Exhibit 2-11 | Cultural Variations: Performance Appraisals | | |
|---|---|---|---|
| **Dimensions, General** | **United States** | **Saudi Arabia** | **Japan** |
| **Objective of performance appraisal** | Fairness, employee development | Placement | Direction of company/employee development |
| **Who does appraisal** | Supervisor | Manager several levels up. Appraiser has to know employee well | Mentor and supervisor. Appraiser has to know employee well. |
| **Authority of appraiser** | Presumed in supervisory role or position. Supervisor takes slight lead. | Reputation important (prestige is determined by nationality, sex, family, tribe, title education. Authority of appraiser important: Don't say, "I don't know" | Respect accorded by employee to supervisor or appraiser. Done coequally |
| **How often?** | Once a year | Once a year | Developmental or periodically once a month. Evaluation appraisal after first 12 years. |
| **Assumptions** | Objective appraiser is fair. | Subjective appraiser more important than objective. Connections are more important | Objective and subjective. Japanese can be trained in anything |
| **Manner of communication and feedback** | Criticism direct. Criticism may be in writing. Objective, authentic. | Criticism subtle. Older more likely to be direct. Criticism not provided. | Criticism subtle. Criticism given verbally. Observe formalities in writing. |
| **The right to challenge** | American will dispute appraisal. | Saudi Arabian will dispute. | Japanese would rarely dispute. |
| **Praise** | Given individually | Given individually | Given to the whole group |
| **Motivators** | Money and position | Loyalty to supervisor | Internal excellence |

Adapted from Cultural Variations: Performance Appraisals, Managing Cultural Differences, 3rd ed., P. Harris and R. Moran, © 1991, with permission from Elsevier.

a rapid international expansion of businesses due to their globalization initiatives. As a result, the workforce is comprised of people who are different and who hold a wide range of attitudes, needs, desires, values, and work behaviors (Deluca & McDowell 1992; Morrison 1992; Rosen & Lovelace 1991). However, this cultural diversity is often perceived differently by managers in organizations. Some managers regard cultural diversity as a problem. For others, cultural diversity presents considerable benefits that organizations need to capitalize on. An analysis of these advantages and disadvantages is surveyed in the following sections.

## Disadvantages of Cultural Diversity

Problems most frequently occur in convergence situations, when the organization needs employees to think and act in similar ways. Communication and integration become more difficult. There is potential for increased ambiguity, complexity, and confusion when single agreement has to be reached or when overall procedures have to be developed (Adler 1997).

Problems may be attitudinal (Hodgetts & Luthans 2000). For example, the attitude that American managers have when they perceive a problem is different from Chinese managers. In the United States, life is seen as the set of problems to be solved. For the Chinese, however, life is seen as a set of situations to be accepted. Americans, then, perceive problems much earlier than Chinese and thus prevent an actual problem from happening. On the other hand, for Chinese problem solvers, the problem exists when it has already happened.

Cultural diversity within an organization, without any strategies or attitudes to accommodate it, may create perceptual (stereotyping, status-related problems, gender role conflicts) and communicational (language and misinterpretation) problems. It can engender increased anxiety among managers because they worry that they lack information essential for effective intercultural interactions. They are afraid that they cannot possibly catch up and learn all there is to know about cultural differences; and intercultural encounters might lead them to make expensive and embarrassing mistakes (Irwin & More 1994). An extreme reaction to cultural difference and to culture shock is fear and even relational paralysis.

## Advantages of Cultural Diversity

Cultural diversity can be seen as advantageous to organizations in a number of ways:

- "Selling goods and services in the increasingly diverse marketplace is facilitated by a well-utilized, diverse workforce" (Cox & Smolinski 1994, 26);
- Competitive advantage can be gained by firms in terms of the insights of employees from various cultural backgrounds who can assist organizations in understanding cultural effects on marketing strategies.
- Sales benefit can be achieved by firms, if consumers have some opportunities to interact with organizational representatives of their own communities (Cox & Smolinski 1994).
- Enhanced creativity, flexibility, and problem solving can be fostered, especially for complex problems involving many qualitative factors (Hayles 1982).
- Acceptance of new ideas is easier when it is proposed by someone from other cultures than it is from someone within one's own culture (Adler 1997),
- "Diversity becomes most advantageous when the organization wants to expand its perspective, its approach, its range of ideas, its operations, its product lines, or its marketing plans" (Adler 1997, 101).

On balance, advantages of diversity far outweigh its disadvantages provided that managers have incorporated diversity within their mainstream activities and managerial processes and functions including their corporate culture, one that values and celebrates diversity. Thus, effective management of cultural diversity in any national and or international organization can produce significant benefits.

# KEY STRATEGIES FOR EFFECTIVE MANAGEMENT OF CULTURAL DIVERSITY ACROSS THE GLOBE

The following managerial strategies are recommended in order to enhance multicultural organizational performance:

1. Management should actively seek to capitalize on the advantages of its organization's cultural diversity, rather than attempting to stifle or ignore the diversity, and to minimize the barriers that can develop as a result of people having different backgrounds, attitudes, values, behavior styles, and concerns.

2. Organizational resources, such as key jobs, income, prerequisite, access to information, and the like, should be distributed equitably and not determined or affected by cultural characteristics such as ethnic background.

3. Decision-making should be shared widely by employees with differing cultural characteristics.

4. Management needs to develop tolerance and acceptance of cultural diversity. The organizational culture (assumptions about people, taken for granted norms, the way work gets done) is pluralistic in that it recognizes and appreciates diversity. It acknowledges both the need for "being the same" in some ways to work together effectively and the need for "being different" in some ways to recognize individual and group interests, concerns, and backgrounds.

5. Institutional policies, practices, and procedures are flexible and responsive to the needs of all employees, regardless of cultural differences.

To effectively manage cultural diversity at work both nationally and internationally, managers should view differences as a challenge and an opportunity rather than as a set of additional problems needing their attention. It also means being continuously sensitive to issues that arise in the management of cultural diversity. On this point, it can be argued that employees and managers must have a high capacity for examination of thoughts and feelings, attitudes, and beliefs about race, sex, or people who are different on any cultural dimension: actively examining personally held assumptions, taking care not to view differences among people as indications that some of these people are inferior or strange. All these require, above all, an honest and dedicated leadership that is committed to the goals and values of a multicultural organization. Also, in order to better manage their culturally diverse organizations, managers need to incorporate cross-cultural training as part of their overall strategic human resource planning. The issues to be addressed in cross-cultural training programs should reflect an understanding of:

1. The concept of "individual culture," which incorporates one's image of self and role. This, in turn, recognizes that personal needs, values, standards, and expectations are in one way or another conditioned by cultural forces beyond the self. Kaye's (1994) adult communication management model provides a

rationale for this argument, since the inner "self" doll is very much influenced by the social and organizational culture enveloping people in systems. Interculturally competent managers, therefore, understand the impact of cultural factors on human relationships and communication, and are willing to adapt to changing "intercultures" as part of their process of growth.

2. The concept of "cultural sensitivity," which involves integrating the characteristics of corporate culture, with experiences of individuals or minority groups in the workplace. Managers who are interculturally competent, therefore, need to develop sensitivity of how cultural diversity can influence individual behavior and communication. Global managers need to apply such cultural awareness to developing effective professional relationships with those who are culturally different.

3. The concept of "acculturation," which refers to effectively adjusting and adapting to a specific culture or subculture. Interculturally competent managers understand what is involved in self and group identity, and are alert to the impact of culture shock or differences upon an individual's sense of identity. When dealing with multicultural employees, these managers make it a basic rule to avoid any hint of ethnocentric values.

4. The concept of "cultural management influences," which connotes the effects of cultural conditioning on the management of information and human or natural resources. One's own culture affects the way a manager views every critical factor in the management process, from decision-making and problem solving to supervision and appraisal. As there are differences underlying cultural diversity, an interculturally competent manager tries to adapt modern principles of management to the realities of a multicultural workforce. This tendency could be labeled "cultural contingency" (Saee 1998).

5. The concept of "effective intercultural performance," which assumes the ability of managers to apply intercultural communication research findings and principles to specific cross-cultural work situations that affect people's performance on the job (Saee 1998).

6. The concept of "problem-solving" in multicultural contexts. Harris and Moran (1991) suggest a five-step method of problem solving across cultures:

   - Describe the problem as understood in both cultures.
   - Analyze the problem from two (or all) cultural perspectives.
   - Identify the basis for the problem from both (or all) viewpoints.
   - Solve the problem through synergistic strategies.
   - Determine if the solution is working multiculturally.

| *Summary* |
| --- |

This chapter explored cross-cultural dimensions and their influences upon management practices around the world. It was established that sound management of cultural diversity calls for a high-level knowledge of various cultural dimensions prevailing in different parts of the world. Important theoretical perspectives, as originally advanced by Kluckhohn and Strodtbeck (1961), Hofstede (1980), Trompenaars (1994), Trompenaars and Hampden-Turner (1997), and Ronen and Shenker (1985), dealing with cross-cultural dimensions and their influence on managerial practices were also discussed. Specific managerial strategies in managing cultural diversity both nationally and internationally effectively were suggested. Finally, it is recommended that cross-cultural skills and training are essential to managers and professionals concerned with increasing understanding, cooperation, productivity, profitability, and organizational cohesiveness within their multicultural workforce both nationally and internationally.

The next chapter discusses worldviews that have considerable influence on the way business is conducted in different parts of the world.

## Critical Discussion Questions

1. What are the main objectives of cross-cultural management?

2. What are the specific dangers of an international manager having parochial or ethnocentric views?

3. Briefly describe six cultural dimensions as outlined by Kluckhohn and Strodtbeck. Provide some examples from an organizational context to illustrate each of these dimensions.

4. Explain the terms: "collectivism," "individualism," "small and large power distance," "weak and strong uncertainty avoidance," "femininity and masculinity," "short-term and long-term orientation." Provide examples.

5. What is the main contribution of Trompenaars relating to cultural dimensions?

6. Define the term "workforce diversity."

7. Examine and critically discuss the statement: "Cultural diversity can be perceived as a major disadvantage for an organization."

8. In what ways does cultural diversity present considerable benefits for an international organization?

9. What are the specific strategies that international managers could adopt with the view to enhancing organizational performance?

## Applications

### Experiential

1. In the light of Hofstede's cultural dimensions, critically describe the culture of your home country with reference to your home country's managerial practices.

2.  Use the model of cultural dimension as suggested by Trompenaars to develop a cultural profile of a country of your choice, using library materials.

3.  Compare and contrast the managerial practices in any two countries of your choice using various models of cultural dimensions described in this chapter.

## Internet

### NESTLÉ, A Truly World Company

Nestlé was founded in 1866 in Switzerland as a family business. Henri Nestlé, the founder, developed the first milk food for infants in 1867. Over the centuries, Nestlé has become the worlds largest food and beverage company. Nestlé's own statistics showed that sales at the end of 2001 were CHF 84.7 billion with a net profit of CHF 6.7 billion. It has a workforce of 230,000 and it has factories and operations in nearly all countries in the world. Some of its product lines are dairy products, baby foods, breakfast cereals, beverages and bottled waters, and pet care products.

In recent years, it has been involved in major acquisitions of companies around the world. Since this company deals with numerous culturally diverse people as consumers, employees, and shareholders, your assignment is to consult the Nestlé website: www.Nestlé.com and other databases available at your school. Then carefully study how Nestlé markets its products in different countries. As well, try to answer the following questions:

1.  In what ways does culture affect its product development?

2.  In what ways does Nestlé respond to the needs of its culturally diverse clientele around the world?

3.  In what ways does Nestlé manage cultural diversity in the workplace?

## References

Adler, N. (1997). *International dimensions of organizational behavior* (3rd ed.). Cincinnati, OH: South-Western College Publishing.

Adler, N.J., Campbell, N.C., & Laurent, A. (1989). In search of appropriate methodology from outside the People Republic of China looking in. *Journal of International Business Studies, 20* (1), 41–60.

Ahiauzu, I.A. (1989). "The Theory A" system of work organization for the modern African workplace. *International Studies of Management and Organization, 19,* 6–27

Atsumi, R. (1979). Tsukiai: Obligatory personal relationships of Japanese employee. *Human Organization, 38,* 63–70.

Beugre, C.D., & Ofodile, O.F. (2001) Managing for organizational effectiveness in sub-Sahara Africa: A cultural fit model. *International Human Resource Management, 12* (4), 535–550.

Child, I. (1981). Culture, contingency and capitalism in the cross-national study of organizations. In L. L. Cummings & B. M. Staw (Eds.), *Research in Organizational behavior* (pp. 3, 30–356). Greenwich, CT: JAI Press.

Child, J., & Tayeb, M. (1983). Theoretical perspectives in cross-national organizational research. *International Studies of Management and Organizations, 7* (3–4), 19–32.

Clark, R. (1979). *The Japanese company.* New Haven: Yale University Press.

Cole, R. (1991). *Cross-cultural training bibliography.* Canberra: Department of the Prime Minister and Cabinet, Office of Multicultural Affairs.

Cox, T., & Smolinski, C. (1994). Managing diversity and glass ceiling initiatives as national economic imperatives. *Report prepared for the U.S. Department of Labor's Class Ceiling Commission.* Washington, DC: U.S. Government Printing Office.

Deluca, J.M., & McDowell, R. N. (1992). Managing diversity: A strategic "grass-roots" approach. In S. E. Jackson (Ed.), *Diversity in the workplace: Human resources initiatives, Society for Industrial and Organizational Psychology— The Professional Practice Series.* New York: Guilford Press.

Dunford, W. D. (1992). *Organizational behaviour.* Reading, MA.: Addison-Wesley.

Fan Ying (2001). The Chinese cultural system: Implications for cross-cultural management. *SAM Advanced Management Journal.*

Form, W. (1979). Comparative industrial sociology and the convergence hypothesis. *Annual Review of Sociology, 5,* 1–25.

Frank, G. (1990). Mergers and acquisitions: Competitive advantages and cultural fit. *European Management Journal, 8* (1), 00–00

Harris, P., & Moran, R. (1991). *Managing cultural differences* (3rd ed.). Houston, TX: Gulf Publishing Company.

Hatvany, N. & Pucik, V. (1981). Japanese Management Practices and Productivity. *Organizational Dynamics, 8* (4), 5-21

Hayles, R. (1982, July 25–31). Costs and benefits of integrating persons from diverse cultures in organization. Paper presented at the 20th International Congress of Applied Psychology, Edinburgh, Scotland.

Hickson, D. J., Hinnings, C.R., McMillan, C. J., & Schweiter, J. P. (1974). The culture-free context of organizational structure: A tri-national comparison. *Sociology, 8,* 59–80.

Hodgetts, R.M., & Luthans, F. (2000). *International Management.* New York: McGraw-Hill.

Hofstede, G. (1980). *Culture's consequences: International differences in work related values.* Beverly Hills, CA: Sage.

Hofstede, G. (1991). *Cultures and organizations: Software of the mind.* New York: McGraw-Hill.

Hofstede, G., & Bond, M. H. (1984). Hofstede's Culture Dimensions: An independent validation using Rokeach's value survey. *Journal of Cross-Cultural Psychology, 15,* 417–433.

Irwin, H., & More, E. (1994). *Managing Corporate Communication*. Sydney: Allen and Unwin.

Kaye, M. (1994). *Communication Management*. Sydney: Prentice-Hall.

Khan, R. P. (1991). Japanese management: A critical appraisal. *Management Decision, 29,*17–23.

Kluckhohn, F. & Strodtbeck, F. (1961). *Variations in value orientation*. New York: Harper and Row.

Lane, H.W., & diStafano, J.J. (1992). *International Management Behavior: From Policy to Practice* (2nd ed.). Boston: PWS-Kent.

Laurent, A. (1983). The cultural diversity of Western conceptions of management. *International Studies of Management and Organization, 13,* (1–2), 75–96.

Limaye, M.R., & Victor, D. A. (1995). Cross-cultural communication. In Jackson, T. (Ed.), *Cross-cultural management*. London: Butterworth Heinemann.

Mann, L., Radford, M., & Kanagawa, C. (1985). Cross-cultural differences in children's use of decision rules: A comparison between Japan and Australia. *Journal of Personality and Social Psychology, 49,* 1557–1564.

Marsh, R.M., & Mannari, H. (1976). *Modernization and the Japanese factory*. Princeton, NJ: Princeton University Press.

Mead, R. (1998). *International management: Cross-cultural dimensions*. Cambridge, MA: Blackwell Publishers.

Morrison, A. (1992). New solutions to the same old glass ceiling. *Women in Management Review, 7* (4), 15–19.

Mukhi, S., Hampton, D., & Barnwell, N. (1988). *Australian Management*. Sydney: McGraw-Hill.

Mushashi, M. (1982). *The book of five rings: The real art of Japanese management*. New York: Bantam Books.

Ouchi, W. (1981). *Theory Z: How American business can meet the Japanese challenge*. Reading, MA: Addison-Wesley.

Ouchi, W.G., & Jaeger, A.M. (1974). Made in America under Japanese Management. *Harvard Business Review, 52* (5), 61–69.

Ronen S., & Shenker O. (1985).Clustering countries on attitudinal dimensions: A review of synthesis. *Academy of Management, 28* (4), 435–454

Rosen, B. & Lovelace, K. (1991). Piecing together the diversity puzzle. *HR Magazine, 36* (9), 78–84.

Saee, J. (1998). Intercultural competence: Preparing enterprising managers for the global economy. *Journal of European Business Education, 7* (2), 15–37.

Saee, J. (1997, May). Cultural diversity and global economy. *Australian Institute of Management Journal, 17* (2), 17–19.

Sheldon R. & Kleiner, B. (1990). What Japanese management techniques can (or should) be applied by American managers? *Industrial Management, 3* (3),17–19.

Schonberger, R.J. (1982). The transfer of Japanese manufacturing processes to United States industry. *Academy of Management Review, 7*, 477–487.

Takezawa, S., & Whitehill, A.M. (1981). *Workways: Japan and America.* Tokyo: Japan Institute of Labour.

Torrington, D. (1994). *International human resource management: Think globally, act locally.* Englewood Cliffs, NJ: Prentice Hall.

Trompenaars, F. (1994). *Riding the waves of culture.* New York: Irwin.

Trompenaars, F., & Hampden-Turner, C. (1997). *Riding the waves of culture: Understanding cultural diversity in business* (2 ed.). New York: McGraw-Hill.

Zavalloni, M. (1980). Values. In H.C. Triandis and R.W. Brislin, (Eds), *Handbook of cross-cultural psychology* (Vol. 5, pp. 73–120). Boston: Allyn and Bacon.

# Chapter 3

*Worldview and Religion*

*History is philosophy teaching by example.*

—Henry St. John Bolingbroke

*There are truths on this side of the Pyrenees which are falsehoods on the other.*

—Blaise Pascal, Pensèes

# WORLDVIEWS: AN OVERVIEW

Since the dawn of civilization, human societies in different regions of the globe have been grappling with complex realities of existentialism and other related "Big Picture" questions such as who are we? Why are we on this earth? What is the meaning of life, and why do we die? Is there an eternal life? What is the origin of the universe? How do we apprehend (or understand) the world? Worldviews and the issues they pose for managers are timeless and represent the most fundamental basis of a culture, including religion. For example, a Hindu, with a strong belief in reincarnation, will perceive his or her time in the world differently from a Christian, Muslim, Jew, Taoist, or atheist (Samovar & Porter 1995). The Islamic worldview, based on the Koran, forbids usury. In keeping with God's law, the Islamic banking sector in a practicing Islamic country does not charge interest on loans provided to their customers.

Segregated geographically, each human community has in isolation advanced its own unique explanations for these philosophical, "big picture" questions over the centuries. One category of explanation is referred to as the *worldview*. For this reason, many worldviews exist capable of explaining complex realities, each developed over time by human societies located in different geographic parts of the globe. More importantly, each community perceived its own worldview to be the "ultimate truth." The worldview of each community was immeasurably shaped by its cultural orientations. This is mainly due to the fact that the human being's inside view of the way things are colored, shaped, and arranged is according to personal cultural preconceptions (Hoebel & Frost 1976). While Pennington (1985), in acknowledging the highly influential role of culture on worldview, held the notion that "if one understands a culture's worldview and cosmology, reasonable accuracy can be attained in predicting behaviors and motivations in other dimensions" (32).

Understanding worldviews help us understand how business is conducted in different parts of the world, because such business activities are fundamentally predicated on worldviews held by the individuals involved on all sides of any transaction. In this chapter, an explanation is provided of how worldviews are formed and transmitted, including sociocultural dimensions; social structure; educational institutions; and, more importantly, religions. The main focus of discussion in this chapter is on world religions—Judaism, Christianity, Islam, Hinduism, Buddhism, and Confucianism—which typically have the most influence on ultimately shaping the worldviews prevailing in different societies. A comparison of Western and Eastern philosophies and their respective worldviews is also presented. Finally, the implications of differing worldviews are discussed with reference to business practices around the world.

# RELIGION

Worldviews are shaped by a number of cultural channels. The one channel that has a predominant role in transmitting and preserving a worldview is one's faith and the institutions that reinforce it whether it be a church, mosque, synagogue, or temple. Research shows that of the existing 6 billion people living on this planet, close to 80 percent of the world population claim some religious affiliation (Mahoney, et al. 1998).

Religion is a socially shared set of beliefs, ideas, and actions that relate to reality. These beliefs, such as the existence of God, good and evil, Creation, and the like, cannot be verified empirically, yet they affect the course of natural and human events. Religion explains the notions that cannot be resolved otherwise. The belief systems that people receive from their religion conditions their motivations and priorities, which, in turn, affect their actions. A sympathetic understanding of religion, then, gives us insight into everyday practice of life in a particular culture (Samovar & Porter 1995). The religious strictures of diet, for example, are particularly illustrating in the cultural sensitivities that such an understanding can provide the manager who must interact with groups who may seem diametrical. The consumption of pork is strictly prohibited in Islam. Practicing Muslim families consider pork an unclean meat and sinful to eat. Even when confronted with an act of hospitality, extended by a family of a different faith who consumes pork, a Muslim will find even their host's kitchen utensils as being unhygienic simply because they have been used for preparing pork. Where Muslims—and most Jewish people who keep kosher—have little reason to esteem the pig, there are religious traditions that have no dietary strictures on pork—Christian, for example—and cultures in which the ownership of pigs is a status symbol. In many Papua New Guinean communities a pig represents real wealth and, as such, pigs are treated with great care and attention, so much so that pigs are even housed within their family homes. (This, of course, does not stop the Papua New Guineans from eating their guests!)

Religious systems are complex. Each has a galaxy of sacred texts, myths, symbols, institution, rites, and rituals. A religion encompasses more than a stipulated set of beliefs and practices; however, within each one of these systems is the genius of a particular worldview (Swearer, 1981). Thus, the complexity and diversity inherent within every religious system have important implications for understanding respective worldviews, which, in turn affects how business is conducted in different parts of the world.

## TYPES OF RELIGIONS

Two types of religions have been identified, *monotheistic*, or the belief in one supreme being, and *polytheistic*, the belief in many supreme beings. The followers of each will have to some degree a different set of attitudes towards work and entrepreneurship. How these believers—and by believer it does not necessarily mean a religious person, but rather one whose secular worldview is consciously or subconsciously informed by a religious culture—conduct themselves in the workplace and in commerce has a direct affect on the cost of doing business and this is of most interest to the manager in the global business environment (Hill 2000).

The monotheist holds the belief that there is only one supreme being who is the Creator of all things. The major monotheistic religions are Judaism, Christianity, and Islam. The polytheist sees each aspect of reality and spirituality controlled by a specific deity, who may be a god, a spirit, an ancestor. The major polytheistic religions encompass Hinduism, Buddhism, the many animist faiths of Africa and the Caribbean, and so-called New Age beliefs, such as Wicca, which revives elements of the pagan religions of pre-Christian Europe.

# MONOTHEISTIC RELIGIONS

The following sections survey the major monotheistic faiths in our world, namely Islam, Christianity, and Judaism. Each section concludes with some of the key implications for business people operating in environments in which such these religions are the predominate shaper of their employees, clients, and customer's worldviews.

## Judaism

Judaism is one of the oldest religions in the world. It origins can be traced back to the year 1300 B.C.E., when a covenant was established between "the one God" and the prophet Abraham.

Today Judaism represents around several million followers and is spread throughout the world.

Major concepts of Judaism are:

- God is one.
- No human will ever be divine.
- Humans are free.
- Humans are the pinnacle of creation.
- Jews are chosen people in terms of serving God.
- Humans must be obedient to God-given commandments, as written in the holy book *Torah,* and that human beings are held personally responsible for their deeds in this life (Samovar & Porter 1995).

### Jewish Religious Groups

The four main groups in Judaism include:

- *Orthodox,* the traditional form of Judaism—The traditionalists consider that God gave the Torah and the Talmud directly to the Jewish people as a guide for them to pursue a life consistent with God's will. This group treats these holy books as being God's actual words and of the highest authority in stipulating the traditions and laws of Judaism.

- Reform (liberal)—Inspired by the 18th century Enlightenment, Jewish immigrants in the United States established a reform movement that modernized ancient Jewish rituals and practices in order to enjoy the freedoms they had experienced in American society—and outside of the European ghetto. This liberal wing of Judaism focuses on adapting to changes in the culture (for example, feminism in that women can be Reform rabbis) as well as maintaining a bond to the Jewish faith and to the Jewish state, Israel.

- Conservative—This group was formed in the 19th century as a reaction to the Reform movement. Conservative Jews, like the Reformists, made changes to the traditional system, but not to the extent of the reformists.

- Hassidim—This group emerged in the 17th century in Eastern Europe. Its difference from the other groups is that Hasidic Judaism places high importance on mysticism. They are to some extent modeled on cults thereby according enormous respect to their respective leaders within their community (McDowell & Stewart 1992). Their religious practice is also very traditional, reviling the Orthodox Jews in strictures and religiousity.

### Business Implications of Judaism

There are no strictures in Judaism against private ownership and commercial activities. Indeed, throughout history, Jewish people in different parts of the world have prospered from business and entrepreneurial applications as they were often prohibited from agriculture and other industries.

Jewish faith does place certain restrictions on the consumption of food items, such as pork and dairy items. Orthodox Jews, for example, do not drive or do any "work" once the Sabbath begins. They cannot even operate a light switch. International managers need to be mindful of these and other faith- or culturally-based practices specific to Jews—and from this understanding know that such cultural sensitivity is applicable to workers and clients so as not to cause offense.

## Christianity

Christianity, with its many branches ranging from Roman Catholicism, Orthodoxy, and Protestantism, could be considered the world's largest religion, and has its origins in Judaism. Its founding is attributed to Jesus of Nazareth in the 1st century C.E. as described in the New Testament, a continuation of the Torah, the Jewish Bible.

### Major Concepts of Christianity

At the center of Christianity is a belief that Jesus is God who was manifested in flesh and dwelled among men (Noss & Noss 1984; Samovar & Porter 1995). Therefore Christ is a portrayal of God. The very essence of Christianity is based on the notion of the Trinity of God. This includes the Father, the Son, and the Holy Spirit. Christian religion sees Christ as their savior. By following Christ's example humans can become one with God. If they go against God's will, they risk guilt and punishment, or life without God. Major conceptions in Christ's teaching embody the following principles:

- The coming Kingdom of God—living a Christian life makes the person belong to this Kingdom.
- Salvation—those who honestly repented of their past errors will be forgiven.
- Ethical system—the Ten Commandments:
  - Worship no God but me.
  - Do not make images of anything in heaven
  - Do not use my name for evil purposes
  - Observe the Sabbath and keep it holy
  - Respect your mother and father
  - Do not commit murder
  - Do not commit adultery
  - Do not steal
  - Do not accuse anyone falsely
  - Do not covet another person's possessions.

Generally speaking, Christianity recognizes hierarchy both in spiritual and human organizational terms. This is particularly manifested in the Catholic faith as the pope, bishops, and priests are considered as intermediaries between the people and God. Further, Christianity stresses the real and meaningful nature of the world and the significance of people as they were created by God. Each and every human being is important to God. Time is also important.

Protestant faith emerged in response to the Catholic domination and ritualized beliefs. Protestants do not believe in the pope as a spiritual intermediary. Religious guidance comes directly from the Bible, and religious hierarchy is not supposed to stand between the people and God. Protestants strongly emphasized the importance of work in this life as a means of salvation (Shelley & Clarke 1994).

### Christian Religious Groups

There are several groups found within the Christian faith who claim that their interpretation of Christianity is more in line with the actual teachings of Jesus than any other Christian group(s), and they include the following:

- Roman Catholic—The traditional form of Christianity with belief in the spiritual leadership of the pope. This Christian group advocates the infallibility of the pope and the hierarchical nature of the religious order as represented by church organization.

- Eastern Orthodox—This traditional form does not recognize the authority of the pope. However, its own religious order is significantly hierarchical.

- Protestant—This group separated from the Roman Catholic church in the 16th century. Protestantism is divided into many branches, including the major "revelations," Lutheran, Anglican, Baptist, and Presbyterian. They have in common no ultimate authority, such as the pope in Rome, and advocate instead salvation based on individual righteous living, as stipulated in the *Holy Bible*. They believe that there is no need for mediation through hierarchy of the church, as is the case with Catholicism.

- Indigenous Christian—These are the Christians from non-Western countries who have over the years combined missionary Christian religious beliefs with their own traditional culture such as Christ Army Church in Nigeria, whose followers believe they have discovered the right way to lead a pious Christian life (Shelley & Clarke 1994; Samovar & Porter 1995).

### Business Implications of Christianity

Christianity recognizes the importance of work and free ownership of property. Protestants, in particular, see the salvation of the individual through hard work and piety. The noted German sociologist Max Weber argued that capitalism rose to prominence due to the *Protestant work ethic*. This is because Protestantism advocated the importance of hard work and the pursuit of economic prosperity, which is consistent with the development of free enterprise based on capitalist ideology (Weber 1930).

On balance, virtually every branch of Christianity endorses free enterprise and business activity. Interestingly, Catholicism holds the notion that a free enterprise should also embody something not unlike social justice in its conduct and in the pricing of goods and services provided to the community—part of a worldview that Catholics have in common to some degree with Islam.

## Islam

Islam is the second largest and fastest growing world religion. It is estimated that approximately 1.2 billion people around the globe believe in Islam. *Islam* means "to submit" in Arabic and *Muslim* means "someone who is surrendering himself or herself to the will of God." The *Holy Koran*, a collection of God's (*Allah,* in Arabic) revelations to Prophet Muhammad around 610 C.E., the founder of Islam, is accepted as God's last testament. However, Muslims believe that God has spoken to human beings many times before (Adam, Moses, Abraham, Jesus are considered divine prophets in Islam).

### Major Concepts of Islam

Allah, according to Islam, rules the universe. Everything good or evil proceeds directly from the divine will. This orientation is responsible for fatalism, because whatever happens is the will of Allah (Samovar & Porter 1995). Love of knowledge, egalitarianism, and tolerance are central to Islam (Irwin 1996). As a way of life, Islam is a personal relationship with God; so Islamic religion is not the compartment of life but an entire way of life for Muslims. The sacred text of Islam is the Koran—or as it is variously spelled in English, Qur'an—which literally means "recitation" and is said to have been dictated to Muhammad by Allah. The Holy Koran is made up of 114 chapters and each chapter is called a *sura*. In Islam there are six main articles of belief:

1. Allah is the only God;
2. Allah sends Angels, spiritual beings, to communicate a message with humans;
3. Muslims believe in the Jewish *Bible* and the Christian *Gospels*, however they believe that their message has been lost. The *Holy Qur'an* which was dictated to Muhammad is the final book and replaces the other books;
4. Muslims believe in all the prophets God sent to mankind as messengers but the last and greatest prophet was Muhammad;
5. Muslims believe in the judgment day;
6. Muslims believe that Allah constructed everything on earth and beyond. God determines who will be saved and who will suffer in hell (Samovar & Porter 1995).

Other major principles of Islam include:

- Honoring and respecting parents.
- Respecting the rights of others.
- Being generous but no squanderer.
- Avoiding killing except for justifiable causes.
- Not committing adultery.
- Dealing justly and equitably with others.
- Being of pure heart and mind.
- Safeguarding the possessions of orphans.
- Being humble and unpretentious (Abbasi, et al. 1990).

### Religious Rituals

The Islamic faith has many rituals and is heavily centered on day-to-day practice. The major practices for Muslims are known as the Five Pillars of Faith, which include:

1. *Repetition of creed (Shahadah)*—meaning the belief that there is no God but Allah and Muhammad is his prophet. The first part of this pronouncement expresses the primary principle of monotheism (belief in one universal God); and the second part reinforces the Muslim belief in Muhammad being the divine prophet, thus validating the holy Koran.

2. *Prayer (Salat)*—a prayer performed five times a day in the mosque or at home.

3. *Charity (Zacat)*—the payment of alms to the destitute. In some Islamic countries *Zacat* is taken out of a person's wages

4. *Fasting (Ramadan)*—during which from sunrise to sunset complete fasting is observed. Even pleasures such as smoking and sex are not allowed.

5. *Pilgrimage (Haj)*—The travel to the holy Mecca. Each Muslim is expected once in his or her lifetime to travel to Mecca, where certain rituals must be performed (Samovar & Porter 1995; Abbasi, et al. 1990).

The most important and fundamental religious concept of Islam is the *Shariah,* the law that embraces the total way of life as explicitly commanded by God. The *Shariah* was formulated by Muslim scholars in the 8th and 9th centuries C.E. In some Muslim nations there is no separation of the church and state, but there is no hierarchy within the church. Moreover, under the Islamic concept of God, all human beings are equal as such. *Shariah*, for some of these states, is also the civil law.

Prayer for a Muslim begins at birth when a parent whispers in a child's ear this prayer (Crotty, et al. 1995): "Allah is great. There are no Gods but the one God (Allah) and Muhammad is his prophet. Come to prayer, come to prayer, come to security, come to security, Allah is great; there are no Gods but Allah."

Mecca is the holiest site for Muslims, and non-Islamic people are not permitted to enter. An example took place in Saudi Arabia, where Swedish engineers were hired to make restoration repairs to the holy Mecca. However they were not allowed to enter Mecca, rather they were made to supervise the project through the use of cameras situated around the work site (*Wall Street Journal*, 1975).

### Business Implications of Islam

Islam stresses fairness and equity in business dealings. Charging of interest is prohibited; so Islamic banking takes the form of something resembling venture capital. In general Islam is supportive of free enterprise. The Koran says nothing against private property and wealth. How the individual uses the wealth for good is the main issue. However, Islam, along with Catholicism, condemns capitalism for distracting individuals from the spiritual life and from the path to God. Material consumption occurs at the cost of one's relationship with God. For many Muslims, the Western world is disliked because secular capitalism threatens this tradition. Nevertheless, there is nothing explicit in the Koran that is antibusiness.

"Given that most Muslim countries favor a free market-based system, their citizens are typically receptive to international businesses—to globalization as such—so long as those businesses behave in a manner that is consistent with Islamic ethics (Hill 2000). With this in mind, there are a number of business prohibitions under Islam. The Koran emphasizes that all trade and business agreements should be made through mutual consent and without any form of coercion by the parties involved in business transactions. However, there are major prohibitions under Islam that international managers need to be aware of so that they conduct their business activities, trade negotiations, and the like in a way that is acceptable to their Islamic counterparts. These prohibitions include:

- Bribery and misappropriation.
- Embezzlement of public and private wealth.
- Larceny.
- Unjust use of the property of an orphan.
- Short weights and measures.
- Trades which promote obscenity.
- Income from prostitution and adultery.
- Manufacture, sale, and importation of alcohol and narcotic drugs.
- Gambling and all those means in which the passing of wealth from one party to another depends upon chance of luck.
- Making and selling of idols and services rendered in or to pagan places of worship.
- Fortune telling.
- The charging of interest.
- Consumption of pig meat and alcohol (Barnwell & Pratt 1998).

# POLYTHEISTIC RELIGIONS

The important polytheistic religions are now surveyed, Hinduism, Buddhism, and Confucianism. Though by no means a complete overview, the same cultural sensitivity that applies to these faiths can also be transferred to religions.

## Hinduism

Hinduism originated in India and is one of the oldest of humankind's religions. Hindus believe in many gods and goddesses. Scholars estimate that there are close to 3 million Hindu deities.

### Major Concepts of Hinduism

For Hindus this world is transient and illusory. Their beliefs emphasize the spiritual progression of each person's soul rather than the material world or the concerns of work and creating wealth (Mead, 1998). Hinduism is most common in India, its birthplace. Its religious texts chronicle the acts and exploits of the gods Brahma, Vishnu, and Shiva, and these accounts are presented as if the gods were persons (McDowell & Stewart 1992). Hindus find divinity—and therefore the incarnations of their deities—in everything, and the practices associated with this belief have impressed many a non-Hindu that they are the most religious people on Earth (Samovar & Porter 1995).

Despite the enormous pantheon of gods, Hindus revere two main gods, Vishnu and Shiva. Vishnu is the god of creation who created the universe by separating Heaven from Earth. Shiva is the god of destruction. There is a hierarchy of gods and goddesses. One of the most famous gods is Ganesh, the god of merchants and business, who is shown in Hindu art as part elephant and human.

The Hindu texts that transfer its sacred knowledge from generation to generation are the Vedas, which date from 1300 B.C.E. The Hindu epics, which contain the exploits of various Hindu deities, are written down in Mahabharta and Ramayna, and are as important to Hindus for conceptualizing the struggle between good and evil as Old Testament to Christians and Jews.

The idea of reality in Hinduism is different from that of Christianity and Islam. Where the Christian or Muslim believes that the reality is Heaven and Earth—for Hindus it is more complex, and the separation between the spiritual and material world is not so clearcut. Every living creature and plant has a soul. Upon death the soul transmigrates into another living thing. This is the cycle of birth and rebirth. All living things are in a constant process of birth, death, and reincarnation. The goal of salvation is to escape from this cycle. The cycle can be broken only through accumulation of *karma* or good deeds or moving into a state of spiritual perfection—*nirvana*. *Nirvana* is the ultimate detachment from the world when all worldly desires are renounced. It is achieved through meditation (Barnwell & Pratt 1998). This way the only reality is that of mind and spirit and that the world, as it is, is an illusion and impermanent.

There is no formal religious hierarchy in Hinduism. However, there are those individuals regarded as holy, such as the spiritual advisors known as *gurus*. Despite this lack of hierarchy in their religion, Hindu society itself is strictly divided into many castes:

- *Brahmins* (priests)
- *Kshatriyas* (soldiers)
- *Vaishyas* (merchants and farmers)
- *Sutras* (laborers, craftsman)
- *Harijians* (descendents of the aboriginal people of the Indian subcontinent and typically poor—also known as the "untouchables") (McDowell & Stewart 1992)

This social hierarchy is governed by purity, with the upper castes being pure and lower considered polluted. A Hindu born within an Indian social group adheres to the rituals and marriage practices of his or her caste and its given prescribed rituals to honor the gods. An individual's position in the caste is inherited and determined not only by religious status but also by occupation and position in society. This has historically constrained the roles that Hindu individuals assume in the society. For the international manager doing business in a modern democratic India, where the caste system is not observed and is even illegal, the lingering effects of caste can still be seen in labor's mobility.

In Hinduism, which is a communal religion, life can be categorized into two forms: the regular order of life through such events as birth, marriage, and death; and that which relies on faith and achieving an individual's goal, which ultimately is *nirvana* (Knott 1998; McDowell & Stewart 1992).

### Business Implications of Hinduism

The Hindu religion itself does not concern itself with the economic activities common in capitalist societies such as investment, wealth accumulation, quest for higher productivity, and efficiency. Max Weber, the theoretician of the Protestant work ethic, argued that "the ascetic principles embedded in Hinduism do not encourage the entrepreneurial activity in pursuit of wealth creation that we find in Protestantism" (Weber 1930, 92). However, the colonial India of Weber's observation is not the same country as the one that exports one of the most skilled and productive labor forces in the world, and which is now the home to many outsourced industries from the United States and Europe, especially in information technology. Paradoxically, Hindus have worldviews that see the material world in which they succeed and its affairs as relatively unimportant.

## Buddhism

Buddhism stresses spiritual fulfillment as the greatest reward of all, not anything that the material world has to offer. This follows from the principles learned through the spiritual journey of its founder, Siddhartha Gautama, who lived in India from 563 to 483 B.C.E. After six years of experimenting with yoga, a physical discipline in Hinduism that supposedly gives one some feeling for what nirvana will be like, he suddenly understood how to break the laws of karma and the endless cycle of rebirth through reaching an actual state of nirvana, the ultimate detachment from the world and the suffering that the world entails. Gautama emerged as the Buddha or Enlightened One and saw his mission as solving the riddle of suffering. According to Hindu beliefs, the religion from which Buddhism grew, suffering is for eternity because of the constant process of rebirth. Gautama, however, taught that all suffering can be brought to an end by overcoming greed, hatred, and delusion whereby the existence is suffering arising from a desire that can be suppressed (Samovar & Porter 1995; Swearer 1981).

### Major Concepts of Buddhism

Buddha's teaching contains four truths:

- Existence is suffering; suffering is unavoidable.
- The suffering arises from a desire. Desire is self-defeating as it can never be completely satisfied. Desire causes suffering because it attaches us to the objects (things and persons).
- Desire can be suppressed, and therefore the suffering will cease.
- The process of suppressing the desire is known as the *Eightfold Path steps* (Swearer 1981; Irwin 1996):
    1. *Right understanding.* This ensures that the person is aware of taking full responsibility for his or her actions by being spiritually minded and knowing the four noble truths so spiritual ignorance can be avoided.
    2. *Right thought.* This concerns the emotions, where they are properly channeled through peace, compassion, and freedom from sensuality and away from ill will and cruelty.
    3. *Right speech.* This means the absence of lying, cheating, backbiting, and vain talking.

4. *Right conduct.* This concerns abstaining from trickery, greed, and harming others and one's self (such as refraining from the use of alcohol and drugs).

5. *Right livelihood.* This is to abstain from making a living through the suffering of others (such as trafficking in arms).

6. *Right effort.* This means to avoid developing an unskillful mind that cannot resist delusion and craving.

7. *Right mindfulness.* This requires the use of meditation to prevent craving and delusion.

8. *Right meditation.* This is complete concentration on a single object and the achievement of purity of thought, free from all hindrances and distractions and eventually all sensations. According to the Buddha, when the mind is still, the true nature of everything is reflected (Swearer 1981; Samovar & Porter 1995; Rimpoche, et al. 1987; McDowell & Stewart 1992).

Buddhists do not believe in a god or gods who created the world. However, they do believe that there is a supreme and wonderful truth that words cannot teach, and rituals cannot attain.

### Business Implications of Buddhism

Buddhism, it appears, is not favorably disposed to the notion of free enterprise and the pursuit of material wellbeing. Seen from a Western worldview, the having of no desires adversely affects motives for personal enrichment and economic growth generally. Thus, little support is accorded to free enterprise.

## Confucianism

Confucianism is considered a religion by many outsiders, but it is more of a philosophy that embodies and perpetrates the Chinese norms for social and personal morality. Like Buddhism, it is named after its founder, the philosopher K'ung-Fu-Tzu, who was born around 551 B.C.E in China's Shantung province. His teachings attracted large number of followers (Shelley & Clarke 1994; Hill 2000).

Confucianism is a set of pragmatic rules for daily life derived from experience. The key tenet of Confucian teachings is that hierarchical relationships between people create stability in society. The five basic relationships are ruler–subject, father–son, older brother–younger brother, husband–wife, and older friend–younger friend. The junior owes the senior respect, and the senior owes the junior protection and consideration. The prototype for all social institutions is the family. A person is primarily a member of his or her family before he or she is an individual.

Harmony in the family must be preserved; and harmony is the keeping one's *face*, that is, one's dignity, self-respect, and prestige. Treating others as one would like to be treated oneself is virtuous behavior. Virtue with respect to one's tasks consists of attempting to obtain skills and education, working hard, not spending more than necessary, being patient, and persevering. It should be noted that individuals may have inner thoughts that differ from the group's norms and values. However, individuals may not act on those thoughts, because group harmony and not shaming the group are of paramount importance (Samovar & Porter 1994). The ideal Confucian reality and worldview is a cohesive social relationship.

### Major Philosophical Principles of Confucianism

Confucianism embodies the following principles (Barnwell & Pratt 1998; Samovar & Porter 1995):

- *Jen,* the love for humankind that has to be cultivated by one's own effort.
- Respect for the past.
- Respect for the acquisition of knowledge and character building. The stress here is on learning from the past, which is why in Confucian societies there is so much memorizing.
- Society is best run by virtue, not by law. Shame for nonvirtuous behavior should lead to correction.
- Responsibility of government to the governed. Government is analogous to the father in the family, an authority that must be obeyed.
- System of hierarchy (husband–wife, father–son, citizen–state, and so on).
- Emphasis on social harmony and obligation. Seniors should look after juniors in return for their loyalty.
- The family institution is strongly supported.
- Work is a moral virtue.

### Business Implication of Confucianism

Scholars argue that Confucianism has an economic dynamic that is as profound as that of Weber's Protestantism (Aoki 1988; Womack, et al. 1990), and this comes from its strong emphasis on fostering relationships. Beyond the extended family lies the domain of friends and social and business connections that form a network called *guanxi*. For cultures informed by Confucianism, networking and cultivating relationships with customers, suppliers, competitors, partners, and government officials, and maintaining good and regular contact with them takes on a philosophical and moral basis rather than simply being just standard business practice in other parts of the world. The nature of business and workplace relationships in much of Asia is that they are personal and reciprocal and not just contractual and transactional in nature (Lassere & Schutte 1995).

# A COMPARISON OF WORLDVIEWS: EAST AND WEST

Religion, as a way of explaining and categorizing the worldviews of clients, customers, business partners, and fellow employees in a global business environment, can further be reduced to two encompassing worldviews that characterize Eastern and Western cultures (Samovar & Porter 1995). The *mechanistic* worldview, which came as a reaction against the limitations of the Judeo-Christian tradition in the West, places reason above intuition and science above the religion. In the American worldview, for example, Hoebel and Frost (1976) noted that people tend to think rationally rather than mystically. To Americans, the universe is a physical system operating in a determinate manner and according to discoverable scientific laws. That is, the universe is a mechanism—and to some degree Americans believe they can manipulate it, that they need not accept it as it is and can, by dint of knowledge and skill, improve and even redesign reality to be more to their liking. Within this worldview is a belief in the dualism of mind and body, God and humankind. The world consists of separate entities that can be manipulated and examined as such and remade.

On the other hand, in cultures that have a nonmechanistic worldview, such as those that predominate in the East, the emphasis is on intuition over logical thinking. Wisdom rises from the depths as a divine voice. The Eastern worldview does not recognize dualism and the world and everything in it is perceived as a unit, as holistic, where people cannot so easily be either mind or spirit but rather one in the same.

# IMPORTANCE OF WORLDVIEWS FOR INTERNATIONAL BUSINESS MANAGEMENT

A worldview based on religion shapes people's values and attitudes in terms of personal responsibility, work, motivation, and the like. For example, observant Hindus are more motivated by pursuing a spiritual life rather than materialism. Jews, as another example, place more emphasis on the individual's obligation to society and have a balanced approach between spiritualism and materialism. Muslims and Christians share some of this balance.

Social restrictions are another consideration for international managers. They need to be culturally aware of hierarchies such as the caste system in India. Dietary laws, for example, can have an impact on what kinds of food products can be sold in a country or what restaurant to choose for a business meeting. Recall that the consumption of pork is prohibited for Jews who keep kosher and for every member of Islam. Hindus, because they revere living things as reincarnated beings, may not eat any kinds of animals. Cows in India are considered sacred for this reason and as the incarnation of a Hindu deity (Mahoney, et al. 1998). Muslims are prohibited from charging interest—a standard banking practice in many other countries that cannot be taken for granted in countries where the *Shariah* is the law of the land. Buddhism discourages the pursuit of materialism and free enterprise in favor of spiritual fulfillment—what motivates the employees of this faith may not always be more money. And the religious holidays and rituals of many faiths can affect employee performance and work scheduling.

When members of different religious groups work together in an organization, it may potentially present hostility, division, and instability within the work force. The way to avoid these cultural clashes is for the management to develop a sophisticated understanding of differing worldviews. It is imperative for the management to be fully committed to respecting, valuing, and accommodating these diverse worldviews within their mainstream managerial philosophy and practice. Only then does the organization begin to enjoy the benefits of cultural diversity in a number of ways including a better team spirit, high labor productivity, and a greater range of innovative ideas for organizational improvement.

## *Summary*

In this chapter we focused on the development of worldviews based on religious systems in different cultures. The major world religions, both monotheistic and polytheistic, were discussed and compared, with examples of how these faiths form an individual's reality or worldview. The diversity of worldviews was finally discussed, with examples that suggest what such cultural differences mean for managers and organizations involved in international business operations.

## Critical Discussion Questions

1. Discuss the notion that all worldviews are valid in their own rights.

2. In what ways does the worldview of Confucianism differ from that of Christianity?

3. Is an Islamic worldview compatible with the Christian worldview?

4. In what ways does the Confucian worldview promote free enterprise?

5. Is Buddhist philosophy compatible with the Confucianism worldview?

6. Can Eastern and Western worldviews ever converge due to increasing globalization of world economy?

## Applications

### Experiential

1. Interview a local priest or minister about his or her worldview on Islam. Do you think that the priest's worldview is found to be in line with the Islamic worldview?

2. Is the media—newspapers, television, film, and the like—responsible for much of the misrepresentation of any worldview that is foreign to the local or national culture? Research your own national media to justify your findings.

3. Interview a local manager about his or her worldview of a foreign religion and culture and see whether it has presented any problem for the manager in terms of his or her globalization strategy.

### Internet

Use your Web browser and navigate to http://www.google.com search engine. Type in the keywords *world religions*. You will be presented with a number of hits for a host of religions from which you choose two polytheistic religions—such as Santeria and Wicca—that are not discussed in this chapter. Critically compare and contrast them with the Christian and Islamic faiths in terms of the following issues:

- Belief systems.

- Ethics.

- Moral philosophies.

- Prohibitions.
- Business practices.

Finally, share your research findings with your classmates as specified by your instructor.

# References

Abbasi, S., Hollman, K., & Murrey, J. (1990). Islamic economics: Foundations and practices. *International Journal of Social Economics, 16* (5), 5–17.

Alexander, P. (1984). *Judaism.* Manchester: Manchester University Press.

Aoki, M. (1988). *Information, incentives, and bargaining in the Japanese economy.* Cambridge: Cambridge University Press.

Barnwell, N., & Pratt, G.R. (1998). *Australian Business: An Asian Pacific Perspective.* Sydney: Prentice Hall.

Crotty, R., Habel, N., Moore, B., & O'Donoghue, M. (1995). *Finding a way: The religious world of today.* Melbourne, Australia: Harper Collins.

Hill, C. (2000). *International business: Competing in the global marketplace* (3rd ed.). New York: McGraw-Hill.

Hoebel, E.A., & Frost, E.L. (1976). *Cultural and social anthropology.* New York: McGraw-Hill.

Irwin, H., & More, E. (1994). *Managing Corporate Communication.* Sydney: Allen and Unwin.

Irwin, H. (1996). *Communicating with Asia. Understanding people and customs.* Sydney: Allen and Unwin.

Knott, K. (1998) *Hinduism: A very short introduction.* Englewood Cliffs, NJ: Prentice Hall.

Lassere, P., & Schutte, H. (1995). *Strategies for Asia Pacific.* Melbourne: Macmillan Business.

Mahoney, D., Trigg, M., Griffin, R., & Pustay, M. (1998). *International business: A managerial perspective.* Melbourne: Addison Wesley Longman.

Masterson, P. (1971). *Atheism and alienation.* Dublin: Gill and Macmillian.

McDowell, J. & Stewart, D., (1992) *Handbook of today's religions.* Nashville, TN: Thomas Nelson.

McManners, J. (Ed.) (1993). *The Oxford history of Christianity.* Oxford: Oxford University Press.

Mead, R. (1998). *International management: Cross-cultural dimensions.* Cambridge, MA: Blackwell Publishers.

Noss, D.S., & Noss, J.B. (1984) *Man's Religion* (7th ed.). New York: Macmillan.

Pennington, D.L (1985). Intercultural communication. In L. A. Samovar & R.E. Porter (Eds), *Intercultural communication: A reader* (4th ed.). Belmont, CA: Wadsworth.

Rimpoche, T.S., Hanh, T.N., & Batcheler, S. (1987). *Buddhism in the West: Spiritual wisdom for the twenty-first century.* Australia: Hay House.

Rule, H., & Goodman, S. (1987). *Gulpilil's stories of the Dreamtime.* Sydney: William Collins Publishers.

Saee, J. (1999). Managing across cultural frontiers. *Journal of European Business Education, 8* (2), 35–59.

Samovar, L.A., & Porter, R.E. (Eds.) (1994). *Intercultural communication: A reader* (7th ed.) Belmont, CA: Wadsworth.

Samovar, L.A., & Porter, R.E. (1995). *Communication between cultures.* Belmont, CA: Wadsworth.

Shelley, F.M., & Clarke, A.E. (1994). *Human and cultural geography.* Dubuque, IA: W.C. Brown.

Swearer, D. (1981). *Buddhism and society in southeast Asia.*, Chamberbourg, PA: Anima.

Triandis, H.C. (1994). *Culture and social behavior.* New York: McGraw-Hill.

Wall Street Journal (1975). September 8. p. 13.

Weber, M. (1930). *The Protestant ethic and the spirit of capitalism.* London: Alen and Unwin.

Womack, J., Jones, D., & Roos, D. (1990). *The machine that changed the world.* New York: Rawson Associates.

# Chapter 4

*Communication and Culture*

## LEARNING OBJECTIVES

After reading this chapter, you should be able to:
- Understand the importance of communication to organizational life.
- Understand the characteristics of communication.
- Understand the nexus between communication and culture.
- Understand intercultural communication.
- Describe major obstacles to intercultural communication.
- Understand the nexus between communication and management.
- Understand e-business and its implications for managerial communications.
- Understand why intercultural communication competence is so critical to international trade and management, both nationally and internationally.

*You cannot speak of oceans to a well frog, the creature of a narrow sphere. You cannot speak of ice to a summer insect, the creature of a season.*

—Chang Tzu

*What sets us against one another is not our aims— they all come to the same thing— but our methods.*

—Antoine de Saint-Exupery

## HUMAN COMMUNICATION: AN OVERVIEW

Communication is central to human life and survival. Moreover, if anything sets human beings distinctively apart from all other animals, it is their ability to communicate their ideas, feelings, and thought processes through language coupled with the concurrent development of human psychological understanding. We learn to communicate from the point of birth. A baby crying is often communicating to his or her parent, saying that it needs feeding or wants attention to his or her emotional or physical need. At the toddler stage, an individual learns to speak in order to get what he or she wants and to communicate in general. By the time persons reach adulthood, chances are that they have learned to speak their language fully and use other forms of communication—nonverbal communication—effectively, including body language and facial expressions to complement written and spoken—verbal—language. Six billion people in our world are engaged in some form of communication, using one or more of 3,000 languages and 10,000 thousand dialects—this includes the media as well—to convey ideas, emotions, beliefs with each other on a daily basis. "Communication—our ability to share our ideas and feelings—is the basis of all human contact" (Samovar & Porter 1995, 25). The centrality of communication in our lives, whether personal, professional, or *intercultural*, cannot be overemphasized. International management is no exception to this—and managers working in a global business environment of client negotiations and international staffs must develop a high-level intercultural communication competence. It is essential to the success of any venture in an international business setting and the strategic continuation of international business.

However, to understand intercultural communication, we must first recognize the role of communication. In this chapter, the nexus of culture and communication is analyzed, as are the obstacles to intercultural communication. How intercultural communication facilitates international management is also discussed as well as its special purpose in electronic communication in a global context, that is, in the context of what we now call *e-business*.

## HUMAN COMMUNICATION: A COMPLEX PHENOMENON

Human communication is a form of human behavior, which is based on a human's innate psychological need to establish social contact with another. However, albeit a natural process, the art of communication is not simple. Consider the bodily activity that accompanies the act of saying "hello." From the secretion of chemicals in your brain to the moving of your lips to produce sound, thousands of mental and physical actions are in operation (and most of them at the same time). As you might suspect, communication becomes even more complex when we add emotional and cultural dimensions (Samovar & Porter 1995).

## DEFINING COMMUNICATION

There is no single definition of communication. Dance and Carlson (1976), in their review of the literature, found 126 definitions of communication—and that is simply one scholarly statistic. For our purposes, communication is the ability to share ideas and feelings and is the foundation of human contact and, therefore, human relationships at all levels. Outlined below are some other definitions that we can also consider as valid, especially for intercultural relationships. Some are derived from psychology, which deals with perception. Others are the definitions of linguists, who focus on the language that people use.

- Communication is a complex process of linking up or sharing perceptual fields between interacting persons (Harris & Moran 1991).

- "Communication occurs whenever meaning is attributed to behavior or the residue of behavior. Behavior residue is what remains as a record of our action" (Samovar & Porter, 1995 27).

- Communication is conceptualized in terms of a two-way process by which information is exchanged between individuals, including any behavior, verbal or nonverbal that is perceived by another (Dwyer 1993).

- "Communication is seen as a two way process involving a dialogue, an exchange, or a transaction between people. The process involves feedback and negotiation of meaning has the intent of building and sharing meanings. There is a strong emphasis upon mutuality, involvement, and context-dependence" (Stewart 1971, 367).

What is evident in these definitions is that communication is a two-way process in which the persons involved in the communication process try to achieve a shared meaning.

---

**EXAMPLE 4-1:** Is English Understood by all English-Speaking People?

One would think that the English language was understood by all English-speaking people in the same way. Well, this is not the case. Not long ago, I attended an international management conference in Los Angeles. Soon after the conclusion of the conference, I had to catch a flight back home to Sydney, Australia at the Los Angeles International Airport. There, while checking in at the counter, I suddenly heard an announcement over the public address system that stated:

Attention passengers, you are not required to give out money to the solicitors, because the airport does not sponsor their activities.

I was astonished by this announcement. It made me think that why on earth do I need to give money out to people in the legal profession and at an airport of all places? Somewhere in that thought, for a split of a second, it dawned on me that I, too, share that perception among Australians that America is a land of litigation, where everybody sues everybody else. Naturally, I thought that this announcement had to do with that. But then I soon doubted that the American lawyers are so desperate as to target international visitors for raising their income levels!

Back in Australia, the word *solicitor* means lawyer, which is a highly regarded profession in our society at least in terms of status and income level. In contrast, solicitors in the United States can be beggars who hassle people for money. Some months later, I recounted this story to an English colleague of mine, and then he began to laugh. I asked why found this so hilarious. He then retorted that the word *solicitor* back in the southeastern part of England where he came from means a sex worker.

# INTENTIONALITY AND UNINTENTIONALITY OF HUMAN COMMUNICATION

There are two different schools of thought conceptualizing human communication, the Intentional School of Thought and Unintentional School of Thought (Samovar & Porter 1995).

The intentional school, as propounded by Gerald Miller and Mark Steinberg, regards communication as the process whereby one person deliberately tries to convey meaning to another. The purpose of an intentional communication is designed to modify the behavior of other people and, therefore, the words and actions that embody such a communication have a degree of consciousness on the part of the person who initiates the message in the first place, that is, the communicator.

The unintentional school of thought, on the other hand, maintains that the notion of intentionality in communication is far too limited due to the fact that it does not take into consideration all circumstances within which many messages are transmitted unintentionally. Scholars who advocate this perspective argue that communication takes place whenever people attach meaning to behavior, even if the sender of the message does not expect his or her actions to be communicated. However, it is noted that communication has an influence on other people, regardless of whether or not such influence is intended.

## Basic Components of the Communication Process

There are seven components of communication that usually operate instantaneously and simultaneously. These components are found in every culture:

- Source
- Encoding
- Message
- Channel
- Receiver
- Decoding
- Feedback (Samovar & Porter 1995).

### Source

The source (sender) can be a person or a group—or even an organization—that devises a message in response to an outside stimulus such as a question, a meeting, an interview, a problem, a report, and so on (Bartol, et al. 1995).

### Encoding

Since a person cannot directly link with another person's internal psychological state, it is logical to deduce that it is not possible to share one's ideas and feelings with another directly. Consequently, one must use symbolic representations, an activity referred to as *encoding*. In encoding, the source selects and arranges verbal and nonverbal symbols. During the encoding, there are three aspects to communication, which the source needs to master in order to ensure clarity of a message.

- *Communication skills.* This is where the source needs to develop good use of grammar, syntax, and composition for his or her written communication;

- *Attitudes*. How one individual feels about himself or herself may induce him or her to formulate communication quite different-ly from someone with a different attitude (Kroeber & Kluckhohn 1952).
- *Knowledge*. This involves understanding of both the communi-cation process and the subject to be communicated.

### Message

*Message* involves three phenomena: content; treatment; and code. The treatment is the way the message is presented: It may be repeated; it may be the subject of a story; it may be humorous; and it may be a series of quotations from celebrities. The code is a group of signs structured to achieve meaning. The code may be a word in a language such as English—or it may be photographs or signs, and so on (Mohan, et al. 1997, 32).

### Channel

A *channel* or medium through which communication flows depends on one or more of the five senses: sight, sound, touch, smell, and taste. The primary channels used in organizational life are sound and sight. We receive messages when we listen to or watch each other (either verbally or nonverbally). The degree to which an individual prefers one channel over another is often determined by his or her culture. Also, selecting the prop-er channel significantly impacts the receiver's perception and acceptance of the message. Since messages can carry emotional and mixed meanings, as well as hidden and ambiguous ones, a fax or e-mail to inform a person that a family member suddenly died would not be appropriate. Nor would announcing reorganization through a voice mail to all employees be an effective medium (Weiss 1996).

### Receiver

A message is normally initiated by a source that uses an appropriate channel in order to reach a receiver: a person or persons for whom the message is intended. The management of a firm develops a strategic plan and makes an announcement about the plan to its employees using their employee forum. In this instance, the source is the management of the firm, the channel used in this instance is the forum, and the intended receivers are the employees.

### Decoding

During this phase of communication, the receiver decodes (interprets) the information that he or she receives and attaches meaning to the source's behavior. Using again the example of management's strategic plan announcement, the employees decode the announcement in terms of attaching their own meanings to what has been announced. However, it should be noted that during any communication phase, there may be interference with exchanging messages and achieving common meaning, which is referred to as *noise*. Noise ranges from interruptions that occur as a sender (source) is encoding to static on telephone lines as the message is being transmitted. It can even include receiver fatigue as decoding takes place. Noise can reduce the probability of achieving common meaning between source (sender) and receiver (Bartol, et al. 1995).

### Feedback

Feedback is a vital element in human communication: It is the response to the source's message. Without feedback, one can never be sure whether the message initially transmitted to the receiver has made an impact during the communication process. Obtaining feedback involves face-to-face communication so as to gauge the reactions of receivers through their words, gestures, and expressions. It would be hard to obtain feedback for management's announcement in our example if impersonal channels, were used such as voice mail and e-mail, which are one-way forms of communication.

# THE CHARACTERISTICS OF COMMUNICATION

Human communication embodies the following characteristics:

- *No direct mind-to-mind contact.* It is not yet humanly possible to establish direct mind-to-mind contact between individuals (telepathy). Therefore, it is not possible to share our feelings and experiences without some physical process. Also, much of what we know and feel remains inside of us; it can only be made known to a large extent through effective communication (Samovar & Porter 1995).

- *We can only infer.* Since we do not have direct access to the thoughts, feelings, and emotions of other human beings, we can only infer what they are experiencing themselves (Samovar & Porter 1995).

- *Communication is a dynamic process.* It is not static and passive, but rather it is continuous and active, often without a definable beginning or end. In this dynamic interplay, communicators are simultaneously perceiving others and expressing bodily signals or information about themselves (Saee & Kaye 1994).

- *We seek to define the world.* We are born into a world that to us is without meaning. Our search for meaning covers every aspect of our existence from the definition of a single word to how we cope with the eventuality of death. It is the role of communication (and the diverse culture norms that it entails) that helps, us discover these meanings (Samovar and Porter 1995).

- *Communication is interactive.* Interaction implies a reciprocal process in which each party attempts to influence the other. That is, each party simultaneously creates messages designed to draw specific responses from the other and vice versa (Samovar & Porter 1995).

- *Communication is inevitable.* Whether intended or not, receivers in the communication process described in this chapter assign meaning to the verbal and nonverbal communication of others. Such meanings form the basis for future action and strategic communication (Saee & Kaye 1994; Watzlawick 1967).

- *Time binding links us together.* Thoreau perhaps best expresses the concept of *time binding*: "All the past is here." It is here for two reasons: We are born into a culture, and we can make symbols. Time binding is therefore another example of how the characteristics of communication and culture are woven together. Not only do we transmit knowledge from person to person, we also pass ideas from generation to generation. For cultures to survive, each new infant must learn from past generations. We are told what from the past we need to know, so that we can live in the present and prepare for the future (Samovar & Porter 1995).

- *Communication is symbolic.* Symbols are used to represent things, processes, ideas, or events in ways that make communication possible. The most significant feature of symbols is their arbitrary nature. For example, there is logical reason why the letters in this book should stand for the printed object you read now (Adler & Rodman 1997).

- *Communication does not necessarily mean understanding.* Even when two individuals agree that they are communicating or talking to each other, this does not mean that they have understood each other. Understanding occurs when two individuals share interpretations of relationships, events, and phenomena in their interpersonal worlds (Saee & Kaye 1994).

- *Communication has a consequence.* When we receive a message, something happens to us. Each one of our messages does something to someone else. This is not a philosophical or metaphysical theory, but a biological fact. It is impossible not to respond to the actions of others (Saee & Kaye 1994).

- *Communication is self-reflective.* That has its roots in our unique ability to think about ourselves and to reflect on our past, present, and future. This lets us be participant and observer simultaneously: We can watch, evaluate, and alter our performance as a communicator at the very instant we are engaged in the act. We are the only species that can be at both ends of the camera at the same time (Ruben 1988).

- *The brain is an open system.* This aspect of communication has its origins in another special feature of the human brain: our ability to learn and never stop learning. If I were to tell you that Confucius lived from 551 to 479 B.C.E and if this were new information to you, I would be adding to your wealth of information. This is why the brain is described as an open system (Samovar & Porter 1995).

- *Communication occurs in a context.* Contextual factors like the time and place of communication may have cultural value and assist the communicators to interpret each other's intentions (Saee & Kaye 1994). This view is further supported by Littlejohn (1989, 152) who states, "Communication always occurs in context, and the nature of communication depends in large measure on this context." Thus context provides us with what Shimanoff (1980, 57) calls "a prescription that indicates what behavior is obligated, preferred, or prohibited."

- *We are alike and we are different.* As human beings we have a lot in common in terms of our physiological make up: We have a heart, lungs, brain, and the like. We experience pleasure and pain. We are faced with the same destiny, namely that life is finite and transitory. On the other hand, as individuals we innately possess a degree of uniqueness and, because of this, we respond to the outside world differently. For example, when we hear a word, or someone touches us, our body reacts from the inside out. Culture influences and defines the conditions and circumstances under which various messages may or may not be sent, noticed, interpreted, and understood. The content of our repertory of communicative behaviors is also contingent largely upon the culture in which we have been raised (Samovar & Porter 1995).

Culture and communication are so inextricably bound that most cultural anthropologists believe the terms are virtually synonymous. This relationship is the key factor to understanding intercultural communication.

## CULTURE AND COMMUNICATION

One way to understand the interplay between culture and communication is through Bourdeau's (1988) metaphor of the journey and the map. Cultures are both the maps of a place (the rules and conventions) and the journeys that take place there (actual practices). Furthermore, "culture and communication are so inextricably linked that most anthropologists believe that the terms are virtually synonymous. This relationship is the key factor to understanding intercultural communication" (Samovar & Porter 1995, 45). This view has been well articulated by the internationally renowned anthropologist Edward T. Hall, who stated that culture is primarily a system for creating, sending, storing, and processing information. As such, communication underlies everything (Hall, 1976). People respond to the world through messages they receive; however it is the culture which determines the form, pattern, and content of those messages. Culture also determines the content and style of the messages we send.

Hall also observed that there is not one aspect of human life that is not touched and altered by culture. Similarly, it can be argued that culture governs and defines the conditions and circumstances under which various messages may or may not be sent, noticed, and interpreted (Samovar & Porter 1995).

The content of our repertoire of communication behaviors depends largely on the culture in which we have been raised. When cultures differ, communication practices also differ. In the context of the global business environment, that people communicate in different ways and in different societies is a crucial concept. In diverse cultures it matters who talks to whom, and in what way, and about what.

## WHAT IS CULTURE?

The meaning of "culture" is wide-ranging in anthropological interpretations. In 1871, the English anthropologist John Tyler defined culture as that complex whole that includes knowledge, belief, art, morals, law, custom, and any other capabilities and habits acquired by a person as a member of society (Adler 1997). In the last century, Kroeber and Kluckhohn (1952) offered one of the most comprehensive and generally accepted definitions:

> *Culture consists of patterns, explicit and implicit, of and for behavior acquired and transmitted by symbols, constituting the distinctive achievement of human groups, including their embodiment in artifacts; the essential core of culture consists of traditional (i.e., historically derived and selected) ideas and especially their attached values; culture systems may, on the one hand, be considered as products of action, on the other, as conditioning elements of future action (181)*

Hofstede (1980) investigated the nature of culture from a psychological perspective, defining it as the collective programming of the mind that distinguishes the members of one category of a people from another.

Culture provides significant knowledge and the techniques that enable humans to survive, both physically and socially, and to control in varying degrees the world around them. More particularly culture provides guidance, direction, and order in all aspects of our lives. Several features of culture are worth mentioning because of their special importance to intercultural communication:

1. Culture is learned from infancy and members of a culture learn their patterns of behavior and ways of thinking until they become internalized. Our cultural learning proceeds through interaction, observation, and imitation. All of this learning "occurs as conscious or unconscious conditioning that leads one toward competence in a particular culture" (Hoebel & Weaver 1979, 58). This process of learning one's culture is referred to as *enculturation*.

2. Cultural values are also expressed through proverbs. Cited below are examples from different world cultures that provide important educational lessons to their respective cultural groupings:

   *A proverb is like a swift horse.* This Yoruba saying calls attention to the importance of proverbs as a teaching aid in this culture.

   *One does not make the wind blow but is blown by it.* This saying is found in many Asian cultures, suggesting that people are guided by fate rather than by their own devices.

   *Order is half of life.* This expresses the value Germans place on organization, conformity, and structure.

   *Woman has but two residences: the house and the tomb.* This expresses an Algerian view of the place of woman within society.

   *The mouth maintains silence in order to hear the heart talk.* This saying expresses the value Belgians place on intuition and feelings in interaction.

   *He who speaks has no knowledge, and he who has knowledge does not speak.* This saying from Japan reinforces the value of silence.

   *How blessed is a man who finds wisdom.* This Jewish saying expresses the importance of learning and education.

   *A zebra does not despise its stripes.* From the Maasai of Africa, this saying expresses the value of accepting things as they are, of accepting oneself as one, and of not envying others.

   *Loud thunder brings little rain.* This Chinese proverb teaches the importance of being reserved instead of boisterous.

   *A man's tongue is his sword.* With this saying, Arabs are taught to value words and use them in a powerful and forceful manner.

   *A single arrow is easily broken, but not a bunch.* This proverb, found in many Asian cultures, expresses the belief that the group is stronger than the individual.

   *He who stirs another's porridge often burns his own.* The Swedish, a very private people, attempt to teach the value of privacy with this proverb.

3. Culture can be transmitted from one member of a society to another. Some elements of culture are transmitted from genera-

tion to generation, such as a parent teaching a child table manners (Mahoney, et al. 1998).

4. Culture is dynamic. As with communication, culture undergoes changes over time. As ideas and products evolve within a culture, they can produce change through the mechanisms of invention such as discovery of new practices, tools, or concepts and diffusion such as borrowing from another culture (Saee 1993).

5. The elements of culture are interrelated. For example, one element of British culture is its class system. Consistent with this system, British education is very elitist and focuses on training a relatively small number of students extremely well (Mahoney, et al. 1998).

6. Culture is ethnocentric. Ethnocentrism is a tendency for any group of people who regard their culture to be far more superior to others.

That "culture is ethnocentric" is a major challenge to effective intercultural communication because of the conflict that can be generated between people of different cultures. Other impediments to effective intercultural communication include fear of change, fear of the unknown, fear of threat to identity, fear of rejection, and fear of contradictions to a belief system. Many of these fears are deeply rooted in people's cultural value systems (Saee 1998). Moreover, in explaining incompetent intercultural communication, one can argue that misunderstandings arise when people are unaware of cultural differences or the possibility of such differences. These misunderstandings reflect a *mono*cultural perspective, which "denies cultural differences, views cultural interactions as filled with errors not diversity, and forms cultural boundaries in which people remain their entire lives, unable to wander out" (Pearce & Kang 1987, 22). Thus, a lack of understanding of the contextual elements of cultural diversity by the participants of a given communication process can be problematic, especially in the international business and management environment.

## MAJOR OBSTACLES TO INTERCULTURAL COMMUNICATION

The primary sources of misunderstanding between people of different cultures arise from values and priorities. Some of the most common misconceptions occur when there are conflicts in the way time is understood, the way people think and reason, in personal space, material possessions, language, and religion, as well as particular ethnocentric beliefs (Saee 1998). That misunderstandings, from harmless ones to those with serious consequences, occur alongside the success stories of globalization, reinforce the need for cultural sensitivity on the part of virtually every stakeholder in the economy.

### Different Modes of Thinking and Reasoning

Intercultural communication can often breakdown between people owing to different structures of reasoning. For example, it has been shown that many Asians and Australians think in different ways when it comes to hierarchies and status. Australians who interact with Japanese have noted that the Japanese frequently appear to change their minds. They often conclude that Japanese are too polite to express their opinions or hold no opinions at all. This interpretation ignores that Japanese reasoning tends to be contextual rather than abstract, which is a characteristic of Western cultures (Irwin & More 1994).

## Stereotyping

Stereotyping is the application of generalizations to an individual or group. Members of one culture may inappropriately stereotype members from another culture rather than accurately seeing them as they really are. Stereotypes present barriers to seeing, communicating, and acting effectively when they are based on erroneous or hurtful misinformation (Weiss 1996). Adler (1997) shows that on one particular management team, members falsely assumed that their American colleagues had more technological expertise than did their Moroccan colleagues simply because Morocco is an economically and technologically less-developed country. In a parallel situation, an Indian manager described the lack of respect granted him by many of his British colleagues who, he believed, "assume that I am underdeveloped simply because I come from an economically underdeveloped country" (133).

## Language

As stated earlier in the chapter, there are over 3,000 languages spoken throughout the world and language differences can produce barriers to cross-cultural understanding and international trade (Saee 1998). Examples of the difficulties associated with the translation of English into a foreign language intended for marketing a product or service include some amusing *faux pas*:

- An American food chain, *Taco Times Restaurant,* decided to expand into the Japanese market. It was discovered that "taco" meant "idiot" in the Japanese language.
- When the Mitsubishi *Pajero* was introduced into South America, it was not received with any great enthusiasm in South American countries. The slogan "Have an affair with a Pajero" translated into a local dialect as "Have an affair with a gay" (Selverajah & Cutbush-Sabine 1991).
- The famous Pepsi-Cola slogan, "Come alive with Pepsi" was translated in Germany as "Come out of the grave" and in Taiwan as "Bring your ancestors back from the dead."
- General Motors' "Body by Fisher" translated as "Corpse by Fisher" in Flemish.
- "Let Hertz put you in the driver's seat" translated literally into Spanish means "Let Hertz make you a Chauffeur."
- "Nova," the name of a car, sounds in spoken Spanish like "It doesn't go."
- "Braniff's 747 Rendezvous Lounge" in Portuguese meant "Braniff's 747 Meet Your Mistress Lounge" (Selverajah & Cutbush-Sabine 1991; Saee 1998).

Businesses owned by non-English speaking persons tend to make linguistic blunders, especially when they try to convey their advertising messages in English language. Exhibit 4-1 shows just some of the many amusing grammar mistakes that travelers sometimes encounter.

| Exhibit 4-1 | Faux pas in the English Language from Around the World |
|---|---|

- "Is forbidden to steal hotel towels please. If you are not a person to do such a thing is please not to read notis."—sign in a Tokyo hotel
- "The lift is being fixed for the next day. During that time we regret that you will be unbearable."—sign in a Bucharest hotel lobby
- "Do not enter lift backwards, and only when lit up." –sign in a Leipzig elevator
- "To move the cabin, push button wishing floor. If the cabin should enter more persons, each one should press a number of wishing floor. Driving is then going alphabetically by national order." —sign in a Belgrade hotel elevator.
- "Please leave your values at the front desk."—sign in a Paris hotel elevator
- "Visitors are expected to complain at the office between the hours of 9 and 11 A.M. daily."—sign in a hotel in Athens
- "The flattening of underwear with pleasure is the job of the chambermaid."—sign in a Yugoslavian hotel
- "You are invited to take advantage of the chambermaid."—sign in a Japanese hotel
- "You are welcome to visit the cemetery where famous Russian and Soviet composers, artists and writers are buried daily except Thursday."—sign in the lobby of a Moscow hotel across from Russian Orthodox monastery
- "Not to perambulate the corridors during the hours of repose in the boots of ascension."—sign in an Austrian hotel catering to skiers
- "Our wines leave you nothing to hope for."—menu of a Swiss restaurant
- "Salad a firms' own make; limpid red beet soup, with cheesy dumplings in the form of a finger; roasted duck let loose; beef rashers beaten up in the country people's fashion."—menu of a Polish hotel
- "Ladies may have a fit upstairs."—sign outside a Hong Kong tailor shop
- "Drop your trousers here for best results."—sign in a Bangkok dry cleaners
- "Dresses for street walking."—sign outside a Paris dress shop
- "Order your summer suit. Because is big rush we will execute customers in strict rotation."—sign in a Rhodes tailor shop
- "There will be a Moscow Exhibition of Arts by 150,000 Soviet Republic painters and sculptors. These were executed over the past two years."—from the Soviet Weekly
- "It is strictly forbidden on our black forest camping site that people of different sex, for instance, men and women, live together in one tent unless they are married with each other for that purpose."—sign posted in Germany's Black Forest
- "Because of the impropriety of entertaining guests of the opposite sex in the bedroom, it is suggested that the lobby be used for this purpose."—sign posted in a Zurich hotel
- "Teeth extracted by the latest Methodists."—advertisement for a Hong Kong dentist
- "Ladies, leave your clothes here and spend the afternoon having a good time."—sign posted in a Rome laundry
- "Take one of our horsedriven city tours–we guarantee no miscarriages."—sign posted Czechoslovakian tourist agency
- "Would you like to ride on your own ass?"—advertisement for donkey rides in Thailand
- "Special today–no ice cream."—Swiss mountain inn
- "We take your bags and send them in all directions." – Copenhagen airline ticket office
- "If this is your first visit to the USSR, you are welcome to it."—door of a Moscow hotel room
- "Ladies are requested not have children in the bar."—Norwegian cocktail lounge
- "Please do not feed the animals. If you have any suitable food, give it to the guard on duty."—sign at a Budapest zoo
- "Specialist in women and other diseases."—sign in an office of a doctor in Rome
- "The manager has personally passed away all the water served here."—sign in an Acapulco hotel
- "Our nylons cost more than common, but you'll find they are best in the long run."—sign in a Tokyo shop
- Cooles and Heates: If you want just condition of warm in your room, please control yourself.—front of a Japanese information booklet about using a hotel air conditioner
- "When passenger of foot heave in sight tootle the horn. Trumpet him melodiously at first but if he still obstacles your passage then tootle him with vigor."—from a Tokyo car rental firm's brochure
- "English well speaking." and "Here speeching American"– two signs in front of a Majorcan shop entrance

Source: Adapted from Funny Translations of Signs in Different Countries, Air France Bulletin, December 1, 1989. Reprinted with permission of Air France.

## Perception

Perception is a process by which individuals view reality and make sense of it. It is an individual's subjective reality. Perception determines how we see ourselves and others. Perception precedes and affects our judgment and decision making (Weiss 1996). Since perception is highly subjective, it can present barriers to intercultural communication. A couple of good examples that follow illustrate with reference to problematic advertising message by the Ford Company.

Ford introduced a low-cost truck, the *Fiera*, into Spanish-speaking countries. Unfortunately, the name is Spanish idiom for an "ugly old woman." Needless to say, this name did not encourage sales. Ford also experienced slow sales when it introduced a top-of-the-line automobile, the *Comet*, in Mexico under the name *Caliente*. The puzzling low sales were finally attributed to the Mexican idiomatic meaning of the word: Caliente is slang for streetwalker (Ricks 1983).

## Materialism

Most Western cultures place importance on material acquisitions and tend to equate materialism with success. By contrast, there are some societies that place little or no value on material acquisitions. They regard materialism as vulgar and greedy. And they resist being identified or relating with people who tastelessly flaunt wealth. (Saee 1998).

## Religion

As discussed in Chapter 3, religion is a major influence in the lives of millions of people around the world, especially in terms of their worldview. It affects the way in which members of a society relate to each other and to outsiders. For example, life in conservative Islamic countries is centered on Islamic religious precepts and laws; therefore, all Muslims are required to observe these laws, including Islamic laws relating to the conduct of their businesses (Saee 1998).

## Ethnocentrism

The most damaging influence on human interactions and intercultural communication arises from ethnocentric values that are predicated on the belief that people of a particular race and religion are superior to all other races and only they are, as it were, "the center of the Universe." This belief can be a major impediment to effective intercultural communication and can ultimately lead to strong prejudice and even hatred towards others (Saee 1998). Lack of understanding of nonverbal communication; differences in religion and values; language; different styles of reasoning; and stereotyping provide a basis for ethnocentric attitudes that become obstacles to effective intercultural communication (Hall 1976; Samovar & Porter 1995; Adler 1997). Facial expressions, distance between people, and the use of space, posture, gestures, personal appearance, clothing, etiquette, and the body require as much attention as that given to the spoken word. "For a stranger entering an alien society, a knowledge of when not to speak may be as basic to the production of culturally acceptable behavior as a knowledge of what to say" (Basso 1990, 305). Nonverbal communication is explored in detail in Chapter 5.

# CULTURAL DIVERSITY AND COMMUNICATION

Misunderstanding between individuals from different cultural backgrounds can lead to confrontation and conflict. In any culture, social expectations accompany communicative practices. Recognizing the reality of such cultural differences, Edward T. Hall (1976) divided world cultures into "high context" and "low context" cultures. A high context culture uses information contained in either the physical context or internalized in the person. High context cultures display the following characteristics:

- There is reliance on nonverbal cues for understanding factual meaning.
- Deliberation and not speed is the essence of business negotiation.
- Relationships are personal and based on trust.
- Change is slow and seen as necessary only if it is essential.
- Seniority is respected and the position of people in companies determines relationships (Selverajah & Cutbush-Sabine 1991).

Research illustrates some of the key characteristics of Japanese communication as a high context culture. The following are examples:

- Indirect and vague communication is more acceptable than direct and specific reference, with ambiguity in conversation preferred.
- Sentences may be left unfinished to leave the other person to draw the conclusion in his or her own mind.
- The context of communication is often vague so as not to preclude personal interpretation.
- The listener may make noises of understanding and encouragement, and "hai" in Japanese rarely means "yes" in agreement, simply a "Yes, I have heard you."
- The real business deals are often struck after the formal deliberations and while entertaining.

Using a more direct communication approach, managers of English-speaking cultures may find that their communication skills, acquired as a result of years of their respective cultural conditioning, do not apply in the high context cultures of Japan, Saudi Arabia, and China.

In contrast, a low context culture employs communication in which most information is contained in explicit codes such as words. There is less reliance on nonverbal cues for understanding factual meanings, except for support or reinforcement. Speed is the essence of business negotiation. The relationship is founded on a contractual basis and changes in work practices and speed and adaptation to changes in work practices are viewed as desirable. Most English-speaking cultures typically engage in low context communication, which makes English a low context language (Saee 1998).

Low context cultures are more individualistic than group-oriented; and their personal nonverbal communication is characterized by large boundaries of personal space, little touching, and so on. High context cultures, on the other hand, are group-oriented. They also feature high sensory involvement; that is, they have much less pronounced interpersonal space defenses and they tend to initiate and receive more bodily contact when talking.

In view of the foregoing, unless international managers are aware of these subtle differences and their origins in a cultural context, communication misunderstandings between them and colleagues, employees, clients, and other stakeholders can easily result (Saee 1998).

# THE NEXUS BETWEEN COMMUNICATION AND MANAGEMENT

Communication is at the heart of successful management (Egan 1988; Irwin & More 1994; Irwin 1996). According to Jackson (1993), a manager is one whose main responsibility is to organize other people's time within an organization in order to pursue the objectives of the organization, and whose primary activity is to communicate with others to achieve these ends. Consequently, communication is central to the successful operation of an organization including interpersonal, face-to-face communication, intergroup and interorganizational communication. Yet "Much of what is written about organizing, managing, and leading in modern organizations either explicitly or implicitly takes for granted a close connection between success in those activities and communication" (Irwin & More 1994, 2). In addition, the importance of communication for managers cannot be overemphasized for one compelling reason: Everything a manager does involve communicating (Robbins, Bergman, & Stagg 1994). It is notable that "Without communication, nothing can be achieved in an organization and that everything an organization does and is, is dependent on communication" (Thayer 1990, 7–8).

The association between management and communication can be approached by determining the amount of a manager's time that is spent on communication. Research shows that managers spend 75 percent of their time each day on communicating. This includes writing, talking, and listening (Harris & Moran 1991). In fact, all business ultimately comes down to transactions and interactions between individuals. The success of the transactions depends almost entirely on how well managers understand each other. Mutual understanding is thus seen as the most vital element in managing an organization, whereas a manager's inability to empathize with other persons can lead to dysfunction in an organization (Saee & Kaye 1994).

Managerial communication involves the use of human, financial, and technical resources to understand and perform the communication function within corporations and between those corporations and their public. Managerial communication requires the administering and managing of communication resources (personal, group, organizational, and technical) to facilitate communication in corporate contexts. The process of managerial communication, that is, the way people perceive and interpret the information presented to them, is critical to the building of successful professional relationships. Accurate and relevant information processing is clearly a crucial aspect of managerial decision-making (Saee & Kaye 1994).

Generally speaking, communication serves four main managerial functions within an organization (Whetten & Cameron 1998):

1. Control
2. Motivation
3. Emotional expression
4. Transference of information/meaning

**EXAMPLE 4-2:** Japanese Pickles and Mattresses Incorporated

It was my first visit to Japan. As a gastronomic adventurer, and because I believe cuisine is one route that is freely available and highly effective as a first step towards a closer understanding of another country, I was disappointed on my first evening when my Japanese hosts offered me a Western meal. As tactfully as possible, I suggested that sometime during my stay I would like to try a Japanese menu if that could be arranged without inconvenience. There was some small reluctance evident on the part of my hosts and due, of course, to their thinking that I was just being polite by asking for Japanese food that I would not really like. So they had to politely find a way of not letting me eat any authentic Japanese food!. Eventually, however, by my starting with Western food that had a slightly Japanese character and gradually breaking myself in for the real thing, my hosts were at last convinced that I really wanted to eat *their* native food and was not "posing." From then on they become progressively more enthusiastic in suggesting even more exotic Japanese dishes. I guess I graduated from this "education" when, after an excellent meal one night (apart from the Japanese pickles) on which I lavished some praise. They said, "Do you like Japanese pickles?" To this, without preamble, I said, "No!" To this reply, with great laughter all around, they responded, "Nor do we!"

During this gastronomic getting-together week, I had also been trying to persuade my hosts that I really did wish to stay in traditional Japanese hotels rather than the Westernized ones they had selected. They thought I would prefer my "normal" lifestyle. (I should add that, at this time, traditional Japanese hotels were still available and often cheaper than, say, the Osaka Hilton.) Anyway, after the pickles joke, it was suddenly announced that Japanese hotels could be arranged. For the remaining weeks of my stay, on most occasions a traditional Japanese hotel was substituted for the Western one on my original schedule.

Now, a traditional Japanese room has no furniture except a low table and a flower arrangement. The "bed" is a mattress produced just before you retire from a concealed cupboard, accompanied by a pillow. One evening, my host and I had finished our meal together in my memorable hotel room. I expected him to shortly say "goodnight" and retire, as he had been doing all week, to his own room. However, he stayed unusually long and was obviously in some sort of emotional crisis. Finally, he blurted out, with great embarrassment, "Can I sleep with you?!" As they say in the novels, at this point I went very still. My mind was racing through all the sexual taboos and prejudices my own upbringing had instilled, and I can still very clearly recall how I thought, "I'm bigger than he is, so I can fight him off. But then he's probably an expert in the martial arts, and, on the other hand, he has shown no signs of being gay up until now. He is my host, after all, and there is a lot of business at risk." It seemed like an eternity had passed, though it had been only a few seconds, before I said, feeling as if I was pulling the trigger in Russian roulette, "Yes, sure."

The look of relief that followed my reply was obvious. Then he looked worried and concerned again, and said, "Are you sure?"

I reassured him and he called in the maid, who fetched his mattress from his room and laid it on the floor alongside mine. We both went to bed and slept all night without any physical interaction.

Later I learned that for the traditional Japanese one of the greatest compliments you can be paid is for the host to ask, "Can I sleep with you?" This goes back to the ancient feudal times when murder and assassination were rife in Japan. What this host's invitation really said was, "I trust you with my life. I do not think that you will kill me while I sleep. You are my true friend."

To have refused the invitation would have been an insult or, at the very least, my host would have been acutely embarrassed because he had taken the initiative. If I refused because I had failed to perceive the invitation as a compliment, he would have been out of countenance on two grounds: the insult to him in the traditional context and the embarrassment he would have caused me by forcing a negative, uncomprehending response from me.

As it turned out, he and I were now "blood brothers," as it were. His assessment that I was "ready for Japanization" had been correct and his obligations under ancient Japanese custom had been fulfilled. I had totally misinterpreted his intentions through my own cultural conditioning. It was sheer luck, or luck plus a gut feeling that I'd gotten it wrong, that caused me to make the correct response to his extremely complimentary and committed invitation.

Source: From *International Dimensions of Organizational Behavior*, 4th ed. by Adler, © 2002. Reprinted with permission of South-Western, a division of Thomson Learning: www.thomsonrights.com. Fax 800-730-2215.

Communication acts to control behavior in several ways. Organizations have authority structures and formal guidelines that employees are required to follow. When employees are required to first communicate any job-related grievance to their immediate supervisor, to follow their job description, or to comply with company policies, communication is performing a control function. Communication also fosters motivation by clarifying to employees what is required of them, how well they are performing, and what can be done by employees to further improve their performance should their performance be inadequate. For many employees, their employment with an organization is a primary source of social interaction. Communication that takes place within the organization is a fundamental vehicle through which members express their ideas. Communication, therefore, provides a release for the emotional expression of feelings and for the fulfillment of social needs.

The final function that communication performs relates to its role in facilitating decision-making. It provides the information that organizations need to make decisions by transmitting the information needed to identify and evaluate alternative choices. Within almost every communication interaction that takes place in an organization, one or more of these functions are being performed.

# DIRECTIONS OF COMMUNICATIONS IN ORGANIZATIONS

In organizations, decisions may be communicated in various manners (Hellriegel, Jackson, & Slocum 1999):

- Downward
- Upward
- Laterally
- Through formal networks
- Through informal networks

In the next sections, each of these decision modes is discussed in some detail.

## Downward Communication

Communication that flows from one level of an organization to a lower level is a downward communication. Downward communication is utilized by management to:

1. Assign goals.
2. Provide job instructions.
3. Inform other employees of policies and procedures.
4. Provide feedback about performance.
5. Stimulate and encourage employees' dedication to organizational mission.

## Upward Communication

Upward communication flows from a lower level to one or more levels higher within organization. It is used for feedback to middle or senior management about many kinds of issues, including (1) the current progress of work; (2) serious unresolved problems; (3) situations in which subordinate, may need help from superiors; (4) suggestions for improvement; and (5) employees attitudes, morale, and efficiency (Bartol, et al. 1995).

## Lateral Communication

Lateral communication or horizontal communication is communication by members of the same team, horizontally equivalent peers, and between management on the same level. In some cases lateral relationships are formally sanctioned by senior management so as to expedite the decision making process. Horizontal communication takes place in many forms including meetings, reports, memos, telephone conversations, and face-to-face discussion (Bartol, et al. 1995).

## Formal versus Informal Networks

Communication networks define the channels by which information flows. These channels are one of two varieties:

1. Formal networks

2. Informal networks

Formal networks are typically vertical, follow the authority chain, and are related to task-related communications. In contrast, the informal network is free to move in any direction and to skip authority levels and is as likely to satisfy organization members social needs as it is to facilitate task accomplishments (Hellriegel, Jackson, & Slocum 1999). Informal communication is occurring without regard to hierarchical or task requirements. Informal communication is related to personal not positional issues (Bartol, et al. 1995).

Effective managerial communication is central to the success of an organization regardless of its geographic locations. An Australian study found that communication was a key factor in explaining the "productivity advance" of National Mutual, a large financial institution, and Mayne Nickless, including Vicstate Railex, and Skyroad, a major transport corporation. The study found that in both corporations, management fostered an environment of openness and trust and used goal-oriented teams that were granted high levels of autonomy. Both corporations used structures to encourage and facilitate communication vertically and laterally between teams and, in each case, delegation of authority necessitated open communication between work groups and between work groups and management. The study also found that National Mutual and Mayne Nickless benefited from enhancement of communication channels by supervisors who believed in and practiced participative management and who met regularly with subordinates. Further the research found that the Dulux company in Australia has achieved an increase in goods delivered in full on time; that is, from 60 percent to 98 percent; a reduction of 49 percent in labor per product batch (from 79 to 40 hours); and a reduction of 88 percent in products reworked (from 4.5 percent to 0.5 percent). These substantial increases were due to the improvements in corporate communication within its culturally diverse workforce (Office of Multicultural Affairs and EMD Consultants 1994).

Similarly, research of an organization survey of 122 white collar employees in an American engineering company (Putti 1990) confirmed that the satisfaction of organizational members concerning the amount of information available to them can enhance their commitment to excellence in work performance. This was largely because satisfaction with information encouraged a sense of belonging and identification with the values and objectives of the organization. This research also found that high levels of commitment were linked to high levels of performance and low levels of turnover and absenteeism.

# THE AGE OF INFORMATION SUPERHIGHWAY AND MANAGEMENT COMMUNICATION

Managerial communication process has been undergoing unprecedented transformations in recent time largely as a result of technological revolution, particularly, with the advent of the Internet, the World Wide Web, and electronic mail. Every conceivable industry in the world has been affected by the emergence of the Internet and the World Wide Web. As part of their competitive marketing strategies, businesses are formulating new ways of reaching out to world markets while successfully overcoming existing impediments to international trade; and this is all made possible via their use of the Internet and the World Wide Web. The purchase, sale, and exchange of goods and services, or information over telecommunication networks such as the internet, is referred to as electronic business (e-business). E-business comprises many types of activities including on-line advertising, distribution, billing, payment, and service.

E-business is not necessarily restricted to businesses—getting a book from the library via the Internet is a form of e-business. And e-business also involves increasing participation of consumers. Over 300 million consumers around the world are already connected to the Internet who make routine purchases of goods and services from around the globe. Business-to-business transactions are also prevalent via the Internet. Business-to-business transactions accounted for $150 billion in 1999 and it is envisaged that this figure will dramatically grow to $3 trillion in 2003 (Wild, Wild, & Han 2001).

Of particular interest to management communication within organizations has been the widespread use of electronic mail—e-mail—in recent years, and it is considered to be the cheapest and fastest means of communication available to management in any organization worldwide. Dissemination of information of all types within and outside an organization can now be done in a most efficient and cost-effective manner using e-mail. E-mail messages can be stored, forwarded, and repackaged very efficiently. What is also striking about e-mail facility is the ability of the users to schedule their communication during a time of a day that is most convenient for them. Increasingly, managers and employees in organizations are accessing their e-mail in other places besides the physical location of their workstations and places of employment—and at a time more convenient for them. E-mail has also made it possible for staff and management to communicate openly and speedily at all levels without having to be hindered by the hierarchical management system in an organizational setting, as was the case before the advent of the Internet and electronic mail.

Having discussed the growing importance of e-mail in management communication, We have still not addressed the issue of how managers should develop competence in cross-cultural communication. In fact, one could argue that e-mail has increased problems that exist already—especially between two cultures, because it is not taking into account the cross-cultural dimensions of the communicators involved in the communication process. Thus, cross-cultural communication competence is a critical managerial skill in the face of increasing globalization of businesses and its culturally diverse workforce.

## CROSS-CULTURAL COMMUNICATION COMPETENCE

Ruben and Kealey (1979) defined intercultural communication competence in terms of an individual's empathy, respect, ability to perform role behaviors, nonjudgmentalness, openness, tolerance for ambiguity, and interaction management. To communicate effectively also requires that we have certain knowledge. The knowledge component of competence refers to what we need to do to communicate in an appropriate and effective way. This includes (1) knowledge of how to gather information; (2) knowledge of group differences; (3) knowledge of personal similarities; and (4) knowledge of alternative interpretations for others' behavior.

Several skills have also been identified (Berger 1979; Coleman & DePaulo 1991; Gudykunst & Kim 1997) that would serve to improve intercultural communication competence by reducing uncertainty and anxiety. To reduce anxiety, managers must be mindful of and tolerate ambiguity—while remaining calm. According to Gudykunst (1993), to reduce uncertainty, managers must anticipate, explain, and make accurate predictions of a behavior displayed by a person of another culture (stranger's behavior).

Three behavioral dimensions associated with perceived competence have been identified (Gudykunst, Wiseman, & Hammer 1977; Gudykunst & Kim 1997):

- *The ability to deal with psychological stress.* This includes the ability to deal with frustration, stress, anxiety, pressures to conform, social alienation, financial difficulties, and interpersonal conflicts.

- *The ability to communicate effectively.* This includes the ability to enter into meaningful dialogue with other people, to initiate interaction with strangers, to deal with communication misunderstandings, and to deal with different communication styles.

- *The ability to establish meaningful interpersonal relationships.* This includes the ability to develop satisfying relationships with others, to understand the feelings of others, to work effectively with others, and to deal with different social customs. (A detailed discussion on the Theory of Intercultural Communication Competence is in Chapter 6).

## SOME STRATEGIES FOR ENHANCING INTERCULTURAL COMMUNICATION COMPETENCE

Learning intercultural communication can be acquired and developed over a period of time (Beamer 1992; Saee 1998). The key to intercultural communication is recognizing that cultures are whole and coherent; all cultures are equally valid in the way they organize and explain human experience; and the interculturally competent communicator acknowledges that a cultural bias always exists (Saee 1998). To this end, five levels of learning can be postulated that can each be represented by a circle. The circles are stacked, like records in an old jukebox. The five levels are (a) acknowledging diversity; (b) organizing information according to stereotypes; (c) posing questions to challenge the stereotypes; (d) analyzing communication episodes; and (e) generating other culture's messages (Beamer 1992).

## Acknowledging Diversity

The first and most basic level in intercultural learning is an awareness of differences; it may be the key organizing concept for intercultural sensitivity to occur (Bennett 1986).

## Organizing Information According to Stereotypes

The second level of intercultural learning is developing basic categories of certain selected characteristics that distinguish a particular culture and its members. Arabs like to stand very near a listener when speaking. Chinese typically refuse hospitality initially when offered. Latin Americans like to do business with people who show consideration for their family affairs. These examples are stereotypes. "Stereotypes are not usually as simple or brief as the examples above. Indeed, they are often multilayered, complex, multidimensional images" (Coleman & DePaulo 1991).

## Posing Questions to Challenge the Stereotypes

At the third level of learning, stereotypes are challenged. The intercultural communicator asks questions about other cultures in order to break out of the stereotypes. Put another way, to communicate competently across cultures one needs ethnographic, (i.e., cultural interpretation) tools as well as business communication tools. One may ask questions, for example, about how members of a business organization describe that organization, about their relationships to one another and to their material environment, or about their position in relation to the universe. Questions reveal attitudes that are important for understanding business activities, such as attitudes toward time, status, and role, obligations in relationships, responsibility and the decision-making processes, the role of law, and the role of technology. Answers to the questions may be sought from various research sources, published and primary (Beamer (1992).

## Analyzing Communication Episodes

Once the learner-manager has actively sought to understand a culture through posing questions to challenge stereotyped categories, the understanding can be used to analyze communication in actual cases. As communication is analyzed, new meanings for communication behavior can be attributed. At this fourth level of learning intercultural communication competence, emphasis is culture-specific; learning focuses on the depth of understanding and the application of the abstractions considered in level three during the plotting of a culture's value orientations (Beamer 1992).

## Generating "Other-Culture" Messages

The communicator becomes interculturally competent when messages are encoded and directed as if from within the "other" culture and when messages from the "other" culture are decoded and responded to successfully. This is similar to the standard suggested by Brislin (1993) in his description of intercultural behavior as an ability to walk in the other person's "moccasins," because the communicator's perceptions are so attuned that he or she has the ability to simulate being the other.

## Summary

Communication is pivotal to human life. Business operations, irrespective of their geographic locations, depend on effective managerial communication competence. However, obstacles to effective managerial communication especially dealing across cultures exist. Some strategic solutions for effective intercultural management communication were discussed.

Given the increasing globalization of the world economy, it is imperative that international managers develop high level intercultural communication competence so that they could use it in varied aspects of their personal, professional, and organizational life as well as their respective international negotiations. Electronic telecommunication via the Internet and e-business were discussed in this respect. It is apparent that the success of any international deal largely depends on how competent managers are in their dealings with their counterparts globally and this involves to a large extent communication competence in their intercultural encounters. Equally, it should be noted that contemporary organizations increasingly embody varying degrees of cultural diversity in terms of their clientele, human resources, and ownership. Thus, intercultural communication competence will be an invaluable asset for international managers to possess, rendering them highly competent in their dealings with people of all social strata around the world. As an essential part of effective managerial intercultural communication, understanding of nonverbal communication is equally necessary, and therefore, the next chapter is devoted to a detailed discussion on nonverbal communication with implications for management communication across cultures.

## Critical Discussion Questions

1. Describe seven components of the communication process. Provide examples.
2. Discuss how context affects intercultural communication.
3. Effective communication is at the core of effective management. Explain.
4. How do you define effective intercultural communication?
5. "Culture and communication are synonymous." Discuss and provide examples.
6. What are the major obstacles to successful intercultural communication?
7. How can intercultural communication be enhanced?

## Applications

### Experiential

1. Ask each of your group members or fellow students to write down cultural traits of a particular ethnic group that they know about. After a few minutes, discuss the sources for their knowledge and the implications of this stereotyping for real-life intercultural communications.

2.  Interview someone who had a recent experience of visiting a foreign country with particular reference to challenges arising from his or her intercultural communication encounters.

3.  Identify a company that employs a culturally diverse workforce and interview a manager of this firm about the issues and problems that he or she encounters in managing people of different cultural backgrounds. Ask what are the managerial communication strategies used to minimize the effects of these problems at the workplace.

4.  Critically examine your own strengths and weaknesses in so far as intercultural communication is concerned and indicate the steps you would like to take to ensure that your weaknesses in communication are overcome.

### Internet

The late Sam Walton opened his first Wal-Mart discount department store in 1962. Since then, Wal-Mart has become the largest chain of stores in the world. According to Wal-Mart's statistics, Wal-Mart now employs more than 1.2 million employees (associates) worldwide. The company has more than 3,000 stores and offices across the United States and more than 1,000 stores internationally. It has also expanded online with Walmart.com. Your assignment is to visit the corporate Wal-Mart Web site at http://www.walmart.com and click the Company News link in the home page's contents bar. Try to find out the following. You can use other Internet and non-Internet sources if desired.

1.  In what ways does Wal-Mart management communicate its business philosophy?

2.  What types of management communications has Wal-Mart formulated in terms of targeting different market segments? Provide examples.

3.  In what ways does Wal-Mart, as part of its promotional strategies, address the question of cultural diversity involving its clientele?

4.  Critically assess Wal-Mart's overall management communications.

5.  Finally, in what ways has Wal-Mart failed to address cultural diversity in its corporate and managerial communication? Provide examples.

## References

Adler, N. (1997). *International dimensions of organizational behavior* (3rd ed.). Mason: OH: South-Western, a division of Thomson Learning.

Adler, R.B., & Rodman, G. (1997). *Understanding human communication* (6th ed.). Austin, TX: Holt, Rinehart and Winston.

Bartol, K.M., Martin, D.C., Tein, M., & Graham, M. (1995). *Management: A Pacific Rim focus.* Sydney: McGraw-Hill.

Basso, K. (1990). To give up on words: Silence in Western Apache culture. In D. Carbaugh (Ed.), *Cultural communication and intercultural* contact (pp. 303–320). Hillsdale, NJ: Lawrence Erlbaum Associates.

Beamer, L. (1992). Learning intercultural communication competence. *Journal of Business Communication, 27*, 285–303.

Bennett, M.J. (1986). A developmental approach to training for intercultural sensitivity. *International Journal of Intercultural Relations, 10* (2), 179–195.

Berger, C.R. (1979). Beyond initial interactions. In H. Giles & R. St. Clair (eds), *Language and social psychology* (pp. 122–144). London: Edward Arnold.

Bourdeau, P. (1988). Viva la crise! For heterodoxy in social science. *Theory and Society, 17* (5), 773–787.

Brislin, R. (1981). *Cross-cultural encounters.* Elmsford, NY: Pergamon.

Brislin, R. (1993). *Understanding culture's influence on behavior.* Fort Worth, TX: Harcourt Brace.

Coleman, L., & DePaulo, B. (1991). Uncovering the human spirit: Moving beyond disability and "missed" communication. In N. Coupland, H. Giles, & J. Wiemann (Eds.), *"Miscommunication" and problematic talk.* Newbury Park, CA: Sage.

Dance, F.E.X., & Carson, C.E. (1976). *The functions of human communication: A theoretical approach.* New York: Holt, Rinehart and Winston.

Dwyer, J. (1993). *The business communication handbook* (2nd ed.). Sydney: Prentice Hall.

Egan, G. (1988). *Change agent skills: Assessing and designing excellence.* San Diego: University Associates.

Gudykunst, W., Wiseman, R., & Hammer, M. (1977). Determinants of a sojourner's attitudinal satisfaction. In Ruben, B. (Ed.), *Communication Yearbook 1.* New Brunswick, NJ: Transaction.

Gudykunst, W.B. & Kim, Y.Y. (1997). *Communicating with strangers* (3rd ed.). Boston: McGraw-Hill.

Gudykunst, W.B. (1993). Toward a theory of effective interpersonal and inter-group communication: An anxiety/uncertainty management (AUM) perspective. In Wiseman, R. and Koester, I. (Eds.), *Intercultural communication competence* (pp. 33–71). Newbury Park, CA: Sage.

Hall, E.T. (1976). *Beyond culture.* New York: Anchor Press.

Harris, P., & Moran, R. (1991). *Managing cultural differences* (3rd ed.). Houston, TX: Gulf Publishing Company.

Hellriegel, D., Jackson, S., & Slocum, J. (1999). *Management* (8th ed.). Mason, OH: South-Western, a division of Thomson Learning.

Hoebel, E.A., & Weaver, T. (1979). *Anthropology and the human experience* (5th ed.). New York: McGraw-Hill.

Hofstede, G. (1980). *Culture's consequences: International differences in work related values.* Beverly Hills, CA: Sage.

Irwin, H. & More, E. (1994). *Managing corporate communication.* Sydney: Allen and Unwin.

Irwin, H. (1996). *Communicating with Asia. Understanding people and customs.* Sydney: Allen and Unwin.

Jackson, T. (1993). *Organizational behavior in international management.* London: Butterworth Heinemann.

Kroeber, A. L., & Kluckhohn, F. (1952). *Culture: A critical review of concepts and definitions.* New York: Random House.

Littlejohn, S.W. (1989). *Theories of human communication* (3rd ed.). Belmont, CA: Wadsworth.

Littlejohn, S.W. (1992). *Theories of human communication* (4th ed.). Belmont, CA: Wadsworth.

Mahoney, D., Trigg, M., Griffin, R., & Pustay, M. (1998). *International business: A managerial perspective.* Melbourne: Addison Wesley Longman.

Mohan, T., McGregor, H., Saunders, S. & Archee, R. (1997). *Communicating theory and practice,* 4th ed. Sydney: Harcourt Brace.

Office of Multicultural Affairs and EMD Consultants (1994). *Best practice in managing a culturally diverse workplace: A manager's manual prepared for the Office of Multicultural Affairs.* Canberra: Australian Government Publishing Services.

Pearce, W.P., & Kang, K. (1987). Conceptual migrations: Understanding "Travelers' Tales" for cross-cultural adaptation. In Y.Y. Kim & W.B. Gudykunst (Eds.), *Cross-cultural adaptation* (Vol. XI of the International and Intercultural Communication Annual, pp. 20–41). Newbury Park, CA: Sage.

Putti, J. (1990). Communication relationship with satisfaction and organization commitment. *Group and Organization Studies, 15* (1), 44–52.

Ricks, D.A. (1983). *Big business blunders: mistakes in multinational marketing.* Homewood, IL: Dow Jones-Irwin.

Robbins, S.P., Bergman, P., & Stagg, I. (1994). *Managers and management.* Upper Saddle River, NJ: Prentice Hall.

Ruben, B. (1988). *Communication and human behavior.* New York: Macmillan.

Ruben, B.D., & Kealey, D.J. (1979). Behavioral assessment of communication competency and the prediction of cross-cultural adaptation. *International Journal of Intercultural Relations, 3,* 15–47.

Saee, J. (1999). Managing across cultural frontiers. *Journal of European Business Education, 8* (2), 35–59.

Saee, J., & Kaye, M. (1994. July 11–15). Intercultural communication competence in management training. Paper presented at the 44th Annual Conference of the International Communication Association. Sydney, Australia.

Saee, J. (1993). Culture, multiculturalism and racism: An Australian perspective. *Journal of Home Economics of Australia, 25,* 99–109.

Saee, J. (1997, May). Cultural diversity and global economy. *Journal of Australian Institute of Management,* 17–18.

Saee, J. (1998). Intercultural competence: Preparing enterprising managers for the global economy. *Journal of European Business Education, 7* (2),15–37.

Samovar, L.A., & Porter, R.E. (1995). *Communication between cultures.* Belmont, CA: Wadsworth.

Selverajah, C.T., & Cutbush-Sabine, K.C. (1991). *International business.* Melbourne: Longman Cheshire.

Shimanoff, S. (1980). *Communication rules: Theory and research.* Beverly Hills: Sage.

Stewart, E. (1971) *American cultural pattern: A cross-cultural perspective.* Pittsburgh, PA: Regional Council for International Education.

Thayer, L. (1990). Corporate communication: Some thoughts on how to think about what needs thinking about. *Australian Journal of Communication, 17* (2), 28–36

Watzlawick, P., Beavin, J.D., & Jackson, D.D. (1967). *Pragmatics of human communication: A study of interactional patterns, pathologies and paradoxes.* New York: W. W. Norton.

Whetten, D.A., & Cameron, K.S (1998). *Developing management skills* (4th ed.). Sydney: Addison Wesley Longman.

Weiss, J.W. (1996) *Organizational behavior and change.* Eagan, MN: West.

Wild, J.J., Wild, K.L., & Han, J. C.Y; (2001) *International business: An integrated approach.* Upper Saddle River, NJ: Prentice Hall.

# Chapter 5

*Nonverbal Communication Across Cultures*

*Do not the most moving moments of our lives find us all without words?*

—Marcel Marceau

*Eyes are more accurate witnesses than ears.*

—Heraclitus

## NONVERBAL COMMUNICATION: AN OVERVIEW

An American's eyebrows are constantly in motion as he or she speaks, and these motions express the inner feelings behind the words. In contrast, the "blank," nearly motionless Japanese forehead reveals very little of a Japanese person's inner feelings to an American (but not necessarily to a Japanese person). Therefore, during a conversation, an American might feel that the Japanese person is not really interested, or (worse yet) that the Japanese person is hiding the truth. (Taylor 1974).

The foregoing is a typical example of how different cultures attach meanings to the same nonverbal cues based on their own cultural frame of reference, which when compared are quite at variance with each other and may potentially lead to conflict.

Edward T. Hall has called nonverbal communication the "silent language." Humans communicate much of what they think and feel through this range of facial expressions, space and distance between people, postures, gestures, personal appearance, clothing, etiquette, and touching. Research shows that the average person speaks words for a total of 10 to 11 minutes daily—the standard spoken sentence taking only about 2.5 seconds. In a normal two-way conversation, verbal components carry less than 35 percent of the social meaning of the situation; more than 65 percent of the social meaning is carried on nonverbally (Knapp 1978). Nonverbal communication plays a crucial role in understanding people from different cultural backgrounds (Triandis 1994)—and an awareness of this significance can lead to competence in the intercultural communication that exists in globalized business, management, and workplace environments. As Basso (1990, 305) suggests, "For a stranger entering an alien society, a knowledge of when not to speak may be as basic to the production of culturally acceptable behavior as a knowledge of what to say."

In this chapter, the importance of nonverbal communication in the human interactions of different cultures is discussed and analyzed—as well as compared to the verbal forms of communication we learned in the previous chapter.

## THE SIGNIFICANCE OF NONVERBAL COMMUNICATION

Our ability to understand nonverbal cues helps us to learn about the emotional and psychological states of the people we communicate with. Indeed, we judge a person's psychological state by his or her nonverbal cues despite what he or she might actually say. Most of us rely on what we learn through our eyes. For example, when we see a man raising a clenched fist to another's face, usually no words are needed to inform us of his aggressive behavior. Research suggests that we believe nonverbal messages over verbal ones when the two contradict each other (Adler & Rodman 1997). This is because nonverbal cues signal what we take to be the real person—his or her emotions, attitudes, and images of self (Argyle 1976).

Nonverbal communication is often the foundation for our first impressions of individuals. Think for a moment of how often you initially judge people on how they look and dress. These are both nonverbal cues and color our perception of everything else that follows. Even how we select employees or friends is grounded in nonverbal communication, that "first impression. One approaches people because of the way they dress, how attractive one finds them" (Samovar & Porter 1995).

Nonverbal communication is, like verbal communication, conveyed both intentionally and unintentionally—the latter being more so. That is, we send countless nonverbal messages of what we never intended to be "part of the conversation." Mehrabian (1972) estimated that the total impact of a message on a receiver is based on 7 percent of the spoken words used and 38 percent of how the words are said (tone of voice, loudness, inflection). The remaining 55 percent is nonverbal: facial expressions, hand gestures, body position, and the like. Another study by Hall and Hall (1987) showed that "80 to 90 percent of all information is transmitted between people in different cultures by means other than language." Further research reveals that up to 90 percent of our emotions are expressed nonverbally—and people also signal, 65 to 93 percent of the time, what they mean during the communication process through nonverbal cues (Axwell 1991).

A failure to understand the often subtle nonverbal content of a message can result in serious comprehension issues. The hand signal for "everything is okay"—a circle made with the thumb and index finger—commonly used in the United States and Australia means something else in France (it signifies worthlessness) and Japan (it symbolizes money). In parts of South America, making the okay sign is a vulgar sexual gesture. One international company unfortunately learned this the hard way when it had an entire catalogue printed with the okay sign on each page. Although the error was discovered in time not to cause offense, it resulted in a costly delay while the catalogues were reprinted (Ricks 1993).

In the following sections, we will look at how nonverbal communication is defined and considered so important in our total understanding of what communication is.

# NONVERBAL COMMUNICATION DEFINED

The literature of nonverbal communication has many definitions for it. Elashmawi and Harris (1993, 50) suggest that *nonverbal* communication "is communication in any form other than words that can produce shared meaning and elicit a response." Samovar and Porter (1995) argue for a more comprehensive definition that includes the source communicator's person as well as external variables such as the distance he or she has from the receiver. Nonverbal communication, in this case, involves those nonverbal stimuli in a communication setting that are generated by the source and his or her use of the environment that have potential message value for both the source or receiver." Of critical importance to note in the foregoing definitions is that nonverbal communication embraces the intentionality and unintentionality of messages during the encoding and decoding phases. In addition, like verbal communication, nonverbal communication is about achieving a shared meaning between the source (the encoder) and the recipient (the decoder) during the nonverbal communication process.

Since nonverbal and verbal communication work in tandem in global management and business settings, it is important to compare the two and understand how they work together.

# SIMILARITIES AND DIFFERENCES BETWEEN VERBAL AND NONVERBAL COMMUNICATION

Nonverbal and verbal messages are both indispensable in how we send and receive interpersonal messages (Vaughan 1995; Samovar & Porter 1995). Both verbal and nonverbal communication are similar when one considers that they both use a culturally agreed upon set of symbols. We generate a message that someone else is going to use to infer something about us. Finally, in both verbal and nonverbal communication, the person involved in the communication process is attaching meaning to the symbols we produce (Samovar & Porter 1995). There are distinct differences between verbal and nonverbal communication. Many of our nonverbal actions are governed biologically—some are even psychosomatic reactions—whereas verbal messages are deliberate. We usually think before we talk or write. Therefore we have much more control over verbal communication. Most nonverbal messages are not deliberate; although we try to control our behavior, like smiling to convince people that we are happy, we cannot think and control all nonverbal channels. Another difference is that nonverbal communication is learned much earlier in life than verbal communication. A nonverbal message can also be more emotional in its appeal and impact. (Compare tears to saying "I'm sad.") Another distinguishing feature of nonverbal communication is that nonverbal communication is more universal. People tend to have similar meanings for some behaviors (laughing, crying, smiling, frowning, and the like). Moreover, we can say that verbal messages are sent through a single channel (one at the time). However, nonverbal messages do not come in an orderly sequential way. They come simultaneously from a multiple of channels. For example, when you meet someone new, little is said, but the many nonverbal messages that you pick up make you form a first impression (posture, clothes, distance) (Adler & Rodman 1997; Deresky 2000; Samovar & Porter 1995). Another distinguishing feature of nonverbal communication is that unlike verbal messages such as words and sentences, which have a clear beginning and end, nonverbal communication is continuous and a never ending process. Even the absence of a message is still a message (e.g., an unreturned phone call). Finally, where the verbal messages can be confusing, the nonverbal messages can be even more so. When your boss is smiling at you during a staff meeting, is it because he or she is happy with your idea or is amused with it? (Vaughan 1995; Samovar & Porter 1995).

# CHARACTERISTICS OF NONVERBAL COMMUNICATION

There are several features inherent to non-verbal communication:

- *Nonverbal communication exists.* Without talking and any formal training, one is able to get an idea about how others are feeling. We can form an opinion about how other people are feeling. You probably notice that some people were in a hurry whereas others seemed happy, confused, withdrawn, or deep in thought (Adler & Rodman 1997).

- *All behavior has communicative value.* It is impossible not to send out messages; no matter what people do they send out messages that say something about them. For instance, an expressionless face still communicates a message. Uncontrollable behaviors can convey messages. Blushing indicates that you are embarrassed. But not all behaviors can be interpreted so accurately. Trembling hands may mean nervousness—or that you are shaking from the cold (Samovar & Porter 1995).

- *Nonverbal messages are primarily attitudinal.* Nonverbal communication is especially well suited to convey attitudes. It is less effective at conveying thoughts or ideas. For example, it would be easier to convey "I am angry at someone in the room" than it would be to convey "Smoking is not good for health." We can understand attitudes and feelings of others as reflected nonverbally (Vaughan 1995).

- *Nonverbal communication is ambiguous.* There are well over 700,000 different physical gestures, facial expressions, and movements (Adler & Rodman 1997). Imagine the possibilities of interpreting silence from a companion. It could range from warmth, anger, preoccupied, bored, or nervous. In laboratory settings, subjects better identified positive facial expressions such as happiness, love, surprise, and interest than negative ones like fear, sadness, anger, and disgust. In real life, spontaneous nonverbal expressions are so ambiguous that observers are unable to accurately identify what they mean (Littlejohn 1992).

## FUNCTIONS OF NONVERBAL COMMUNICATION

There are several main functions that can be attributed to nonverbal communication across cultures. These include repeating, complementing, substituting, regulating, contradicting. deception, and leakage, which are described in the following sections (Knapp 1980; Adler & Rodman 1997; Samovar & Porter 1995).

- *Repeating.* In many cultures, people use nonverbal communication to repeat, clarify, and emphasize their point of views. For example, if someone asks us for direction, we might tell him or her "to go this way or that way;" at the same time we repeat our instructions nonverbally by pointing in a certain direction.

- *Substituting.* We can substitute nonverbal messages for verbal ones when we perform some actions in lieu of speaking. For example, one may place one's index finger to one's lips as an alternative to saying: "Please keep quiet."

- *Complementing.* This is closely related to repeating. For example, when a supervisor tells an employee that he is happy with his or her productivity. The same message, however, may take on an emphatic meaning if the supervisor pats the employee on the shoulder at the same time.

- *Regulating.* Adler and Rodman (1997) suggest that nonverbal behaviors can help control verbal interactions by regulating them, such as turn-taking signals in conversations to indicate the speaker has finished talking and is ready to listen: changes in vocal intonation. Examples would be:
  - A rise and fall in pitch at the end of a clause
  - A drawl on the last syllable or the stressed syllable in a clause
  - A drop in vocal pitch or loudness when speaking a common expression such as "you know."

Eye contact is another way of regulating conversations. Breaking eye contact with someone in the course of a conversation is a way of "taking turns."

- *Contradicting.* Contradiction is another function of nonverbal communication. Certain nonverbal behaviors can contradict spoken words. For example, to indicate our disbelief about what someone is saying, we roll our eyes in their presence. Another example is yawning as someone talks nonstop. The yawn suggests that you are getting bored. A nonverbal contradiction can also be used in double meanings. The same yawn can be employed, but as you say "Really," so as to soften the impolite yawn with politeness. Hopefully, the nonstop talker will pick up the double meaning—the nonverbal cue of the yawn and the verbalized one—and stop talking (Adler & Rodman 1997; Mohan, et al. 1997).

- *Deception and leakage.* Nonverbal behaviors can reveal information that a communicator does not disclose verbally, such as raised eyebrows to connote that something is not exactly true about something one is saying ("This dessert [eyebrows raise] is wonderful!"). Some nonverbalisms may get lost—or "leaked"—because people are more likely to pay attention to controlling their faces. A person trying to convey that "there's no problem" either verbally or nonverbally (with a smile) might be shifting his or her feet all the while, conveying that there is a problem.

## NONVERBAL COMMUNICATION AND CULTURE

We learn nonverbal communication—and our different cultures influence that learning process. Moreover, culture is primarily a nonverbal phenomenon because nearly every aspect of one's culture is learned through observation and imitation rather than explicit verbal instructions or expression (Anderson 1994). The primary level of culture is communicated implicitly, without awareness, by primarily nonverbal means (Hall 1984).

Culture also affects emotional expressions. Lustig and Koester (1993) suggest that individualism, collectivism, and status differentiation have an effect on emotional expressions. Westerners such as Americans value freer, more favorable, more accurate expressions of self-emotions via nonverbal behavior. The Japanese prefer moderate expressivity, reflecting a greater deal of control. Such differences in nonverbal "languages" can make cross-cultural interactions difficult—and many do exist in expression, regulation, and interpretation of nonverbal cues (Elashmawi & Harris 1993).

The significance of many nonverbal behaviors varies from one culture to another. Less obvious cross-cultural differences can damage relationships without people ever recognizing exactly what went wrong. This highlights the importance of nonverbal communication competence within the business world and this is why managers and companies today should become familiar with the meanings that different cultures attach to nonverbal cues. For example, in parts of the Middle East and Central Asia, when two male friends meet each other in the street, they often greet each other by hugging and simultaneously kissing each other on the cheeks. The same men, both heterosexual, could also walk holding each other's hands. This display of emotion in public may, of course, mean something entirely different to someone from a Western country. He or she may falsely assume that the two gentlemen are gay and are openly expressing their affections for each other in public. But this is not to be the case. In the Middle East, friendships can be emotionally profound and long-lasting. Such friendships between two men are as important as the relationship they have with a brother or other family member. There is nothing in their culture, such as men having to signify that they are straight, by maintaining a distance from each other. In Australia, where friendships are easily made and broken, there is no such display of emotions between two close male friends in public—unless they are gay and are not inhibited by what is, in Australia, still regarded as culturally inappropriate.

The example of two Middle Eastern men holding hands is one of many nonverbal cues for which one culture attaches its meaning to the cue and a different culture attaches another. In high context cultures such as South Korea or Taiwan, people rely less on verbal communication and more on the content of nonverbal actions and environmental settings to convey meaning. On the other hand, in a low context culture such as the United States or Germany, people rely more on explicit communication and less on circumstances and implied meaning. Expectations are usually spelled out in a low context culture through explicit statements, such as "Please wait until I'm finished" (Mahoney, et al. 2002). Imagine the confusion and frustration of someone from a low context culture trying to negotiate about a business proposition with businesspersons from high context culture. This is where an understanding of how nonverbal communication can be interpreted or conveyed differently becomes important.

## CATEGORIES OF NONVERBAL COMMUNICATION

Nonverbal communication is divided into two categories: those the individual combines with the setting, such as time, space, silence, and those produced by the body, such as facial expressions, posture, gestures, touch, appearance, body movements, eye contact, dress, and voice (Samovar & Porter 1995).

### Time

According to Hall (1976), cultures organize time in one of two ways: monochronic or *M-time* and polychronic or *P-time*. These two views of time affect important temporal concepts, such as:

- Appointments
- Schedules
- Discussion time
- Acquaintance time (Mead 1990)

A monochronic view of time can be seen through the Western cultures; Western cultures are obsessed with time. Westerners tend to view time as inescapable, linear, and fixed in nature (Deresky 2000; Dodd 1998; Samovar & Porter 1995). Good examples of time-driven countries include Germany, Austria, Switzerland, and the United States. These countries are renowned for their punctuality.

People from polychronic time cultures live their lives quite differently. These cultures include Chinese, Indians, Arabs, Latin Americans, and

Mediterraneans. They tend to view time more flexibly. A number of Southeast Asian cultures view time cyclically rather than linearly, and thus they attach less importance to time consciousness (Dodd 1998).

The timing of appointments is very important to members of monochronic cultures. In Swedish terms the allowance that an American or Australian might allow of, say five minutes, for arriving at an appointment is lax. Swedes are more particular about appointments. An appointment at ten o'clock means ten o'clock on the dot (Mead 1990). People of Middle Eastern and Latin American cultures attach less urgency to appointments; people come late to appointments—or they may not come at all—and it is not considered especially inconsiderate. There are cultural differences in understanding of schedule time, referring to the time when a job should be finished. In Western European countries, time is a valuable and limited resource, to be saved, scheduled, and spent with precision. Whereas in polychronic cultures, constant pressure may be needed to persuade the employee to meet the deadline. In Latin America, for example, a common attitude towards time is *mañana*, a word that literally means "tomorrow"; a person in Peru or Mexico using this word usually means an indefinite time in the near future, not literally the next day (Deresky 2000).

In Anglo-societies, it is generally supposed that a meeting will cover the main points in as short time as possible without 'time wasting.' In Brazil, you must expect to spend at least two hours and in Bolivia three hours in general discussion before mentioning the topic of your business—to do otherwise would be impolite (Mead 1990). In such countries, the feeling is that one should know one's business partner on a personal level before transactions can occur. Therefore rushing straight to business will not be appreciated and rewarded because deals are made not only on the basis of the best product or price, but also on the business or person deemed most trustworthy (Axell 1991). In Arab countries, personal relationships between people take precedence over the job or business as well.

## Space

Space is related to *proxemics*, Hall's term for the study of humankind's perception and use of space, which focuses on how people use space to communicate (Hall 1984). We use space and distance to convey messages. Proxemics is concerned with such things as:

- Personal space.
- Seating.
- Furniture arrangement (Mohan, et al. 1997; Samovar & Porter 1995).

Human beings use space to convey a communicated message to others. This space is divided up into personal space in which only those with close relationships such as family, lovers, and friends are allowed to invade. Next is social space, for work colleagues, and finally, public space, intended for strangers. The amount of space one needs to feel comfortable during interaction with others depends largely on culture. Thus each culture has appropriate distances for various levels of communication, and most people are uncomfortable if those distances are ignored (Mahoney, et al. 2002).

Cultures that stress individualism, such as England, the United States, and Australia, generally demand more personal space—and tend to take an active aggressive stance when space is violated—than do collectivist cultures such as those in the Middle East and Asia (Samovar & Porter 1995). North Americans are most comfortable with 20 inches, while people from Latin and Arab cultures generally prefer a closer spacing. It is not uncommon to see an Anglo-American continuously back up to maintain his or her comfort zone (Mahoney, et al. 2002)—something perceived by a collectivist culture member incorrectly as a negative reaction. Space can also have a cultural dimension in, for example, a seating arrangement that can reflect status and role distinctions. In Korea and Japan, sitting on the right hand side of a car, in an office or home is considered an honor. Culture can also influence the manner and meaning in furniture arrangement. In France, space is a reflection of its culture and institutions. Everything is centralized spatially—like the entire country is laid out around Paris (Hall & Hall 1987; Mead (1990)).

## Material Possessions

In many cultures, power is symbolized by material possessions, and in the workplace, these may be prominently displayed in the manager's office. In Arabic countries, it is bad manners to admire another person's possessions. The rules of courtesy bind the owner to give it to you if you admire it (Mead 1990; Samovar & Porter 1995).

## Silence

Even silence has meaning. Australians tend to abhor silence at meetings or in private conversation, believing that silence reflects an inability to communicate or to empathize (Mahoney, et al. 2002). In Far Eastern countries, silence is taken differently. People in China, Japan, and elsewhere in Asia do not feel uncomfortable with the absence of noise or talk—and they are not compelled to fill every pause when they are with people.

## Kinesics

Nonverbal messages are communicated by means of body movements known as *kinesics*. Samovar and Porter (1995) outline three *kinesic* cues that send a message through body movements:

1. Our attitude toward the other person: direct body orientation.
2. Our emotional state: tapping on the table or fidgeting (a sign of being nervous).
3. Our desire to control our environment: motioning someone to come closer means we want to talk to him or her.

In the United States, managers have been known to relax by putting their feet up on a desk in an office environment; this is considered a major insult to an Arab or a Thai. Most Germans would consider this an uncivilized behavior (Ferraro 1994).

## Facial Expression

Every culture uses facial expressions to communicate nonverbally. Facial expressions occur in every human interaction: people smile, frown, squint, sneer, and engage in a range of facial movements (Mahoney, et al. 2002). According to Ruben (1988), humans can create 250,000 facial expressions. There are a great variety of characteristics, which an individual in each culture can use to communicate from one person to another.

There are different ways of judgment and actions that would be appropriate for each culture. There are seven emotions that can be expressed by facial expression: happiness, sadness, fear, surprise, anger, disgust, and interest (Ekman 1973). The interpretations that people of different cultures have for facial expressions are difficult to assess because anatomically similar expressions occur in everyone, yet the meanings attached to them can differ from culture to culture (Samovar & Porter 1995). The Chinese do not readily show emotion for reasons that are deeply rooted in their culture—the Chinese custom of keeping face being one of the most important. For the Chinese, displaying too much emotion violates this norm that signifies more than just personal stability and strength of character—doing otherwise disrupts harmony and cause conflict. In many Mediterranean countries, such as Italy, however, the demonstration of one's emotions is socially accepted for the way it authenticates an emotion. Exaggerating the outward signs of grief or sadness in one's face is not considered weakness; and it is not uncommon in this region to see men crying over something enormously sad or even happy.

A simple smile has many meanings across cultures, in Australia, a smile is a sign of happiness or friendliness; however, in the Korean culture too much smiling is often perceived as the sign of a shallow person.

## Posture

Body posture relates to the way people stand, walk, sit, and even the way they lie down. Posture and sitting habits offer insight into a culture's structure of respect and status. In many Asian cultures, bowing is much more than a greeting. It signifies that culture's concern with status and rank. In Japan, for example, low posture is an indicator of respect. The manner in which one sits can also communicate a message. A trip on a Japanese subway, for example, will quickly reveal the proper way of sitting—straight forward, legs together, head slightly down and for women hand bag placed squarely on lap (Mahoney, et al. 2002). People in Thailand believe that since the bottom of one's feet are the lowest part of the body, they should never be pointed in the direction of another person (Samovar & Porter 1995). In Ghana and Turkey, sitting with ones' legs crossed is extremely offensive, while putting one's hands in pocket is a sign of disrespect in Turkey.

## Gestures

A gesture includes how you use your hands, head, shoulders, and other parts of the body to reflect, reinforce, or substitute verbal messages (Mead 1990). Hand gestures have been studied exclusively. Morris (1994) isolated twenty common hand gestures that have a different meaning in a range of cultures.

In Australia, when a person wants to signal a friend to come, he or she makes the gesture with one hand up, palm down, fingers more or less together, and moving toward his or her body. In parts of Burma, the summoning gesture is made palm down and fingers moved as though playing the piano. Filipinos often summon people with a quick nod of the head. In Germany and Scandinavia, a beckoning motion is made by tossing the head back. For many Arabs, nonverbally asking someone to "come here" is performed by holding the right hand out, palm outward and opening and closing the hand (Samovar & Porter 1995; Deresky 2000).

## Eye Contact

The number of messages we can send with our eyes is almost limitless. Eye movement includes length of gaze, maintaining eye contact, dilation, and blinking (Samovar & Porter 1995; Basso 1990; Deresky 2000). There are six communication functions that relate to the eye contact; eyes:

1. Indicate degrees of attentiveness, interest, and arousal.
2. Influence attitude change and persuasion.
3. Regulate interaction.
4. Communicate emotions.
5. Define power and status relationships.
6. Assume a central role in impression management (Samovar & Porter 1995; Mohan, et al. 1997).

Eyes are used to convey messages differently across cultures. In most Asian countries, for example, it is considered polite and respectful not to look a person in the eyes during conversation. This is particularly the case if the person is of higher status. In Western societies including Australia, such a mannerism implies a totally different meaning. It can indicate a guilty conscience or devious behavior (Saee 1993). A male–female relationship in a culture also determines customs of eye contact and gaze. In many Asian and Arab societies, it is considered taboo for women to look straight into men's eyes. Most men, in accordance with this custom, do not stare directly at women. This is in stark contrast to men in France and Italy who stare at women in public (Deresky 2000). Generally speaking, people in Western societies expect the person with whom they are interacting to look them in the eye. If the person fails to look at you, there is a tendency to be suspicious towards that person. However, direct eye contact is not a custom in every culture. The Japanese consider staring into ones eyes for a prolonged time rude, threatening, and disrespectful. The traditional Indian woman avoids looking into the eyes of a man to whom she is not related. An Egyptian stands close in order to read the other persons eyes (Mead 1990).

## Touch

Touching is also proxemic—and we communicate a variety of feelings with it including anger, interest, trust, warmth, love, and fear. Tactile communication is a powerful nonverbal communication signal (Mohan, et al. 1997). Different meanings are conveyed by means of touch across different cultures. For example, Asian men, particularly Vietnamese men, express their friendship by touching and holding during conversation. This is not an accepted custom in Australia, as discussed earlier. Men there tend to keep their distance from one another. And where, in Australia, it is customary to wave a greeting to one another and to use hands to accompany and emphasize speech, neither of these customs would be considered polite in Vietnamese culture (Saee 1993; 1998)—a difference that would make for some embarrassing moments in a cross-cultural incident. In the Middle East, men greet each other by kissing and hugging. Yet such behavior in Australia may be totally inappropriate (Saee 1993; 1998). In Thailand and in other Asian countries, the head is sacred, and it is offensive to touch someone's head. For Muslims, the shoulder is an approved zone of contact, and it is used for hugging, a sign of brotherhood (Saee 1998). In Korea, on the other hand, young people are socially forbidden from touching the shoulders of their elders (Samovar & Porter 1995).

## Dress

People's clothing conveys to us messages about who they are. In different cultures styles of dress signal degrees of formality, informality, and social status. Most occupations have their official and unofficial uniforms in Western cultures. For example, doctors and nurses normally dress in white. In Western societies such as Germany, Britain, and the United States, it is not uncommon for people of high status to wear a suit and a tie during working hours (Saee 1998). In Indonesia, however, a good quality long sleeved batik shirt, which appears almost casual by Western standards, is worn as formal attire.

## Paralanguage

The voice itself is another form of nonverbal communication. Social scientists have identified a range of nonverbal communication behaviors, or *paralanguage*, associated with the human voice in terms of its use and meanings across cultures:

- Voice quality—harshness, hardness, stridency, breathiness, strength
- Tempo
- Pitch variation
- Volume

In Anglo societies, a deep male voice is associated with masculinity and is favored, whereas a high pitched male voice may be mocked. In Iran, females are expected to be relatively unemotional and to speak with a more restricted pitch (Mead 1990).

## Smell

A sense of smell can also be a conduit for different meanings across cultures. In Bali, when lovers greet one another, they often breathe deeply in a kind of friendly sniffing. Burmese, Samoans, Mongols, Lapps, and some Filipinos smell each other's cheeks to say "Hello." It is not uncommon for young Filipino lovers to trade small pieces of clothing on parting, so that the smell of the other person will evoke their affection for each other (Samovar & Porter 1995).

In the Arab world, a person's smell is regarded as an extension of the person. To the Arab, good smells are pleasing and a way of being involved with each other. To smell one's friends is not only desirable, but to deny your friend your breath is to act ashamed. Americans, on the other hand, learn not to breathe in people's faces and to avoid being breathed on, which would strike an Arab as impolite (Samovar & Porter 1995).

# NONVERBAL COMMUNICATION: IMPLICATIONS FOR INTERNATIONAL MANAGERS

International managers, workers, and entrepreneurs operating in a globalized business economy and community need to develop a high degree of understanding and sensitivity to nonverbal cues and their meanings across cultures. They need to be culturally aware of their own nonverbal communications as well as people in different countries and societies, especially when it comes to interacting effectively with their multicultural employees and clientele. There are two types of misunderstandings that can occur in intercultural nonverbal communication. The first is misinterpretation, that "one gesture has two or more meanings between cultures." The second is misunderstanding or a lack of comprehension as when a Chinese employee does not look directly into the eyes of his Western manager because doing so signifies disrespect—not a lack of interest on his part, as such a nonverbal cue might signify in the manager's native culture (Southworth 1999).

The idea that these silent cues across cultures signify different meanings has been and continues to be a great challenge to communication—especially in the global business environment. There are two possible reasons for this. The first is that people believe that everyone communicates in the same fashion they do, which is known as *projected similarity* (Cruz, 2002). The second reason is that people are not familiar with the nonverbalisms used in different cultures. Overt misunderstandings, which occur frequently through verbal communication, are often correctable. However, covert misunderstandings, which frequently occur through nonverbal communication, are much harder to correct (Southworth 1999). One possible explanation for this is that through verbal communication, where we express our thoughts and ideas, we can have a degree of control in terms of what we say and how say it. Much of nonverbal communication is, however, is "primarily attitudinal," and it is conveyed subconsciously, rendering it very difficult to control.

## Summary

People convey their thoughts and feelings through nonverbal communication. Nonverbal communication includes facial expressions, distance between persons or the use of space, posture, gestures, personal appearance, clothing, etiquette, and body contact. People in different cultures can interpret different meanings in nonverbal cues that appear analogous. An effective manager should be aware of the importance of nonverbal communication and recognize its potential impact. The inability to understand or recognize differences and interpret them objectively could negatively impact business relations because we make judgments and decisions about others based on their nonverbal behavior.

Awareness of the cultural nuances of nonverbal communication is one part of being interculturally competent as an intercultural communicator. This is particularly important for international business people who must deal with clientele and human resources of culturally diverse backgrounds.

## Critical Discussion Questions

1. Nonverbal signals principally communicate emotional states, interpersonal attitudes, and images of self across cultures. Discuss why this is so.

2. Describe the key components of nonverbal communication. Provide examples.

3. Discuss how context affects nonverbal communication across cultures.

4. Effective understanding of nonverbal communication across cultures is at the core of effective global management. Give your reasons.

5. How do you define nonverbal communication?

6. Describe the main functions of nonverbal communication across cultures. Provide examples.

7. In what ways does cultural difference pose challenges for understanding of nonverbal communication? Provide examples.

8. In what ways has this chapter helped to identify your own shortcomings when interacting with people of diverse cultural backgrounds, particularly with reference to their nonverbal cues?

# Applications

### Experiential

1. Ask each of your group members or class members to write down why and in what ways does nonverbal communication differ across cultures. After they have finished, discuss the results.

2. Interview someone who had the recent experience of visiting a foreign country and noted some kind of difficulty in understanding the nonverbal communication that he or she encountered.

3. Interview a manager of multinational company with regard to the challenges arising from the nonverbal cues of employees and clientele from different cultures.

### Internet

The following web site addresses contain some insightful articles on nonverbal communication across cultures. Your task is to select and browse one web site address and read the relevant article. In addition, summarize your findings and discuss them in class.

1. Bee, M. (2001). *Non-Verbal Communication*
   http://www.hunnybee.com.au/non-verbal-communication.html

2. Cruz, W. (2002). *Differences in non-verbal communication styles between cultures: The Latino-Anglo perspective.*

   http://www.rochesterdiversitycouncil.com/docs/
   article_NonverbalCommunication.pdf

3. McGovern, L. (1998). *When "Yes" means "No" or "Maybe"- Avoiding Cross-Cultural Misunderstandings in Global Business.* http://www.frugalmarketing.com/dtb/xcultcomm.shtml

4. Southworth, H. (1999). *Nonverbal communication in a cross-cultural context.* http://www.gsb.columbia.edu/cis/training/acrostuff/tooHOT.research.pdf

5. Vandenabeele, B.(2003). *The importance of non verbal communication in first contacts between different cultures.* http://www.uia.ac.be/apil/apil101/vandenabeele.pdf

6. YoungEntrepreneur.com. (2003). *Non-Verbal Communication.* http://www.uncstudent.com/cec/business/management/non-verbal-communication.html

# References

Adler, R.B. & Rodman, G. (1997). *Understanding human communication* (6th ed.). New York: Harcourt Brace College.

Adler, R.B., Rosenfeld, L.B., & Towne, L.B (1992). *Interplay: The process of interpersonal communication* (5th ed.) Forth Worth, TX: Harcourt Brace Jovanovich.

Andersen P. (1994). *Explaining intercultural difference in nonverbal communication.* In Samovar, L. A. & Porter, R. E. (Eds.), *Intercultural communication: A reader* (7th ed.) (pp. 229-239 ). Belmont, CA: Wadsworth.

Argyle, M. (1976). *Bodily communication.* London: Methuen.

Axell, R. (1991). *Gestures, the do's and taboos of body language around the world.* New York: John Wiley & Sons.

Basso, K. (1990). To give up on words: Silence in Western Apache culture. In D. Carbaugh (Ed.), *Cultural communication and intercultural contact* (pp. 303–320). Hillsdale, NJ: Lawrence Erlbaum Associates.

Burgoon, J.K. & Hale, J.L. (1984). The fundamental topoi of relational communication. *Communication Monographs, 151,* 193–214.

Cruz, W. (2002). *Differences in non-verbal communication styles between cultures: The Latino-Anglo perspective.* Greater Rochester [NY] Diversity Council. http://www.rochesterdiversitycouncil.com/docs/article_NonverbalCommunication.pdf

Czinkota, M.R. & Ronkainen, I.A. (1998). *International marketing* (5th Ed.) Orlando, FL: Harcourt Brace.

Deresky, H. (2000). *International management: Managing across borders and cultures.* Upper Saddle River: Prentice Hall.

Dodd, C.H. (1998). *Dynamics of intercultural communication.* New York: McGraw-Hill.

Ekman, P. (1973). Cross-cultural studies of facial expression. In P. Ekman (Ed.), *Darwin and facial expression* (pp. 169–222).San Diego, CA: Academic Press.

Elashmawi, F., & Harris, P.R. (1993). *Multicultural management: New skills for global success.* Houston: Gulf Publishing.

Ferraro, G. (1994). *The cultural dimension of international business* (2nd ed.). Englewood Cliffs, NJ: Prentice Hall.

Hall, E.T. & Hall, M.R. (1987). *Understanding cultural differences.* Garden City, NY: Doubleday.

Hall, E.T. (1959). *The silent language.* Garden City, NY: Doubleday.

Hall, E.T. (1976). *Beyond culture.* New York: Anchor Press.

Hall, E.T. (1984). *The dance of life: the order dimension of time.* New York: Anchor Press.

Kaye, M. (1994). *Communication management.* Sydney: Prentice Hall.

Knapp, M.L. (1978). *Nonverbal behavior in human communication.* New York: Holt, Rinehart and Winston.

Knapp, M.L. (1980) *Essentials of nonverbal communication.* New York: Holt, Rinehart and Winston.

Littlejohn, S.W. (1992). *Theories of human communication* (4th ed.). Belmont, CA: Wadsworth.

Lustig, M., & Koester, I. (1993). *Intercultural competence: Interpersonal communication across cultures.* New York: Harper Collins.

Mahoney, D., Trigg, M., Griffin, R., & Pustay, M. (2002). *International business: A managerial perspective.* Melbourne: Addison Wesley Longman.

McGovern, L. (1998). When "Yes" means "No" or "Maybe": Avoiding Cross-Cultural Misunderstandings in Global Business. FrugalMarketing.com. http://www.frugalmarketing.com/dtb/xcultcomm.shtml.

Mead, R. (1990). *Cross-cultural management communication.* New York: John Wiley & Sons.

Mead, R. (1998). *International management: Cross-cultural dimensions.* Cambridge, MA: Blackwell.

Mehrabian, A. (1972). *Nonverbal communication.* Chicago: Aldine.

Mohan, T., McGregor, H., Saunders, S., and Archee, R. (1997) *Communicating theory and practice* (4th ed.). Sydney: Harcourt Brace.

Morris, D. (1994). *Body language: A world guide to gestures.* New York: Random House.

Pease, A. (1981). *Body language.* Sydney: Camel.

Pease, A., & Pease, B. (1998). *Why men don't listen and women can't read maps.* (Melbourne, Australia): Harper Collins.

Ricks, D.A. (1993). *Blunders in international business.* Cambridge, MA: Blackwell.

Ruben, B. (1988). *Communication and human behavior.* New York: Macmillan.

Saee, J. (1993). Culture, multiculturalism and racism: An Australian perspective. *Journal of Home Economics of Australia, 25,* 99–109.

Saee, J. (1998). Intercultural competence: Preparing enterprising managers for the global economy. *Journal of European Business Education, 7* (2), 15–37.

Samovar, L.A. & Porter, R.E. (1995). *Communication between cultures.* Belmont, CA: Wadsworth.

Samovar, L.A., & Porter, R.E. (Eds.) (1994*). Intercultural communication: A reader* (7th Ed.). Belmont, CA: Wadsworth.

Southworth, H. (1999). *Nonverbal communication in a cross-cultural context.* Columbia Business School. http://www.gsb.columbia.edu/cis/training/acrostuff/tooHOT.research.pdf.

Taylor, H. (1974). Misunderstood Japanese nonverbal communication. *Gengo Seikatsu (Language Life).* Cited in Southworth, H. (1999). *Nonverbal communication in a cross-cultural context.* Columbia Business School. http://www.gsb.columbia.edu/cis/training/acrostuff/tooHOT.research.pdf

Triandis, H.C. (1994). *Culture and social behavior.* New York: McGraw-Hill.

Vaughan, G., & Hogg, M. (1995) *Introduction to Social Psychology.* Sydney: Prentice Hall.

# Chapter 6

*Theoretical Perspectives on Intercultural Communication*

## LEARNING OBJECTIVES

*After reading this chapter, you should be able to:*
- Understand the need for theories of intercultural communication.
- Understand the theories of intercultural communication.
- Understand why language acquisition is an indicator of intercultural communication competence.
- Describe psychological theories of intercultural communication.
- Describe General Systems Theory.
- Describe Uncertainty Reduction Theory.
- Describe sociological theories of intercultural communication.
- Describe Convergence Theory.
- Describe Interpersonal Theory.
- Understand the importance of perception in intercultural communication.
- Define intercultural communication competence.
- Understand the implications of these theories for managers in achieving communication competence in the global business environment.

*Theories [. . .] are nets cast to catch what we call "the world": to rationalize, to explain. We endeavor to make the mesh ever finer and finer.*

—Karl Popper

## OVERVIEW

In Chapters 4 and 5 the central role of verbal and nonverbal communication within contemporary society and of organizational life was discussed as were the important differences in communication styles, contexts, and content prevailing across global cultures with an emphasis on what the implications are for international management in all manners of organizational settings in the global business community. In this chapter we learn the major theories that are important to our understanding and achieving intercultural communication competence. Becoming familiar with these theories performs a number of vital functions including:

- It helps to *organize and summarize* the knowledge arising from differences in attitudes, behaviors, feelings, and thoughts found among peoples in different cultures in a systematic manner. This, in turn, informs a worldview that distinguishes intercultural patterns and linkages.
- It *focuses on* what are important variables and relationships.
- It plays a considerable role in *clarifying*. The clarification not only helps the observer understand relationships but also interpret specific events. Theories provide guideposts for interpreting, explaining, and understanding the complexity of human relations.
- It provides aids in terms of not only what to observe, but how to observe—and interpret what is observed.
- It gives us the ability to *predict* without having to rely on guesswork and ad hoc impressions of social phenomena (Littlejohn 1996).

With this in mind, this chapter critically examines current theoretical perspectives on intercultural communication that have considerable implications for global management communication competence. These theoretical perspectives on intercultural communication include the psychological theories—such as Culture Shock Theory; General Systems Theory; Uncertainty Reduction Theory—and the sociological theories, namely Convergence Theory and Interpersonal Theory. The psychological theories are relevant to expatriate workers and international managers in the overseas business and workplace environments, especially in regard to the development of intercultural communication competence needed to function in a host culture and for interacting with the workers and clients encountered in the host country's society. For convenience, the term "sojourner" is used throughout this chapter to refer to these expatriate workers and international managers as well as multicultural workforce clients living overseas.

## LANGUAGE ACQUISITION AS A "PANACEA" FOR INEFFECTIVE INTERCULTURAL COMMUNICATION

With the rapid globalization of businesses and cultures, intercultural communication skills have become essential. The need for communication competence in culturally diverse workplaces has forced changes in communication training programs around the world. Often intercultural communication competence is seen by organizations as competence in the host (local) language. For example, in Australia, to improve communication within their culturally diverse workforce, Australian organizations tended to focus on English-language training to remedy ineffective intercultural problems between managers and their foreign workers. Such a solution was initially promulgated by government policymakers and researchers who have emphasized the acquisition of English language competence by a multicultural workforce. Learning English then became a panacea, *the* way to overcome the communication barrier between management and ethnic workers (Eyles & Davis 1989; Harris 1996; Jupp 1989). This view is clearly evident in the *Report of the Committee for the Review of Migrant and Multicultural Programs and Services* released in 1986, which stated that "Proficiency in English is central to all aspects of life in Australia. Ideally, all immigrants should have the opportunity to learn English on their arrival to meet their employment and living requirements" (ROMMPAS 1986, 1). This centrality implies that an immigrant from a non-English speaking background (NESB) can only adapt quickly and competently to his or her new environment and workplace in Australia by gaining language skills. This "language acquisition is enough" thesis has its origins within the field of linguistics, initially pioneered by Sapir and Whorf, who advocated that our thought processes and the way we see the world are shaped by the grammatical structure of the language. "All one's life one has been tricked by the structure of language into a certain way of perceiving reality" (Whorf 1956, 27). While an organization's focus on language training to remedy communication problems is laudable, language training is only a partial solution. As a primary strategy for facilitating communication in a multicultural workplace, host language skills training is based on false assumptions:

- That efficient communication between cultures is solely based on linguistic competence.
- That communication, like typing, is purely a mechanical skill, unrelated to emotional and other interpersonal factors (Gouttefarde-Claire 1992; Saee 1998).

An exclusive emphasis on language training will not necessarily enhance workplace communication. Speaking a language cannot be considered synonymous with communicating effectively in it. The ability to communicate competently in a particular context goes far beyond syntax and vocabulary and includes many cultural dimensions.

Maurice Bloch (1991), in writing about cognitive anthropology, has investigated the relationship of language to understanding culture, and has concluded:

- That much knowledge is fundamentally nonlinguistic.
- That concepts involve implicit networks of meanings that are formed through the experience of, and practice in, the external world.
- That, under certain circumstances, this nonlinguistic knowledge can be rendered into language and thus take the form of explicit discourse. In other words, competence in speaking a host language at an appropriate level for the workplace may not guarantee that meanings are exchanged effectively about workplace knowledge, skills, and attitudes.

By emphasizing that *sojourners* should master skills in written and spoken host language, both training and responsibility are deflected away from the members of the host society. Language training does not address the dynamics of intercultural communication processes and lacks a framework for international managers to develop and assess their *own* intercultural communication competence. The range of theoretical approaches to intercultural communication discussed in the following sections demonstrates that the "Host language is enough" view is inadequate.

# PSYCHOLOGICAL THEORIES OF INTERCULTURAL COMMUNICATION

Psychological theories of intercultural communication explain intercultural communication in terms of individual rather than group behavioral adaptation (Bochner 1981; Bochner 1982; Brislin 1979; Gudykunst 1984). These studies emphasized personal and interpersonal traits and attributes as integral parts of intercultural communication processes. These theories proposed that variables in the individual person determined stages of acculturation, alienation, assimilation, or adaptation to a dominant culture. Consequently, these theories provided an insight into the individual internal psychological responses when participating in intercultural communication settings.

## Culture Shock Theory

Psychologists (Lysgaard 1955; Oberg 1960; Selltiz, et al. 1963; Furnham & Bochner 1989; Searle & Ward 1990; Harris & Moran 1991) have observed that when a sojourner enters a foreign culture for the first time, he or she undergoes several recognized stages of cross-cultural learning (acculturation) and adaptation—this is called the "culture shock" theory. The stages of adaptive change through which an individual progresses are shown in Figure 6-1. A "U" curve or "W" curve indicates the way the sojourner undergoes the acculturation process (Gudykunst & Hammer 1988; Gudykunst 1995). These curves indicate patterns of change over time from living in the alien environment. The sojourner's level of adjustment, adaptation, and well-being produces a W-shape curve, where satisfaction and well being gradually decline but then increase again.

The typical stages of adjustment are identified in the following sections.

### Initial Contact

At the point of initial contact with a different culture, the sojourner fails to recognize new realities. The sojourner's own culturally influenced worldview persists; the sojourner sees one's own initial worldview in the second culture. The differences experienced by the sojourner may not be threatening, but intriguing instead. In other words, the sojourner feels a high degree of excitement and euphoria during this stage (Furnham & Bochner 1989; Harris & Moran 1991).

### Initial Culture Shock

This stage is characterized by a sense of increasing confusion and loss. The sojourner experiences disorientation because of a lack of familiarity with every day cues such as language, gestures, foods, and customs. The individual lacks points of reference, social norms, and rules to guide his or her actions and to understand others' behavior. A sojourner undergoing culture shock displays certain symptoms. Some of the symptoms of culture shock are: excessive washing of the hands; excessive concern over drinking water, food, dishes, and bedding; fear of physical contact with

**EXAMPLE 6-1:** Language Acquisition versus Communication Competence.

A Chinese MBA graduate studying at an Australian university recounted his experience in an MBA class to one of my Australian colleagues. Before coming to Australia, the Chinese MBA graduate remembered, "I had managed to master English language at a sufficiently high level in order to pursue my postgraduate study in Australia. In fact, I had to attain a high score in a Toefel test in English being a partial requirement for my admission into the MBA program."

During the first semester, one professor lectured to us for nearly 10 minutes, and then suddenly stopped the lecture and started by asking us: Are there any questions? In my mind, I began to seriously doubt the academic rigor of this class, and I was thinking to myself, "I paid a lot of money to come to study in Australia, and here's a lecturer who stops the class after 10 minutes of lecture. It is not fair!"

| **Figure 6.1** | The Culture Shock Theory Curve |

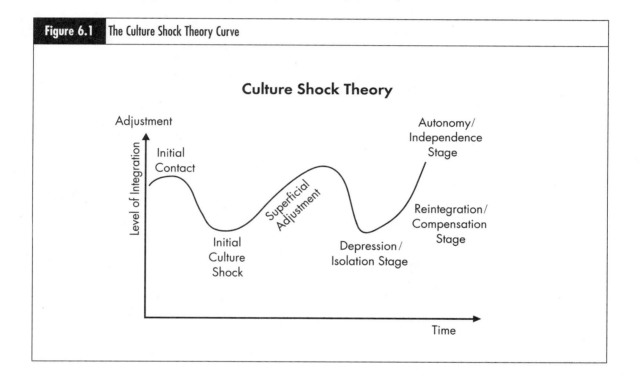

Thus, the sojourner may experience periods of depression, withdrawal, severe homesickness, mounting tension, frustration and fatigue. This stage is also referred to as the "disintegration stage" (Furnham & Bochner 1989; March 1995).

attendants; an absent-minded, faraway stare; feelings of helplessness and a desire for dependence on long-term residents of one's own nationality; fits of anger over delays and other minor frustrations; delay and outright refusal to learn the language of the host country; excessive fear of being cheated, robbed, or injured; great concern over minor pains and eruptions of the skins; and finally, that terrible longing to be back home, to be able to have a cup of coffee and a piece of apple pie, to walk into that corner drugstore, to visit one's relatives, and, in general, to talk to people who really make sense (Oberg 1960).

### Superficial Adjustment

This stage is marked by the sojourner's attempt to find a solution to a difficult situation as he or she temporarily overcomes the negative effects of culture shock and has learned how to "survive" in the host culture. The sojourner can communicate basic needs in the host language and appears to be settled. However, cultural differences begin to intrude and the foreigner experiences a loss of ties with his or her own culture.

### Depression/Isolation Stage

The foreigner experiences a growing loss of self-esteem because of awareness of deep cultural differences. The foreigner feels alienated from members of the host culture. Frequent misinterpretation of cultural cues and lack of ability to "fit in" occur because the foreigner feels a loss of control over his or her environment. His or her sense of identity and personality are threatened (Furnham & Bochner 1989; Harris & Moran 1991).

### Reintegration/Compensation Stage

The sojourner develops coping behavior to deal with self-esteem. Cultural differences continue to cause the sojourner to make negative judgments; however, he or she may develop strategies to help deal with anxiety, nervousness, frustration, and anger (Furnham & Bochner 1989; March 1995).

### Autonomy/Independence Stage

The sojourner accepts and sometimes even values differences between his or her own and the host culture. During this stage, the sojourner feels more relaxed and demonstrates self-confidence. The sojourner is capable of interacting socially in the host culture.

Church (1982) reported seven studies that found some evidence for these stages depicted in Figure 6-1. Torbiorn (1982) studied the psychological adjustment of Swedish expatriate managers working abroad and his findings confirmed the figure's U-curve model. In Australia, there has been a major study (Taft 1988) of psychological adaptation of Soviet immigrants to Australia. This study revealed similar types of psychological adaptation experienced by Soviet immigrants.

In terms of a managerial context, let's take a hypothetical Japanese manager on his first assignment to work in France. During his first weeks of settling in, he discovers new things in the French environment including the culture, history, food, architecture, and language. This manager understandably feels a degree of excitement due to his new environment and any problems arising from his intercultural encounters may be overlooked.

As the Japanese manager begins to settle in, he finds problems having tasks completed successfully and trouble interacting with both French colleagues at the workplace and, generally, the French citizens he encounters outside the workplace stemming from his lack of knowledge of the appropriate cultural cues and norms—that is, reference points. This causes him a varying degree of personal stress.

As time goes on, the manager may find ways of coping with certain day-to-day issues, and feel a heightened sense of integration and a better ability to communicate with his colleagues (the artificial integration stage). But later on, due to his increasing awareness of cultural differences, he may fall into periods of depression, which are characterized by feelings that he does not fit into his French environment and a lack of identity with either subordinates or superiors resulting in severe feelings of isolation.

As this Japanese expatriate tries to reintegrate, he may find ways to cope with these feelings, would begin, bit by bit, to solve interpersonal problems as he learns the necessary cultural cues, and thus he becomes more relaxed in interacting with members of the host culture. During the last two stages, projects and tasks would be completed more successfully, and the Japanese manager would feel a higher sense of confidence in his abilities once again.

Thus, intercultural competence by international managers and their staff on overseas assignments means more than acquiring the host language. More importantly, managers should prepare themselves for the challenges of cross-cultural adaptation based on culture shock theory. They should undergo a rigorous and comprehensive cross-cultural training program either conducted in their own home country or through an intensive cultural immersion program in the host country over an extended period of time.

## General Systems Theory of Intercultural Communication

One leading theory of intercultural communication is General Systems Theory as formulated by Y.Y. Kim (Kim 1988; Kim & Rubin 1988). It is deeply rooted in the disciplines of psychology and sociology and is predicated on a set of "open-systems" assumptions about the nature of humans as adaptive living entities. Individuals are viewed as open systems, which function through ongoing interaction with the environment and other people. In particular, human beings are seen as having an inherent drive to adapt and grow. Adaptation is considered to be a fundamental life goal for humans, something that people do naturally and continually as they face the challenges from their environment (Kim, 1988; Slavin & Krugman 1992).

Upon entering a new and unfamiliar culture, sojourners are faced with situations that deviate from their familiar and internalized original cultural scripts. Sojourners discover that they lack a level of understanding of the communication system of the new host culture, and must therefore manage key challenging features of intercultural communication: namely, cultural differences, unfamiliarity, and intergroup posture. According to Kim, stress results from these cultural experiences:

> Because a sojourner's cultural identity and attributes are placed against the backdrop of the systematic forces of the host culture, the cross-cultural experiences of new comers are unsettling. Sojourners are, at least temporarily, in a state of disequilibrium, which is manifested in many emotional "lows" of uncertainty, confusion and anxiety. In the present open systems perspective, such disruptive experiences of a person reflect stress. (Kim 1995, 1).

Under stress, a so-called defense mechanism is activated in sojourners to hold the internal structure in balance by some form of protective psychological maneuvering. They attempt to avoid or minimize the anticipated or actual "pain" of disequilibrium by selective attention, self-deception, denial, avoidance, and withdrawal as well as by hostility, cynicism, and compulsively altruistic behavior (Lazarus 1966). International managers are especially exposed to unsettling, puzzling, and indeed hostile interactions with members of the host culture in which they will experience these psychological effects.

In the General Systems theoretical perspective, the capacity to manage intercultural challenges is referred to as *adaptability*—the capacity of individuals to alter some of their old cultural ways to learn and accommodate some of the demands of the host environment. Generally speaking, an individual's adaptability within intercultural encounters affects the cognitive dimension (sense-making of cues inherent within such an encounter), the affective dimension (motivational and attitudinal predisposition in responding to intercultural encounters), and the operational or behavioral dimensions (abilities to be flexible and resourceful in carrying out what the individual is capable of in the cognitive and affective dimensions).

Stress and adaptation responses are followed by a subtle internal transformation as the individual grows in his or her host environment. Growth can be attributed to the development of increasing degrees of intercultural transformation (Kim 1988). Intercultural communication competence is explained not as communication competence in dealing with a specific culture but as the cognitive, affective, and operational adaptability of an individual in all intercultural communication contexts.

Three interrelated aspects of the sojourner's intercultural transformation are also specified in this theory, as the key outcomes of the cross-cultural adaptation process (Kim 1995). The first aspect is increased functional fitness. Through repeated activities, resulting in new cultural learning and internal reorganizing, sojourners achieve an increasing "synergy" over time between their internal responses and the external demands in the host environment (Kim 1990). Successfully adapted sojourners have accomplished competence in communicating *and* developing a satisfactory relationship with the host society.

Closely related to increased functional fitness, the second aspect is increased psychological health in relation to the host environment. The psychological health of sojourners is directly linked to their ability to communicate an accompanying functional fitness in the host society. Finally, the development of functional fitness and psychological health in sojourners is likely to produce the third aspect of an emergent intercultural identity. This emergent intercultural identity is based "not on belongingness which implies either owning or being owned by a single culture, but on a style of self-consciousness that situates oneself neither totally a part of nor totally a part from a given culture" (Adler 1976, 391).

Kim previously conducted a major study on communication patterns of foreign immigrants in the process of acculturation in the United States in which she empirically confirmed General Systems Theory of intercultural communication. Results from this study showed that the effects of three main causal factors—language competence, acculturation motivation, and channel accessibility were all significantly related to intercultural communication. The study also showed that sex, age at the time of migration, time spent in the host culture, and education were the most important factors in predicting a sojourner's language competence, acculturation motivation, and accessibility to host communication channels (Kim 1988; Gudykunst & Kim 1997). It would seem that the influence of interpersonal communication is stronger than that of the mass media in developing a subtle, complex, and refined system for perceiving the host society. This may have significant implications for this study of the role and competence of international managers in intercultural communication. (This issue will be considered in the last section of this chapter.)

One major limitation inherent within Kim's General Systems Theory is that while her explanation of the stress, adaptation, and growth dynamics of intercultural encounters is an incisive conceptual tool, the direction of analysis (sojourner to host society) is one-way, whereas the process of intercultural communication is two-way (sojourner to host and host to sojourner). A notable limitation of Kim's analysis is her lack of emphasis on the nature of appropriate cross-cultural skills and relational competencies required for sojourners and members of the host culture. Consequently, General Systems Theory does not provide a comprehensive model for it fails to acknowledge that the responsibility for adaptation and for developing intercultural communication competence should not only include the sojourner but also the role of the host culture (Saee & Kaye 1994).

## Uncertainty Reduction Theory of Intercultural Communication

Closely related to the General Systems Adaptation Model of intercultural communication is the theoretical perspective of Uncertainty Reduction (Berger & Calabrese 1975; Berger 1979; Gudykunst 1983; Gudykunst, Wiseman, & Hammer 1977). According to this theory, a primary motivation for communication is the need to reduce uncertainty. Uncertainty is a cognitive phenomenon and uncertainty affects the way we think about sojourners. According to this approach, there are two types of uncertainty present in initial interactions with sojourners:

- *Predictive uncertainty* is the uncertainty that we have about predicting a sojourner's attitudes, feelings, beliefs, values, and behavior. We need, for example, to predict which of several alternative behavior patterns sojourners will choose to employ;

- *Explanatory uncertainty* involves the uncertainty that we have about explaining a sojourner's attitudes, feelings, and thoughts. Whenever we try to figure out why sojourners behave the way they do, we are engaging in explanatory uncertainty reduction. It is important to note that we can never totally predict or explain another person's behavior (Gudykunst & Kim 1997; Wiseman & Koester 1993).

According to the Uncertainty Reduction theory, we all have a maximum threshold (i.e., the highest amount of uncertainty we can tolerate for predicting sojourners' behavior sufficiently so that we feel comfortable interacting with them) and a minimum threshold for uncertainty (i.e., the lowest amount of uncertainty we can tolerate and not feel bored or overconfident about our interactions with others). If our uncertainty is above the maximum threshold or below the minimum threshold, we will have difficulty in communicating effectively. Our uncertainty level should be between the minimum and maximum thresholds for effective, satisfying communication (Gudykunst 1993; Gudykunst & Kim 1997).

Uncertainty reduction theory regards anxiety as the affective (emotional) equivalent of uncertainty, which is experienced any time when we, as members of the host society, communicate with sojourners. Anxiety is perceived as a "generalized or unspecified sense of disequilibrium; imbalance" (Gudykunst & Hammer 1988, 61). Anxiety is an emotional response to situations based on the anticipation of negative consequences (Stephan & Stephan 1985). Anxiety is one of the fundamental problems with which all humans must cope (May 1977; Lazarus 1991) and it tends to be higher in intergroup than interpersonal encounters (Ickes 1984).

Managing anxiety can thus be related to developing trust, which, in turn, may reduce uncertainty. Trust is "confidence that one will find what is desired from another, rather than what is feared" (Deutsch 1973, 149). When members of the host society trust others (in this case, the sojourners), they expect positive outcomes from their interactions with them; when they have anxiety about interacting with others, they fear negative outcomes from their interactions with them. Essentially, hosts fear four types of negative consequences when interacting with sojourners:

- Negative consequences to self-concept.
- Negative behavioral consequences.
- Negative evaluations by sojourners.
- Negative evaluations by members of our in-group (Stephan & Stephan 1985).

It is important to be aware that the amount of anxiety individuals experience when interacting with sojourners can be argued to be, in part, a function of our host intergroup attitudes. For example, the greater the prejudice and ethnocentrism, the greater could be their anxiety from interacting with sojourners—this is especially critical when the host members are international managers.

Reducing uncertainty and controlling anxiety are necessary and sufficient conditions for intercultural adaptations (Gudykunst & Hammer 1988; Gudykunst 1993). To do this, Gudykunst postulated eight variables that reduce both uncertainty and anxiety: knowledge of host culture; shared networks; intergroup attitudes; favorable contact; stereotypes; cultural identity; cultural similarity; and second language competence. He also claimed that only four variables influenced uncertainty reduction: intimacy, attraction, display of nonverbal affiliative expressiveness, and the use of appropriate uncertainty reduction strategies (Gudykunst 1983). Another four variables were associated with reducing anxiety: the sojourners' motivation to live permanently in the host culture; host nationals' intergroup attitudes; host culture policy toward sojourners; and sojourners' psychological differentiation. All these conditions must be satisfied for intercultural adaptation to take place effectively and competently (Gudykunst 1983).

In a detailed discussion of the theoretical perspective of uncertainty/anxiety reduction and intercultural communication, Gudykunst (1988) upholds the view that the necessary and sufficient conditions for intercultural adaptation included both interpersonal and intergroup factors.

To manage our uncertainty and anxiety, we must be conscious of our communication (Gudykunst 1993). Communication is a process of involving the exchange of messages and the creation of meaning. When we communicate, we attach meaning to the messages that we construct and transmit to others and we interpret the messages that we receive from others. Most of the time, we are not aware of our cognitive processing. One reason we are not highly aware of the nature of cognitive processing is that much of our everyday communication is based on our unconscious and implicit assumptions about how communication takes place that we have learned in the past. In other words, we often communicate automatically.

Bargh (1989) has argued that automatic information processing can involve various combinations of attention, awareness, intention, and control. On the other hand, when we are aware of our communication behavior, we become conscious—*mindful*—to some extent. Mindfulness involves "(a) creation of new categories; (b) openness to new information; and (c) awareness of more than one perspective" (Langer 1989,62). One condition that contributes to not being mindful is the use of broad categories. Categorization often is based on characteristics such as physical (gender, race) or cultural (ethnic background). In addition, we categorize others in terms of their attitudes (liberal or conservative) or religion or worldview (Christian, Muslim, Buddhist). Langer pointed out that "categorizing is a fundamental and natural human activity. It is the way we come to know the world. Any attempt to eliminate bias by attempting to eliminate the perception of differences is doomed to failure" (Langer 1989, 154). Thus being mindful involves making more, not fewer, distinctions. When we are on automatic pilot, we tend to use broad categories to predict other people's behavior, for example, their culture, ethnicity, or sex, or the role they are playing. When we are mindful, we can create new categories that are more specific.

Mindfulness involves being open to new information (Langer 1989). When we behave on automatic pilot in a particular situation, we tend to see the same thing occurring in the situation that we saw the previous time in the same situation. If we are consciously open to new information, however, we are more able to see the subtle differences in our own and other people's behavior. It has been argued that the more we think about how to behave in situations, the more appropriate and effective our behavior tends to be (Cegala & Waldron 1992).

In addition, to be mindful, we must also recognize that there is more than one perspective that can be used to understand or explain our interaction with others (Langer 1989). When we communicate on automatic pilot, we do not recognize alternative perspectives. The mindset we bring to communication situations can limit our ability to recognize the choices that we actually have about how to behave in most situations. When we communicate mindfully, however, we can look for the options that are available to us and not be limited by only those that immediately come to mind in the situation. When we are communicating mindfully, we have the potential to use all the communication resources available to us rather than to limit ourselves to our usual responses.

Recent research has tended to show that the reduction of uncertainty and anxiety exerts independent influences on cultural adaptation and that the reduction of uncertainty and anxiety is a necessary and sufficient condition for adaptation (Gao & Gudykunst 1990). The effects of other factors (e.g., knowledge of the host culture) seem to be mediated through reduction of uncertainty and anxiety. However, a major limitation of Uncertainty Reduction Theory concerns the chief cause of miscommunication or maladaptation. According to Gudykunst, the cause of cultural maladaptation can be traced to the sojourner who has not learned or interpreted the host culture sufficiently to adapt to cultural differences (Gao & Gudykunst 1990). The need to focus on the onus and responsibility of members of the host culture for developing competence in intercultural communication is lacking in Gudykunst's theory of uncertainty reduction, as it was in General Systems Theory (Saee & Kaye 1994; Saee 1998).

Notwithstanding this limitation, Gudykunst has made a significant contribution in the literature in terms of understanding issues of uncertainty and anxiety management. As noted earlier, in all initial interactions involving sojourners and members of the host culture, there is a differing degree of uncertainty and anxiety experienced by those involved and dealing with uncertainty/anxiety is a fundamental concern in intercultural communication (Lazarus 1966). Management of anxiety and uncertainty is one of the major influences on effective communication.

Gudykunst's assumptions and axioms (Gudykunst & Hammer 1988) help us to understand the complexity of the nature of intercultural communication competence from an assimilationist perspective in which reduction of uncertainty features primarily. However this perspective is limited by its focus on adaptation by the sojourner rather than the host and is not able to explain the role of the host culture in the process of cultural adaptation.

# SOCIOLOGICAL THEORIES OF INTERCULTURAL COMMUNICATION

The following sections discuss the sociological theories of intercultural communication, which include convergence theory, the interpersonal theory of intercultural communication.

## Convergence Theory of Intercultural Communication

Another theory of intercultural communication is convergence theory as advanced by Kincaid, which overcomes many of the biases that have been evident in the traditional linear, transmission models of communication. This theoretical perspective was derived from the basic concepts of information theory, cybernetics, and general theory systems theory. Its foundations can be traced to symbolic interactions sociology, and to small-group dynamics in psychology, and, at a macro level of analysis, to Durkheim's theory of collective consciousness (1987). Convergence theory describes the fundamental self-organizing process of social systems. Convergence principles and the network perspective are integrated into a single, coherent theory of communication, organization, and culture by means of the application of concepts and principles from nonequilibrium thermodynamics. The concept and measure of entropy is applied directly to the statistical distribution of beliefs, values, and behaviors of intact cultures and to the structures of their communication networks. This allows the development of a general mathematical model of communication, organization, and culture, which is consistent with network-convergence theory. According to Convergence Theory, communication creates a network of relations among people that makes up the structure of society. Networks connect groups with one another and enable them to exchange information. Groups cluster together according to common beliefs, values, and behavior (Littlejohn 1996). There are two key elements in Convergence Theory: (1) Communication is a dynamic process of convergence; and (2) social systems are networks of interconnected individuals who are linked by patterned flows of information (Kincaid 1987). Individuals give different meanings to the information that they share with others. Initial differences in mutual understanding are reduced through a dynamic process of feedback. Although feedback processes reduce differences in meaning among people, the inherent uncertainty involved in information exchange including the feedback process itself implies that some differences in interpretation of meaning will always remain.

It is important to note that the underlying assumption of Convergence Theory is that the communication process results in a change in the statistical distribution of beliefs, values, and behavior of a particular culture. The essence of Convergence Theory is that if communication in a society is unrestricted, then convergence among members in terms of beliefs will be evident. However, if information sharing is restricted, then differences among communicators will be evident, resulting in the rise of entropy and disorder. Kincaid cited an extensive list of bipolar opposites to delineate the entropy concept, as shown in Exhibit 6-1.

In Convergence Theory communication may be described as a series of converging cycles of information exchanged among participants who, through their unrestricted interactions, would converge over time toward a greater degree of mutual understanding, agreement, and collective action (Kincaid 1987). From the viewpoint of intercultural communication, Convergence Theory examines the conditions that affect the degree of convergence (commonness) and entropy (disorder) in a cultural system. However, communicators in a social system cannot openly discuss and analyze issues about all topics all the time. Thus, in Convergence Theory, an examination is made of conditions like time and energy that put restrictions on the degree of convergence that can be reached at any one time by communicators in a cultural system. Four principles of communication embodied within Convergence Theory include:

- Social psychological (personal interdependencies)
- Cognitive (mutual agreement)
- Behavioral (collective action)
- Organization

All these principles are relevant for analyzing the managerial functions of international managers and their intercultural communication competence.

The principle of convergence states that if two or more individuals share information with one another then, over time, they will tend to converge toward one another, leading to a state of greater uniformity.

| Exhibit 6-1 | List of Bipolar Opposites Delineating the Entropy Concept |
|---|---|
| Random | Nonrandom |
| Disorganized | Organized |
| Disordered | Ordered |
| Mixed | Separated |
| Equiprobable | Divergence from equiprobability |
| Independent | Divergence from independence |
| Configurational variety | Restricted arrangements |
| Freedom of choice | Constraint |
| Uncertainty | Reliability |
| Higher error probability | Fidelity |
| Potential information | Stored information |

Source: Adapted from *List of Bipolar Opposites Delineating the Entropy Concept*. Reprinted from *Communication Theory: Eastern and Western Perspectives*, Kincaid, D.L. (ed.), 1987, with permission from Elsevier.

Based on this principle, Convergence Theory has been concerned with determining factors that facilitate or inhibit convergence. With particular reference to intercultural communication, convergence theory advocates that "divergence leads to cultural diversity which in turn results in marked entropy within interpersonal systems or organizations. Conversely, convergence within systems leads to uniformity which ultimately serves to weaken entropic forces" (Kincaid 1987, 289).

It is important to note that convergence emphasizes the provision of opportunity for unrestricted communication between members of the minority culture groups and the host culture. Such unrestricted communication is presumed to maximize the likelihood of convergence of the immigrant group's values with those of the host culture. As a result, it has been argued that both immigrant and host groups would in turn converge toward a state of greater uniformity. However, this theory is debatable, particularly as it requires people to renounce their cultural heritage. In addition, Convergence Theory places a great deal of emphasis on the "unrestricted" flow of information, stating that dialogue is a less restrictive stream of information than monologue. Convergence Theory specifies conditions that lead to a level of similarity. One implication associated with this perspective is that, as with everything in life, there are limits. So, there are limits on the degree of convergence that can be achieved in a certain topic. There is a certain amount of time and energy that can be applied to increasing convergence in a society. Thus, there is a significant cost in keeping the same level of convergence let alone attempting to increase it.

The theoretical construct of convergence is also flawed in terms of its lack of emphasis on the influence of cultural diversity within intercultural communication settings, as all interactants undoubtedly bring with them their own "cultural baggage" when interacting and communicating with each other. In addition, Convergence Theory does not address the issue of power relationships between people and the impact of power differences in a communication process involving two or more individuals of dissimilar cultural heritage (e.g., between expatriate staff—sojourners—and members of the host culture).

In summary, General Systems Theory, Uncertainty Reduction Theory and Convergence Theory tend to emphasize the sojourners' assimilation to the host culture. These theories of intercultural communication also neglect the two-way process inherent in communication as well as the responsibility for developing competence by all parties involved in the communication process, especially the member(s) of the host culture. However, intercultural communication processes can be further understood in terms of interpersonal theory.

## Interpersonal Theory of Intercultural Communication

Interpersonal communication theory is informed and sustained by the concepts of intimacy (closeness) and performance (competence). The concept of intimacy, which holds that closeness between people is a moral good, leads to interest in openness, authenticity, honesty, trust, and empathy. The concept of performance, which holds that improved performance is desirable and possible, leads to interest in communication and relational competence (Irwin 1996). This is especially relevant to the management of a team or organization, for "interpersonal communication is central to effective management" (Jackson 1993, 3). According to interpersonal theory, there are three key features of the communication process: the "context" of the communication, the behavior or "conduct" of the individuals who communicate, and, arguably the most important, the different perceptions of people when they communicate: what we call the "content" of communication. The latter is key in this definition and has great bearing on cross-cultural communication.

In this model of interpersonal communication, "context" is the framework of rules, culture, social structure, and technology within which people live and work—and the context may be quite different from one culture to another. "Conduct" is what one sees or the behavioral aspects of communication: what people actually do. This can also include the skills which people require in order to communicate effectively. These aspects of behavior might be different between individuals of different cultural backgrounds. "Content" is what one does not see. Content includes the perceptions, motivations, attitudes, and objectives of the individuals that are prerequisites to acting in a particular way. These aspects are part of the person which have been acquired or generated through the experiences of living and working in a particular culture and environment and might be quite different between people from different cultures and countries (Jackson 1993). These three interrelated aspects/features of interpersonal communication are important for explaining the dimensions of intercultural communication competence.

Other communication researchers have also focused on the nature of communication relationships. For example, Littlejohn (1996) conceptualized interpersonal communication in terms of three elements: "(1) the communicators; (2) their discourse; and (3) their relationship." Understanding interpersonal communication is important because it helps us to define our relationships with other people, moreover, we have some kind of relationship with everyone around us (Dimbleby & Burton 1992). This focus on relationship, as expressed by Forgas, maintains that "true interpersonal communication takes place at the level of mutuality where there is some degree of real personal involvement and intimacy exists between partners" (1985, 226). Other theorists have defined interpersonal communication as communication that occurs between individuals who consider one another as unique (Adler, Rosenfeld, & Towne 1992).

According to Littlejohn, (1996) the nature of the "relationship is at the heart of interpersonal communication." This is because when two people communicate, in addition to whatever else they may be doing and achieving, they are also defining their relationship. People in a relationship are always creating a set of expectations, reinforcing old ones, or changing existing patterns of interaction.  Littlejohn identified five basic axioms about communication that have direct implications for intercultural communication. The first axiom states that one cannot communicate. We are always affecting others' perceptions, whether we want to or not. Any perceivable behavior is potentially communicative. The second axiom states that every conversation, no matter how brief, involves two messages: (1) a content message and (2) a relationship message. When two people are interacting, each is relating information to the other, and simultaneously each is reacting to perceived changes in the relationship. This simultaneous relationship "talk," which is often nonverbal, is *metacommunication*. This encompasses varying dimensions of dominance, intimacy, affection, involvement, inclusion, trust, superficiality, emotional arousal, composure, similarity, formality, and orientation toward task versus social elements of the relationship. These can be further arranged into four basic, independent dimensions of relational communication:

- Emotional arousal, composure, and formality
- Intimacy and similarity
- Immediacy (liking)
- Dominance–submission (Bochner 1982)

Four behaviors appear to be related to metacommunication. Proximity can be crucial in communicating intimacy, attraction, trust, caring, dominance, persuasiveness, and aggressiveness. Smiling appears particularly important in communicating emotional arousal, composure, and formality, as well as intimacy and liking. Touching, too, communicates intimacy. Eye contact is like an exclamation point intensifying the effect of other nonverbal behaviors (Burgoon & Hale 1984).

Littlejohn's third axiom states that interaction is always organized into meaning patterns by the communicators. This is referred to as *punctuation*. Interaction sequences, like sentences, cannot be understood as a string of isolated elements. To make sense they must be punctuated.

The fourth axiom is that people use both digital and analogic codes. Digital coding is arbitrary, because the sign and the referent, though associated, have no intrinsic relation to each other. The most common digital code in human communication is a language. Sounds, words, and phrases are digital signs arranged to communicate meanings. The analogic code is different. Analogic signs are not arbitrary as digital ones are. Analogic signs can actually resemble the object, as in the case of drawing a picture in the air with your hands, or they can be part of the object or condition being signified, as in the case of crying.

The fifth axiom of communication relates to the matching and meshing of messages in an interaction. The axiom states that where communicators in a relationship behave similarly and differences are minimized, the relationship is said to be symmetrical. When communicator responses are not similar and differences are maximized, a complementary relationship is said to exist.

Other scholars present a meaning-centered approach to interpersonal communication and the nature of relationships. They conceptualized three key characteristics underlying communication: (1) Communication is a process not a product (i.e., a continuing event); (2) communication is a set of constructed meanings (i.e., messages have layers of meanings); and (3) communication involves the use of shared meanings (Martin & Nakayama 1997). However, sharing meanings does not necessarily involve gaining agreement. When communicating is thought of as the sharing of meanings, what is meant is that each participant in communication becomes aware of the meanings about a matter or issue held by the other participant(s). While sharing meanings may bring about agreement, it can just as readily and appropriately lead to disagreement. What is important is that communicating will lead to clarification and enhanced understanding. And communication is both verbal and nonverbal. Thus, negotiation of meaning is another feature of intercultural communication competence.

# PERCEPTION

Perception also plays a crucial role in communication and in the negotiation of meaning. There are two primary ways in which perception is part of communication:

- We communicate mainly about things, events, and people external to us. We have to perceive the external world before we can communicate about it.

- When we communicate with other people, we are involved in a perceptual process through listening or looking, or perhaps reading. We perceive other people's messages and the way they communicate (Jackson 1993).

A person's communicative behavior is affected by his or her perception of the relationship with the other communicator. A person interacting with another has two levels of perception, which R.D. Laing (1967) called "perspectives," where one can observe and interpret another person's behavior in a direct perspective:

*I cannot avoid trying to understand your experience, because although I do not experience your experience, which is invisible to me (and nontastable, nontouchable, nonsmellable, and inaudible), yet I experience you as experiencing. I do not experience your experience. But I experience you experiencing. I experience myself as experienced by you. And I experience you as experiencing yourself as experienced by me, and so on (Laing 1967, 5).*

One also experiences the experiences of other people when one assigns meaning to what one imagines they are thinking and feeling. Laing called this a "metaperspective."

Since our perception of other people influences how we communicate with them, psychological researchers have advanced the notion of person perception. This is predicated on Implicit Personality Theory. According to Hartley (1993) individuals have a coherent picture of which personality characteristics tend to go together in other people. For instance, if one hears someone described as warm, then one is also liable to perceive that person is popular, happy, successful, and so on. It is argued that some of these associations seem to be strong, whereas others are relatively weak. For example, if one asks people to judge the intelligence of others based on a selection of photographs, they will tend to choose people wearing glasses as more intelligent than those without. This has implications for intercultural communication competence.

Overall, engagement in interpersonal communication is central to developing a relationship through the exchange of personal information. Personal information exchange is a two-way process involving information seeking and self-disclosure. According to humanistic psychologists, interpersonal understanding occurs through self-disclosure, feedback, and sensitivity to the disclosures of others. Misunderstanding and dissatisfaction in relationships are promoted by dishonesty, lack of congruence between one's actions and feeling, poor feedback, and inhibited self-disclosure (Cissna & Anderson 1990).

Relational development is also said to be affected by social penetration. This means that relationships become more intimate over time when partners disclose more and more information about themselves. Miler and Sunnafrank (1982) defined interpersonal communication in terms of penetration in that they argued that if the communicators continue their relationship—that is, if they are sufficiently motivated to exert the effort to continue it and if their interpersonal skills are tuned finely enough to permit its growth—then their relationship may undergo certain qualitative changes. When such changes accompany relational development, communicative transactions become increasingly interpersonal.

As relationships develop, communication can move from relatively shallow, nonintimate levels to deeper, more personal ones (Altman & Taylor 1987). As the relationship develops, the partners share more aspects of the self, providing breadth as well as depth through exchange of information, feelings, and activities. In his later work, Altman suggested a modification to social penetration theory by pointing out that relationships generally do not progress simply toward greater openness. "Rather, partners go back and forth between sharing and distance as they manage the tension between the need for privacy and the need for connection" (Altman 1993, 26). Thus, interpersonal communication is an ever-changing transactional sharing that develops between people who are constructing meaning with each other and come to know one another better as their relationships tends to move from impersonal to personal (Caputo 1994).

There has been much debate over the definition of an interpersonal communication event. However, it is generally agreed that there are, in addition to the points raised previously, two features, which separate interpersonal communication events from other types of communication contexts: (1) The participants must be able to receive and provide immediate feedback; and (2) they must be able to adapt to each other in an instant (Gibson & Hanna 1992).

Gudykunst believes that both interpersonal and intergroup factors influence all of our communication. He further suggests that the identity that we use when communicating helps to determine whether it is interpersonal or intergroup (intercultural) communication (Gudykunst 1995). By this he means that if we predominantly use our personal identity when communicating with someone then we are engaging in interpersonal communication. If we use our social identity predominately, however, then it is an intercultural communication.

Since communication in interpersonal relationships is central to life, individuals for this reason seek to develop their relationships with others. Effective communication in this relationship is particularly vital to a sojourner's cognitive, affective, and behavioral learning. Through formal and informal contacts and relationships, sojourners can also find social support for handling difficulties as well as seeking opportunities for making additional contacts (Adelman 1988; Wellman 1992). Interpersonal networks exert social control by determining the language that sojourners must use and by conveying implicit or explicit messages of social approval and disapproval (Heckathorn 1990; Ho & Sung 1990).

Considerable evidence exists to link a sojourner's adaptation to a new culture and his or her interpersonal relationship patterns. Studies of international students and visitors have indicated a positive association between the number of host members (natives) in a sojourner's relational networks and his or her positive feelings towards the host society at large. Also, the degree of interpersonal involvement with members of a host culture has been found to be an important indicator of a sojourner's cognitive learning. One classic study reported that international students in the United States who associated extensively and formed close friendships with host nationals scored higher on measures of adjustment than those who had less association with host nationals or who did not have host friends (Selltiz, et al. 1963). In another study, it was found that students who were high on measures of social relations with host nationals scored high on an index of satisfaction with various aspects of their experience in the host country (Morris 1960).

A similar linkage between interpersonal communication and elements of host communication competence has been observed in studies of long-term settlers in the United States and elsewhere (Kim 1988; Kim & Gudykunst 1988; Kim 1990; Oehlkers 1991; Searle & Ward 1990; Shah 1991). A consistent finding from these studies is that there is a positive relationship between participation in host interpersonal communication activities and other aspects of adaptation, such as the variables of host communication competence and psychological health.

## INTERCULTURAL COMMUNICATION COMPETENCE DEFINED

Intercultural communication competence is a difficult concept to define. Communication researchers have proposed numerous conceptualizations of intercultural communication competence. One kind of consensus is that people who are effective in communicating with sojourners possess (1) an unusual degree of integration or stability; (2) a central organization of the extrovert type; (3) a value system that includes the value of all men and women; (4) a character socialized on the basis of cultural universals; and (5) a marked telepathic or intuition sensitivity (Gudykunst & Kim 1997).

An effective communicator is also perceived as someone who (1) sees people first and representatives of cultures second; (2) knows people are basically good; (3) knows the value of other cultures as well as that of his or her own; (4) has control over his or her visceral reactions; (5) speaks with hopefulness and candor; and (6) has inner security and is able to feel comfortable being different from other people (Gudykunst & Kim 1997). This view of intercultural communication competence is in keeping with Kim's psychological definition of intercultural communication competence, in which she argued that intercultural communication competence should be located within a person as his or her overall capacity to facilitate the communication process between people from differing cultural backgrounds and to contribute to successful interaction outcomes. Here intercultural communication competence is considered a necessary—but not sufficient—condition for achieving success in intercultural encounters since accidents such as a verbal or nonverbal faux pas can occur (Kim 1988, 1990). In other words, intercultural communication competence is intrinsic to the psychology of a person.

Gudykunst took another approach to the concept of competence by arguing that judgments of competence emerge from the interactions in which we engage, pointing out that one communicator's view of his or her communication competence may not be the same as that of the person with whom he or she is communicating. To complicate the matter further, the outsider observing the two parties (i.e. involved in the communication process) might have quite a different perception of their competence (Gudykunst 1995). Together, Gudykunst and Kim state that "Understanding communication competence, therefore, minimally requires that we take into consideration our own and the other person's perspective" (Gudykunst & Kim 1997, 252). Gudykunst further maintained that if we can have views of our competence different from those of the people with whom we are communicating, then competence is an impression we have of others and ourselves. That is, "competence is not something intrinsic to a person's nature of behavior" (Spitzberg & Cupach 1984, 115). There are several implications of this view of competence. First, competence does not actually reside in the performance; it is an evaluation of the performance by someone. Second, the fact that someone is making the evaluation means that it is subject to error, bias, and judgment inferences; different judges using the same criteria may evaluate the performance differently. Third, since the evaluation always must be with reference to some set of implicit or explicit criteria, the evaluation cannot be understood or validated without knowledge of the criteria being employed. Thus, the same performance may be judged to be competent by one standard and incompetent by another (McFall 1982). This view of competence suggests that specific skills we have do not ensure that we will be perceived as competent in any particular interaction.

Additional research has further identified a number of behavioral dimensions necessary for intercultural communication competence: (1) display of respect involves the ability to show positive regard and express respect for another person; (2) interaction posture is the ability to respond to others in a descriptive, nonevaluating, and nonjudgmental way; and (3) interaction management is displayed through taking turns in discussion and initiating and terminating interaction based on a reasonably accurate assessment of the needs and desires of others (Ruben 1976). Ruben and Kealey (1979) further defined intercultural communication competence in terms of an individual's empathy, respect, ability to perform role behaviors, nonjudgmentalness, openness, tolerance for ambiguity, and interaction management.

Other researchers isolated three key variables of perceived competence: motivation, knowledge, and skills (Spitzberg & Cupach 1984). Motivation implies fundamental states of being in humans which, if unsatisfied, generate feelings of deprivation. The needs that propel humans to communicate include: (1) the need for a sense of security as a human being; (2) the need for predictability; (3) the need for a sense of group inclusion; (4) the need to avoid anxiety; (5) the need for a sense of a common shared world; (6) the need for symbolic/material gratification; and (7) the need to sustain our self-conceptions/self-identity (Turner 1988).

To communicate effectively also requires that we have particular knowledge. The knowledge component of competence refers to our awareness of what we need to do to communicate in an appropriate and effective way. This includes (1) knowledge of how to gather information; (2) knowledge of group differences; (3) knowledge of personal similarities; and (4) knowledge of alternative interpretations for others' behavior. Several skills have also been identified (Berger & Calabrese 1975; Coleman & DePaulo 1991; Gudykunst & Kim 1997) that can be applied to improve our intercultural communication competence by reducing uncertainty and anxiety. To reduce our anxiety, we must tolerate ambiguity—and be calm. According to Gudykunst to reduce our uncertainty, we must make accurate assessments of a sojourner's behavior (Gudykunst 1993). That is, intercultural communication should be a "symbolic, interpretive, transactional, contextual process in which people create shared meanings" (Lustig & Koester 1993, 25). Communication is symbolic because it uses symbol systems such as language and nonverbal actions. It is interpretive because individuals interpret and create their own meanings from the communication behavior of others and, in this sense, create their own meanings. It is transactional because constant interaction involving feedback and negotiation is the process by which shared meanings are created. Finally it is contextual because it occurs within a setting or situation which has social, cultural, and possibly historical characteristics that influence the process. What is important to note in this definition is that reaching agreement is not a necessary objective of communicating. Sharing meanings does not necessarily involve gaining agreement. When communicating is thought of as the sharing of meanings, what is meant is that each participant in the communication context becomes aware of the meanings about a matter or issue held by the other participant(s). While sharing meanings may bring about agreement it can just as readily and appropriately lead to disagreement. What is important is that communicating will lead to clarification and enhanced understanding (Irwin 1996).

Essentially, intercultural communication competence is about minimizing misunderstandings.

Finally, intercultural communication competence is "an individual's ability to adapt effectively to the surrounding environment over time" (Spitzberg & Cupach 1984, 35). The central feature of this definition is the focus on adaptability. Thus, for a manager interacting with a workforce and clientele of culturally diverse backgrounds, whether nationally or internationally, it is important to develop an ability to be flexible and adaptable to different cultural contexts, by being sensitive to the cultural situation and acting accordingly (Jackson 1993).

## *Summary*

This chapter discussed intercultural communication theories and their implications for international managers in regard to developing competence in communicating in a global business environment. The emphasis here is that simply knowing the host language is not enough in developing intercultural communication competence. What is needed is a process that incorporates into management training programs what sojourners experience: culture shock, stress, adaptation, and growth. Similarly, there is a need on the part of host society members to develop their intercultural communication competence.

The centrality of interpersonal communication for defining and developing relationships raised this as an issue when it is applicable to host members who are managers and sojourners who are a culturally diverse workforce. As a result, appropriate management training modules based on these theories can be developed with the particular view of providing high level understanding of the complexities of the intercultural communication dimensions.

Understanding of intercultural communication competence will help international managers to be effective in their intercultural encounters including cross-cultural communication and negotiation involving international deals coupled with day-to-day international managerial functions.

## Critical Discussion Questions

1. "To communicate effectively with a person from another culture, is it enough for you to be fluent in their native language?" Is this true or false? Explain.

2. Briefly describe the stages of cross-cultural learning or adaptation as outlined by the Culture Shock Theory.

3. What is the main postulate of General Systems Theory of intercultural communication? And what are the limitations of this theory?

4. Explain the notion of minimum and maximum threshold for uncertainty.

5. What are the different ways of managing uncertainty and anxiety in the cross-cultural context?

6. How does Convergence Theory explain the dynamics of cross-cultural communication? Do you agree with this explanation?

7. "Human relationships are at the core of intercultural communication competence." Is this true or false? Explain.

8. Define intercultural communication competence.

9. Of all the major theories of intercultural communication, which one(s), would you think, will best explain an individual's intercultural communication competence? Provide a detailed justification for your considered view.

## Applications

### Experiential

1. Interview a person who had an experience of settling down in a foreign country with particular reference to different stages of adaptation as outlined by Culture Shock Theory.

2. Try to recall and describe your personal experiences when your ability to communicate effectively was affected by anxiety or uncertainty that you have experienced during your initial intercultural encounters at some point in your personal life.

3. In what ways, is your intercultural communication suffering from deficiencies or weaknesses?

4. List major variables in intercultural communication theories that would help you to be become an effective intercultural communicator.

5. Interview a manager of multinational company in your city and elicit his or her responses in terms of what are the main features of an intercultural communication competence? Then compare and contrast the manager's understanding of intercultural communication competence in terms of theories discussed in this chapter.

### Internet

1.  Visit the following Web site and read and summarize the critique of Uncertainty Reduction Theory as advanced by Berger and Gudykunst.

    http://oak.cats.ohiou.edu/~nw583098/unc.htm

2.  Visit the following Web site and read and summarize the key points about sojourners adapting within a host culture. Try to relate this perspective to how managers can improve their intercultural competence while operating in the global business environment. Discuss your findings in class.

    http://www.interculturalrelations.com/v2i1Winter1999/w99hart.htm

# References

Adelman, M.B. (1988). Cross–cultural adjustment. *International Journal of Intercultural Relations*, 12, 183–204.

Adler, P.S. (1976). Beyond cultural identity: Reflections on cultural and multicultural man. In L. Samovar & R. Porter (Eds.), *Intercultural communication: A reader*, 2nd ed. Belmont, CA: Wadsworth, 362–378.

Adler, R.B., Rosenfeld, L.B., & Towne, L.B (1992). *Interplay: The process of interpersonal communication*, 5th ed. Forth Worth, TX: Harcourt Brace Jovanovich.

Altman, I. & Taylor, D. (1987). Communication in interpersonal relationship: Social penetration theory. In Roloff, M.E and Miller, G.R., (Eds.), *Interpersonal processes: New directions in communication research*. Newbury Park, CA: Sage, 257–277.

Altman, I. (1993). Dialectics, physical environments, and personal relationships. *Communication Monograph*, 60, 26–34.

Bargh, J. (1989). Conditional atomacity. In J. Uleman & J. Bargh (Eds.), *Unintended thought*. New York: Guilford, 3–51.

Berger, C.R. & Calabrese, R. (1975). Some explorations in initial interactions and beyond. *Human Communication Research*, 5, 99–112.

Berger, C.R. (1979). Beyond initial interactions. In H. Giles & R. St. Clair (Eds.), *Language and social psychology*. London: Edward Arnold, 122–144.

Berger, J. & Zelditch, M. (Eds.) (1985). *Status, rewards and influence*. San Francisco: Jossey–Bass.

Bloch, M. (1991). Language, anthropology and cognitive science. *Man*, 26 (2), 183–198.

Bochner, S. (Ed.) (1981). *The mediating person: Bridges between cultures*. Cambridge, MA: Schenkman.

Bochner, S.A. (1982). The social psychology of cross-cultural relations. In S. Bochner (Ed.), *Cultures in contact: Studies in cross–cultural interactions*. Oxford: Pergamon.

Brislin, R. (1981). *Cross–cultural encounters.* Elmsford, NY: Pergamon.

Brislin, R.W. (1979). Orientation programs for cross-cultural preparation. In A.J. Marsella, R.G. Tharp & T.J. Giborowski (Eds.), *Perspectives on cross–cultural psychology.* New York: Academic Press.

Burgoon, J.K. & Hale, J.L. (1984). The fundamental topoi of relational communication. *Communication Monographs,* 151, 193–214.

Caputo, J.S. (1994). *Interpersonal communication: Competence through critical thinking.* Upper Saddle River, NJ: Prentice Hall.

Cegala, D. & Waldron, V. (1992). A study of the relationship between communicative performance and conversational participants thoughts. *Communication Studies,* 43, 105–123.

Church, A.T. (1982). Sojourner adjustment. *Psychological Bulletin,* 91, 540–572.

Cissna, K.J. & Anderson, R. (1990). The contributions of Carl Rogers to philosophical praxis of dialogues. *Western Journal of Speech Communication,* 54, 125–147.

Coleman, L. & DePaulo, B. (1991). Uncovering the human spirit: Moving beyond disability and "missed" communication. In N. Coupland, H. Giles, & J. Wiemann (Eds.), *"Miscommunication" and problematic talk.* Newbury Park, CA: Sage.

Detweiler, R. (1980). The categorization of the actions of people from another culture: A conceptual analysis and behavioral outcome. *International Journal of Intercultural Relations,* 16, 295–310.

Deutsch, M. (1973). *The resolution of conflict.* New Haven, CT: Yale University Press.

Dimbleby, R. & Burton, G. (1992). *More than words: An introduction to communication,* 2nd ed. London: Routledge.

Duran, R.L. (1992). Communicative adaptability: A review of conceptualization and measurement. *Communication Quarterly,* 40 (3). 253–268.

Eyles, Miltenyi, Davis Pty Ltd (1989). *English in the workplace: A shrewd economic investment,* Vol. 1. Canberra: Australian Government Publishing Service.

Fogel, A. (1993). *Developing through relationships.* Chicago: University of Chicago Press.

Forgas, J.P. (1985). *Interpersonal behavior: The psychology of social interaction.* Sydney: Pergamon.

Furnham, A. & Bochner, S. (1989). *Culture shock: Psychological reactions to unfamiliar environments.* London: Routledge Kegan Paul.

Gao, G. & Gudykunst, B. (1990). Uncertainty, anxiety and adaptation. *International Journal of Intercultural Relations,* 14, 301–317.

Gibson, J.W. & Hanna, M.S. (1992). *Introduction to human communication.* Dubuque, IA: W.M.C. Brown.

Gouttefarde, Claire (1992). *European Business Review,* 92 (4). pp. i–iii.

Gudykunst, W. & Ting-Toomey, S. (1988). *Culture and interpersonal communication.* Newbury Park, CA: Sage.

Gudykunst, W., Wiseman, R. & Hammer, M. (1977). Determinants of a sojourners attitudinal satisfaction. In B. Ruben, B. (Ed.), *Communication Yearbook 1.* New Brunswick, NJ: Transaction.

Gudykunst, W.B. & Hammer, M. (1988). Strangers and hosts. In Y. Kim and W.B. Gudykunst (Eds.), *Cross-cultural adaptation.* Newbury Park, CA: Sage.

Gudykunst, W.B. & Kim, Y.Y. (1997). *Communicating with strangers,* 3rd ed. Boston: McGraw-Hill.

Gudykunst, W.B. (1983). Uncertainty reduction and predictability of behavior in low- and high-context cultures: an exploratory study. *Communication Quarterly,* 31, 49–55.

Gudykunst, W.B. (1984). *Communicating with strangers.* New York: McGraw–Hill.

Gudykunst, W.B. (1993). Toward a theory of effective interpersonal and inter-group communication: An anxiety/uncertainty management (AUM) perspective. In R. Wiseman & I. Koester (Eds.), *Intercultural communication competence* (pp. 33–71). Newbury Park: Sage.

Gudykunst, W.B. (1995). Anxiety/uncertainty management (AUM) theory: Current status. In Wiseman, R. (Ed.), *Intercultural communication theory. International and intercultural annual* (Vol. XIX, pp. 8–59). London: Sage.

Gullahorn, J.T. & Gullahorn, J.E. (1963). An extension of the U-curve hypothesis. *Journal of Social Issues,* 19 (3), 33–47.

Harris, F. (1996). *Productive diversity— employer perception.* Sydney: NSW Department of Training and Education Coordination, NSW Migrant Skills and Qualification Branch.

Harris, P. & Moran, R. (1991). *Managing cultural differences.* Houston, TX: Gulf Publishing Company.

Hartley, P. (1993). *Interpersonal communication.* London: Routledge.

Heckathorn, D. (1990). Connective sanctions and compliance norms. *American Sociological Review,* 55, 366–384.

Hellriegel, D. & Slocum, W.J. (1978). *Management: Contingency approaches.* Reading, MA: Addison-Wesley.

Ho, T. & Sung, K. (1990). Role of infrastructure networks in supporting social values to sustain economic success in newly industrialized nations. *International Journal of Psychology,* 25, 887–900.

Hofstede, G. (1980). *Cultures consequences: International differences in work related values.* Beverly Hills, CA: Sage.

Ickes, W. (1984). Composition in black and white. *Journal of Personality and Social Psychology,* 47, 330–341.

Irwin, H. & More, E. (1994). *Managing Corporate Communication.* Sydney: Allen & Unwin.

Irwin, H. (1996). *Communicating with Asia: Understanding people and customs.* Sydney: Allen & Unwin.

Jackson, T. (1993). *Organizational behavior in international management.* London: Butterworth Heinemann.

Jupp, J. (Ed.) (1989). *The challenge of diversity.* Canberra: Office of Multicultural Affairs/Australian Government Printing Services.

Kaye, M. (1992). Intercultural communication competence in vocational education systems: organizational implications for training strategies. *Australian Journal of Communication,* 19, 107–125.

Kim, Y.Y. & Gudykunst, W.B. (Eds.) (1988). *Theories in intercultural communication.* Newbury Park, CA: Sage.

Kim, Y.Y. & Ruben, B.D. (1988). Intercultural transformation: A systems theory. In Kim, Y.Y. & Gudykunst, W.B. (Eds.), *Theories in intercultural communication* Newbury Park, CA: Sage.

Kim, Y.Y. (1980). *Psychological, social and cultural adjustment of Indochinese refugees,* Vol. IV of *Indochinese refugees in the State of Illinois.* Chicago: Travelers Aid Society of Metropolitan Chicago.

Kim, Y.Y. (1988). *Communication and cross-cultural adaptation: An integrative theory.* Clevedon Hall, England: Multilingual Matters.

Kim, Y.Y. (1990). Communication and adaptation: the case of Asian-Pacific refugees in the United States. *Journal of Asian Pacific Communication,* 1, 1–17.

Kim, Y.Y. (1995). Cross-cultural adaptation. In R. Wiseman (Ed.). *Intercultural communication theory.* Thousand Oaks, CA: Sage.

Kincaid, D.L. (1987). *Communication theory: Eastern and Western perspectives.* London: Academic Press.

Kluckhohn, F. & Strodtbeck, F. (1961). *Variations in value orientation.* New York: Harper & Row.

Knapp, M.L. & Miller, G.R. (Eds.) (1985). *Handbook of interpersonal communication.* Beverly Hills, CA: Sage.

Laing, R.D. (1967). *The politics of experience.* New York: Pantheon.

Langer, E.J. (1989). *Mindfulness.* Reading, MA: Addison-Wesley.

Lazarus, R. (1966). *Psychological stress and the coping process.* St. Louis, MO: McGraw-Hill.

Lazarus, R. (1991). *Emotion and adaptation.* New York: Oxford University Press.

Littlejohn, S.W. (1996). *Theories of human communication,* 5 ed. Belmont, CA: Wadsworth.

Lustig, M. & Koester, I. (1993). *Intercultural competence: Interpersonal communication across cultures.* New York: Harper Collins.

Lysgaard, S. (1955). Adjustment in a foreign society. *International Social Science, 7* (1). 45–51.

March, R.M. (1995). Asian literacy and Australia–Asia business relationships. *Napean Working Paper, Department of Marketing, University of Western Sydney.*

Martin, J.N. & Nakayama, T.K. (1997). *Intercultural communication in context.* Mt. View, WA: Mayfield Publication Company.

May, R. (1977). *The meaning of anxiety.* New York: Ronald.

McFall, R. (1982). A review and reformulation of the concept of social skills. *Behavior Assessment, 4,* 1–33.

McPherson, K. (1983). Opinion-related information seeking. *Personality and Social Psychology Bulletin, 9,* 116–124.

Mead, R. (1990). *Cross–cultural management communication.* New York: Wiley & Sons.

Miler, G.R. & Sunnafrank, M.J. (1982). All is one but one is not for all: A conceptual perspective of interpersonal communication. In F.E.X. Dance (Ed), *Human communication theory: Comparative essays* (pp. 220–242). New York: Harper and Row.

Morris, R.T. (1960). *The two–way mirror.* Minneapolis, MN: University of Minnesota Press.

Oberg, K. (1960). Cultural shock: Adjustments to new cultural environments. *Practical Anthropology, 7, 177–82.*

Oehlkers, P. (1991). Networks of social support and adjustment of Japanese sojourners in the United States. Paper presented at the Speech Communication Association Convention, Chicago.

Rogers, E.M. & Kincaid, D.L. (1981). *Communication networks: A new paradigm for research.* New York: Free Press.

ROMMPAS (Review of Migrant and Multicultural Programs and Services) (1986). *Don't settle for less.* Canberra: Australian Government Printing Services.

Ruben, B.D. & Kealey, D.J. (1979). Behavioral assessment of communication competency and the prediction of cross-cultural adaptation. *International Journal of Intercultural Relations, 3,* 15–47.

Ruben, B.D. (1976). Assessing communication competency for intercultural adaptation. *Group and Organizational Studies, 1,* 334–354.

Saee, J. & Kaye, M. (1994). Intercultural communication competence in management training, Paper presented at the 44th Annual Conference of the International Communication Association Co–Host Australian and New Zealand Communication Association Conference on Communication and Diversity, Darling Harbour, July 11–15, Sydney, Australia.

Saee, J. (1998). Intercultural competence: Preparing enterprising managers for the global economy. *Journal of European Business Education, 7* (2), 15–37.

Sapir, E. (1921). *Language: An introduction to the study of speech.* New York: Harcourt Brace & World.

Searle, W. & Ward, C. (1990). The prediction of psychological and sociocultural adjustment during cross-cultural transitions. *International Journal of Intercultural Relations, 14*, 449–464.

Selltiz, C., Christ, J., Havel, J., & Cook, S. (1963). *Attitudes and social relations of foreign students in the United States.* Minneapolis, MN: University of Minnesota Press.

Shah, H. (1991). Communication and cross-cultural adaptation patterns among Asian Indians. *International Journal of Intercultural Relations, 15* (3). 311–321.

Slavin, M. & Kriegman, D. (1992). *The adaptive design of human psyche.* New York: Guilford.

Sorrentino, R.M. & Hewitt, E. C. (1984). The uncertainty reducing properties of achievement tasks revisited. *Journal of Personality and Personal Psychology, 47,* 884–899.

Spitzberg, B. & Cupach, W. (1984). *Interpersonal communication competence.* Beverly Hills, CA: Sage.

Stephan, C. & Stephan, W. (1985). Intergroup anxiety. Journal of Social Issues, 41, 157-166Taft, R. (1988). The psychological adaptation of Soviet immigrants in Australia. In Y. Y Kim & W. B. Gudykunst (Eds.), *Cross-cultural adaptation: Current approaches* (pp. 150–167). Newbury Park, CA: Sage.

Torbiorn, I. (1982). *Living abroad.* New York: Wiley.

Triandis, H.C. (1980). Values, attitudes and interpersonal behavior. In M. Page (Ed.), *Nebraska Symposium on Motivation, 1979* (Vol. 27, pp. 195-260). Lincoln, NE: University of Nebraska Press.

Triandis, H.C. (1994). *Culture and social behavior.* New York: McGraw Hill.

Turner, J.H. (1988). *A theory of social interaction.* Stanford, CA: Stanford University Press.

Ward, C. & Kennedy, A. (1996). Crossing cultures: The relationship between psychological and socio–cultural dimensions of cross–cultural adjustment. In J. Pandley, D. Sinha, & D.P.S. Bhawuk (Eds.), *Asian contributions to cross–cultural psychology* (pp. 289-306). New Delhi: Sage.

Wellman, B. (1992). Which types of ties and networks provide what kinds of social support? *Advances in Group Processes, 17* (2), 28–45.

Whorf, B.L. (1956). Language, mind and reality. In J.B. Carrol (Ed.), *Language, thought and reality* (pp. 246-270). New York; Wiley.

Wiseman, R. & Koester, I. (1993). *Intercultural communication competence.* Newbury Park: Sage.

# Chapter 7

*Organizational Culture*

*The key to successful organizational transformation lies in an understanding of organizational culture.*

—*Edgar Schein*

## OVERVIEW

Organizations like people have a personality or consistent patterns of behavior (Collins 1993). This is referred to as *organizational culture* or *corporate culture*. Every organization's "culture" represents a degree of uniqueness. It is an adaptive system shaped by the values and visions of the organization's founder, the external environment in which the organization operates, the internal strategies the organization selects to succeed, and the larger national culture or cultures of the people who make up its workforce (Johnson & McDougall 2002).

Corporate and organizational culture is pivotal for success nationally and internationally, especially in regard to global management and management of multicultural domestic organizations. This chapter defines organizational culture and surveys its common features. How organizational culture is developed and transmitted is also discussed with an emphasis on the organizational culture of the multinational corporation. Examined as well is the challenge of managing competently in a global business environment marked by multiculturalism and cultural diversity.

## ORGANIZATIONAL CULTURE DEFINED

Management scholars and social scientists have a number of ways to define organizational culture.

Schein (1985, 9), a leading organizational theorist defines organizational culture as a:

> *Pattern of basic assumptions—invented, discovered, or developed by a given group as it learns to cope with its problem of external adaptation and internal integration—that has worked well enough to be considered valuable and, therefore, to be taught to new members as the correct way to perceive, think, and feel in relation to those problems.*

Other researchers (Ouchi 1981; Pascale & Athos 1982; Deal & Kennedy 1982) conceptualize corporate culture as a set of assumptions or an ideology shared by members in an organization. These assumptions are used by people to identify what is important and how things work in that organization. Robbins, Millet, and Cacoppe (1998, 566) see organizational culture as the "sense making and control mechanism that guides and shapes the attitudes and behavior of employees."

These definitions, considered together, suggest that organizational culture reflects shared values, beliefs, norms, expectations, and assumptions that bind people and systems together. Organizational culture, like an iceberg, has both visible and invisible elements. The observable aspects include the physical setting, language, stories, legends, myths, heroes and heroines, ceremonies, behaviors, and dress. The visible aspects are indicative of the underlying dimensions; that is, the values, assumptions, beliefs, attitudes, and feelings of members as well as unwritten rules about the environment, time, space, relationships, and activities (Weiss 1996). Organizational members share in these dimensions and use them in a normative fashion to guide their behavior. They are the "social glue" that binds the organization (Smircich 1983; Golden 1992).

Although there is as yet no single, widely agreed upon definition of culture, however, there is some consensus that organizational culture is holistic, historically determined, and socially constructed; and it involves beliefs and behavior that exist at a variety of levels and manifests itself in a wide range of features of organizational life (Pettigrew 1990; Hofstede 1991).

## COMMON FEATURES OF ORGANIZATIONAL CULTURE

A number of common characteristics in the various ways of seeing organizational culture can be drawn from its research:

- Organizational culture defines a boundary in creating distinctions between one organization and another; that is, each organization projects its uniqueness in terms of who it is and what it stands for.

- Organizational culture conveys a sense of identity for organizational members.

- Organizational culture facilitates the generation of commitment to something larger than interest in one's self (Mead 1998).

- Organizational culture provides the necessary standard that an employee recognizes and is willing to honor. This is related to the employee's code of conduct and general philosophy about customer service. It is the organizational ethos.

- Management relies on its organizational culture (or ethos) as the driving force behind the successful operation of an organization rather than the formal, traditional structures of control.

In regard to the last point, researchers have recognized a relationship between organizational culture and the success of an organization. For example, in their seminal study *In Search of Excellence,* Peters and Waterman (1984, 75) concluded: "Without exception, the dominance and coherence of culture proved to be an essential quality of the excellent companies." Kotter and Heskett (1992) advocate that corporate culture can have a significant impact on a firm's long-term economic performance. For example, the secrets of success for Japanese companies such as Sony are not entirely attributable to specific technical areas such as finance, production, or marketing, but rather to the overall way the organization operated as cultural systems (Ouchi 1981; Pascale & Athos 1982). Research conducted on Banker's Trust Australia revealed that Banker's Trust Australia is regarded as one of Australia's leading merchant banks because of its strong corporate culture (Ivancevich, Olekans, & Matteson 1997).

## STRONG VERSUS WEAK ORGANIZATIONAL CULTURES

Mead (1998) lists the following characteristics as indicative of a strong organizational culture:

- It is cohesive. Group members share the same values, beliefs, and attitudes.

- Members can easily communicate with each other.

- Members can depend on one another in meeting individual needs.

Another and more comprehensive list of characteristics is provided by Deal and Kennedy (1982). They describe a strong organizational culture as having:

- A strong, unifying corporate philosophy and mission.
- Trusted and trusting leaders.
- Open communication channels and access to top management.
- An emphasis on the importance of people and productivity relationship—and an emphasis on the customer and on service.
- A general sense of accomplishment and belonging by all.
- Commonly shared rites, rituals, and ceremonies.
- An uplifting general feeling about employees' work, the place, and the future.
- Satisfaction with rewards, performance, and efforts.

A strong (positive) organizational culture is one in which its members support senior management and the relationship between senior management and workers is good (Trompenaars 1993; Mead 1998). This positive state takes place in organizations when:

- Members perceive that they have a stake in company outcomes: When the company benefits, they benefit and when it fails, they fail.
- Profits expressed in pay and other benefits and losses are perceived to be shared fairly.
- Demands for productivity are considered reasonable.
- Official relationships are considered reasonable: Top management communicates effectively and fairly with members; grievances are listened to, and given a fair response.

In contrast, a weak (negative) culture is one in which there are incongruous and often-contradictory value systems and a lack of unified organizational directions. There may even be disunity, mistrust, and a lack of communication among its members. When the culture is negative, relations with management are bad and the opposite conditions to the foregoing ones prevail. Overall when the culture is strong and positive, relations between management and workforce are good. Communication is easy, open, and fruitful; morale is high and productivity climbs (Mead 1998). Manpower Scandinavia, a Swedish service sector company, focused on developing, maintaining, and ensuring that its employees have healthy and productive values—that is, a positive organizational culture. Unconditional customer satisfaction was guaranteed as part of the focus. Production defects eventually came close to zero. The company also experienced a customer satisfaction rate of 97 percent (Harung & Dahl 1995).

Conversely, a weak, negative organizational culture can inhibit productivity and positive change in an organization, as Sam Malone, Worldwide Marketing Manager at *Xerox Quality Solutions* found out: "The one common denominator that led to failure in all of our previous quality efforts [prior to the mid-1980s] was that we did not change the culture or the environment in which all these tools and processes were being used. We had a 'flavor of the month mentality'" (Brennan 1994, 36).

A major report on management skills (AIM & NBEET 1991) explored weak organizational culture in various Australian organizations that lagged behind their counterparts in other countries. The report stated that the Australian workforce is plagued by hierarchical management styles, long production cycles, quality control only after the work is completed, poor recognition of the upgrading of skills, a tendency for initiative to come from management, and a short-term focus. Exhibit 7-1 shows the difference between the organizational culture of a typical Australian company and a world-class organizational culture.

# TRANSMISSION OF ORGANIZATIONAL CULTURE

Organizational cultures are primarily transmitted through the socialization process—that is, the ways employees learn, adopt, and pass on knowledge and organizational culture. An essential part of the socialization process is made up of "rites of passage," those designated occasions that reinforce particular values and create a bond among employees and between them and the organization (Weiss 1996). The first passage—the *induction process*—helps new employees take on their new roles and statuses. This is followed by an "enhancement rite," which further strengthens the emotional bond. Organizations often hold annual meetings to recognize high performers and send messages to other employees. The "renewal rite" rejuvenates and maintains the employees' identity with the organization. This is achieved through retreats, training, and trips. IBM, for example, awards trips to Hawaii for high sales performers. Lastly, there is an "integration rite," which is marked by events, promotion ceremonies, and other special occasions such as holiday parties designed to help foster the employees' loyalty to the firm.

# ORGANIZATIONAL CULTURE AND NATIONAL CULTURE

Organizations typically operate within a national cultural context and it follows that national culture influences organizational culture. In other words, the way of doing things in an organization is subject to a set of national cultural values, beliefs, and attitudes. National culture determines how members of a culture view the role of business (Weiss 1996). National culture influences the extent to which teams and employee involvement activities are socially valued and meaningfully supported.

| **Exhibit 7-1**   Australian Organizational Culture and a World-Class Organizational Culture | |
|---|---|
| **Typical Australian Organizational Culture** | **World-class Organizational Culture** |
| Hierarchical management | Open style, participative management |
| Long-run production cycles; high stock levels; production focus | Flexible, learning organization; customer focus |
| Quality maintained by postwork checking and rework | Quality mind-set; every employee is a "supplier" and a "customer;" quality problems handled at the source |
| Single skilling/deskilling; directing, task-oriented work | Multiskilling employees self-compartmentalization group |
| Initiatives for improvement usually emanate from management | Innovative organization, initiatives for improvements in all directions |
| Many unions, demarcations; antagonism; disputes | Industry-based unions; shared values; shared goals |
| Short-term focus, day-to-day mentality dominated by the "bottom line" | Short-term and long-term focus strategic thinking and management rewarded |

Source: Adapted from Australian Organizational Culture and a World-Class Culture, Report of National Summit on Management Skills, discussed in *Business Review Weekly*, 11 October 1991. Reprinted with permission.

The cultures of Sweden and Japan, for example, are conducive to employee involvement in organizational activities. The Japanese Union of Scientists and Engineers, for example, promotes quality circles, and helps install them in private firms. Sweden supports employee involvement programs through the Swedish Employers' Federation (Weiss 1996).

Hofstede (1991) revealed an interesting insight into this challenging problem of contrasting cultures within an international organizational context: that national cultural values always overrule contrasting organizational values. The national cultural values also have a significant impact on employees' organizational performance; and the cultural values that employees bring with them to the organization are not easily changed by the organization's intent to instill its organizational culture, which may deviate from the national culture. Similarly, an international study (Laurent 1986) found that organizational culture is unlikely to modify national cultural values; and when national and organizational cultures are in conflict, the first is likely to override the second. The employees of multinational corporations, such as Germans, Americans, and Swedes, demonstrated more loyalty for their national cultures than their organizational cultures in terms of German employees becoming more German; Americans becoming more American; and Swedes becoming more Swedish. This is because everyone is "enculturated" into their respective cultures, thereby developing a worldview based on their own cultural understandings.

National cultures can vary on several dimensions: individualism versus collectivism, power distance, uncertainty, masculinity versus femininity, and long-term orientation versus short-term orientation, as previously discussed in Chapter 2. This has considerable implications for organizational culture.

## ORGANIZATIONAL CULTURE IN MULTINATIONAL CORPORATIONS

Organizational culture is influenced not only by technologies and markets, but also by the cultural priorities of senior managers (Hofstede 1980; Hofstede, et al. 1990; Hofstede 1991; Trompenaars & Hampden-Turner 1997). This explains why some international companies have European, Asian, American, or Middle Eastern subsidiaries, which would be unrecognizable as the same company save for their logo and reporting procedures. Often these are fundamentally different in the logic of their structure and the meanings they bring to common activity (Trompenaars & Hampden-Turner 1997). Hofstede (1980; 1991) made a similar finding, having studied the culture of foreign subsidiaries of IBM, that a variety of cultures exist within a multinational corporation as discussed in the following paragraphs.

- *Process-Orientated versus Result-Orientated Culture.* In a process-orientated organizational culture, one finds the existence of rigid technical and bureaucratic routines, which, in turn, are intolerant of diversity. In a result-orientated organizational culture, there is a common concern for outcomes in which management allows for a range of approaches as long as results are achieved in a satisfactory manner. This includes being supportive of diversity.

- *Job-Orientated versus Employee-Orientated Culture.* In a job-orientated organizational culture, emphasis is placed on getting the job done without regard for employees' well-being. In an employee-orientated organizational culture, management feels responsible for the well-being of employees—and this includes equal opportunities for all including culturally diverse employees.

- *Professional versus Parochial Culture.* In a professional organizational culture, management appears to be more cosmopolitan in its worldviews. Such a state of mind serves the interests of diversity within the organization as there is an appreciation of diversity based on this management–cosmopolitan perspective. In a parochial organizational culture, management is inclined to be narrow-minded and, for that reason, outsiders are not trusted. Seen in this context, there is little appreciation and support for diversity within the latter organization.

- *Open-System versus Closed-System Culture.* In an open-system organizational culture, management is sensitive to both its internal and external environments and it is demonstrably more open to communication and dialogue. In a closed-system organizational culture, one finds that management appears to be insensitive to its environment and, as a consequence, is not open to outsiders and or diversity.

- *Tightly versus Loosely Controlled Culture.* In a tightly controlled organizational culture, there exists a high degree of formality and punctuality. This is due to the fact that tight control is required to ensure that all employees conform to a single model or "fit the slot." The opposite applies to a loosely controlled organizational culture that, in turn, is supportive of cultural diversity.

- *Pragmatic versus Normative Cultures.* In a pragmatic organizational culture, management displays a great deal of flexibility in the conduct of their business. In a normative organizational culture, there is a tendency to rigidly adhere to rules and policies.

## How to Examine the Organizational Culture of Multinational Corporations

In examining the organizational culture of different multinations, three aspects need to be looked at (Trompenaars 1993; Janssens, Brett, & Smith 1995; Hodgetts & Luthans 2000):

- The general relationship between employees and their organization.
- The vertical or hierarchical system of authority that defines superiors and subordinates.
- The general views that employees have about MNC's purpose, destiny, goals, and their places in it.

In the research of Trompennars and Hampden-Turner (1997), such an examination can be used to identify and describe the four types of organizational culture: Family, Eiffel Tower, Guided Missile, and Incubator, as shown in Exhibit 7-2. These types can further be distinguished by equity and hierarchy.

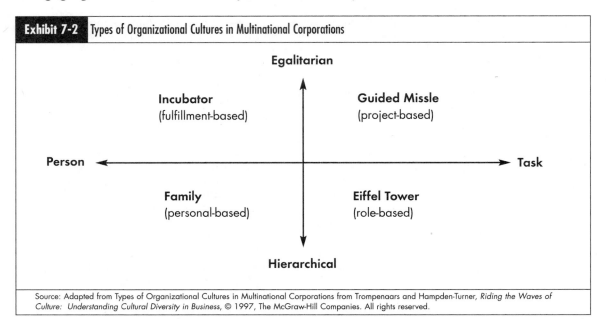

**Exhibit 7-2** | Types of Organizational Cultures in Multinational Corporations

Egalitarian

Incubator
(fulfillment-based)

Guided Missle
(project-based)

Person ←→ Task

Family
(personal-based)

Eiffel Tower
(role-based)

Hierarchical

### Family Culture

In using *family* as a metaphor for describing one type of organizational culture, Trompenaars and Hampden-Turner (1997) argue that the work relationship involves close interpersonal contacts. However, like a family, it is hierarchical. It is headed by the leader who is regarded as a caring parent and the one who knows what is the best for employees. The head is respected; everybody looks up to him or her for guidance and approval. The work of the corporation is carried forward in an atmosphere that in many respects mimics the family home. Many Japanese corporations do this in the practice of the business virtue *amae*, a kind of love between persons of different rank, with indulgence shown to the younger and respect reciprocated to the elder. The idea is always to do more than a contract or agreement obliges you. The idealized relationship is *sempai-kokai;* that is, between an older and younger brother. Promotion by age means that the older person will typically be in charge. The relationship to the corporation is long term and devoted.

Other features of a family culture include the emphasis given to intuitive knowledge rather than rational knowledge. More attention is paid to the development of people rather than their deployment or use. Personal knowledge of others is more important than empirical knowledge about them. Conversations are more important than research questionnaires; and subjective data is superior to objective data. The way that an employee is motivated in a corporation based on family culture is more by praise and appreciation than by monetary rewards (Hodgetts & Luthans 2000).

### Eiffel Tower Culture

An organization that has an *Eiffel Tower* culture has characteristics, which resemble closely a bureaucracy as conceptualized by Max Weber in that it is primarily based on hierarchy; division of labor; and employees' orientation to the prescribed tasks. Each job is clearly defined and every employee knows what he or she is supposed to do while everything is coordinated from the top. Each higher level has a clear and demonstrable function of holding together the levels beneath it. The boss has a legal authority over his or her subordinates arising from him or her holding the position. However, the person holding the top position can be easily replaced with no effect on organization, since the entire running of the organization is based on a set of clearly defined roles and procedures and is therefore impersonal. Status in an Eiffel Tower organization remains within a specified role.

Learning is seen as an accumulation of skills necessary to fit the role. In German and Austrian companies, which are typically Eiffel Tower models, the titles of Professor or Doctor are common on office doors; and professionals and managers in these organizations tend to address each other in an honorific fashion ("Herr Professor, Dr. Schmidt," and so on). An Eiffel Tower firm uses job qualifications in deciding how to schedule, deploy, and reshuffle employees to meet its organizational needs.

A methodical approach based on rational procedures is applied to performance appraisal, training, motivating, rewarding, and conflict resolution in these organizations. Duty is important for the role-oriented employee in an Eiffel Tower organization. He or she sees the responsibilities of the job as an obligation, not as responsibility to any particular individual.

Change in an Eiffel Tower company is immensely complex and time consuming. As such, manuals must be rewritten, procedures changed, job descriptions altered, promotions reconsidered, qualifications reassessed. Consequently, initiating certain kinds of change is not welcome in an Eiffel Tower organization and is often resisted. Trompenaars and Hampden-Turner (1997) observe:

> An American manager responsible for initiating change in a German company described [. . .] the difficulty he had in making progress, although the German managers had discussed the new strategy in depth and made significant contributions to its formulation. Through informal channels he had eventually discovered that his mistake was not having formalized the changes to structure or job descriptions. In the absence of a new organization, this Eiffel Tower company was unable to change (174–175).

### Guided Missile Culture

A Guided Missile organizational culture emphasizes equality among its members in the work place and orientation to the task undertaken by teams or project groups. Assignments are not fixed and limited like in an Eiffel Tower; but people are required to do whatever it takes to get the job done. In a Guided Missile culture, formal hierarchical considerations are given low priority, but the most important is individual professional expertise. Everyone in the team is equal, as his or her contributions to the project are not yet known. This type of organizational culture derived its name from the high-tech organizations that represent this type such as the National Aeronautics and Space Administration (NASA), which pioneered the use of project groups working on space probes. Other features of Guided Missile culture include:

- Peers and not bosses conduct individual performance appraisal.
- Organizational change comes quickly, and unlike in Eiffel Tower culture, is welcome.
- Teams accomplish goals, and teams are reassigned to achieve new objectives.

- Loyalty to one's profession and projects is greater than those to the corporation per se.
- Motivation is inspired not only by money, but more importantly by identifying oneself with attaining the goal (Trompenaars & Hampden-Turner, 1997).

Trompenaars and Hampden-Turner (1997) maintain that a Guided Missile culture tends to be individualistic. It allows for a wide variety of differently specialized people to work with each other on a temporary basis. The scenery of faces keeps changing. Only the pursuit of chosen lines of personal development is constant. The team is a vehicle for the shared enthusiasm of its members, but is itself disposable and will be discarded when the project ends. Members are garrulous, idiosyncratic, and intelligent, but their mutuality is a means, not an end. It is a way of enjoying the journey. They do not need to know each other intimately and may avoid doing so. Management by objectives is the language spoken, and people are paid by performance.

### Incubator Culture

The Incubator culture is predicated on the idea that organizations are secondary to the fulfillment of individuals. This culture is premised on the notion that organizations are there to serve as incubators for the self-expression and self-fulfillment of their members. As a result, the organization contains very little formal structure. There is a strong emphasis on equality among its members. This type of organizational culture is often found in startup companies that are entrepreneurial and made up of creative teams. An example of this type of organization are the kind that thrived in Silicon Valley. Members in an Incubator culture tend to operate in an environment of intense emotional commitment due to the

---

**EXAMPLE 7-1** Nokia Corporation

Nokia is a company that represents a guided missile corporate culture. Nokia Corporation was founded in Finland in 1967 with the merger of three Finnish companies. Starting in the early 1980s, Nokia started to grow through acquisitions of various European telecommunications companies (such as Mobira, Salora, Televa, and Luxor of Sweden), and eventually, at the end of the 1980s, it emerged as the largest information technology corporation in Scandinavia with the acquisition of Ericsson data systems division. Presently, it is currently the world leader in mobile communications and provides quality mobile phones and mobile, fixed broadband, and IP networks to the world.

It is evident that Nokia's corporate culture is extremely important to its organization as it believes it is providing *"a platform for personal growth in a challenging environment with a clear vision, goals, and shared management principles,"* which is defined as "the Nokia Way." It consists of a set of values that characterizes Nokia's corporate philosophy and the driving force behind all of Nokia's activities. The Nokia Way definitely reflects the Guided Missile culture's individualistic aspect in the sense that it places great importance on self-guidance and a responsibility for each employee's own development. For instance, the Nokia Web site mentions that "personal growth through self-leadership provides the foundation for successful management," allowing individual workers to make their own independent decisions. Nokia also places an emphasis on teamwork and trust between workers. At Nokia, there is a non-hierarchical system, where managers and employees work together and collaborate. Open discussion and debate are encouraged, and every employee can comment on what goes on in the firm. Everyone's views and opinions are considered equally.

Source: Adapted from Nokia, Inc. (2003). Company Information: History, http://www.nokia.com/.

creative nature of the work involved. Change in the Incubator culture can be fast and spontaneous where the members are working towards a common objective. Work-related motivation is wholehearted, intrinsic, and intense with work becoming an existential attitude captured in a popular t-shirt at Apple Computer, "70 hours and loving it" (Trompenaars & Hampden-Turner, 1997).

Exhibit 7-3 summarizes and compares the Trompenaars and Hampden-Turner's classification of organizational cultures.

### Understanding Basic Organization Cultural Typologies

The organizational cultures defined by Hofstede (1991) and Trompenaars and Hampden-Turner (1997) are "pure" types and seldom exist in reality, for no contemporary organizations can neatly fit into any of these types. However, it is useful in terms of helping us to understand the basis of how individuals relate to each other; think; learn; change; are motivated; and resolve conflict in an organizational context. Each organizational culture described previously may be effective in its own cultural context; but it is wrong to assume that an organizational culture that is effective in one place is bound to be successful everywhere else.

## MODALITY OF ORGANIZATIONAL CULTURE AND NATIONAL PREFERENCES

In addition to defining certain organizational culture types, Trompenaars and Hampden-Turner (1997) identified national patterns of corporate culture. They surveyed 13,000 respondents across 42 countries. The results of this study are represented in the Exhibit 7-4. It is important to note that the pattern of national preferences identified in this figure reflects only the dominant ethnic cultural values, as national culture is one among a number of factors shaping organizational culture. (Not all companies in Denmark, for example are Incubator types, and those in France are not all the Family type.)

---

**EXAMPLE 7-2** Booster Juice

Booster Juice, a juice and smoothie company throughout Canada, represents an Incubator culture very much like other small entrepreneurial startup companies. The first Booster Juice bar was opened in November 1999 in Edmonton, Canada by Dale Wishewan and Jon Amack, who wanted to "provide consumers a healthy and convenient alternative to traditional fast food." It soon gained popularity with its delicious signature smoothies made from a mixture of different fruits and juices, including exotic types like guava and passion fruit. Since then, 75 stores have opened across Canada, using franchising as its primary growth strategy.

The company still reflects the university students who founded it. It encourages creativity within its workforce. Management structure is nonhierarchical and managers typically work side by side with their employees in an attempt to produce quality products.

Source: Adapted from *Canadian Franchise* (2003). Booster Juice. http://www.canadianfranchise.com/; and Booster Juice (2003). The Business. http://www.BoosterJuice.com

| Exhibit 7-3 | Characteristics of the Four Corporate Cultures | | | |
|---|---|---|---|---|
| | **Family** | **Eiffel Tower** | **Guided Missile** | **Incubator** |
| **Relationships between workers** | Diffuse relationships to organic whole to which one is emotionally attached | Specific role in mechanical system of required interactions | Specific tasks in cybernetic system aimed at common goals and objectives | Diffuse, spontaneous relationships growing out of common creative process |
| **Attitude to authority** | Status is ascribed to parent figures who are close and powerful | Status is ascribed to superior roles that are distant yet powerful | Status is achieved by project group members who contribute to organizational goals | Status is achieved by individuals exemplifying creativity and growth |
| **Ways of thinking and learning** | Intuitive, holistic, lateral and error-correcting | Logical, analytical, vertical and rationally efficient | Problem-centered, professional, practical, trans-disciplinary | Process-oriented, creative, ad hoc; inspirational |
| **Attitudes to people** | Family members | Human resources | Technocrats and experts | Co-creators |
| **Ways of changing** | "Father" changes course | Change rules and procedures | Shift aim as target moves | Improvise and adapt |
| **Mechanisms for motivating and rewarding** | Intrinsic satisfaction in being loved and respected; management by subjectives | Promotion to greater position, larger role; management by job description | Pay or credit for performance and problems solved; management by objectives | Participating in the process of creating new realities; management by enthusiasm |
| **Criticism and conflict resolution** | Turn other cheek; save others' faces; do not lose power game | Criticism is accusation of irrationality unless there are formal procedures to arbitrate conflicts | Constructive task-related only, then admit error and remedy fast | Must improve creative idea, not dismiss it |

Source: Adapted from Characteristics of the Four Corporate Cultures from Trompenaars and Hampden-Turner, *Riding the Waves of Culture: Understanding Cultural Diversity in Business*, 2e © 1997, The McGraw-Hill Companies. All rights reserved.

Trompenaars and Hampden-Turner (1997) concluded that multinational corporations operating in a number of countries should adjust their local organizational cultures to fit the cultures of the countries in which they have operations. At the same time, subsidiaries have to be able to coordinate their local operations with other organizational groups within the company so that all units operate in harmony and therefore have a shared vision and purpose. This is because a strong national identity can

| **Exhibit 7-4** | National Patterns of Corporate Culture |
| --- | --- |

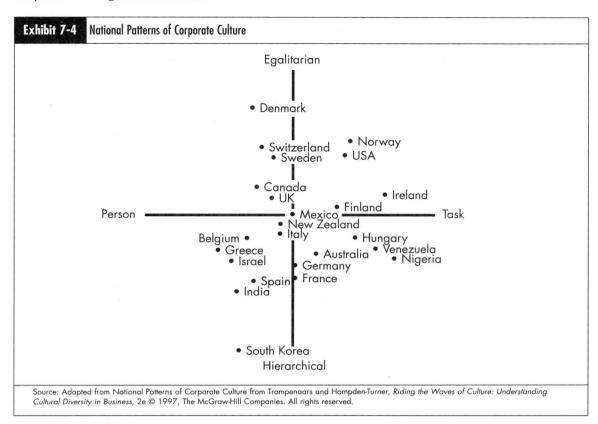

cause divisions in the workforce of a multinational corporation. This, in turn, adversely affects other parts of the organization (Yip 1995). Hence, the corporate culture of a multinational must be adaptive to different local culture. This strategy is confirmed by a study of 176 work units of one multinational corporation located in 18 European and Asian countries. It found that when management practices are congruent with a local and national culture, work unit performance is higher (Newman & Nollen 1996).

## ORGANIZATIONAL CULTURE AND CULTURAL DIVERSITY

To be successful strategically, international managers not only have to adapt their corporate culture to national values and practices, but also they have to manage culturally diverse employees' groups that may be present within their organizations. Managers who are culturally sensitive to their employees substantially contribute to business success (Saee 1998). However, managers are not well equipped to deal with the cultural diversity in their organizations. Ineffective management vis-à-vis cultural diversity stems from the nature of corporate culture, which is basically monocultural. An Australian study (Karpin 1995) found that Australian management tends to value sameness rather than differences. Another Australian study (Saee & Saunders 2000) revealed that most organizations lacked a coherent corporate strategy capable of dealing with cultural diversity.

## Appropriateness of Organizational Culture Types for Effective Management in a Culturally Diverse Workplace

What type of corporate organizational culture is ideally suitable to the cultural diversity that many kinds of corporations experience at home and in the global business environment? What type can achieve corporate goals? Reviewing the Hofsted's typologies of organizational culture described in this chapter, the following types would be congenial to effective management in the presence of workforce (and business environment) cultural diversity:

- Result-orientated culture, since it allows for all types of approaches as long as the organizational goal is achieved.
- Employee-orientated culture, because this approach takes into account the needs of and concern for all employees.
- Professional culture, as it values and recognizes all contributions made by all employees irrespective of their cultural backgrounds.
- Open-system culture, as it fosters free interactions within and outside the company.
- Loosely controlled culture, as conformity to organizational norms is not necessarily an issue.
- Pragmatic culture, as it encourages flexibility within its organizational processes.

Of the types of organizational cultures described by Trompenaars and Hampden-Turner, perhaps only the Incubator and the Guided Missile would be prescriptive as they both foster a climate of openness and interaction among management and their employees—and this is the ideal climate where cultural diversity is likely to be valued and embraced because of its perceived contributions to organizational performance.

## Strategies for Managing Cultural Diversity both Nationally and Internationally

Not all types of organizational culture possess the features deemed necessary for successful incorporation of cultural diversity within an organization. Yet no multinational corporations can afford to ignore cultural diversity, since cultural diversity is seen as a competitive advantage. In other words, cultural diversity can be a source of strength for an organization, provided the organization manages its cultural diversity within its workforce effectively. To do this, an organization needs to adopt cultural synergy as an essential part of its organizational culture and strategy, where managers form organizational strategies, policies, structures, and practices based on, but not limited to, the cultural patterns of individual organization members and clients (Adler 1997). Both similarities and differences between the cultures are recognized, and cultural diversity is seen as a resource in designing and developing organizational systems. The assumption is that there are many culturally distinct ways to reach the same goal. This cultural synergistic approach to organizational culture embodies a systematic process for increasing the options open to international executives, managers, and employees working in an increasingly global business environment (Adler 1997). Similarly, it is an effective approach for multicultural business environments.

## Summary

The focus of this chapter was organizational culture and its relevance and causality to the success of corporations operating in an increasingly global economy. The types and common features of organizational culture were surveyed and described. Strong and weak organizational cultures were also discussed. Finally, the importance of cultural diversity in an organizational culture was examined. The conclusion drawn is that for an organization to succeed in the contemporary global economy, it needs to adopt a synergistic organizational culture, one that highly values cultural diversity in all its organizational processes and business practices.

## Critical Discussion Questions

1. What are the similarities and differences between the definitions of national culture and corporate culture?
2. Briefly describe the functions performed by an organizational culture.
3. "Strong organizational culture is always behind the success of the organization." Is this a true assertion? Discuss.
4. "National culture greatly influences organizational culture." In what ways? Use outside sources and discuss.
5. When examining organizational culture in a multinational corporation, which aspects and functional areas would need to be considered?
6. Briefly describe four types of organizational culture outlined by Trompenaars and Hampden-Turner in this chapter. You should also look at the original source, which is listed in the References.
7. "National culture is the only factor shaping organizational culture." Is this true or false? Explain your answer.
8. What is the link between the corporate culture and management of cultural diversity within an organization?
9. Explain how cultural synergy may be used as a strategy to manage cultural diversity within an organization effectively.

## Applications

### Experiential

1. Interview managers of a local company in relation to the organizational culture. Analyze the company's culture in the light of knowledge gained from this chapter.
2. Interview a manager employed in a multinational company operating in your region. Discuss his or her views about the organizational culture of the company. Then analyze your findings in terms of its appropriateness to your national culture.

### Internet

IKEA, an international home furnishings company based in Sweden that specializes in affordable, well-designed furniture and articles for the home, commenced operations in 1943. Currently, the IKEA group employs 70,000 co-workers and has a turnover of over €11 billion. THE IKEA GROUP has 154 stores in 22 countries. In 2001, a total of 286 million people visited IKEA stores around the world. The IKEA catalog was printed in 118 million copies in 45 editions and 23 languages. In addition, IKEA has franchisees in Australia, United Arab Emirates, Greece, Hong Kong, Iceland, Israel, Kuwait, Malaysia, the Netherlands, Saudi Arabia, Singapore, Spain, Taiwan, and the United States. This is a grand total of 175 IKEA stores in 31 countries and territories. IKEA Group works with 1,800 different suppliers across the world and produces many of its own products through saw mills and factories in the IKEA industrial group.

## Assignment

Visit the IKEA Web site at: http://www.ikea-usa.com/

### Then answer the following questions:

1. What are the key aspects of IKEA corporate culture?
2. How is IKEA Group organized around the world?
3. In what ways does IKEA organization represent cultural diversity?
4. In what ways does IKEA communicate its core values to its stake holders, including employees and customers?
5. How would you typify IKEA corporate culture in the light of Trompenaars and Hampden-Turner and Hofstede's examples of corporate culture as described in this chapter? Justify your explanation.

## References

Adept Consulting (2000). The Cultural Minefield. *ADEPT Advisor* no. 5, http://www.adept-consulting.co.uk/advisor5a.html.

Adler, N. (1997). *International dimensions of organizational behavior* (3rd ed.). Cincinnati, OH: South-Western College.

Alexander, J.C. (1990). Analytic debates: Understanding the relative autonomy of culture. In J.C. Alexander & S. Seidman (Eds.), *Culture and society: Contemporary debates* (pp. 1–27). Cambridge: Cambridge University Press.

Australian Institute of Management (AIM) & National Board of Employment, Education and Training (NBEET) (1991, October 11). *Report on National Summit on Management Skills*. In *Business Review Weekly*, pp.68-70.

Brennan, N.E. (1994). *Lessons taught by Baldrige winners*. New York: The Conference Board.

Canadian Franchise (2003) Booster Juice. CandianFranchise.com, http://www.canadianfranchise.com.

Collins, R. (Ed.) (1993). *Effective Management*. Sydney: CCH International.

Cooke, R. & Rousseau, D. (1988). Behavioral norms and expectations: A quantitative approach to the assessment of organizational culture. *Group and Organizational Studies, 13*, 245–273.

Deal, T.E. & Kennedy, A.A. (1982). *Corporate cultures: The rites and rituals of corporate life*. Reading, MA: Addison-Wesley.

Denison, D. & Mishra, A. (1995). Toward a theory of organizational culture and effectiveness. *Organizational Science, 6*, 204–224.

Fulop, L. and Linstead, S. (Eds.) (1999). *Management: A critical text.* South Yarra, Australia: Macmillan Education.

Golden, K.A. (1992). The individual and organizational culture: Strategies for action in highly-ordered contexts. *Journal of Management Studies, 29,* 1–21.

Gordon, G.G. & DiTomaso, N. (1992). Predicting corporate performance from organizational culture. *Journal of Management Studies, 29,* 783–798.

Guirdham, M. (1999). *Communicating across cultures.* London: Macmillan.

Harung, H.S. & Dahl, T. (1995). Increased productivity and quality through management by values: a case study of Manpower Scandinavia. *The TQM Magazine, 7* (2),13–22.

Hellriegel, D. & Slocum, J. (1996). *Management* (7th ed.). Cincinnati, OH: South Western College.

Hodgetts, R.M. & Luthans, F. (2000). *International Management.* New York: McGraw-Hill.

Hofstede, G. (1980). *Culture's consequences: International differences in work related values.* Beverly Hills, CA: Sage.

Hofstede, G. (1991). *Cultures and organizations: Software of the mind.* London: McGraw-Hill.

Hofstede, G., Neuijen, B., Ohayv, D.D., & Sanders, G. (1990). Measuring organizational cultures: A qualitative and quantitative study across twenty cases. *Administrative Science Quarterly, 35,* 286–316.

Ivancevich, J., Olekans, M., and Matteson, M. (1997). *Organizational behavior and management.* Sydney: McGraw-Hill.

Janssens, M., Brett, J.M., & Smith, F.J. (1995). Confirmatory cross-cultural research: testing the viability of a corporation-wide safety policy. *Academy of Management Journal, 38,* Issue 2, April, 364–382.

Johnson, J. & McDougall, L. (2002, September). Workplace Design and Organizational Culture, Part II. *ISdesignNet,* http://www.isdesignet.com.

Karpin, D.S. (1995). *Enterprising nation: Report of the industry task force on leadership and management skills,* Vols. 1, 2, & 3. Canberra: Australian Government Printing Services.

Kotter, J.P. & Heskett, J.L. (1992). *Corporate culture and performance.* New York: Free Press.

Laurent, A. (1986). The cross-cultural puzzle of international human resources management. *Human Resources Management, 25* (1), 91–102.

Mead, R. (1998). *International management: Cross-cultural dimensions.* Cambridge, MA: Blackwell.

Newman, K. & Nollen, S. (1996). Culture and congruence: The fit between management practices and national culture. *Journal of International Business Studies, 27* (4), 753–780.

Ouchi, W. (1981). *Theory Z: How American business can meet the Japanese challenge.* Reading, MA: Addison-Wesley.

Pascale, R.T. & Athos, A. (1982). *The art of Japanese management.* London: Penguin.

Peters, T.J. & Waterman, R.H. (1984). *In search of excellence: Lessons from America's best-run companies.* New York: Harper and Row.

Pettigrew, A.M. (1990). Conclusion: Organizational climate and culture: Two constructs in search of a role. In B. Schneider (ed.), *Organizational climate and culture* (pp. 413–434). San Francisco: Jossey-Bass.

Robbins, S., Millett, B., Cacioppe, R. & Waters-Marsh, T. (2001). *Organizational behaviour: Leading and managing in Australia and New Zealand* (3rd ed.). Sydney: Prentice Hall.

Rossman, G.B., Corbett, H.D., & Firestone, W.A. (1988). *Change and effectiveness in schools: A cultural perspective.* Albany, NY: State University of New York Press.

Rousseau, D.M. (1990). Assessing organizational culture: The case for multiple methods. In B. Schneider (Ed.), *Organizational climate and culture* (pp. 153–192). San Francisco: Jossey-Bass.

Saee, J. (1998). Intercultural competence: Preparing enterprising managers for the global economy. *Journal of European Business Education, 7* (2), 15–37.

Saee, J. & Saunders, S. (2000). Intercultural communication competence and managerial functions within the Australian hospitality industry. *Australian Journal of Communication, 27* (1), 111–129.

Schall, M. (1983). A communications-rules approach to organizational culture. *Administrative Science Quarterly, 28,* 557–581.

Schein, E.H. (1992). *Organizational culture and leadership* (2nd ed.). San Francisco: Jossey Bass.

Schwartz, H., & Davis, S.M. (1981). Matching corporate culture and business strategy. *Organizational Dynamics, 10* (1), 30–38.

Smircich, L. (1983). Concepts of culture and organizational analysis. *Administrative Science Quarterly, 28,* Issue 3, 339–358.

Trompenaars, F. & Hampden-Turner, C. (1997). *Riding the waves of culture: Understanding cultural diversity in business* (2nd ed.). New York: McGraw-Hill.

Weiss, J. (1996). *Organizational behavior and change: Managing diversity, cross-cultural dynamics, and ethics.* Eagan, MN: West.

Yip, G.S. (1995). *Total global strategy: Managing for worldwide competitive advantage.* Englewood Cliffs, NJ: Prentice Hall.

# Chapter 8

*Leadership Across Cultures*

## LEARNING OBJECTIVES

*After reading this chapter, you should be able to:*
- *Understand the importance of leadership in a successful organization.*
- *Describe the differences that exist between a leader and a manager.*
- *Understand the good leader's characteristics.*
- *Describe different styles of leadership.*
- *Describe different theoretical paradigms of leadership.*
- *Understand different approaches to leadership across cultures.*

[. . .] *global business now requires all leaders to be explorers, guided by only the faintest glimmer of unfamiliar stars and excited by the opportunity and uncertainty of untapped markets.*

—H. Gregersen, A.J. Morrison, and J.S. Black (1998)

## OVERVIEW

It takes dynamic leaders to play the pivotal roles in our contemporary global economy—and leadership is a crucial function in organizations and a critical ingredient for organizational success:

> "Organizations worldwide strive to fulfill their missions. They select leaders who articulate a vision that guides them towards achieving long-term goals and short-term objectives. They expect their leaders to motivate the workforce in consistent and effective ways. Corporate leaders continually make decisions that influence the success of entire operations" (Adler 1997, 151).

Leadership has a long history. As Sarros and Woodman (1993, 3) observed, "Leaders have existed for as long as mankind has been civilized. Egyptian hieroglyphs around 5,000 years ago differentiated among leaders, leadership, and followers. For almost as long, Taoism has emphasized leadership qualities in terms of guiding and nurturing followers." Historical leaders such as Alexander the Great, Moses, Jesus, and Mohammad are clear examples of great leaders who inspired millions of people for their respective visions. Considering leadership within a business organizational context, leadership styles that were practiced in traditional hierarchies and that relied on authoritarian controls are seldom applicable to the changing workforces of the 21st century. Instead, new styles of leadership are needed in contemporary organizations, ones that inspire trust and creativity and motivate the workforce. However, leadership is not an easy task when challenged with a culturally diverse workforce.

Many situational factors contribute to the effectiveness of managerial leadership. These include the leader's characteristics, the followers' expectations, the task, organizational policies, and top management values and philosophies. An ever-present factor which influences the other situational factors is the host culture. Without a thorough understanding of cultural differences, a leader who may be quite effective in his or her own culture may be doomed in a different culture. An examination in this chapter is made of different styles of leadership that would prevail across cultures. Leaders and managers of a corporation intent on globalizing its operations successfully need to adapt leadership style(s) to local conditions present in overseas countries.

## MANAGEMENT AND LEADERSHIP

Leaders create vision, the meaning within which others work and live. Managers, by contrast, act competently within the vision (Adler 1997). Traditionally, we think of leadership as being associated with the role of managers. However, leader and manager are not necessarily the same. Someone may be an outstanding manager without being a workgroup or team leader. While a manager performs planning, organizing, coordinating, and controlling activities deemed as essential managerial functions, leadership goes beyond management in that leaders act as role models, coaches, and mentors for team members. A manager gets his or her authority from a formal managerial position. Leaders, on the other hand, emerge without necessarily holding a manager's position or authority. Leadership implies something more than mere managerial or supervisory responsibility or formal authority. It consists of influence that extends beyond the usual influence that accompanies legitimacy as a supervisor. Organizations usually manage complexity first by planning and budgeting (setting targets and goals within a specific time frame, that is, quarterly; semi-annually, yearly, and so on) and by establishing detailed steps to achieve those targets and allocating resources. In contrast, Kotter (1990) suggests that leading an organization to constructive change begins by setting a direction, developing a vision, along with strategies for reducing the needed changes to achieve the vision. He developed a comparison between leadership and management shown in Exhibit 8-1.

It can be said that leadership is the incremental influence or additional influence that a person has beyond his or her formal authority (Hellriegel & Slocum 1996). Anita Roddick, the founder and CEO of the Body Shop, a highly successful international retail store, describes what constitutes sound business leadership:

> *Leaders in the business world should aspire to be true planetary citizens. They have global responsibilities since their decisions affect not just the world of business, but world problems of poverty, national security, and the environment. Many, sad to say, duck these responsibilities, because their vision is material rather than moral (Roddick 1991, 226).*

## LEADERSHIP DEFINED

Leadership is defined in a number of ways. The following are some that will be useful in our context of a leader in a global business environment and in a culturally diverse workforce:

- The process of influencing people to direct their efforts toward the achievement of some particular goal (Hodgetts & Luthans 2000).
- Getting the best out of subordinates individually and collectively, achieving objectives in the most effective way.
- A leader shows skills in directing group activity, has a natural authority, and gains respect of others, is capable of building effective teams involves all team members, and gives advice and help when required (Weiss 1996).

| Exhibit 8-1 | Comparison of Leadership and Management | |
|---|---|---|
| **MANAGEMENT** | ← → | **LEADERSHIP** |
| Planning and Budgeting | DECIDING WHAT TO DO | Establishing the Direction |
| Organizing and Staffing | CREATING HUMAN SYSTEM FOR ACCOMPLISHING ORGANIZATIONAL GOALS | Aligning People |
| Controlling and Problem Solving | EXECUTION | Motivating and Inspiring |

Source: Adapted from *A Force For Change: How Leadership Differs from Management*, John P. Kotter, with permission of The Free Press, a Division of Simon & Shuster Adult Publishing Group, © 1990 by John P. Kotter, Inc. All rights reserved.

- Leadership is about the ability to effectively use strategic competencies, power, and influence to accomplish organizational goals (Sethi, Namiki, & Swanson 1984).

From these definitions a number of features common to leadership can be identified:

- Leadership is an influencing process.
- Leadership requires at least two people, a leader and a follower(s).
- Leadership occurs when attempting to achieve specific objectives or goals, either explicit or implied.

## QUALITIES OF A LEADER

Jackson (1993) has isolated a number of abilities that make for effective leaders:

- The ability to build effective teams.
- The ability to listen.
- The capability to make decisions on their own.
- The ability to retain good people.
- The ability to surround themselves with good people (Jackson 1993).

The traits of a good leader, as identified by Kirkpatrick and Locke (1991) also add to his or her effectiveness:

- Drive, high desire for achievement; ambition to get ahead in work and career.
- Leadership, the desire and willingness to lead.
- Motivation, the ability and willingness to assume responsibility.
- Honesty and integrity.
- Self-confidence, needed to withstand setbacks and persevere through hard times and lead others in the right direction.
- Cognitive ability and above average intelligence to analyze situation and solve problems.
- Knowledge of business.

## MAJOR SOURCES OF LEADERSHIP POWER AND INFLUENCE

Effective leadership begins with an understanding of power. Leadership also depends on the responsible use of power—and influence with followers and external constituencies. Power and influence are interrelated. Power is the ability to control behaviors and outcomes in a given direction. Influence depends on the followers' acceptance of the influences and the types of influence used. Influence is related, in this sense, to authority; that is, the power granted to leaders by followers (Sethi, Namiki, & Swanson 1984). According to McLaughlin (1993), leaders have four core sources of power and influence available to them:

- *Formal or legitimate power.* This comes from being appointed by the organization to a leadership position (as a manager). Cultural norms tend to reinforce the view that a manager has the right to lead subordinates.

- *Expert power.* This sort of power comes from having knowledge, skills, and expertise that are regarded as important by the leader's followers. With a formal leader, this expertise is usually associated with goal achievement.

- *Reward/punishment power.* This comes from the leader having the ability to reward and punish followers. That is, they have influence over promotion and recognition of followers.

- *Personality power.* Many personal characteristics come into this category. If a leader is liked and respected by subordinates and peers, he or she will have more influence over them. This is sometimes called the *power of charisma.* A charismatic leader is one who inspires his or her subordinates to achieve goals, essentially through force of personality.

Given the power and influence that leaders have, they have the authority over the following responsibilities—which can, of course, be the manager's task as well:

- To sort and control agendas.

- To build and cultivate strategic alliances and networks.

- To control the interpretation and flow of information in the organization, and in the roles of president, CEO, and chairperson, to influence the vision, culture, and strategies of his or her organization (Sethi, Namiki, & Swanson 1984; Kotter 1990).

Cohen, et al. (1992) and Sethi, Namiki, and Swanson (1984) in their research see organizational leaders and followers as having different categories of influence that they can exert (or fail to exert):

- *Legitimate influence.* This is based on orders, instructions, directions, or by example, which are accepted as proper by followers.

- *Illegitimate Influence.* This is based on orders, instructions, directions, or by example, which are not accepted as proper by followers. Both legitimate and illegitimate influences may refer to a leader's individual or personal experience, qualities, profile, and/or to a process (policy, directives, goal implementation) established or directed by the leader.

- *Formal (assigned) legitimate influence.* This is attributed to position, title, assigned authority.

- *Legitimate informal (unassigned) influence.* This comes from authority given to a leader by followers not because of a title or position, but because of personal characteristics such as charisma, experience, skills, or attractive personality traits.

- *Formal illegitimate influence.* That is when a leader orders or requests an activity that is not within his or her formal position description or boundary to do so. For example, a company's managing director requests a supervisor to contribute a sum of money to charity fund.

- *Informal illegitimate influence.* This can be illustrated by means of an example. A supervisor on probation threatens an employee to decrease his higher-than-average productivity output in order not to threaten the supervisor's already poor status in the factory.

John Scully initially had significant legitimate influence at Apple Computer. Yet after several years his influence as a visionary waned.

Critics claimed that he lost touch with the technology market. President Mitterand of France exemplified a presidential leader whose influence resided in his position and his formal use of it.

# LEADERSHIP BEHAVIORS AND STYLES

There are three recognized leadership styles and behaviors: (1) authoritarian. (2) paternalistic, and (3) participative (Hodgetts & Luthans 2000). They are described in detail:

- *Authoritarian leadership* is where the leader typically uses one-way communication from superior to subordinate. The focus here is on work progress, work procedures, and goal attainment.
- *Paternalistic leadership* style can be summarized by the statement: "Work hard and the company will take care of you." The organization culture of Japanese firms typically has this kind of leadership model.
- *Participative leadership* is the use of both work-centered and people-centered approach. Such leadership has been widely espoused in the United States, the United Kingdom, and in other English-speaking countries. This style is popular in Scandinavian countries as well.

Burns (1978), in looking at older and newer leadership modes, sees a move from a *transactional* style of leadership to a *transformational* one. Transactional leaders motivate subordinates to perform at expected levels by helping them recognize task responsibilities, identify goals, acquire confidence about meeting desired performance levels, and understand how their needs and the rewards that they desire are linked to goal attainment. Transformational leaders, in contrast, motivate subordinates to perform beyond normal expectations by inspiring them to focus on broader missions that transcend their own immediate self-interests; to concentrate on intrinsic, higher level goals such as achievement and self-actualization, to use Maslow's terms, rather than extrinsic, lower level goals such as safety and security; and to have confidence in their abilities to achieve the extraordinary missions articulated by the leaders. Key behaviors of transformational leaders may include:

- *Charisma.* A leader's ability to inspire faith, pride, and respect in followers.
- *Individualized consideration.* A leader pays personal attention to each follower's needs and treats each follower as an individual worthy of respect.
- *Intellectual stimulation.* A leader offers new ideas to stimulate followers to rethink old ways of doing things and fosters creative breakthroughs in obstacles that seemed insurmountable (McLaughlin 1993).

Max Weber's historical view of leadership styles is a continuum that runs from charismatic to traditional to legal/rational (see Exhibit 8-2). Basi (1983), in the light of recent societal and technological transformations, has added two additional leadership styles to Weber's continuum:

- *Supportive Leadership Style.* A leader gains power and the status is earned from the demonstration of his or her knowledge and willingness to be helpful.

- *Facilitative Leadership Style.* A leader empowers employees and removes hurdles to accomplish outcomes.

Goleman (2000) reported that leaders use six styles, each springing from different components of emotional intelligence. Exhibit 8-3 illustrates a summary of these styles, their origin, when they work best, and their impact on an organization's performance. He found that many

---

| Exhibit 8-2 | Weber's Continuum of Leadership |
| --- | --- |

| CHARISMATIC | TRADITIONAL | LEGAL/RATIONAL |
| --- | --- | --- |
| Calls for obedience to leaders because of personal trust, power, or exemplary character | Demands obedience to boss who occupies the traditionally sanctioned position of authority | Calls for obedience to the legally established impersonal order |

Source: Adapted from *Contextual Management: A Global Perspective*, 241-263, R.S. Basi, © 1998, with permission of Haworth Publishing, International Business Press, NY.

---

| Exhibit 8-3 | The Six Leadership Styles |
| --- | --- |

|  | Coercive | Authoritative | Affiliative | Democratic | Pace-setting | Coaching |
| --- | --- | --- | --- | --- | --- | --- |
| **The leader's style of doing things** | Requires immediate and absolute compliance | Mobilizes people toward a future vision | Establishes harmony and fosters emotional ties | Builds consensus through participation | Sets high standards for performance | Develops people for the future |
| **The style in a phrase** | "Do what I tell you" | "Come with me" | "People come first" | "What do you think?" | "Do as I do, now" | "Try this" |
| **Underlying emotional intelligence competencies** | Drive to achieve, initiative, self-control | Self-confidence, empathy, change catalyst | Empathy, building relationships, and good communication | Collaboration, team leadership and communication | Conscientiousness with a drive to achieve and initiate | Developing others, empathy, and self-awareness |
| **When this style of leadership is most effective** | In a crisis like a hostile takeover to break failed business habits or with problem employees | When changes require a new vision, or when a clear direction is needed | To heal rifts in a team or to motivate people during stressful circumstances | To build buy-in or consensus or to get input from valuable employees | To achieve quick results from a highly motivated and competent team | To help an employee improve performance or develop long term competencies |
| **Overall impact on working environment** | Negative | Most strongly positive | Positive | Positive | Negative | Positive |

Source: Adapted and reprinted by permission of *Harvard Business Review*. From "The Six Leadership Styles" adapted from Goleman, D., Leadership that Gets Results, HBR, March-April, 78-90. © 2000 by the Harvard Business School Publishing Corporation; all rights reserved.

studies, including his own, show that the more styles a leader exhibits, the better it would be for the organizational performance. The leaders who have mastered four or more styles—especially the authoritative, democratic, affiliative, and coaching styles—are the most effective when they can switch flexibly among their different leadership styles as needed.

# LEADERSHIP THEORIES

Historically, the literature of leadership focused on the "Great Man theory," that is, leaders are born, not made. Since leadership was innate, early social scientists tried to isolate the appropriate characteristics. Robbins, Bergman, and Stagg (2000), however, like other contemporary researchers and behavioral scientists, have found no consistent set of traits differentiating leaders from other people. Americans value charisma in their leaders and identify such business and political leaders as Lee Iacocca, Sam Walton, and John F. Kennedy as charismatic leaders. Contemporary Germans are suspicious of charisma given their experience with the evil charisma of Adolf Hitler (Adler 1997).

## Theory X and Y

The way leaders direct their subordinates is a relatively newer avenue in the study of leadership. Douglas McGregor (1960) showed that there are two schools of thought attributable to leadership and managers. The first school of thought is premised on *Theory X*, which assumes that people, by their very nature, do not like to work and will avoid work whenever possible. Workers, that is, have little ambition; try to avoid responsibility—and like to be directed. The primary need of employees, in Theory X, is job security; to get the people to do their work, Theory X leaders believe they must direct, control, and coerce people in order to motivate them to work. Theory Y takes a different view of people and the way to lead them in the workplace. Its primary assumption is that people are basically good and trustworthy (Adler & Bartholomew 1992). Theory Y leaders believe that they must give employees freedom, autonomy, and responsibility in their work to motivate them:

- The expenditure of physical and mental effort at work is as natural to people as resting or playing.
- External control and threats of punishment are not the only ways of getting people to work toward organizational objectives.
- If people are committed to the goals, they will exercise self-control; commitment to objectives is determined by the rewards associated with their achievement.
- Under proper conditions, the average human being learns not only to accept but to seek responsibility.
- The capacity to exercise a relatively high degree of imagination, ingenuity, and creativity in the solution of organizational problems is widely distributed throughout the population.
- Under conditions of modern industrial life, the intellectual potential of the average human being is only partially utilized (Adler 1997; Hodgetts & Luthans 2000).

Leaders from different cultures can be classified as falling under Theory X and Theory Y. A "Theory Y" manager in the United States may believe that most people can and want to develop interpersonal relationships characterized by trust and open communication. A Theory Y manager in China, who is influenced by the egalitarian philosophy of Chairman Mao, would believe that all employees had to improve their lot together, both economically and culturally. Though worlds apart ideologically, the American and Chinese managers are Theory Y leaders because they see that workers can perform efficiently and productively without being dehumanized.

## Behavioral Theory of Leadership

The Behavioral Theory of leadership resulted from research at The Ohio State University during the 1940s. It classified two ways of identifying leaders. A leader who shows a high degree of *initiating* is concerned with detailing task requirements, clarifying and emphasizing standards of work assignments, and schedules. This *task-oriented leader* places more importance on the performance of tasks than on maintaining a good relationship with subordinates. In contrast, there is the leader who shows a high degree of *consideration,* is sensitive to employees' ideas, emphasizes trust, and seeks to communicate. This *relationship-oriented leader* places much more emphasis on maintaining a bond with his or her subordinates than he or she does on the performance of tasks. In the real world, a leader can choose and adopt both an initiating structure and consideration style of management as appropriate to the situational requirements of his or her workforce and its tasks. Blake and Mouton (1964) and their research support this. They surveyed 2,500 managers from six countries and found that most managers agreed that the ideal leadership style is the integration of relationship and task orientation. However, when managers were asked to describe their actual style, they admitted to being more task- than relationship-oriented. Indeed, there is no conclusive evidence to support the notion that a particular combination of initiating structure and consideration will result in optimum group performance (Weiss 1996).

## Contingency Leadership Theory

Fiedler (1967) pioneered the Contingency Theory that postulates that leadership can be measured with the Least Preferred Coworkers (LPC) scale. Those with a high LPC scale are relationship-oriented; those with a low LPC scale are task-oriented. There are also those who straddle both styles.

Fiedler argued that leadership style depends on three major contingency variables: task structure, leader–member relations, and the leader's position power. Task structure refers to the extent that the task is routine or nonroutine. A routine task has well-defined goals and procedures. The outcomes are verifiable and the means of performing the work is specific. Nonroutine tasks have the opposite characteristics. Leader–member relations refer to the extent to which a group accepts a leader. Acceptance leads to commitment and loyalty, unacceptance leads to friction and tension. Leader position power refers to the extent that a leader can hire, fire, reward, and discipline subordinates. Organizations, Fiedler claims, should match tasks and work environments with an individual's leadership style to ensure high group performance—however, in the context of cross cultural reliability, questions remain over the selection and measurement of Fiedler's variables (Weiss 1996).

## Path-Goal Theory

The Path–Goal theory of leadership, from House's research (1971), states that leaders are effective if they can clarify goals for subordinates and assist them in attaining these goals. The ideal Path–Goal leader provides training, coaching, and guidance and removes obstacles to goal attainment. There are four leadership styles that House identifies that mark such a leader:

- *Directive.* The leader informs about what to do and when to do it. This is a *telling* style.
- *Supportive.* The leader is friendly with followers and shows them what to do. This is a *sharing* style.
- *Participative*: The leader is friendly with followers and solicits their ideas and suggestions. This is a *consultative* style.
- *Achievement-oriented.* The leader sets challenging goals and shows confidence in employee performance. This is a delegating style.

Research findings regarding the validity of the Path–Goal theory are mixed (Fulk & Wendler 1982). Like the "Great Man" theory, Theory X and Theory Y, Behavioral theory, and Contingency theory, it is a universalist approach to leadership and, like these other theories, developed in the United States. It would seem that, for this reason, such theories of leadership can be "universally" applied to other cultures and to the organizations that exist in them. This is critically examined in the next section.

## Cultural Relativity of Leadership

For managers to be effective in leadership roles transplanted into the business and workplace environments of another culture, their leadership styles should be adaptive to their host culture; that is, they should develop a culturally contingent approach to leadership style. International study demonstrates that there are more similarities than differences among the leaders and their styles, as was the case in a study of 14 countries (even though the countries studied were clustered along ethnic rather than industrial lines) (Haire, Ghiselli, & Porter 1963). Still, Hofstede (1980b) found that participative management approaches, including Theory Y, strongly encouraged by American managerial theorists, were not suitable for all cultures. People in power-distance societies such as Germany, Austria, and Switzerland believe in a hierarchical power distribution in which everyone has a rightful place and everyone is protected by this order, where managers perceive themselves different from subordinates and vice versa. The difference between superiors and subordinates leads to inaccessibility of superiors. Power entitles people to certain privileges that include obedience and respect from others and subordinates. Powerful people will not hide their powers and, in fact, use various trappings to signal their power. Officeholders can be identified by the mode of dress, type of office, and their entourage. Employees in high power-distance cultures expect managers to act as strong leaders; they become uncomfortable with leaders delegating discretionary decisions.

Cultures with strong uncertainty avoidance such as France, Iran, Japan, Argentina, Pakistan, Turkey, Spain, and Thailand consider the uncertainty of life as a continuous threat that they have to resist. They avoid conflict and competition and strive for consensus. Security in life is valued greatly, which leads to the search for truth and values. People in these cultures are risk averse and worry about the future. To avoid uncertainty, there is a heavy reliance on written rules and regulations. Matters of importance are left to the authorities, which relieve subordinates from assuming the responsibility. To manage in uncertainty-avoidance societies is to deal with doubt, indecision, and the like in running an organization. A critical aspect of managing and leading is dealing with uncertainty by providing subordinates with direction and instructions for task performance. The payback in this relationship, as Hofstede discovered, is that in countries with a high uncertainty-avoidance factor, loyalty to employers is considered a virtue (Fatehi 1996).

# LEADERSHIP IN DIFFERENT CULTURES AND THE IMPLICATIONS FOR INTERNATIONAL MANAGEMENT

Because of the diverse values and core beliefs of different societies, leadership and organizations are inevitably culture bound. No two cultures view the essence of authority, hierarchy, or optimum structure in an identical light (Lewis 1996). Culture plays a strong role in the content of *leadership* prototypes (Lord & Maher 1991). To date, a study by Gerstner and Day (1994) is the most widely cited for its focusing on cross-cultural comparisons of *leadership* prototypes. Respondents completed a questionnaire asking them to assign ratings to 59 *leadership* attributes. Comparing the ratings from a sample of American students to smaller samples of foreign students from seven countries, they found that the traits considered to be (1) most, (2) moderately, or (3) least characteristic of business leaders varied by respondents country or culture of origin. This study had several limitations, among them small sample sizes (35 American and 10–22 foreign students), and that only foreign students currently in the United States represented their respective cultures in the sample. The study also employed an English language test that, for this reason, was not cross-culturally validated. Despite these shortcomings, reliable differences in *leadership* perceptions by members of various countries were found (Hartog, et al. 1999). Nevertheless, there is still no cross-cultural leadership theory to explain leadership with reference to cultural differences in the face of the fact that the use of authority varies across cultures. Given this state of affairs, we must adapt existing leadership theories despite their provenance, which is so often American.

The conspicuous use of power and authority is frowned upon in some cultures and encouraged in others. Cultures vary in their practice of delegating authority and responsibility. Subordinates in some cultures are not comfortable in participating in decision-making (such as Indonesia). The meaning of work also varies by cultures. For some, work is a necessary evil; for others it is a source of pride and purpose. Dealing with each culture requires a different leadership approach. An essential aspect of leadership is the role and behavior of the subordinates.

Leadership centers on the relationship between the managers and the followers. The manner of relating to employees, the style of projecting and using power, and the method of dealing with conflict and crisis set the stage for managerial leadership. The boundaries in which these issues are dealt with vary among cultures (Fatehi 1996). The way in which a cultural group goes about structuring its commercial and industrial enterprises and other kinds of organizations usually reflects to a considerable degree the cultural orientation and accordingly the manner in which it is organized. The basic questions to be answered are how is authority organized and what is authority based on. Western and Eastern answers to these questions vary enormously. In the West alone, there are striking differences in attitude. There is, for instance, little similarity in the organizational patterns of French and Swedish companies. Germans and Australians have almost diametrically opposing views as to the basis of authority for leaders. In the following sections different leadership styles and behaviors that prevail in different countries and societies are surveyed.

## France

Despite the internationally famous French slogan "freedom, equality and brotherhood," the French management system is, nonetheless, both elitist and autocratic. In France, businesses and the civil service are run by elites who are graduates of the *grandes écoles* (elite schools), which produce a high proportion of the best brains who lead business enterprises and civil service in France.

French organizations are highly centralized and hierarchical, and decisions are made at the very apex (Phillips 1994). French managers see their work as an intellectual challenge, requiring the remorseless application of individual brainpower. The design of French organizations reflects and reinforces the cerebral manager. France has a long tradition of centralization, of hierarchical rigidity, and of individual respect for authority. French company law resembles the country's constitution in conferring power on a single person. At the helm of French companies is the *president-directeur-general* (PDG), who decides, executes, and controls company policy. The PDG is what Australian, British, and U.S. companies would regard as chairperson of the board and chief executive rolled into one, or the German *Vorstandsvorsitzender* (chairperson of the executive committee) plus operating executive. The PDG is not answerable to anyone. Votes are rare; and if a proposal is put to vote, it is tantamount to a vote of no confidence in the PDG (Barsoux & Lawrence 1991).

The French chief executive's status is attributed on grounds of family, age, education, and professional qualifications preferably from one of the grandes écoles with an emphasis on oratorical ability and mastery of French language. Unlike companies in the United States, in French companies, such managers are allowed to accumulate all the responsibilities they feel capable of handling (Barsoux & Lawrence 1991). They have less specialization than their counterparts in the United States, Britain, and Australia; but they generally have a wider horizon and grasp of issues facing their company. While mistakes by German executives are not easily forgiven and American managers are summarily fired, there is a high tolerance in French companies of blunders on the part of managers. French managers who relish the art of commanding are encouraged to excel in their work by the very intensity of expectation on the part of their subordinates. French managers debate issues at length with their staff, often examining all aspects in detail. Their decisions, however, are usually made alone. If the chief executive's views are known in advance, it is not easy to reverse them—or to know about them. Information is not allowed to filter down below certain levels in French organizations (Rodrigues 1996). Nevertheless, French managers have a great affinity for written communication that reinforces a formality that permeates their relationships (Fatehi 1996).

## United States

American managers typify a free enterprise economy coupled with a frontier spirit: They are competitive, assertive, goal and action oriented, confident, vigorous, optimistic, friendly and informal, and value innovation. American managers aspire to the highest level of society through their own accomplishments and hard work (Fatehi 1996). They possess a strong work ethic and are very time conscious in just about everything they do (Harris & Moran 1991). Management in the United States is about efficiency; and there is a great deal of competition in evidence within American organizations. American managers deeply value individual freedom above the welfare of the company and their first interest is furthering their own careers. Control for American management is very explicit; people know precisely what to control and how to do it. Responsibility for a task is assigned by a manager to an individual employee (Hodgetts & Luthans 2000). Thus, leadership in America means getting things done, improving the standard of living, making money for oneself, one's firm, and its shareholders. With status accorded almost exclusively based on demonstrable achievement (Hall & Hall 1987), American managers and their staff are usually motivated by monetary incentive to perform at a high level. The pace of life and decision making is fast in American organizations. Leaders in American organizations are expected to help subordinates solve problems. For that reason, there is a democratic style of leadership prevailing within the American organizations. Although, it should be noted that ultimate decision-making, in many aspects of organizational life, still rests with the American managers.

## Asia

Asian cultural values are highly influential on every aspect of structure, organization, and behavior in the business enterprises of China, Taiwan, Hong Kong, Singapore, Japan, and Korea. Much of business practice is still centered around Confucian social philosophy or its influence. Organizational leadership is expected to demonstrate virtues, namely, humanity, patience, integrity, compassion, and humility. Based on Confucian philosophy, a leader's authority is sanctioned by becoming worthy of respect and providing a good role model for subordinates. Chinese values emphasize self-effacing behavior and propriety that fosters trust and confidence. Although, national differences account for variations in the concepts of leadership, there is a clearly discernible Eastern model. Virtuous behavior, protection of the weak, harmony, loyalty, moderation and calmness, conflict avoidance, face saving, and didactic roles are part and parcel of Asian leadership makeup. Asian ideal leadership represents men (and women) of higher education achievement and of sound morality. Japanese and Korean business leaders flaunt qualifications such as university and professional connections more than family name or wealth. Many of the traditional Japanese companies are classic models of Confucian theory, where paternalistic attitudes to employees and their dependents are top-down and to a greater degree than in China itself. In the decision-making process, the Japanese leader typically employs consensus in building a system of reverential inquiry about a superior's intention (Hofstede 1980b; Sarros & Woodman 1993; Fatehi 1996). Authority is also considered benign, and the benevolence attributed to the leader permeates organizations from Singapore to Tokyo as well as Thailand, Malaysia, and Indonesia with only slight variations in degree (Hofstede 1980b).

The Asian leader is expected to diffuse any disruptive behavior within an organization and, like a family head, infuse employees with standards for socially accepted behavior that will not prompt confrontation (Holt & Wigginton 2002). There is, for that reason, a considerable degree of emphasis on social harmony by the Asian managers at the work place.

## *Summary*

In this chapter, a broad range of leadership theories were discussed, and it was established that leadership is the art of influencing others to accomplish goals. Effective styles of leadership vary and will vary as much in the context of different cultures. While managers in all countries must lead, motivate, and make decisions, the way in which they approach these core managerial responsibilities remains, in part, determined by their own cultural dimension and that of their work environment. The questions raised about leadership are universal, but the solutions remain culturally specific. The approaches to leadership have been divided into two main types that are universalistic and contingency. A number of the leadership theories and models were advanced over time, but their application remains to be seen in the context of culturally diverse workforces.

Leadership behaviors are also translated into different leadership styles including authoritarian, paternalistic, and participative. Within the frameworks and the cultural contexts, various societies and their organizations have varying conceptualizations and styles of leadership. The more styles a leader exhibits, the better. Leaders who master four or more leadership styles have a greater chance of being effective in their organizational context. And the most effective leaders switch flexibly among the leadership styles appropriate to each prevailing situation and cultural dimension across the globe. Finally, there is no universally agreed definition of leadership that can capture every aspect of effective leadership. International managers should develop high level knowledge of cross-cultural dimensions that affect their managerial and leadership responsibility taking what they can from the different theories and styles presented here and prescriptively applied.

## Critical Discussion Questions

1. Good management is all about leadership. Is this true or false? Explain your answer.

2. What are the essential qualities of a good leader in a multinational company?

3. "Transformational approach to leadership reflects today's societal trends." Is this true or false? Explain your answer.

4. "Good leaders are born not made." Is this true or false? Explain your answer.

5. "The best leader integrates variety of leadership styles depending upon the situation." Do you agree with this statement? If yes, why?

6. What does cultural relativity approach to leadership advocate?

7. What are the implications of cultural relativity of leadership for international managers?

8. Compare and contrast leadership styles between French and American leaders.

9. "Asian approach to leadership is largely bound by Confucian values of the society." Expand on this with your own research.

10. Cultural contingency approach to leadership is appropriate when managing a business enterprise internationally. Is this true or false? Explain your answer.

# Applications

## Experiential

Interview the manager(s) of a multinational company in your home country with reference to his or her leadership style practiced. Try to compare and contrast his or her leadership style(s) to the cultural values prevailing in your country.

## Internet

Conduct secondary research on the leadership philosophies and styles of a business leader and a political leader of your choice (such as Ghandi), using Internet search engines such as Google and Alta Vista as well as databases available at your business school. Critically compare and contrast them. Discuss your findings.

# References

Adler, N. (1997). *International dimensions of organizational behavior* (3rd ed.). Cincinnati, OH: South-Western College.

Adler, N.J. & Bartholomew, S. (1992). Academic and professional communities of discourse: Generating knowledge on transnational human resource management. *Journal of International Business Studies, 23* (3), 551–569.

Barsoux, J.L., & Lawrence, P. (1991). The Making of a French manager. *Harvard Business Review, 69* (4), 58–60.

Basi, R.S. (1998). *Conceptional management: A global perspective.* New York: International Business Press 30 (1983). 241–263

Bass, B.M. (1985). *Leadership and performance beyond expectations.* Mahwah, NJ: Lawrence E. Erlbaum Associates.

Bass, B.M. (1998). *Transformational leadership.* Mahwah, N J: Lawrence E. Erlbaum Associates.

Bennis, W. & Nanus, B. (1985). *Leaders: The strategies for taking charge.* New York: Harper & Row.

Beyer, J.M. (1999). Taming and promoting charisma to change organizations. *Leadership* Quarterly, *10* (2), 307–330.

Blake, R.R. & Mouton, J.S. (1964). *The managerial grid.* Houston, TX: Gulf.

Burns, J.M. (1978). *Leadership*. New York: Harper & Row.

Cohen, A., Fink, S., Gadow, H., & Josefowitz, N. (1992). *Effective behavior in organization* (5th ed.). Homewood, IL: Dow Jones Irwin.

Collins, R. & McLaughlin, (1996). *Effective management* (2nd ed.). Sydney: CCH Australia.

Collins, R. (ed.) (1993). *Effective management*. Sydney: CCH International.

Fatehi, K. (1996). *International management: A cross culture and functional perspective*. Upper Saddle River, NJ: Prentice Hall.

Fiedler, F.E. (1967). *A theory of leadership effectiveness*. New York: McGraw-Hill.

Fulk, J. & Wendler, E.R. (1982). *Dimensionality of leader-subordinate interactions: a path-goal investigation. Organisational Behaviour and Human Performance, 30*, 241–264.

Fulop, L. & Linstead, S. (Eds.). (1999). *Management: A Critical Text*. South Yarra, Australia Macmillan Education.

Gerstner, C.R. & Day, D.V. (1994). Cross-cultural comparison of *leadership* prototypes. *Leadership Quarterly, 5,* 121–134.

Goleman, D. (2000). Leadership that gets results. *Harvard Business Review, 78* (2), 78–90.

Gregersen, H., Morrison, A.J., & Black, J.S. (1998). Developing leaders for the global frontier. *Sloan Management Review, 40* (1), 21–32.

Haire, M., Ghiselli, E., & Porter, L. (1963). Cultural patterns in the role of the manager. *Industrial Relations, 2* (2), 95–117.

Hall, E.T. & Hall, M.R. (1987). *Understanding cultural differences*. Garden City, New York: Doubleday.

Harris, P. & Moran, R. (1991). *Managing cultural differences* (3rd ed.). Houston, TX: Gulf.

Hartog, D., Deanne, N., House, R.J., Hanges, P.J., Ruiz-Quintanilla, S.A., and Dorfman, P.W. (1999). Culture specific and cross-culturally generalizable implicit *leadership* theories: Are attributes of charismatic/transformational leadership universally endorsed? *Leadership Quarterly*, 10 (2), 219–238.

Hellriegel, D. & Slocum, J. (1996). *Management* (7th ed.). Cincinnati, OH: South-Western College.

Hodgetts, R.M. & Luthans, F. (2000). *International Management*. New York: McGraw-Hill.

Hofstede, G. (1980a). Motivation, leadership and organization: Do American theories apply abroad? *Organizational Dynamics*, 9 (2), 42–63.

Hofstede, G. (1980b). *Culture's consequences: International differences in work-related values*. Beverly Hills, CA: Sage.

Holt, D.H. & Wigginton, K.W., (2002). *International Management* (2nd ed.). Orlando, FL: Harcourt College.

House, F.J. (1971). A path goal theory of leadership effectiveness. *Administrative Science Quarterly*, 16, 321–338.

House, R.J. & Aditya, R.N. (1997). The social scientific study of leadership: Quo vadis? *Journal of Management*, 23, 409–473.

House, R.J. (1977). A 1976 theory of charismatic leadership. In J.G. Hunt & L.L. Larson (Eds.), *Leadership: The cutting edge* (pp. 189–207). Carbondale, IL: Southern Illinois University Press.

House, R.J., Hanges, P.J., Ruiz-Quintanilla, S., Dorfman, P., Javidan, M., Dickson, M., & Associates. (1999). Cultural influences on leadership and organizations. In W. H. Mobley (Ed.), *Advances in global leadership* (Vol. 1, pp. 171–233). Greenwich, CT: JAI.

Jackson, T. (1993). *Organizational behavior in international management.* London: Butterworth Heinemann.

Kirkpatrick S. & Locke, E.A. (1991). Leadership: do traits matter? *Academy of Management Executive*, 5 (2), 48–60

Kotter, J. (1990). *A force for change.* New York: McMillan.

Lewis, R. (1996). Take the "big" out of big projects: Break them into manageable chunks. *Infoworld*, 18 (20), 24.

Lord R.G., & Maher, K.J. (1991). *Leadership and information processing.* London: Routledge.

McGregor, D. (1960). *The human side of enterprise.* New York: McGraw Hill.

McLaughlin, Y. (1993). Corporate leadership: putting it together. In R. Collins (Ed.), *Effective Management.* Sydney: CCH International.

Mole, J. (1995). *Mind your manners: Managing business cultures in Europe.* London: Nicholas Brealey.

Phillips, N. (1994). *Managing international teams.* Burr Ridge, Il: Richard D. Irwin.

Robbins, S., Bergman, R., & Stagg, I. (2000). *Management* (2nd ed.). Upper Saddle River, NJ: Prentice Hall.

Roddick, A. (1991). *Body and soul.* New York: Crown.

Rodrigues, C. (1996). *International management: A cultural approach.* St. Paul, MN: West.

Sarros, J.D. & Woodman, D.S. (1993). Leadership in Australia and its organizational outcomes. *Leadership and Organizational Journal*, 4 (4), 3–9.

Sethi, S.P., Namiki, N., & Swanson, C.L. (1984). *The false promise of the Japanese miracle.* Boston: Pitman.

Weiss, J. (1996). *Organizational behavior and change: Managing diversity, cross-cultural dynamics, and ethics.* St. Paul, MN: West.

# Chapter 9

*Motivating Across Cultures*

## LEARNING OBJECTIVES

*After reading this chapter, you should be able to:*
- *Understand the importance of motivation to organizational performance.*
- *Describe different theories of human motivation.*
- *Understand how human motivation differs across cultures.*
- *Understand how motivational tools are applied within human resources management practices worldwide.*

*A gentleman understands what is moral. A base man understands what is advantageous or profitable.*

—*Confucian proverb*

*To get anything done here, the manager has to be more of an instructor, teacher, or father figure than a boss.*

—*Robert Hoskins on Mexico*

# OVERVIEW

Motivating culturally diverse human resources is becoming increasingly significant as more firms set up operations overseas in the global business environment. Similarly, firms must also motivate an increasingly diverse workforce in their home operations as well. In both these domestic and international settings, motivation has linkage to productivity, creativity, job turn over, absenteeism, and the like—all of which are crucial for effective management. In this chapter motivation is discussed in light of its differing cultural orientations with the aim of providing an understanding of human motivation across cultures and within organizational life. The motivational theories introduced in this chapter include Maslow's Hierarchy of Needs, Herzberg's Two-Factor Theory, McClelland's Achievement Motivation Theory, and Hofstede's cultural dimensions.

# MOTIVATION DEFINED

Research has provided us with a number of ways to define human motivation:

- "Motivation is a psychological process through which unsatisfied wants or needs lead to drives that are aimed at goals or incentives" (Hodgetts & Luthans 2000, 372).

- "Motivation is defined as the process through which behavior is mobilized to reach certain goals" (Fatehi 1996, 229).

- Motivation is an assumed force operating inside an individual inducing him or her to choose one action or another (Hofstede 1991).

- "Motivation is process which energizes and directs behavior" (Avery & Baker 1990, 368).

# UNIVERSALITY OF MOTIVATION

There is a widely held view among management scholars and social scientists that the human motivation process is universal in the sense that all people, irrespective of their geographic locations, are motivated to pursue the goals they value. However, the motivation process itself and the goals that are pursued are influenced by the respective national cultures. Research shows that money motivates American workers, whereas, respect and power motivate Japanese workers. Latin American workers are motivated by family connections (Hodgetts & Luthans 2000). In Norway and Sweden workers are motivated by improvements to their quality of life such as paid vacations or memberships to a prestigious club. South African workers are motivated by welfare of the community. For Chinese workers, group affiliation and social harmony are more important. As can be seen in these random examples, one cannot assume that a motivator that works for the members of one culture will work for another culture. Thus, it is important that international business managers find motivators that reflect the cultural values and priorities held by their workforce with respect to culture in order to improve performance and productivity (Mead 1998).

# APPLYING ANGLO THEORIES

The study of human motivation and the various kinds of recommendations for management that arise from them reflect the Anglo-American culture of their researchers. Their theories all tend to show the following emphases:

- Masculinity.
- A Protestant work ethic.
- Individualism.
- Narrow power distances.
- A low need to avoid uncertainty.
- A high need for continual streams of explicit information (Hofstede 1991; Mead 1998).

There is no doubt as to the value of the motivational research that has been carried out in the United States and in other similarly developed societies. Nevertheless, the utility of its application in the management and motivation of workforces with cultural dimensions that differ from the cultural context of this pioneering research and its results can be highly questionable. Different cultures have different priorities that do not fit Anglo-American models—and the members of these different cultures typically do not abandon their own cultural priorities and values.

## Cross-cultural Comparison of Mainstream Motivational Theories

Human motivation can be explained in terms of two distinct categories: *content* and *process*. Content theories explain motivation in terms of what arouses, energizes, or initiates employee behavior. Process theories of motivation explain how employee behavior is initiated, redirected, and halted. Much of the research conducted on human resources has been content-orientated. It examines motivation in more general terms and is useful in developing a composite picture of employee motivation in a particular country or region. Process theories are more sophisticated and tend to focus on individual behavior in specific settings—and they have less value to the study of employee motivation in an international setting (Hodgetts & Luthans 2000). For this reason, we will now examine three leading content theories of motivation in the following sections and relate them to the needs of motivating workforces in different cultures: Maslow's Hierarchy of Needs, Herzberg's Two-Factor Motivation theory, and McClelland's Achievement Motivation theory.

## Maslow's Hierarchy of Needs

Abraham Maslow identified five basic human needs, which are hierarchical in nature, that motivate people to meet them. Lower needs have to be met before a person moves to the next higher levels of needs—and acts to fulfill them. Therefore, lower-level needs have to be satisfied before higher-level needs can be motivators (Maslow 1954). This principle is shown in the five levels of Maslow's classic figure depicting his hierarchy of needs:

- *Level 1: Physiological (existence) Needs.* These needs consist of food, clothing, and other physical needs such as water and air. Translated into work motivation, these physiological needs can be addressed through wages and salaries paid by the firms.

- *Level 2: Safety and Security Needs:* Safety and security needs are characterized by the desire for security, stability, and the absence of pain. Organizations tend to address these employee needs through providing good working conditions, such as workers compensation, medical insurance, retirement plans, holiday pay, and other kinds of benefits.

- *Level 3: Belonging and Social Needs.* These include the need to socialize and the desire to feel wanted by others including family and friends. Organizations tend to fulfill employees' social needs by creating an organizational structure that fosters teamwork and a high degree of lateral and vertical communication across the organization among its employees.

- *Level 4: Esteem Needs.* This involves the need for power and status. This comes about as a result of an individual wanting to feel important and achieve public recognition. Viewed from an organizational context, promotions, awards, titles, company car, expense accounts, and praise and recognition for a job well done from his or her manager tend to fulfill this need.

- *Level 5: Self Actualization and Achievement Needs.* This represents an individual's ultimate desire to reach one's full potential by becoming everything one is capable of becoming. Viewed from an organizational context, this may not be a promotion, but, instead, may involve mastering one's environment as well as setting and achieving attainable goals (Maslow 1954; Hodgetts & Luthans 2000).

### Applying Maslow's Hierarchy of Needs Across Cultures

Maslow' Hierarchy of Needs theory has been the basis for several studies conducted in different parts of the world, with the intent of examining its applicability and any recommendations for management across different cultures. Most concluded that a motivator that applied to culture A was unlikely to succeed in culture B. This is because the priorities in culture A would be different from culture B. Research found that less-developed countries had similar priorities that differed from those of developed nations and which reflected their stage of economic growth. Managers in Australia and Papua New Guinea both regarded self-actualization as their most important need. However, unlike Australians, the Papua New Guineans were most dissatisfied with their levels of security and placed security needs higher than autonomy needs. This corresponds to studies conducted in Argentina, Chile, India, Malawi, and Kenya (Onedo 1991; Mead 1998). Several studies in the People's Republic of China, Hong Kong, Taiwan, and Singapore as well as other Southeast Asian societies have revealed a need hierarchy that is dramatically different from Maslow's hierarchy of needs. For example, Hofstede and Bond (1984) found more importance for social factors based on Confucian philosophy in Chinese societies, where loyalty to one's referent group and obedience to one's social order were prevalent within their hierarchical social systems. In many Asian cultures, the prevalence of self-effacement often allows individuals to deny basic physiological needs if their sacrifices serve the larger needs of families and like referent groups. Self-actualization does not imply achievement in the Western sense, but rather it can mean many different things, from self-control to humility, which is seen as a virtue. Validation studies by Redding and Richardson (1986), in which they compared East Asian and Chinese managers with managers in the United States, support the foregoing.

Researchers such as Nevis (1983) have suggested modifying Maslow's hierarchy to reflect needs in the Asian cultures. Nevis proposes four levels of needs in a Chinese hierarchy, in which the lowest order need is (1) *belonging,* a sense of social acceptance; followed by (2) *physiological needs;* then a higher order need of (3) *safety,* that is security for self and family; and finally (4) *self-actualization* defined in collective terms of contribution or service to society. In Africa, where collective cultures predominate, the motivation of employees varies from the individualist cultures of North America or Australia. A strong sense of community-mindedness is present in East African nations. Thus "the community dominates all aspects of African thought. Dances are communal and worship is communal. Property was held communally before the colonial era and there are attempts today to reinstate that practice. This inbuilt bias toward the community means that individualism is always seen as a deviance" (Mutiso 1974, 35).

### Herzberg's Two-Factor Theory of Motivation

Herzberg (1966) conceived motivation as two distinct sets of variables: *hygiene factors* and *motivators.* According to his Two-Factor theory, if the "hygiene" factors are absent, the employee will be dissatisfied; but their presence does not guarantee satisfaction. Only by providing the "motivators" can satisfaction be achieved. The hygiene—job context—factors are made up of wages, security, working conditions, company policy and administration, and relationships with supervisors and peers. These hygiene factors are very much similar to Maslow's lower order needs; and they are considered extrinsic factors—those outside of the job itself. Motivators—job content factors—however, include intrinsic value of the work and they are characterized by achievement, responsibility, and recognition. Herzberg's motivator factors are, in turn, compatible with Maslow's higher order needs; and they are considered intrinsic factors. The Two-Factor theory has received criticism for a number of reasons (Hodgetts & Luthans 2000; Fatehi 1996; Mead 1998):

- That the distinction between hygiene factors and motivators is a matter of degree and not an absolute difference—and international operations can further obscure the distinction.

- That job-context and job-content factors may not be independent or mutually exclusive elements. Herzberg's model regards advancement and achievement as separate aspects of job content, yet they are often interdependent in practice.

- That Herzberg's classifications are not uniformly predictable in the nature or intensity of their effect. Younger workers likely value job context factors, such as salaries and status, more than established workers do, although job content factors such as advancement and growth retain their importance. In contrast, older workers value security, relationships, and the intrinsic rewards associated with their jobs. Therefore, a factor that may be a source of dissatisfaction in one person may motivate another.

### Global Application of Herzberg's Two-Factor Theory

When Herzberg's Two-Factor theory is taken out of its original Anglo-American cultural context and used for the workforces of other cultures, it has been shown to have limited application. Kanungo and Wright (1983) concluded that the orientations and values that managers hold with respect to job outcomes are, to a large extent, culturally determined,

---

**EXAMPLE 9-1** What Motivates a Person? A New Hotel in Tahiti

A major hotel chain chose to develop a new hotel in Tahiti. The developer contracted with a Tahitian skilled in carving large wooden totems. The hotel desired a number of these totems to provide the site with "atmosphere." The Tahitian quoted a price for carving the first totem and then higher and higher prices for each succeeding totem. This, of course, astonished the hotel developer, who asserted that this was "no way to do business." The developer did not see why, as in Western economic practice, a quantity of items entailed a discount rather than an increase in price for each item. The Tahitian artisan, equally mystified, tried to explain: "Carving the first totem is fun. Carving each additional totem becomes less fun."

Source: Adapted from *International Dimensions of Organizational Behavior*, 4th edition by Adler, © 2002. Reprinted with permission of South-Western, a division of Thomson Learning: www.thomsonrights.com. Fax: 800-730-2215.

---

particularly with respect to the relative importance of intrinsic and extrinsic job outcomes. Their study showed that in France job context factors such as security and fringe benefits were more highly valued. Meanwhile, Hofstede (1991) pointed out that Herzberg's Two-Factor theory fits an environment in which power distances are small and uncertainty avoidance is weak. Neither dependence on more powerful superiors nor a need for rules is supposed to be functional or necessary to make people act. This is characteristic of an individualist culture. In the societies with a large power distance, dependence on more powerful people is a basic need that can be a real motivator. This can be applied to a collectivist culture (Hofstede 1991).

## McClelland's Achievement Motivation Theory

David C. McClelland, in his classic book, *The Achieving Society*, traces different dominant motivation patterns in different countries. As a result, he distinguished three types of motives: (1) achievement, (2) affiliation (i.e., associating with other people), and (3) power (1961):

- *Need for achievement* is defined as a desire to take on tasks and to accomplish them in a satisfactory manner. It characterizes individuals who enjoy challenges and thrive on stimulating environment. They prefer independent responsibility and autonomy to pursue self-determined goals, and they garner strength from constructive feedback. McClelland provides the profile of high achiever as someone who:
  - Takes personal responsibility for finding solution to problems.
  - Has a preference for taking moderate risks (does not like insufficient rewards).
  - Has a need for immediate and frequent feedback on performance so as to modify his or her actions.

- *Need for power* refers to a sense of desiring influence and control over events and, in particular, responsibility over the people. Individuals who score high on need for power are comfortable with executive positions where they can make decisions in highly competitive situations. They place high value on status and advancement opportunities. Such behavior often suggests an autocratic mindset, but a high power orientation also suggests strong leadership behavior and a willingness to accept unilateral responsibility. Notable is the fact that unlike achievement, the need for power is not associated with creativity or entrepreneurship, yet many successful new ventures have resulted when power-focused people pursued risky enterprises.

- *Need for affiliation* is characterized in terms of social norms. Need for affiliation is a desire for belonging; and participating with other people, creating friendships, and seeking social interactions are all part of the need for affiliation. People who score high on need for affiliation display aversion to risk and discomfort with managerial responsibilities. They seldom become involved in difficult decisions such as enforcing policies or disciplining subordinates, but they work extremely well in egalitarian situations and team environments (Holt 1998).

Overall, Achievement Motivation Theory holds that individuals have a need to attain success and reach objectives. Like Maslow's higher order needs and Herzberg's motivator factors, the need for achievement is learned. McClelland made a significant contribution in understanding human motivation and how it can be understood by managers concerned about achieving high labor productivity and job satisfaction—that is, what questions need to be asked:

- What energizes employees to behave in a productive way?
- What directs and channels their behavior to accomplish organizational goals?
- How do organizations maintain desired behavior?
- What factors in employees and in their environment reinforce or discourage them from following a particular course of action? (Steers & Porter 1975; Adler 1997).

McClelland's model, however, like Maslow' Hierarchy of Needs, is a product of Anglo-American culture. In choosing an individualist achievement motive, as Hofstede points out (1980; 1991), McClelland has elevated a largely American set of values to a universal one for economic success that may not be applicable to collectivist cultures. Hofstede went on to argue that in individualist culture, achievement motive is derived from individual achievement "doing one's own thing." Individual personality in the West is seen as a separate entity and, for that reason, an ultimate aspiration is self-actualization by every individual. In a collectivist culture members derive self-actualization from contributing to the success of the in-group. The idea of "doing one's own thing," for example, is not translatable into Chinese collectivist culture. In more feminine societies, in which uncertainty avoidance is strong and belongingness (human relationships) prevail, safety and security are needs ranked above other needs; whereas in a masculine culture self-esteem dominates (Hofstede 1991).

## EMPIRICAL EVIDENCE FOR DIFFERING MOTIVATIONS ACROSS CULTURAL FRONTIERS

As we now know, workforces in different cultures have different needs and motivations for their work. England (1986) found that employees' work goals and motivation varied in Germany, Japan, and the United States in responding to questions about the nature of their work and what aspects of it was important to them (see Exhibit 9-1).

| Exhibit 9-1 Comparative Work Goals for German, Japanese, and American Workers | | | |
|---|---|---|---|
| **Work Goals** | **Germany** | **Japan** | **USA** |
| Interesting work | 3 | 2 | 1 |
| Good pay | 1 | 5 | 2 |
| Good interpersonal relations | 4 | 6 | 7 |
| Good job security | 2 | 4 | 3 |
| A good match between you and your job | 5 | 1 | 4 |
| A lot of autonomy | 8 | 3 | 8 |
| Opportunity to learn | 9 | 7 | 5 |
| Variety in terms of job content | 6 | 9 | 6 |
| Convenient work hours | 6 | 8 | 9 |
| Good physical working conditions | 11 | 10 | 11 |
| Good opportunity for promotion and personal growth | 10 | 11 | 10 |

Source: Reprinted from *Comparative Work Goals: German, Japanese, and American* adapted from England, G.W., *National Work Meanings and Patterns: Constraints on Management Action,* 4(3) 176-184, © 1986, with permission from Elsevier.

# DESIGNING MOTIVATORS FOR INTERNATIONAL HUMAN RESOURCE MANAGEMENT

The challenge for the human resource (HR) manager responsible for recruiting, retaining, and developing a workforce in a business that hires from a culturally diverse pool of individuals as it does business in the contemporary global economy is to discover what motivators elicit the desired productivity and job satisfaction. Hofstede's model (1984; 1991) provides a basic conceptual tool for predicting motivations in different cultural contexts for HR managers to consider before developing appropriate incentive programs for employees. This tool is surveyed in the following sections. (This discussion also includes other kinds of managers who are also stakeholders in motivated and productive workforces that are marked by cultural diversity.)

## Individualism versus Collectivism Dimension

The more collectivist a culture, the greater the degree to which the individual is motivated by group membership and group decisions. Financial rewards as a motivator are more effective when promised as an obvious benefit to the group. Since opportunities to belong to a supportive group are valued more highly, it is important for global managers operating in such a cultural context to devise a reward system that rewards group performance rather than individual worker's performance. By contrast, in individualist cultures, in which opportunities for individual promotion, growth, and autonomy are valued more highly, more attention needs to be paid by the global manager to individual motivational needs to stimulate high level individual work performance.

### Uncertainty Avoidance Dimension

For Hofstede (1991), designing permanent jobs should be a priority by global managers in a high uncertainty-avoidance culture where job security is valued more highly by the workforce—and is, for that reason, a motivator. In a low uncertainty-avoidance culture, the global HR manager needs to design, as part of a motivational incentive program, a job with variety as the motivator.

### The Femininity versus Masculinity Dimension

In feminine cultures, such as Scandinavian countries, quality of life, including relationships between people, is more significant than money. HR managers can design shorter and convenient working hours and paid holidays for workers in such a culture so as to get the best out of them in terms of motivation and performance. By contrast, members of a masculine culture are more materialistic and enjoy the game of competition. Here HR managers need to pay particular attention to individualized incentive program as a way of stimulating a high employee productivity level.

### Power Distance Dimension

Cultures that have a narrow power distance tend to value cooperation with peers and, as such, HR managers may need to create organizational ethos and processes that will increase opportunities for employees to cooperate with each other while managers themselves need to maintain a consultative decision making process. On the other hand, high power-distance cultures value personal loyalty shown by superiors to subordinates. In this instance, managers may need to cultivate loyalty and paternalism with their employees as well as provide more explicit instructions in order for employees to follow.

In Mexico, where a rigid hierarchy of power prevails, subordinates are rewarded according to their submissive behavior and personal service (allegiance) to authority figures. Managers are expected to make paternalistic gestures to protect their employees and to ensure equitable compensation without singling out individual employees. This collective-reward-based system affects Mexican workers' motivation to work productively (Holt 1998).

### Motivators: Some National Preferences

An international study by Sirota and Greenwood (1971) came up with the following findings describing major differences in motivation found among cultural groups:

- Workers in English-speaking countries ranked higher on individual achievement and lower on the desire for security.
- Workers in French-speaking countries, although similar to the English-speaking countries, gave greater importance to security and somewhat less to challenging work.
- Workers in Northern European countries expressed less interest in "getting ahead" and work recognition goals and put more emphasis on job accomplishment; in addition, they showed more concern for people and less for the organization as a whole. It was important for them that the job did not interfere with their personal lives.

- Workers in Latin American and Southern European countries found individual achievement somewhat less important. Southern Europeans placed the highest emphasis on job security, while both groups of countries emphasized fringe benefits.

- German workers ranked security and fringe benefits high and were the highest on "getting ahead."

- Workers in Japan, although low on advancement, also ranked second highest on challenge and lowest on autonomy, with a strong emphasis on good working conditions and a friendly working environment.

# MOTIVATION APPLIED GLOBALLY

The content theories discussed previously provide insight into how managers motivate their employees to get the best out of them in terms of high productivity level and job satisfaction. Other motivator categories that have received considerable attention in the literature are money, job enrichment movement, job design, and work centrality. The following sections survey these.

## Monetary Incentives

Monetary rewards play an important role in fulfilling both physiological and psychological human needs. Money enables individuals to purchase the necessities of life, including food and clothing and other items that meet physiological needs. Money can also buy prestigious cars and high-class residential homes and the like. Earning a substantial amount of money justifies a sense of self-worth, which also reflects our sense of self-esteem and high achievement, an essential ingredient for meeting psychological needs at workplace. As McClelland notes:

> The person with high needs works hard anyway provided there is an opportunity of achieving something. He is interested in money rewards or profits primarily because of the feedback they give him as to how well he is doing. Money is not the incentive to effort but rather the measure of its success to the entrepreneurs (1961, 65).

According to Mead (1998), increasing pay is not the only possible motivator of effective behavior and often not the most valued motivator. However, so much emphasis is placed upon pay raises by both employees and employers because monetary incentives are the easiest to specify and quantify—and the easiest to administer. Kovach (1987) showed that to motivate employees, monetary rewards may be complemented by the following motivational incentives:

- Encouraging promotion and growth within the organization showing appreciation of the work done.
- Giving the employee a feeling of being in on things.
- Improving working conditions.
- Showing personal loyalty to employees.
- Using tact when disciplining, improving interpersonal relationships.
- Improving job security.
- Improving the quality of work.
- Giving variety in work; where this is desired.

• Providing autonomy in work-where this is desired.

The foregoing incentives and, particularly, monetary rewards are generally applicable to individualist cultures, where individual achievement and materialism are highly valued (Hofstede 1980, 1991). However, it is instructive to note that research revealed that both workers in less-developed countries and workers in developed countries—during economically distressed periods such as recession—attach more importance to monetary rewards including good pay, benefits, and security factors than to promotion or recognition rewards (Westwood 1992).

## The Job Enrichment Movement

The Job Enrichment Movement emerged in response to increasing specialization and a division of labor that has degraded the experience of work by creating mundane and repetitive task environments. Although specialization and the division of labor led to a dramatic increase in productivity, especially in factories, it has over the years also led to a decline in worker motivation and more importantly job satisfaction—which, of course, can undermine the very improvements in production that had been achieved. The managerial philosophy of job enrichment, which includes such strategies as job rotation, job enlargement, and job design, came about to stimulate motivation and improve the quality of working life.

### Job Rotation

*Job rotation* involves planning the employee's time so that he or she performs a variety of tasks and thereby reduces the boredom associated with repetitive work. This job rotation system is also designed to increase the skill base of employees, thus enabling firms to maximize and optimize their human resources in terms of internal flexibility and competencies, labor productivity, and labor mobility. This is of particular significance to global managers who want to increase the talent base of employees in a culturally diverse workforce while improving the relational skills needed to interact with them. The individual employee, it is hoped, will perceive job rotation as a way to enhance job security, status, and self-esteem through growth and job recognition of achievements (Holt & Wigginton 2002).

Job rotation is unlikely to succeed among workforces that have high uncertainty avoidance and among those marked by a high power distance or where group membership is significant such as the collectivist societies in China and Mexico.

### Job Enlargement

*Job enlargement* involves reorganizing the job specification so that all the tasks required to produce one unit are performed by an individual worker (Mead 1998). According to Herzberg (1966), as an individual employee gains responsibility for a broad new range of tasks, this added responsibility should enhance motivators such as status, job security, and self-esteem. However, this result does not always come out (Mead 1998). Employees may view an enlargement program as an effort to get them to do more work without corresponding increases in benefits. Some societies value job specialization and its members may view job enlargement as a loss of identity. Kanungo and Wright (1983) maintain that in some instances job enlargement is seen as manipulation by management to break down group identity or devalue individual roles within the group. Job enlargement, essentially, is a product of individualist culture that may have difficulty gaining acceptance in a collectivist culture with a strong focus on group identity and a commensurate reward mechanism.

### Job Design

*Job design* consists of a job's content, the methods that are used on the job, and the way in which the job relates to others in the organization. Job design is different for the same type of work depending on the quality of work life, which is, in turn, determined by cultural profile of the country (Hodgetts & Luthans 2000). For example, assembly line workers in Japan can work a rapid pace for hours, where they have no control over their activities. Japanese society, having high power distance and a strong uncertainty avoidance while being low on individualism, emphasizes job security and the group success and, therefore, individual risk taking is discouraged. In Japan, workers are accustomed to taking orders from superiors, and they have very little say in what actually goes on in the organization (Hodgetts & Luthans 2000).

By contrast, in Swedish workforces, which have low uncertainty avoidance, employees perform jobs at a more relaxed pace, and they are more in control over work activities. Given their low distance power culture, Swedish managers display consultative decision-making and further encourage workers to take risks and decisions. At the same time, interpersonal relations among workers and managers are emphasized because of their more feminine culture.

The challenge for global managers is to adjust job design to meet the motivational needs of the host country vis-à-vis its cultural values.

## Performance Evaluation

Many cultures are not particularly concerned with performance evaluation as it is understood by Western managers. In China, for example, there is distrust in performance appraisal because of its ideological principles and *guanxi* (Sergeant & Frenkel 1998). Performance evaluations are complicated by different cultural values and attitudes. An attempt to evaluate performance of individuals in a Japanese subsidiary will encounter resistance in a culture that values group efforts above individual achievement.

## The Role of Feedback in Individualist and Collectivist societies

Some studies point out that U.S. respondents desire more success feedback and perceive direct feedback better than Japanese or Chinese employees. There is a difference between Chinese and Japanese in communicating negative feedback. In Japan it should be done in confidence; but in China it is done in public, because subtle criticism is seen as sneakiness. This, of course, suggests that members of individualist societies seek more feedback about their performance than do the members of collectivist societies (Bailey, et al. 1997). This is because of the need of individualists who want to distinguish themselves as strong, independent persons. Successful feedback is more important for individualists to protect their self-esteem. Feedback about failure, for them, could prove quite demotivational. Thus, in an individualist society, to accept credit for oneself and distance oneself from failure is a norm. In a collectivist society, however, it is norm to accept failure and distance oneself from accepting credit for one's success. To act otherwise may be perceived as deviant. This might explain why American workers seek feedback; the question being often asked of their respective managers is "How am I doing?" This is in contrast to workers from a collectivist culture such as China or Japan who might ask the question from their superiors: "How are we doing?"

# MOTIVATION AND GLOBAL CULTURES: IMPLICATIONS FOR INTERNATIONAL MANAGERS

It is clear that cultural dimensions influence effective motivation. When international managers fail to recognize this, it can potentially create organizational dysfunction. An Italian computer firm that received advice from an international management consulting firm for its restructuring into a matrix organization failed because the task-oriented approach to a matrix organization challenged loyalty to the company head—and in Italy "bosses are like fathers and you cannot have two fathers" (Trompenaars & Hampden-Turner 1997, 5). Many Australian, New Zealand, and American managers who work for Japanese multinational companies have had difficulty with the seniority-based, group-performance-oriented compensation systems of their employers. The Japanese high-tech conglomerate NEC realized that to exploit the core competencies held by Australian workers, it would need a different approach to that of their traditional team-oriented approach common in Japanese organizations. Rather than motivate employees through increased pay or benefits, NEC Japan has given the Australian management more autonomy in designing and developing communication products for the rest of the world. This has not only satisfied the employees' need for individual achievement, but has resulted in the production of world class communication products that the parent company was unable to match. Such competencies are also being discovered and exploited by Fujitsu's and Sony's Australian operations to benefit these organizations on a global basis while satisfying the motivational needs of its Australian managers and workers.

## Summary

Different motivational theories have been examined that have considerable implications for international human resource managers involved in managing culturally diverse workforces. The key to successful motivation is to develop a deeper understanding of host cultures. At the same time, international managers should relate this understanding to those motivational incentives that work best in a given culture and adapt their managerial strategies to these needs accordingly. In other words, international managers, above all, need to be creative in designing flexible incentive programs aimed at addressing both individualized as well as collectivized needs of their respective culturally diverse employees, where appropriate.

## Critical Discussion Questions

1. "The human motivation process is universal, but its content may vary across cultures." If this is true, discuss why and give evidence. Use outside sources if necessary.

2. Briefly describe Maslow's Hierarchy of Needs.

3. Explain Herzberg's concept of *motivators* and *hygiene factors*. Are they the same for the employees around the world?

4. What motivates humans according to McClelland's Achievement Motivation theory?

5. Discuss the ethnocentric nature of Maslow's Hierarchy of Needs.

6. How can Hofstede's cultural dimensions be applied in terms of the design of motivators for international human resource management practices?

7. What are the alternatives to pay increases as a motivator?

8. How can job enrichment be used in different countries to motivate workforce?

9. Is the role of a supervisor's feedback the same across the cultures?

10. In what ways, can McClelland's Achievement Motivation theory be applied across cultures? Provide examples.

# Applications

## Experiential

1. Conduct an interview with a manager of a multinational corporation about his or her managerial strategies in terms of what motivational tools work best for management of an international workforce.

2. Identify a domestic multicultural organization and interview a human resource manager with a view to identifying motivational tools in relation to a culturally diverse workforce.

3. Consider this hypothetical scenario: You are appointed as a human resource manager for a multinational company and you have an important managerial role to ensure that your culturally diverse staff, who have until now been somewhat unmotivated due to this company's ill-conceived management practices based on ethnocentrism, become motivated.

   In this regard, what specific motivational tools would you apply in order to achieve high level work performance? Please outline your managerial strategies and discuss them in class.

## Internet

Research American and Chinese management practices when it comes to motivating employees using Internet search engines such as Google and Alta Vista as well as databases available at your school. Critically compare and contrast them. Discuss your finding.

# References

Adler, N. (1997). *International dimensions of organizational behavior* (3rd ed.). Cincinnati, OH: South-Western College.

Avery, G. & Baker, E. (1990). *Psychology at work* (2nd ed.). Englewood Cliffs, NJ: Prentice Hall.

Bailey, J.R.C., et al. (1997). Conception of self and performance-related feedback in the U.S., Japan, and China. *Journal of International Business Studies*, Vol. 28, Issue 3, pp. 605-624.

England, G.W. (1986). National work meanings and patterns: Constraints on management action. *European Management Journal, 4* (3), 176–184.

Fatehi, K. (1996). *International management: A cross culture and functional perspective*. Upper Saddle River, NJ: Prentice Hall.

Herzberg, F. (1966). *Work and the nature of man*. Boston: World.

Hodgetts, R.M. & Luthans, F. (2000). *International management*. New York: McGraw–Hill.

Hofstede, G. & Bond, M.H. (1984). Hofstede's culture dimensions: An independent validation using Rokeach's value survey. *Journal of Cross-Cultural Psychology, 15*, 417–433.

Hofstede, G. (1980). Motivation, leadership and organization: Do American theories apply abroad? *Organizational Dynamics, 9*, 42–63.

Hofstede, G. (1984). *Culture's consequences: International differences in work–related values*. Beverly Hills, CA: Sage.

Hofstede, G. (1991). *Cultures and organizations: Software of the mind*. London: McGraw-Hill.

Holt, D.H. & Wigginton, K.W. (2002). *International management* (2nd ed.). Orlando, FL: Harcourt College.

Kanungo, R.N. & Wright, R. (1983). A cross–cultural comparative study of managerial job attitudes. *Journal of International Business Studies, 14* (2), 115–129.

Kovach, K.A. (1987). What motivated employees? Workers and supervisors give different answers. *Business Horizons, 30*, 58–65.

Maslow, A. (1954). *Motivation and personality*. New York: Harper and Row.

McClelland, D. (1961). *The achieving society*. New York: Irvington.

Mead, R. (1998). *International management: Cross-cultural dimensions*. Cambridge, MA: Blackwell.

Mutiso, G.C.M. (1974) *Socio-political thought in African literature: Weusi*. New York: Barnes and Noble.

Nevis, E.C. (1983). Cultural assumptions and productivity: The United States and China. *Sloan Management Review, 24* (3), 17–29.

Onedo, A.E.O. (1991). The motivation and need satisfaction of Papua New Guinea managers. *Asia Pacific Journal of Management, 8* (1), 121–129.

Plunkett, S. (1993, January 22). Parents slowly let subsidiaries off leash. *Business Review Weekly*, 10.

Redding, S.G. & Richardson, S. (1986). Participative management and is varying relevance in Hong Kong and Singapore. *Asia Pacific Journal of Management, 3* (2), 76–98.

Sergeant, A. & Frenkel, S. (1998). Managing people in China: Perception of expatriate managers. *Journal of World Business, 33* (1), 17–34.

Sirota, D. & Greenwood, M. (1971). Understanding your overseas workforce. *Harvard Business Review, 14,* 53–60.

Sisk, H. & Clifton, W.L. (1985). Management and organizations. Cincinnati, OH: South-Western College.

Steers, R. & Porter, L.W. (Eds.) (1975). *Motivation and work behavior.* New York: McGraw-Hill.

Trompenaars, F. & Hampden–Turner, C. (1997). *Riding the waves of culture: Understanding cultural diversity in business* (2nd ed.). New York: McGraw-Hill.

Westwood, R.I. (1992). *Organizational behavior: Southeast Asian perspectives.* Hong Kong: Longman.

# Chapter 10

*International Negotiation*

*Let us not be blind to our differences—but let us also direct attention to our common interests and the means by which those differences can be resolved.*

John F. Kennedy, Former President of the United States

## OVERVIEW

The 21st century is witnessing spectacular growth in the globalization of trade across national boundaries made possible through the exporting of products and services, offshore operations, strategic alliances and joint ventures, mergers and acquisitions, and licensing and distribution agreements. Much of this involves face-to-face negotiations between the stakeholders in the global economy, which includes managers, sales representatives, clients, government officials, and the workforce. In this setting, arguably, those who become successful negotiators display what we have already called intercultural communication competence. International negotiation is complex and difficult. It involves different laws, regulations, standards, business practices, and, above all, cultural differences. That is why negotiation, in the context of the global business environment, is such an important skill. The saying "when in Rome, do as the Romans do" is still good advice for it means that to succeed in negotiations in different societies, cultures, and across borders, we need to suppress ethnocentric tendencies and replace them with an awareness and sensitivity for cultural diversity that, in turn, lead to appropriate strategies and tactics to suit a particular situation.

To successfully conclude a business deal, a labor agreement, or a government contract with people who are different from us requires a considerable amount of communication skill. To successfully manage such negotiations, business people need to know how to influence and communicate with members of the culture other than their own (Adler & Graham 1989). This chapter examines negotiation styles that can be adopted under different conditions and cultural settings to reach an agreement while conducting business across cultures.

## NEGOTIATION DEFINED

Negotiation is conceived as "a process in which at least one individual tries to persuade another individual to change his or her ideas or behavior and it often involves one person attempting to get another to sign a particular contract or make a particular decision. Thus, negotiation is the process in which at least two partners with different needs and viewpoints need to reach an agreement on matters of mutual interest" (Casse 1981, 152).

Another way of looking at negotiation is as a process of communicating back and forth for the purpose of reaching a joint agreement about differing needs or ideas—that is, a process in which two or more parties exchange goods or services and attempt to agree upon the exchange rate for them (Acuff 1993).

## CROSS-CULTURAL NEGOTIATION DEFINED

All global negotiations are cross-cultural—and they contain all of the complexity of domestic negotiation, with the added dimension of cultural diversity (Adler 1997). A negotiation becomes cross-cultural when the parties involved belong to different cultures and therefore do not share the same ways of thinking, feeling, and behaving (Casse 1981). Negotiation, therefore, can significantly vary from one culture to another; and this does not exclude domestic negotiations when they span two or more ethnic groups. Americans view negotiations as an opportunity to resolve contentious issues. However, Japanese, Chinese, and Mexican businesspeople view negotiations as a vehicle to establish a relationship. For them, resolving problematic issues is never the first goal (Perlmutter & Heenan 1974).

Cross-cultural negotiations can be very intricate. Every culture, whether it is a high- or low-context one, has a distinctive approach to the negotiating process that may also include the consideration of various norms, values, laws, and beliefs that can impact on the outcome of the agreement. Negotiators from different cultures will focus on different aspects of an agreement, with more of an emphasis on the legal side; whereas the other party might focus on certain idiosyncratic, personal, or even religious aspects. In some cultures, documenting the agreement is significant while in others the process and actual implementation are the focal point (Gulbro & Herbig 1995). Americans negotiate a contract, while the Japanese negotiate a personal relationship, is an illustration of the dissimilarity between the individualistic culture of the United States and Japan's collectivist culture (Mead 1998).

Cross-cultural negotiations consume a great deal of the global manager's time—as much as 50 percent—which is why it is ranked as one of the most imperative skills for global managers to have (Adler 1997; George, Jones, & Gonzalez 1998). From small domestically oriented firms to multinational corporations, face-to-face and technology-facilitated cross-border and cross-cultural negotiations are becoming increasingly widespread. Negotiations are undertaken for numerous purposes, such as international joint ventures, licensing agreements, seller–buyer relationships, and mergers and acquisitions to name just a few.

## COMPONENTS OF NEGOTIATION

In any negotiation there are three components:

- The process.
- The parties.
- The agreement or outcome.

Complications in negotiation arise when the parties have different objectives. These objectives can be different from what each party requires from the agreement—or different in that one party may not even want an agreement. Another issue that can lead to complications is the routes that the parties take to arrive at their objectives, which might be quite different—and this often happens in a cross-cultural context.

## TYPES OF NEGOTIATION

In a cross-cultural context, there are two types of negotiations: intracultural and intercultural negotiations (Fatehi 1996). *Intracultural negotiations* assume a similarity in the culture and fields of experience between negotiating parties. Here, according to Goldman (1991), negotiating strategies are devised to influence the other party's position—and much of the negotiation skill involves accomplishing three tasks:

- Bringing your own perceptions in line with reality.
- Ascertaining the other side's perceptions of the proposed transaction and the available alternatives.

• Finding ways to favorably alter the other side's perceptions.

*Intercultural negotiations* encompass all the challenges arising from intracultural communication while involving effective intercultural communication that bridge the difficulties relating to cultural diversity.

## CROSS-CULTURAL INFLUENCES ON NEGOTIATIONS

Cultural differences play into all the variables of negotiation. They can, for example, influence the size of the team directly involved in the negotiation. Negotiating teams from a collectivist society tend to be large. Japanese businesses often use a large contingent in their negotiating teams. Businesses from an individualistic culture such as the United States, however, may send a single person to represent them at the negotiating table. Robbins, Bergman, and Stagg (2000) showed that younger negotiators are common among American teams—and they are often given the authority to make the final decision. An Asian team, from a collectivist culture that respects seniority, is more likely to be led by a senior negotiator who has high status in his or her company. This person may play little part in the actual negotiations, but his presence provides a necessary "figurehead" role (Markus & Kitayama 1991). Further, in an Asian, collectivist culture, subordinates brief superiors who, in turn, use their influence to negotiate and make decisions. Everyone affected by the decision is included in the process (Robbins, Bergman, and Stagg 2000). Collectivist societies consider people important. It is difficult for collectivists to separate people from the issues. For the same reason, collectivists are very much reluctant to express disagreement openly. Consequently, nonverbal and indirect communication cues play an important role in negotiation with collectivists. To succeed in business in Korea, for example, a person needs an extraordinary skill to read *nunchi,* which means the look in a person's eyes (De Mente 1991; Fatehi 1996). As such, an understanding of cultural differences based on individualism/collectivism is essential for a cross-cultural negotiator who may need to incorporate these aspects as part of his or her overall negotiating strategies.

In an analysis of Hofstede's cultural dimensions, negotiations between people of masculine and feminine cultures also present challenges to overcome. For the negotiators of masculine societies, ego preservation is essential. For them to compromise may signal giving in, which would be a sign of weakness. On the other hand, negotiators from a feminine culture may not be aware of the importance of ego for the people of masculine cultures—thus, building the ego of their counterparts and focusing on the task at hand can help advance their negotiations faster (Fatehi 1996).

The different value systems that exist between negotiators from different cultures also play a role. Negotiators from a high power distance culture may need more information to convince their superiors of the value of the agreement. They may also take a longer time because they have to clear decisions with those in the position of power.

The expected outcomes between culturally dissimilar parties in negotiation can also differ as either integrative or distributive. *Integrative outcomes,* or win-win situations, produce mutual benefits to both the parties. Integrative outcome negotiations result in great benefit for both parties (and usually entail longer, stable relationships between them (Bazerman & Neal 1982; Fatehi 1996). *Distributive outcomes* result from competition between negotiators. Distributive outcome negotiation is a win-lose scenario, in which the negotiators believe that they have opposing interests and incompatible alternative choices (Phatak 1997). American negotiators, for example, tend to have a short-term, distributive way of negotiation, for they are concerned with their interests and view negotiations competitively, often arriving at distributive outcomes. In contrast, Asian negotiators may view negotiation as a long-term relationship and a cooperative task (Lewicki & Litterer 1985). Japanese negotiators emphasize harmonious interdependence and a distributive way of negotiating indicative of a collectivist culture (Lituchy 1993).

## THE NEGOTIATION PROCESS

Process is the single most important factor predicting the success or failure of a negotiation. An effective process includes managing the negotiation's overall strategy or approach, its stages, and the specific tactics used. As with other aspects of negotiating, process varies markedly across cultures. An effective strategy reflects the situational characteristics and personal backgrounds of the negotiators involved. It balances the position, procedure, timing, and roles of the negotiating partners (Adler 1997). To successfully negotiate the global business environment, Fisher and Ury (1981) advocate a culturally synergistic approach, based on principled negotiation method, which could lead to fruitful cross-cultural negotiations. This approach involves four steps:

1. Separating the people from the problem.
2. Focusing on interests, not on positions.
3. Insisting on objective criteria (and never yielding to pressure).
4. Inventing options for mutual gain.

Principled negotiation provides participants to the negotiation with a method of focusing on the basic interests and the mutually advantageous solutions. It enables parties to reach agreement without all the haggling and posturing (Fatehi 1996).

## STAGES OF A NEGOTIATION

There are basic steps involved in managing the negotiation process. The following sections discuss them in detail, the first phase being planning.

### Planning

Planning begins with negotiators identifying the objectives that they want to attain. This involves considering the areas of common ground between the parties and the following major areas:

- Setting limits on single point objectives.
- Dividing issues between short term and long term considerations.
- Determining the sequence in which to discuss various issues (Chaney & Martin 1995).

Raider (1982), in comparing successful experienced negotiators to less skilled ones, lists other criteria for a successful outcome:

- *Planning time.* Successful negotiators use time in ways that are more fruitful to negotiation outcome than average negotiators, and this is where successful negotiators tend to pay a lot of attention on how to use available time so as to advantage their negotiations.

- *Exploring options.* Successful negotiators are inclined to come up with more wide-ranging options than the average negotiators, thereby increasing their chances for success.

- *Establishing common ground.* Unlike the average negotiators, successful negotiators are more focused on developing common ground than paying attention to areas of conflict than of agreement.

- *Focusing on long- versus short-term horizons.* Successful negotiators are strategically focused and therefore they spend more time on long-term issues than short-term issues. The average negotiators do not spend a substantial amount of time on strategic issues.

- *Setting limits.* Unlike the average negotiators, successful negotiators are focused on developing a range of objectives, providing them with flexibility necessary to succeed in their bargaining.

- *Using sequence versus issue planning.* In contrast to the average negotiators, successful negotiators discuss each issue under negotiation independently with no preconceived sequence or order of priority during the negotiation process.

## Interpersonal Relationship Building

The second phase of the negotiation process is getting to know the members of the other party or parties to the process. This "feeling out" period is characterized by the desire to identify those who are reasonable and those who are not. This is particularly important for collectivist culture, where trust in interpersonal relationship is required between partners involved in negotiation.

## Exchanging Task-Related Information

In this part of the process, each group sets forth its position on the critical issues. Each party finds out what the other party wants to attain and what it will give up. In negotiating, cross-cultural miscommunication can give rise to numerous hurdles for the parties involved. Example 10-1 illustrates what happened in a political context when the Iranians misinterpreted a bargaining offer in English. The lack of a proper understanding of language within its cultural context—on the part of both parties—posed a serious hindrance to successful cross-cultural negotiations.

## Persuasion

This is the most important step. The success of the persuasion often depends on:

- How well the parties understand each other's position.
- The ability of each to identify the areas of similarity and differences.
- The ability to create new options.
- The willingness to work towards a solution.

---

**EXAMPLE 10-1** Persian versus English

In Persian, the word *compromise* apparently lacks the positive meaning it has in English (a "midway solution both sides can live with") and has only a negative meaning ("her virtue was compromised" or "our integrity was compromised"). Similarly, the word *mediator* in Persian suggests "meddler," someone who is barging in uninvited. In early 1980, United Nations Secretary General Waldheim flew to Iran to intercede on behalf of the American Embassy hostages. His efforts were seriously set back when Iranian national radio and television broadcast in Persian a remark he reportedly made on his arrival in Tehran: "I have come as a mediator to work out a compromise." Within an hour of the broadcast, his car was being stoned by angry Iranians.

Source: Excerpt from *Getting To Yes* 2/e by Roger Fisher, William Ury and Bruce Patton, © 1981, 1991 by Roger Fisher and William Ury, (9:34). Reprinted by permission of Houghton Mifflin Company. All rights reserved.

---

Goldman (1991) suggests that in negotiation what counts is not the reality but the party's perception of reality. Also, there are two extreme negotiating positions: hard and soft. Negotiators who take hard positions see every negotiation as a contest of wills. They believe that by taking extreme positions and holding out longer, they fare better. The other party responds by taking an equally hard position. This exhausts both parties and damages their long-term relationship. Negotiators who take soft positions, however, may create a one-sided deal and ill feelings. Avoiding confrontation and taking a more accommodating soft position may result in an undue advantage for the other party. Neither perfectly hard nor soft approaches to negotiation are constructive. The best way is negotiating on merits or principled negotiations (Fisher & Ury 1981). Such posturing styles play a crucial role in persuasion, especially cross-cultural negotiations. For example, Americans push hard for direct answers and fill potential periods of silence with rhetorical embellishments. Latin Americans may simply change the topic when it becomes too pointed or uncomfortable. Chinese negotiators try to avoid conceding any points until negotiations near their culmination point. Japanese seem unemotional in their persuasive techniques. Yet Korean, Italian, and Middle Eastern negotiators often rely on bravado and intimidation tactics (Holt & Wigginton 2002).

### Agreement

The final phase is the granting of concessions and hammering out a final agreement. To negotiate effectively in the international areas, it is necessary to understand how cultural differences between the parties affect the process. The way Americans negotiate is different from Russians and Asians in that Americans negotiate one issue at a time and then once it is resolved, they move on to focus on the next issue. Asian and Russian parties tend to negotiate a final agreement on everything and few concessions are given until the end (Reardon & Spekman 1994).

## CROSS-CULTURAL DIMENSIONS AFFECTING NEGOTIATIONS

To negotiate effectively, it is important to have a sound understanding of the other side's culture. This includes consideration of areas such as communication pattern, time orientation, and social behaviors—variables covered in detail in Chapter 4—from which Weiss (1994) has made the following recommendations:

- Do not identify the counterpart's home culture too quickly. Common cues such as name, physical appearance, language, accent, and location may be unreliable. The counterpart probably belongs to more than one culture.

- Beware of the Western bias toward "doing," In Arab, Asian, and Latin American societies, the ways of "being," including feeling, thinking, and talking, can shape relationships more powerfully than doing.

- Try to counteract the tendency to formulate simple, consistent, stable images. Not many cultures are simple, consistent, or stable.

- Do not assume that all aspects of the culture are equally significant. In Japan, consulting all relevant parties to a decision is more important than presenting a gift.

- Recognize that the norm for interactions involving outsiders may differ from those for interactions between compatriots.

- Do not overestimate your familiarity with your counterpart's culture. An American studying Japanese wrote New Year's wishes to Japanese contacts in basic Japanese characters but omitted one character. As a result, the message becomes "Dead man, congratulations."

## WHEN TO NEGOTIATE?

Many experts who study global business negotiations take the view that negotiation is not always the best approach to doing business. In some cross-cultural transactions, the best strategy may be "take it or leave it" or "this-for-that" bargaining (Raider 1982). Complex negotiations, involving intricate, time-consuming problem solving can add costs. However, when the value of the exchange and of the relationship are important; international managers need to commit to negotiating as the preferred strategy with the need of creating win-win solutions. This is especially the case, according to Adler (1997), when any of the following conditions apply in negotiations:

- When the power position is low relative to a counterpart.
- When the trust level is high.
- When the available time is sufficient to explore each party's multiple needs, resources, and options.
- When commitment—not mere compliance—is important to ensure that the agreement is carried out.

## WHO NEGOTIATES?

Who represents the parties at the cross-cultural negotiating table is an important consideration and it varies from culture to culture, country to country. (Greek and Latin American top managers prefer to maintain personal control of all aspects of the process and so may head the team rather than delegate to a subordinate.) Mead (1998) relates how the composition of the team can be formed in terms of number and functions, gender, age, and rank:

- *Number and functions*. A single negotiator faces obvious difficulty if sent up against a team representing the full range of functions in the other organization. A team from China or Japan may represent a wide range of constituent groups within the organization. Its counterpart, an American team, may only include a legal representative—which can be perceived as hostile and threatening by the Japanese.

- *Gender*. A team that includes women may be at an advantage in feminine cultures, such as in Scandinavian countries, but not where women are normally unaccepted in business such as in Arab societies.

- *Age*. An American company may make a mistake in selecting a young "high-flier" to head a team negotiating with a Chinese or Japanese team. The Asian team is likely to be led by a senior and older person, the "figurehead" as previously discussed.

- *Rank*. The problem of matching team leaders is complicated by the far wider currency of the title "Vice President" in the United States than in Japanese organizations. In the American companies, there can be as many as 20 Vice Presidents, whereas a Japanese company of equal size may have three or four. Moreover, these ranks do not always match up across cultures.

## DEVELOPING EFFECTIVE NEGOTIATION SKILLS

According to Fisher and Ury (1981), the essence of effective negotiation can be achieved by following these steps that entail (1) researching your opponent; (2) acquiring as much information as you can about your opponent's interests and goals for the purpose of understanding his or her or their behavior; and (3) predicting responses to your options and to frame solutions. Furthermore, negotiations skills should include:

- Beginning with a positive overture.
- Addressing problems not personalities.
- Paying little attention to initial offers. (Treat an initial offer as merely a point of departure as they tend to be extreme and idealistic.)
- Emphasizing win–win solution when conditions support it— that is, look for an integrative solution.
- Being open to accepting third-party assistance.

## INDIVIDUAL QUALITIES OF A NEGOTIATOR

The role that individual qualities play varies across cultures. Favorable outcomes are most strongly influenced by the negotiator's own characteristics in Brazil; the opponent's characteristics in the United States; the role in Japan; and a mixture of negotiator's and opponent's characteristics in Taiwan (Graham 1983). Brazilian negotiators achieve higher profits when they act more deceptively and in their own self interest. American negotiators do better when their counterparts are honest, not self-interested and introverted. In Taiwan negotiators do better when they act deceptively and when their counterparts are neither self-interested nor have particularly attractive personalities. Exhibit 10-1 shows the key individual characteristics of negotiators for these four countries.

| Exhibit 10-1 | Key Individual Characteristics of Negotiators Representing Four Nationalities | | |
|---|---|---|---|
| **American Negotiator** | **Japanese Negotiator** | **Chinese (Taiwan) Negotiator** | **Brazilian Negotiator** |
| Preparation and planning skills | Dedication to job | Persistence and determination | Preparation and planning skills |
| Thinking under pressure | Perceive and exploit power | Win respect and confidence | Thinking under pressure |
| Judgment and Intelligence | Win respect and confidence | Preparation and planning skills | Judgment and intelligence |
| Verbal expressiveness | Integrity | Product knowledge | Verbal expressiveness |
| Product expertise | Demonstrate listening skills | Interesting | Product expertise |
| Perceive and exploit power | Broad perspective | Judgment and Intelligence | Perceive and exploit power |
| Integrity | Verbal expressiveness | | Competitiveness |

*Source:* Adapted from *International Dimensions of Organizational Behavior*, 4th ed. by Adler, © 2002. Reprinted with permission of South-Western, a division of Thompson Learning: http://www.thompsonrights.com. Fax 800-730-2215.

## DIFFERENT APPROACHES TO NEGOTIATION

There are two general approaches to negotiation, and they include *distributive bargaining* and *integrative bargaining*. *Distributive bargaining* refers to the negotiations that seek to divide up a fixed amount of resources and is a win-lose solution. When engaged in distributive bargaining, the negotiator should focus on trying to get the opponent to agree to his or her specific target point or to get as close to it as possible (Robbins, Bergman, & Stagg 2000). This style of negotiation is most common among Americans. It is indicative of an approach recommended by one business negotiation primer which terms it as: "Don't worry what others get. Don't worry what others think. Just know what *you* want to accomplish" (Kuhn 1988, 27). However, this approach to negotiation may not be strategically fruitful in a cross-cultural business negotiation. In contrast, *integrative bargaining* operates under the assumption that there is at least one settlement that results in a win–win situation for the parties involved in the negotiation. This is indicative of Japanese, Chinese, and South Americans—that is, it is a collectivist culture approach. In general, integrative bargaining is preferable to distributive bargaining as it builds long-term relationships and facilitates working together in the future. It bonds the negotiators and allows them to leave the bargaining table feeling that they have both achieved victory. Such an integrative strategy is recommended for cross-cultural negotiations. Both strategies are compared in Exhibit 10-2.

| Exhibit 10-2 | Distributive Bargaining Versus Integrative Bargaining | |
|---|---|---|
| **Bargaining Characteristics** | **Distributive Bargaining** | **Integrative Bargaining** |
| Available Resources | Fixed amount of resources to be divided | Variable amount of resources to be divided |
| Primary Motivation | "I win, you lose" | "I win, you win" |
| Primary Interest | Opposed to each other | Compatible with each other |
| Focus of relationship | Short – term view | Long – term view |

Source: Adapted from *Negotiation* by R.J. Lewicki and J.A. Letterer, ©1985, Irwin. Reprinted with permission from The McGraw-Hill Companies.

# NEGOTIATION STRATEGIES: SOME GUIDELINES

Acuff (1993) suggests that the following ten negotiation strategies will work anywhere in the world:

- Plan the negotiation.
- Adopt a win-win approach.
- Maintain high aspirations.
- Use language that is simple and accessible.
- Ask a lot of questions then listen with your eyes and ears.
- Build solid relationships.
- Maintain personal integrity.
- Conserve concessions.
- Be patient.
- Be culturally literate and adopt the negotiating strategies of the host country environment.

Kirkbride and Tang (1995), with more specific research from behind the "Bamboo Curtain" of Asian countries, have suggestions that supplement Acuff's universal list of rules with a more cross-cultural emphasis:

- Always set explicit limits or ranges for the negotiation process.
- Always seek to establish general principles early in the negotiation.
- Always focus on potential areas of agreement and seek to expand them.
- Avoid taking the negotiation issues in sequence.
- Avoid excessive hostility, confrontation, and emotion.
- Always give the other party something to take home.
- Always prepare to negotiate as a team.

# NEGOTIATION TACTICS

Negotiation includes verbal, nonverbal, and situational tactics. Australian and American businesspeople, who represent individualist cultures, would consider verbal tactics to be most important. Businesspeople from the collectivist cultures of Asia prefer nonverbal tactics during their cross-cultural negotiations. The following explains some of these in more detail.

## Verbal Tactics

Negotiators can use many verbal tactics such as promises, threats, recommendations, warnings, rewards, punishments, normative appeals, commitments, self-disclosure, questions, and commands. The use and meaning of many of these tactics vary across cultures. Hodgetts and Luthans (2000) have shown that the profits of a negotiating party increase when they (1) make a high initial offer; (2) ask a lot of questions; and (3) do not make many verbal commitments until the end of the negotiating process. In short, verbal behavior is critical to the success of negotiations.

## Nonverbal Tactics

Nonverbal behavior represents communication other than verbal as we learned in Chapter 5. It includes how the negotiators express the words rather than the words themselves. Nonverbal behavior includes tone of voice, facial expressions, body distance, dress, gestures, timings, silences, and symbols. Nonverbal behavior conveys multiple messages, many of them are responded to at a subconscious level. Counterparty negotiators frequently respond more emotionally and powerfully to the nonverbal than the verbal message. As with verbal behavior, nonverbal behavior also differs considerably across cultures. Japanese use the silence effectively as do Americans to a lesser extent. Americans often respond to silence by assuming that the other team disagrees or has not accepted their offer. Moreover, they tend to argue and make concessions in response to silence. This response does not cause problems in negotiating with Brazilians, who use almost no silence at all in negotiations; but it would put Americans at a disadvantage when dealing with Japanese. While the Japanese silently consider an American offer, the Americans interpret their silence as rejection and respond by making concessions such as lowering the price (Adler 1997).

## Situational Tactics

Another set of tactics can be classified as *situational tactics,* which include location, time limit, and physical arrangement. These are discussed in the following sections.

### Location

Where should negotiations be held is a significant consideration in terms of a successful outcome. Most negotiators select neutral locations for various forms of negotiations. Business entertainment has become a main feature of neutral location, used by the negotiating team primarily to become acquainted with members of the opposing team. However, using a neutral site results in a number of benefits such as each party having a limited access to its home office for what is perceived by both as an unfair and advantageous access to precious information. Secondly, cost of staying at the site often is quite high, so both sides have an incentive to conclude negotiations quickly (Hodgetts & Luthans 2000).

### Time Limit

Setting a time limit is an important negotiation tactic when one party is under time constraints. The duration of a negotiation can vary markedly across cultures. Americans, being particularly impatient, often expect negotiations to take a minimum amount of time (see Example 10-2). Concessions in negotiations are usually made towards the time deadline of the party making the concession. This obviously puts members of a

**EXAMPLE 10-2** The Paris Peace Talks

During the Paris Peace Talks to negotiate an end to the Vietnam War, the American team arrived in Paris and made hotel reservations for a week. Their North Vietnamese counterparts leased a chateau for a year. As the negotiations proceeded, the frustrated Americans were forced to continually renew their weekly reservations to accommodate the more measured pace of the North Vietnamese.

Source: Adapted from *International Dimensions of Organizational Behavior*, 4th edition by Adler, © 2002. Reprinted with permission of South-Western, a division of Thomson Learning: http://www.thomsonrights.com. Fax: 800-730-2215.

more time-conscious culture such as the Americans at a disadvantage (Jackson 1993).

### Physical Arrangements

Sitting around a boardroom table at opposite sides emphasizes a confrontational situation—this is typical of American negotiations, such as those between labor and management. Sitting at a right angle and facing the problem to solve rather than the counterparty engenders cooperation—which is typical of Japanese business negotiations and shows the emphasis on harmony in their approach to negotiation and is indicative of their collectivist culture.

## *Summary*

Negotiation and cross-cultural negotiation were defined and their importance established in conducting business in a culturally diverse environment at home and abroad. Negotiation can be classified into *intracultural* and *intercultural*. To negotiate a business deal, international managers need to recognize the cultural differences in communication and negotiation styles. Some cultures view negotiation is a competitive game, whereas others view negotiations as a relationship building exercise. Such different views call for flexible types of negotiations and skills on the part of international managers—this is especially true in regard to intercultural communication competence, a key contributing factor to successful international business negotiations.

## Critical Discussion Questions

1. "Any negotiation is a complicated process. However, cross-cultural negotiation is even more complex." Is this statement true or false? Explain your answer.

2. What is the difference between intracultural and intercultural negotiations?

3. In what ways is intercultural cultural communication important to international negotiations? Provide examples.

4. Describe cross-cultural influences on negotiation using Hofstede's cultural dimensions.

5. Outline the different cultural perspectives that may apply to negotiation.

6. "Principled negotiation method allows for a culturally synergistic approach to negotiation." Use outside sources to explain why this is the case.

7. Briefly describe the planning behavior of a successful negotiator.

8. Why is building of an interpersonal relationship deemed to be an important part of the cross-cultural negotiation process?

9. Describe the different stages of a cross-cultural negotiation.

10. In what ways does culture influence the composition of negotiating teams?

11. Provide some examples of verbal and nonverbal tactics used during an international negotiation.

# Applications

## Experiential

Interview a manager of a multinational company located in your home country about his or her views on: (1) challenges arising from a cross-cultural negotiation process; and (2) strategies for successful cross-cultural negotiation. Discuss your findings during tutorial or seminar time.

## Internet

Conduct a secondary research on American and Japanese styles of negotiation using Internet search engines such as Google and Alta Vista as well as databases available at your business school. Critically compare and contrast them. Discuss your findings during tutorial or seminar time.

# References

Acuff, F.L. (1993). *How to negotiate anything with anyone anywhere around the world*. New York: American Management Association.

Adler, N. (1997). *International dimensions of organizational behavior* (3rd ed.). Cincinnati, OH: South-Western College.

Adler, N.J. & Graham, J.L. (1989). Cross–cultural interaction: The international comparison fallacy. *Journal of International Studies, 20* (3), 515–537.

Bazerman, M.H. & Neal, M.A. (1982). Improving negotiations effectiveness: Under final offer arbitration: the role of selection and training. *Journal of Applied Psychology, 67*, 543–554.

Casse, P. (1981). *Training for the cross-cultural mind* (2nd ed.). Washington, DC: Society for Intercultural Education, Training and Research.

Chaney, L.H. & Martin, S.J. (1995). *International business communication*. Englewood Cliffs, NJ: Prentice Hall.

De Mente, B. (1991). *Japanese etiquette and ethics in business*. Lincolnwood, IL: NTC Business Books.

Fatehi, K. (1996). *International management: A cross-culture and functional perspective*. Upper Saddle River: NJ: Prentice Hall.

Fisher, R. & Ury, W. (1981). *Getting to Yes.* New York: Penguin.

George, J.M., Jones, G.R., & Gonzalez, J.A. (1998). The role of affect in cross-cultural negotiations. *Journal of International Business Studies, 29, 749–772.*

Goldman, A.L. (1991). *Setting for more.* Washington DC: Bureau of National Affairs.

Graham, J. (1983). Brazilian, Japanese and American business negotiations. *Journal of International Business Studies, 14* (1), 47–56.

Gulbro, R. & Herbig, P. (1995). Differences in cross-cultural negotiation behavior between manufacturers and service-oriented firms. *Journal of Professional Services Marketing, 13, 23–29.*

Hodgetts, R.M. & Luthans, F. (2000). *International Management.* New York: McGraw-Hill.

Holt D.H. and Wigginton, K.W. (2002). *International management* (2nd ed.). Orlando, FL: Harcourt College.

Jackson, T. (1993). *Organizational behavior in international management.* London: Butterworth Heinemann.

Jackson, T. (1995). *Cross-cultural management.* London: Butterworth Heinemann.

Kirkbride, P.S. & Tang, S.F.Y. (1995). Negotiations: Lessons from behind the bamboo curtain. In T. Jackson, T. (Ed.), *Cross-Cultural Management* (pp. 293–304). Oxford: Butterworth Heinemann.

Kuhn R.L., *Dealmaker: All the negotiating skills and secrets:* New York: John Wiley and Sons.

Lewicki, R.J., & Litterer, J.A. (1985). *Negotiations.* Homewood, IL: Irwin.

Lituchy, R. (1993). Negotiating with Japanese: Can we reach win-win agreement? Paper presented at the Academy of International Business Conference, October 21–25.

Markus, H.R. & Kitayama, S. (1991). Culture and the self-implications for cognition, emotion, and motivation. *Psychological Review, 98, 224–253*

Mead, R. (1998). *International management: Cross-cultural dimensions.* Cambridge, MA: Blackwell.

Menger, R. (1999). Japanese and American negotiators: Overcoming cultural barriers to understanding. *The Academy of Management Executive, 13,* 100–101.

Perlmutter, H.V. & Heenan, D.A. (1974). How multinational should your top manager be? *Harvard Business Review, 52* (6), 121–132.

Phatak, A.V. (1997). *International management: Concepts and cases.* Cincinnati, OH: South-Western College.

Pruitt, D.G. (1981). *Negotiation behavior.* New York: Academic Press.

Raider, E. (1982). *International negotiations: A training program for corporate executives and diplomats.* New York: Ellen Raider International, Inc.

Reardon, K.K. & Spekman, R.E. (1994). Starting out right: Negotiating lessons for domestic and cultural business alliances. *Business Horizons*, January–February, 1–9.

Robbins, S., Bergman, R., & Stagg, I. (2000). *Management* (2nd ed.). Upper Saddle River, NJ: Prentice Hall.

Samovar, L.A. & Porter, R.E. (1995). *Communication between cultures*. Belmont, CA: Wadsworth.

Thompson, L. (1998). *The mind and heart of the negotiator*. Upper Saddle River, NJ: Prentice Hall.

Weiss, S.E. (1994). Negotiating with Romans: Parts 1 & 2. *Sloan Management Review, 35,* 51–61, 85–99.

# Chapter 11

*Cross-Cultural Conflict and Conflict Resolution*

## LEARNING OBJECTIVES

After reading this chapter, you should be able to:
- Understand why conflict exists within contemporary organizations.
- Describe how conflict is viewed within contemporary organizations.
- Understand the difference between functional and dysfunctional conflicts.
- Describe different sources and types of conflict.
- Understand different approaches to conflict resolution.
- Understand conflict mediation across cultures.

The natural philosophers believe that if the forces of conflicts and discord were eliminated from the universe, the heavenly bodies would stand still, and in the resulting harmony the processes of motion and generation would be brought to a dead stop.

—Plutarch

# OVERVIEW

Since the beginning of time, conflict has always been part and parcel of human life. In some cultures, thinkers have praised the virtues of conflict for its capacity to drive progress and innovation in society. In other cultures, such as the collectivist cultures of Asia, conflict is considered a destructive force to social harmony and a cohesive community and, therefore, it should be avoided at all costs. Philosophers down through history such as Plutarch, Hegel, and Marx have been interested in the paradox of conflict and its role as an impetus of progress, innovation, and development. Hegel propounded the notion of dialectical idealism, that new ideas are created as a result of the inner conflict occurring within the mind. Marx declared that dialectical materialism is the impetus of progress in human civilization, that class conflict is the engine of change that would ultimately pave the way for a better and fairer society with unfettered opportunities and prosperity for all.

In the management of organizations, the question of how to interpret and deal with conflict is also an important issue. Moreover, how is conflict dealt with in the global business environment, where conflict can take on a cross-cultural dimension that it would not have in a domestic setting? This chapter will explore this issue.

# CONCEPTUALIZATIONS OF CONFLICT

Conflict occurs because of disagreements or incompatibilities between individuals, or between groups and entire organizations (Weiss 1996). Conflict also results from perceived or experienced differences over essential or emotional issues. Pondy (1967) and Thomas (1992) identified the stages of the entire conflict process, rather than attempting a definition, which may be confined to any one stage such as *conflictful* behavior. Thomas devised the process model of conflict in terms of the following components: antecedent conditions, thoughts and emotions, behavior, and outcomes. Antecedent conditions represent goal incompatibility, differences in judgment, or a combination of the two in which judgments differ because of incompatible goals. A concern for satisfying personal needs, achieving delegated responsibilities, or obtaining scarce resources between people contributes to goal conflicts. Cultures differ in the degree to which their members allow goal conflicts and differences of opinion by restricting competition. Among organizational members or units, Japanese and Chinese organizations have been shown to be different from American organizations in this regard (Moran, et al. 1994; Redding, Norman, & Schlander 1994). Conflict is associated with mostly negative emotions that are felt and expressed differently across cultures due to different interpretations and appraisal of the same situation. From one culture to another, very different behavioral modes and regulative mechanisms are used for the expression of emotions (Mesquite & Frijda 1992; Kozan 1997).

## Traditional Managerial Perspective on Conflict

Traditional managerial perspective saw most conflicts in terms of labor versus management and to be avoided or eliminated wherever possible. Such conflicts were considered a malfunction within the organization that negatively affected productivity and organizational life and morale.

Typically, when conflict erupted between individual workers or between workers and managers, the response was to ignore the situation or dismiss the individual worker or workers involved. Gradually, during the course of the last century, an evolution in managerial thought took place that gave rise to a new appreciation of conflict and its place within contemporary organizational life, which is explored in the next section.

## Contemporary Managerial Perspective on Conflict

The contemporary managerial perspective sees conflict as neither good nor bad, but as a fact of organizational life. Conflict is inevitable given the differing personalities and the social and cultural dimensions of employees in a contemporary organization. Conflict can even be perceived as a good thing, for having too little conflict in an organization can lead to apathy and lethargy among employees. Conflict can have positive results that stimulate creativity within the workforce. Thus, it would profit the organization more to manage conflict rather than seek its elimination; that is, to define conflict in terms of its effects. Nevertheless, that is not to say that conflict is a problem that should not be solved—conflict still can divert energy and precious resources in an organization.

Viewed in this way, conflict can spawn either functional conflict or dysfunctional conflict as described in the next sections.

### Functional Conflict

Functional conflict occurs when employees disagree on the best means to achieve a goal, not on the goal itself, and it leads the way for the selection of a better alternative. It plays an essential role in preventing organizational stagnation and resistance to change. It leads to an increased awareness of problems that need to be addressed and results in a broader and more productive search for solutions, facilitating innovation and adaptation. Some companies deliberately encourage functional conflict between its teams so that they compete in creating innovations, improving sales performance, and the like. Dunford (1992) identified conflicts as functional when they:

- Bring up rather than hide issues over which there are differences.
- Force individuals to be direct and accelerate problem solving.
- Attack issues rather than individuals.

Managers need to be mindful that too much or too little conflict can lead to negative and even unethical results and destructive behaviors within an organization. It is their responsibility to decide how much functional conflict is needed in order to create, enhance, and sustain the productivity and to make sure it does not degenerate into dysfunctional conflict, which is discussed next.

### Dysfunctional Conflict

Dysfunctional conflict is conflict that hinders the achievement of organizational goals. When management perceives conflict in this light, it is usually under the following conditions:

- Participants refuse to collaborate to find a solution.
- A superior is unwilling or unable to arbitrate.
- Participants refuse to accept the superior's arbitration.
- Rules and dispute-resolution procedures are inadequate, ambiguous, or contradictory.

- Communication is poor; that is, when the participants are unable to communicate essential information, or they disagree on how it should be interpreted.

## SOURCES AND TYPES OF CONFLICT

Conflict manifests itself in a variety of ways in an organization. The conditions—different kinds of actions and nonactions—that can trigger conflict include the following:

- *Structural conflict* occurs because of cross-functional departmental differences about goals, time horizons, rewards, authority, status, and resources such as when the Research and Development Department and the Finance Department clash over the allocation of financial resources and timelines.

- *Intrapersonal conflict* occurs within an individual. This can be expressed in a number of distinct ways:

  - *Intrarole conflict* is when an employee is receiving conflicting information about his or her performance over a particular role such as an employee rewarded for outstanding service while being the subject of complaints from customers for incompetence.

  - *Interrole conflict* comes about as a result of pressure over the need to perform several roles by an individual employee such as a working mother who has to reconcile her differing roles of motherhood and career.

  - *Person-role conflict* occurs when an individual finds his or her values clashing with job requirements such as a practicing Muslim employee working for a bank that charges interest on loans to its customers.

  - *Intrapersonal value conflict* takes place when individuals experience a gap between the values they believe to be important and conflicting values held by coworkers or managers. For example, this could take place when Muslim workers, who are forbidden to work on Friday, are threatened with dismissal by non-Muslim managers who insist that they show up to work on that day irrespective of their employees' religious beliefs.

  - *Cognitive dissonance* occurs when an individual perceives inconsistencies in his or her own thoughts and behaviors. The existence of considerable and unrecognized inconsistencies can be stressful and it may motivate an individual to reduce it: (a) by changing thought or behavior or; (b) by obtaining more information about the issue that is causing the dissonance (Hellriegel, Slocum, & Woodman 1995).

- *Interpersonal conflict* occurs between two or more individuals. The nature of interpersonal conflict in organizations can be emotional or content-based and is caused by many factors such as personality differences, values, judgments, perceptions, competencies, and management styles. Cross-cultural misunderstandings based on stereotyping and prejudice can also play a role in an interpersonal conflict.

- *Interorganizational conflict* occurs between enterprises and external stakeholders (Ivancevich, Olekans, & Matteson 1997).

It often results from mergers and acquisitions—or controversial business practices in a competitive market. Microsoft was taken to court by the U.S. Government in the 1990s after its competitors accused the software giant of being a monopoly.

# FACTORS THAT INFLUENCE PERCEPTION AND TOLERANCE OF CONFLICT

Mead (1998) identifies a number of factors that influence human perception and the tolerance of conflict—and one of these factors is a cross-cultural dimension while others include:

- *Industrial and occupational factors.* Some organizations are regarded as more tolerant of conflict than others. Ben & Jerry's, the ice cream manufacturer, is more tolerant of conflict than the U.S. Army. For example, a political organization in a democratic society is more tolerant than its army in that society.

- *Organizational culture.* Some organizational cultures tolerate and even encourage competition among their employees as a way of stimulating creativity and innovation. Other organizations have cultures that demand strict compliance with their rules and value system.

- *Urgency.* A military command tolerates conflict among its members less in time of war than in peacetime.

- *Personal interest.* What motivates a person can affect his or her tolerance of conflict.

- *Individual psychology.* Some personalities are more tolerant of conflict than others.

- *Culture.* Conflict is tolerated differently in different societies and cultures.

# THE MEANING OF CONFLICT IN CROSS-CULTURAL CONTEXTS

Conflict is a fact of organizational life in a contemporary global economy, but what is important to note is how conflict is appreciated and handled by management varies across cultures. Hofstede (1984, 1991, 1995), in studying cultural differences, considered four dimensions that can induce conflict: (1) individualism versus collectivism; (2) large power distance versus small power distance; (3) high versus low uncertainty avoidance; and (4) masculine culture versus feminine culture. Understanding these cultural dimensions can help in what style of conflict management should be utilized in different cultural settings.

In collectivist societies—most Asian countries—harmony is maintained and direct confrontation is avoided. This translates into the conflict management of Asian companies where direct confrontation is not evident between workers and managers. In individualist societies—the United States and the United Kingdom, for example—the workforce is encouraged to speak its mind and confront problems head-on.

In large power distance cultures, latent conflict between ranks is normal and conflict is expected. As such, peers are reluctant to trust each other. In small power distance cultures, harmony is valued between the powerful and powerless and peers are willing to cooperate with each other.

In high uncertainty avoidance cultures, conflict in the organization is considered undesirable; it is disapproved of and the readiness to compromise with opponents is low. In low uncertainty avoidance cultures, conflict in the organization is considered natural; and competition between employees can be fair. There is also a far greater degree of readiness to compromise with opponents.

Masculine cultures see competition encouraged and, therefore, conflicts are resolved by fighting them out. A feminine culture, which places a high premium on quality of life for the community, tends to resolve conflicts by means of compromise and negotiation.

## CONFLICT AND THE CONCEPT OF FACE IN DIFFERENT CULTURES

Research by Ting-Toomey (1988) cross-culturally compared the United States, Japan, South Korea, China, and Taiwan in the way members of these societies preserve or save *face*—in the sense of assurance and confidence—in conflict situations. For Americans, keeping *face* is done as a matter of selfhood, of maintaining and showing pride, reputation, credibility, self-respect, and the like. They have a self–face bond that is used in the confrontational, win-lose conflict strategies that mark their culture. They do not consider whether the other side is saving face, only that it loses the conflict. Collectivist Asians, however, understand the notion of face to be related to honor, claimed self image, and the family/organization. For them, there is awareness of relational dynamics in saving face. They are thus motivated by the mutual preservation when it is met by the same in their opponents. Again, conflict avoidance is a common strategy for Asian managers since it is part of their culture. Lebra. (1971), in researching collectivist Japanese subjects, saw some of the strategies of indirection that were used to "protect one's face":

- *Mediated communication.* Asking someone to else to transmit a message.
- *Refracted communication.* Talking to a third person in the intended hearer's presence.
- *Acting as if a delegate.* "Pretending" to be a messenger from a third person.
- *Anticipatory communication.* Not expressing wishes explicitly, but expecting the other person to understand.
- *Corresponding by letter.* So as to avoid meeting face to face. E-mail, voicemail, and the like would now also fall into this category.

Confrontation occurs in collectivist cultures only when it carries little risk of losing face or when the other side is a powerless outsider—or the member of an *outgroup*—and an open disagreement does not threaten the loss of face between the parties involved in a conflict (Leung 1988; Khoo 1994). Members of individualist cultures are more likely to use integrating, compromising, and obliging conflict resolution styles when dealing with members of an outgroup. In this case, task accomplishment overrides national cultural predilections.

In the conflict-avoiding cultures of Asia, managers are expected to show strength and authority in dealing with conflict and imposing their will. If there is the likelihood that one side or the other will lose face, conflict avoidance strategy may be an option.

Because conflict is conveyed in a different manner across cultures, international managers who have culturally diverse workforces have to spot the expressions of disagreement and recognize that conflict has emerged. International managers must avoid communicating messages that can be interpreted as, for example, confrontational to members of a collectivist culture with a large power distance and high uncertainty avoidance.

# MANAGERIAL CONFLICT RESOLUTION APPROACHES

Conflict management in modern organizations should exercise the following principles of mediation:

- Prevent negative (dysfunctional) conflict from occurring in an organization.
- Encourage healthy conflict as a way of stimulating innovation and creativity in an enterprise.
- Minimize and eliminate the dysfunctional conflict within an organization as it is seen to be destructive to the workings of an efficient organization.

Kilmann and Thomas (1975) identified the following conflict management styles, differentiated by the concern for self and the concern for others prevalent in most organizations:

- *The integrating style* involves a high concern for self as well as the other party involved in the conflict. It is concerned with collaboration between parties.
- *The obliging style* involves low concern for self and high concern for others. It involves smoothing over differences and focusing on areas of agreement.
- *The dominating style* involves a high concern for self and a low concern for the other party involved in the conflict. It has been described as forcing one's viewpoint at the expense of others.
- *The avoiding style* is associated with low concern for self as well as the other party. It has been associated with withdrawing from the conflict situation.
- *The compromising style* involves moderate concern for self as well as the party involved in the conflict. It is associated with give-and-take or sharing the search for a middle-ground solution.

A number of studies have been conducted that explore the use of different interpersonal conflict-handling styles (Cosier & Ruble 1981; Rahim 1985; Rahim 1986; Rahim & Blum 1994; Rahim & Magner 1995; Elsayed-Ekhouly & Buda 1996). In general, they maintain that management tends to use compromising or collaboration more often than other styles.

# CROSS-CULTURAL CONFLICT RESOLUTION: MEDIATION AND CULTURAL AWARENESS

In a collectivist culture, such as Asian culture, in which conflict is seen as undesirable, involvement of a third party is seen as a favorable option.

A neutral third party—a *mediator*—does not impose the decision but lets parties decide for themselves and achieve a harmonious win-win solution. This method of handling conflict is becoming increasingly popular in the Western countries. According to Fisher and Ury (1981), mediators perform the following in conflict resolution:

- Separating the people from the problem.
- Focusing on interests, not on positions.
- Insisting on objective criteria and never yielding to pressure.
- Inventing options for mutual gain.

In organizations that are culturally diverse, irrespective of their geographical locations, mediators—and managers—must minimize interpersonal and intergroup conflict related to group and cultural identity. They should instead promote a better understanding of cultural differences prevalent in their organizations. More importantly, international managers need to provide a systematic training program for their culturally diverse workforce that focuses on identifying stereotypes while eliminating stereotypes and inaccurate assumptions about outgroup members representing minority cultures within their respective workplace.

## Summary

Conflict is always present in organizations and managing it has important implications for organizations in a culturally diverse business and workforce environment. Managerial strategies dealing with conflict are most differentiated in collectivist and individualistic cultures. Lastly, the phenomenon of mediation, which originated in collectivist cultures, is making inroads to the West was discussed as prescriptive along with greater awareness of cultural differences in the context of conflict resolution.

## Critical Discussion Questions

1. What is the traditional perspective on conflict? How does it differ from a contemporary understanding of the role of conflict within an organization?

2. What are the attributes of functional conflict and dysfunctional conflict?

3. Briefly describe the main sources and types of conflict.

4. Name the factors that influence the perception and tolerance of conflict within an organization. Provide examples.

5. Analyze the meaning of conflict across cultures.

6. How does the Western understanding of face-saving differ from the Asian perspective on saving face?

7. How is conflict communicated in different cultures? Use examples.

8. Briefly discuss various conflict resolution management styles that can be used within an organization. Provide some examples that may be considered as appropriate choices for conflict resolution management styles to suit the situation at hand.

9. Why is conflict mediation used more in collectivist societies?

# Applications

## Experiential

1. Choose any two countries with different cultural orientations. Undertake research in a library and on the Internet to compare how conflict-related issues are viewed and handled in these two countries. Discuss your findings during tutorial or seminar time.

2. Interview a manager of a local company about his or her views on: (1) conflict related issues within the organization; and (2) how conflict is managed and resolved in his or her organization.

3. Write a research paper discussing why conflict is essential for the development of an organization.

## Internet

Access the following Web site and read the article on conflict resolution and mediation processes and techniques based on the Chinese philosophical paradigm. Then summarize your findings for discussion with particular reference to Western approaches to conflict resolution and mediation.

http://www.cardozojcr.com/vol3no2/notes01.html

# References

Ben-Ari, E., Moeran, B., & Valentine, J. (Eds.) (1990). *Unwrapping Japan: Society and culture in anthropological perspective.* Manchester, England: Manchester University Press.

Blake, R.R. & Mouton, J.S. (1964). *The managerial grid.* Houston, TX: Gulf.

Brislin, R. (1993). *Understanding culture's influence on behavior.* Fort Worth, TX: Harcourt Brace.

Cosier, R.A. & Ruble, T.L. (1981). Research on conflict handling behavior: An experimental approach. *Academy of Management Journal, 24,* 816–831.

Cox, T. & Blake, S. (1991). Managing cultural diversity: Implications for organizational competitiveness. *Academy of Management Executive, 5* (3), 45–56.

Deutsch, M. (1973). *The resolution of conflict.* New Haven, CT: Yale University Press.

Dunford, W.D. (1992). *Organizational behavior.* Reading, MA: Addison-Wesley.

Elsayed-Ekhouly, S.M. & Buda, R. (1996). Organizational conflict: A comparative analysis of conflict styles across cultures. *International Journal of Conflict Management, 7* (1), 71–88.

Fatehi, K. (1996). *International management: A cross culture and functional perspective.* Upper Saddle River, NJ: Prentice Hall.

Fisher, R. & Ury, W. (1981). *Getting to Yes.* New York: Penguin.

Guirdham, M. (1999). *Communicating across cultures.* London: Macmillan.

Gulbro, R. & Herbig, P. (1995). Differences in cross-cultural negotiation behavior between manufacturers and service-oriented firms. *Journal of Professional Services Marketing, 13,* 23–29.

Hellriegel, D. & Slocum, J. (1996). *Management* (8th ed.). Cincinnati, OH: South Western College.

Hellriegel, D., Slocum, J., & Woodman, R.W. (1995). Organizational behavior (7th ed.). St. Paul, MN: West.

Hofstede, G. (1984). *Culture's consequences: International differences in work-related values.* Beverly Hills, CA: Sage.

Hofstede, G. (1991). *Cultures and organizations: Software of the mind.* London: McGraw-Hill.

Hofstede, G. (1995). The business of international business is culture. In T. Jackson (Ed.), *Cross-cultural management* (pp. 150–165). Oxford: Butterworth Heinemann.

Hofstede, G. & Bond, M.H. (1984). Hofstede's Culture Dimensions: An independent validation using Rokeach's value survey. *Journal of Cross-Cultural Psychology, 15,* 417–433.

Ivancevich, J., Olekans, M., & Matteson, M. (1997). *Organizational behavior and management.* Sydney: McGraw-Hill.

Jackson, T. (1993). *Organizational behavior in international management.* London: Butterworth Heinemann.

Jackson, T. (1995). *Cross-cultural management.* Oxford: Butterworth Heinemann.

Khoo, G.P.S. (1994). The role of assumptions in intercultural research and consulting: Examining an interplay of culture and conflict at work. Paper presented at Pacific Region Forum on Business and Management Communication.

Kilmann, R.H. & Thomas, K.W. (1975). Interpersonal conflict-handling behavior as a reflection of Jungian personality dimensions. *Psychological Reports, 37,* 971–980.

Kozan, M.K. (1989). Cultural influences on styles of handling interpersonal conflicts: Comparisons among Jordanian, Turkish, and U.S. managers. *Human Relations, 42,* 787–789.

Kozan, M.K. (1997). Culture and conflict management: A theoretical framework. *International Journal of Conflict, 8* (4), 338–360.

Laurent, A. (1983). The cultural diversity of Western conceptions of management. *International Studies of Management and Organization, 13* (1–2), 75–96.

Lebra, T. (1971). The social mechanism of guilt and shame: The Japanese case. *Anthropological Quarterly, 44* (4), 241–255.

Leung, K. (1988). Some determinants of conflict avoidance. *Journal of Cross-cultural Psychology, 19* (1), 125–136.

Mead, R. (1998). *International management: Cross-cultural dimensions* (2nd ed.). Cambridge, MA: Blackwell.

Mesquite, B. & Frijda, N.H. (1992). Cultural variations in emotions: A review. *Psychological Bulletin, 112*, 179–204.

Moran, R.T., Allen, J., Wichman, R., Ando, T., & Sasano, M. (1994). Japan. In M.A. Rahim & A.A. Blum (Eds.), *Global perspectives on organizational conflict* (pp. 33–52). Westport, CT: Praeger.

Phatak, A.V. (1997). *International management: Concepts and cases.* Cincinnati, OH: South-Western College.

Pondy, L.R. (1967). Organizational conflict: Concepts and models. *Administrative Science Quarterly, 12*, 296–320.

Rahim, M.A. (1983). A measure of styles of handling interpersonal conflict. *Academy of Management Journal, 26*, 368–376.

Rahim, M.A. (1985). A strategy of managing conflict in complex organizations. *Human Relations, 38*, 81–89.

Rahim, M.A. (1986). Referent role and styles of handling interpersonal conflict. *Journal of Social Psychology, 125*, 79–86.

Rahim, M.A. & Blum, A.A. (Eds.) (1994). *Global perspectives on organizational conflict.* Westport, CT: Praeger.

Rahim, M.A. & Magner, N.R. (1995). Confirmatory factor analysis of the styles of handling interpersonal conflict: First order factor model and its invariance across. *Journal of Applied Psychology, 80* (1), 122–132.

Redding, G. (1995). *International cultural differences.* London: Dartmouth.

Redding, S.G., Norman, A., & Schlander, A. (1994). The nature of individual attachment to the organization: A review of East Asian variations. In M.D. Dunnette & L.M. Hough (Eds.), *Handbook of industrial and organizational psychology* (Vol. IV, pp. 674–688). Palo Alto, CA: Consulting Psychologists Press.

Saee, J. & Saunders, S. (2000). Intercultural communication competence and managerial functions within the Australian hospitality industry. *Australian Journal of Communication, 27* (1), 111–129.

Thomas, Jr., R.R. (1990). From affirmative action to affirming diversity. *Harvard Business Review, 90*, 107–117.

Thomas, K.W. (1992). Conflict and negotiation processes in organizations. In M.D. Dunnette & L.M. Hough (Eds.), *Handbook of industrial and organizational psychology* (Vol. 3, pp. 651–717). Palo Alto, CA: Consulting Psychologists Press.

Ting-Toomey, S. (1985). Toward a theory of conflict and culture. In W. B. Gudykunst, L. P. Stewart, & S. Ting-Toomey (Eds.), *Communication, culture, and organizational processes.* Beverly Hills, CA: Sage, 71–86.

Ting-Toomey, S. (1988). Intercultural conflict styles: a face-negotiation theory. In Y.Y. Kim & W.B. Gudykunst (Eds.), *Theories of cross-cultural communication* (pp. 213-233). Newbury Park, Sage.

Ting-Toomey, S. & Korzenny, F. (1991). *Cross-cultural interpersonal communications.* Newbury Park, CA: Sage.

Ting-Toomey, S., Gao, G., Trubisky, P., Yang, Z., Kim, H. S., Lin, S.-L., & Nishida, T. (1991). Culture, face maintenance, and styles of handling interpersonal conflict; a study in five cultures. *The International Journal of Conflict Management, 2,* 275–296.

Weiss, J. (1996). *Organizational behavior and change: Managing diversity, cross-cultural dynamics, and ethics.* St. Paul, MN: West.

# Chapter 12

*Global Business Ethics*

## LEARNING OBJECTIVES

*After reading this chapter, you should be able to:*
- *Understand the importance of ethical behavior for international business.*
- *Understand moral philosophies and their relevance to business ethics.*
- *Understand the notion of cultural relativism.*
- *Understand the difference between ethical and legal behaviors.*
- *Describe different types of unethical dilemmas in global business practices.*
- *Understand the importance of corporate social responsibility.*

*One ought always act so as to treat humanity, in oneself or in another, as an end in itself, and not as a mere means.*

*—Immanuel Kant*

## OVERVIEW

There are ethical norms held in common by people around the world. The major religions all condemn murder, theft, lying, and so on (Mead 1998). Philosophers and prophets such as Plato, Aristotle, Confucius, Spinosa, Moses, Jesus, Muhammad, and others have established or inspired standards of behavior that constitute ethics (Caroll & Gannon 1997). Ethics—and the systems of morality and the laws that evolve from them—are central to human existence and for that reason businesses, which are human institutions, are expected to be socially responsible and conduct themselves in an ethical manner—an expectation that has intensified with the rise of consumerism and environmentalism. In this era of the global economy, international organizations must engage in both business and social responsibility—or face government prosecutions, negative consumer reaction, and other problems that can run from bad public relations to costly international litigation. Headlines in the world's newspapers are full of examples. Nike, due to the management practices of its supplier factories in the Far East, has been accused of allowing poor working conditions, low wages, enforced overtime, and harsh, even brutal, discipline. The maker of Levi jeans has been accused of condoning child labor in its Bangladesh facilities. Lockheed has made $12.5 million in illegal payments to Japanese agents and government officials to secure an important order from Nippon Air. Nestle's marketing of baby formula in Africa has resulted in that company being accused of undermining the custom of breastfeeding African children to the detriment of their health (Buller, Kohls, & Anderson 2000). The Bhopal disaster in India was the worst industrial accident in history. It forced Union Carbide's managers to confront a host of difficult ethical, moral, social, and legal issues—and to cease operations in India (Velasquez 1992).The Australian multinational company BHP is seen as responsible for environmental degradation in Papua, New Guinea, where it had a major mining operation.

Bribery, patent and copy right infringements, lying, and deceit about product performance and safety, deliberate use of harmful substances, intentional environmental pollution, discrimination, dangerous working conditions, violation of promises, and other similar types of unethical behavior exist, yet many companies operating in the global economy incorporate a range of cross-cultural ethical practices to regulate themselves and ensure against the costly ramifications of violating them.

## THE NATURE OF BUSINESS ETHICS

Baumhart (1968), in a major study of business ethics, asked more than a hundred business managers the question: "What does *ethical* mean to you?" Fifty percent of the respondents perceived "ethical" as "What my feelings tell me is right." Twenty-five percent viewed it in terms of their religious beliefs. Eighteen percent saw ethical as what "conforms to the golden rule." As can be seen, there are a variety of perceptions and further studies reveal more based on different societal moral standards (Saee 1993; 1994). Ethics are concerned with human relationships, duties, and obligations: how we think about and act towards each other; and what are the consequences of our decisions and actions in terms of human outcomes as opposed to mere profit. Ethics are an important dimension of international management because ethical behavior in one country is sometimes viewed as unethical in another country.

The complexity and interdependency involved in international business management spill over the area of social responsibility as well. While the impact of obligations and the responsibilities of a domestic business are limited to its home environment, those firms involved in international business create a web of interdependent and often conflicting responsibilities that are not easily resolved. For international management, there is a wider area of potential misunderstanding, disagreement, and dispute. Society—which differs from culture to culture—allows organizations to operate within certain parameters; and businesses are expected to operate in a manner consistent with the societal norms and value systems placed upon them (Fatehi 1996).

# HOW ETHICS ARE LEARNED

Individuals are not born with an ability to understand and apply ethical standards. Just as people's physical, emotional, and cognitive abilities develop, so does their ability to understand and apply ethical standards throughout their lives (Velasquez 1992). Ethics are learned through a number of channels, including:

- *Family groups,* which play a crucial role in the development of ethical beliefs learned through family experience and family influence.
- *Religious beliefs,* which shape behavioral guidelines.
- *Educational institutions,* which shape perceptions about right and wrong.
- *Reflections of social values,* as expressed through media and the like, which reinforce beliefs of right and wrong that arrive via the first three channels.

# MORAL PHILOSOPHIES AND THEIR RELEVANCE TO BUSINESS ETHICS

A moral philosophy is a set of principles or rules used to decide what is right or wrong (Taylor 1975). Moral philosophies help explain why a person believes that a certain choice among alternatives is ethically right or wrong (Amba-Rao 1993). Four categories of moral philosophical thought can be related to the ethical conduct of business: (1) teleology, (2) deontology, (3) the theory of justice, and (4) cultural relativism (Phatak 1997). These are discussed in the following sections.

## Teleology

Teleological philosophy, or *consequentialism,* evaluates the morality of an action by examining its consequences (Phatak 1997). A behavior or action, therefore, is considered acceptable if it produces desired outcomes such as a promotion at work or a bigger market share for a product or service. There are two key teleological approaches that have implications for contemporary management practices, *egoism* and *utilitarianism.*

### Egoism

*Egoism* is based on the pursuit of maximizing individual self-interest and is the determinant of individual behavior. In other words, any action taken by an individual in order to further his or her self-interest is ethically justified. Thus an act contrary to one's self-interest is an immoral act (Hoffman & Moore 1990). Naturally, self-interest varies among individuals. For some, money is the most important goal in life, while for others it is the acquisition of power and prestige.

**Utilitarian View**

The utilitarian approach, initially advanced by the English philosopher Jeremy Bentham, sees decisions as made solely on the basis of their outcome or consequences toward maximizing the greatest good for the largest number of individuals. Although utilitarianism seems on the surface to be more socially responsible than egoism, it is not a perfect ethical system. John Stuart Mill (1957) objected to Bentham for not taking into account the difference between an honest and a dishonest act that produces the same result. Also, utilitarianism tells us nothing about the distribution of this greater good (Hoffman & Moore 1990). There is a problem of social justice. It "is perfectly justifiable, using these principles, to persecute the minority in the interest of the majority" (Jackson 1993, 279).

## Deontology: The Theory of Rights

Deontology (derived from the Greek word for duty, *deon*) is an ethical theory holding that acting from a sense of duty rather than concern for consequences is the basis for establishing our moral obligations (Mill 1957). The German philosopher Immanuel Kant, who devised a deontological approach to a universal moral philosophy, held that all morality depends on a *single categorical imperative* that applies across the entire range of human behavior. People have the capacity to will, they have will power, and it is free. Therefore, they are able to regulate their own behavior in accordance with their own law, which is moral law. We demonstrate our freedom when we act in accordance with our moral law. The basis of moral law is formulated in categorical imperative. According to Kant (1962): One should only act on a principle that one can will to be universal law. One should always act so as to treat humanity, in oneself or in another, as an end in itself, and not as a mere means. Individuals should be treated with respect and dignity as an end in itself; they should not be used as the means to reach the end. A person should not be done harm even if the end aim is good.

Deontology, as promulgated by Kant, is all about "doing the right thing" as a universal moral duty, which is a lot easier to follow both in business and personal life. On the other hand, teleology, in particular, egoism, is problematic in the sense that it ultimately advocates that any means justifies the end—even the Machiavellianism of deceit and ruthlessness in the pursuit of self-interest. Given the heightened awareness and expectations of sound ethical business behavior among modern consumers, *egoistic* corporate behavior will not make business sense for any contemporary organization. There are competitors who are too keen to satisfy consumers' needs and expectations by offering products and services in a responsible manner. Businesses that conduct themselves unethically can be the ultimate losers.

## The Theory of Justice

There are three guiding principles underlying the theory of justice which provide managers with reference points in terms of making ethical decisions:

- Be equitable
- Be fair
- Be impartial (Phatak 1997)

Managers must establish standard rules that are equity-based and transparent. At the same time, these rules should be administered to all employees in the same way, and thus no individuals should be held responsible for actions over which they have no control—that is, those actions that may fall outside the clearly defined and delegated responsibility of individual workers.

## Cultural Relativism in Ethical Decision-Making

In cultural relativism, there is no single right way because all cultures are different and no culture is any better or worse than any other (Donaldson 1989). It is then correct to accept a culture and its values for what they are and not to be judgmental about them. For the relativists, no culture is wrong and no one is right and the standard by which others should conform. However, there is room for moral reform in most societies. Furthermore, the teachings of many religions have to some degree parallels that establish a kind of standard "right way." Buddhism, Christianity, Confucianism, Hinduism, Judaism, and Islam subscribe to something like the "Golden Rule": Do as you would be done by others (Fulop & Linstead 1999).

# BUSINESS ETHICS DEFINED

Business ethics are shaped by societal ethics and scholars have formulated a number of ways to define them:

- A non-mandatory system of certain standards of behavior (Crawford 1974).
- Commercial behavior guided by a slowly accumulated set of guidelines, which have been found to be necessary for the continuous conduct of commercial relationships (Dirksen & Kroeger 1973).
- Standards for conduct perceived as right and moral by individuals within an enterprise, taking into account the human welfare of those affected by decisions and behavior (Holt & Wigginton 2002).
- Applied ethics that study the relationship of what is good and right for business (Hoffman & Moore 1990).
- A complex issue that covers the interactions between firms, individuals, industries, and society (Grace & Cohen 1998).

# ETHICAL VERSUS LEGAL BEHAVIOR

There is a widely held view, recognized by management scholars, that as long as a business operates within the law, it has conducted itself ethically and morally (Fulop & Linstead 1999). However, it is insufficient for a business to *only* act in accordance with laws because (1) not all of a society's norms regarding moral behavior will be codified into law; and (2) many new business activities emerge and develop before there are legal boundaries to protect society (e.g., genetic engineering and e-commerce). There are many instances of unethical behavior that are not illegal and ethical behavior that may be illegal such as the activities of Green Peace whose activists break laws in order to protect the environment (Fulop & Linstead 1999).

## WHY BUSINESS ETHICS ARE NEEDED

For businesses to exist and coexist in contemporary global markets, they must incorporate ethical behaviors into their business practice. The reasons for this are:

- To protect the general public. For example, in the case of defective products; a business should take the ethical responsibility of recalling such products.
- To protect employees. This can range from maintaining a safe work environment to having policies in place that prevent employees from being forced into unethical behaviors (such as sales representatives having to meet quotas).
- To ensure businesses remain economically viable by complying with the value system of the society in which they operate. That is, for businesses to be successful, they must abide by the established ethics of society.
- To protect business itself from unethical practices of employees. If a business has its own set of ethical guidelines in place, unethical employees will not be able to harm the good name of the business. Such guidelines also provide security against unethical competitors.
- To act as major motivator for ethical employees to achieve a high degree of productivity, meaning that employees will be proud to belong to a company where sound ethical behavior is the prevailing norm. (Jefkins 1973)

Becker and Fritzche (1987) found that French, German, and American managers overwhelmingly agreed that sound ethics were good for business, and that a business cannot afford to have a reputation for *not* behaving ethically, which can damage its business interests. For multinational corporations, De George (1993, 3–4), articulated what kinds of ethical behaviors, especially in third world countries, should be observed to achieve such reputations:

- Do no intentional harm. This includes respect for the integrity of the ecosystem and consumer safety.
- Produce more good than harm for the host country.
- Contribute by their activity to the host country's development.
- Respect the human rights of their employees.
- To the extent that local culture does not violate ethical norms, respect the local culture and work with it and not against it.
- Pay a fair share of taxes.

- Cooperate with the local governments in developing and enforcing just institutions (laws, governmental regulation, unions, and consumer groups) that serve as a means of social control.

Also, companies that operate in cross-cultural business environments should:

- Strictly adhere to the local laws while making every effort to be seen to be truthful in the conduct of business affairs.
- Earn the respect of the host culture and show respect for the people and the environment in which they live.
- Practice the Golden Rule, "Do as you would be done by others."

# ETHICAL DILEMMAS IN BUSINESS PRACTICES AROUND THE GLOBE

With the increasing globalization of the world economy, companies ranging from small, domestic operations to multinational corporations must coexist with or in diverse social and cultural environments. This gives rise to many ethical problems that include bribery, deceit, anti-competitive behavior, discrimination, environmental degradation, and the avoidance of social responsibilities.

## Bribery

Businesses around the world face the problem of bribery, which is remuneration for the performance of an act that is inconsistent with the work contract or the nature of the work one has been hired to perform (Shaw & Berry 1989). Bribery is often seen as a problem that originates within the host culture, especially in the developing nations of Asia, Africa, and the Middle East, where government officials often supplement their income with bribes as a common and acceptable practice (Kohls & Butler 1994). In a number of African nations, bribery is such a strong and common norm that it overrides the law (Shaw & Berry 1989). Overall, it is estimated that approximately $85 billion is involved in bribes from developed countries to developing nations. Yet countries such as France, Belgium, Greece, Germany, and Luxembourg allow firms to deduct foreign bribes as business expenses from their taxable income. (In Germany, this tax deduction goes by the euphemism nützliche Ausgaben or "useful expenditure.") This perfectly legal practice, however, gives a degree of legitimacy to bribery and extortion—and many critics, especially in the host countries themselves, feel that corruption does not originate so much in their societies as it is corruption exported to their societies by outsiders (Holt & Wigginton 2002). Unlike their European counterparts, American executives can be prosecuted within the United States if they are found guilty of bribery in another country (Vogel 1992). This comes at some expense to American businesses. A recent report issued by the U.S. Commerce Department estimates that since 1994, foreign firms have used bribes to edge out U.S. multinational companies on some $45 billion of international deals (Hodgetts & Luthans 2000). Exhibit 12-1 provides a survey of the top ten most and least corrupt countries.

| Exhibit 12-1 | Ten Countries with the Low Levels of Corruption and Ten Countries with the High Levels of Corruption (from a survey of 102 nations) | | |
|---|---|---|---|

| Lowest Levels of Perceived Corruption | | Highest Levels of Perceived Corruption | |
|---|---|---|---|
| Rank | Country | Rank | Country |
| 1 | Finland | 90 | Nigeria |
| 2 | Denmark | 89 | Yugoslavia |
| 3 | New Zealand | 87 | Ukraine |
| 3 | Sweden | 87 | Azerbaijan |
| 5 | Canada | 85 | Indonesia |
| 6 | Iceland | 85 | Angola |
| 6 | Norway | 84 | Cameroon |
| 6 | Singapore | 82 | Russia |
| 9 | Netherlands | 82 | Kenya |
| 10 | United Kingdom | 81 | Mozambique |

Source: Adapted from the Transparency International Corruption Perceptions Index 2002, http://www.transparency.org.

## False Information

One serious detriment to the expansion of international business is the degree to which various nations condone the practice of falsifying information. Lying is a particularly complex phenomenon: the person lying must intend to deceive the person with whom he or she is communicating (Agar 1994).

In the area of advertising, nations seem to differ in their reactions to deception. In collectivist cultures such as Hong Kong and Malaysia, managers view deceptive advertising as acceptable. On the other hand, the managers in individualistic cultures such as the United Kingdom and the United States view it as a major problem (Robertson & Schlegermilch 1993). In Venezuela, fraudulent advertising is considered a very grave problem in the business world but not highly unethical when compared to the ranking of other ethical issues (Perdomo 1990).

Falsifying reports for Chinese managers in Hong Kong is a highly unethical practice. Malaysian managers also consider falsifying reports as highly unethical. In Canada, many corporations stress the integrity of books and records (Lefebvre & Singh 1992).The abuse of expense accounts was considered more of an ethical issue among employees of American firms than of firms in the United Kingdom. Padding expense accounts is also considered by Hong Kong Chinese and Malaysian managers as one of the most unethical practices (McDonald & Zepp 1988).

## Dealing with Competitors

If international managers feel that a nation does not provide a leveled playing field for all competitors inside its border, they are less inclined to do business there. This can be seen in the concern over the violation of patents and copyrights and obtaining information about competitors. Violations of patents and copyrights that occur in some nations impede international trade. The International Trade Commission estimated that the United States alone loses $40 billion annually in sales and royalties from the theft of intellectual property (Kohls & Butler 1994). Asia is the region where the most incidents of software piracy occur. (Piracy is even considered legal in Indonesia and Thailand!) However some Asian countries such as Japan and the Philippines have passed legislation against software piracy, even though a high tolerance level still exists for software piracy (Swinyard, Rinne, & Kau 1990).

Industrial espionage, the obtaining of secret information about competitors, is another concern of international companies when a host country condones it. Millions or perhaps billions of dollars may be lost as a result of such illegal activities. There are, however, gray areas in business ethics in regard to competitor information. Managers from different countries accept some form of information gathering as a fact of doing business. Indeed, there is very little cultural difference in this respect between the collectivist cultures of Asia and the individualistic cultures of North America and the United Kingdom in this practice. Flax (1984) identifies the many ways that companies use for obtaining information about competitors, some of which are not overtly criminal, but may be unethical in certain contexts:

- Milking potential recruits who have worked for competitors.
- Picking brains at conferences.
- Conducting phony job interviews.
- Hiring people away from competitors to obtain information.
- Interviewing competitors under false pretences.
- Debriefing design consultants who have served with competitors.
- Grilling suppliers.
- Infiltrating customer business operations.

---

**EXAMPLE 12-1:** Ethical Dilemma of Piracy

During one of my MBA classes in an Asian country, the issue of pirating copyrighted materials came up. I explained to the students that it is not ethical to buy pirated materials such as software, DVDs, and the like. The businesses that develop these materials spend literally millions of dollars a year designing, developing, and marketing such products. I compared piracy to the theft of private property and that to condone piracy amounts to condoning a thief who takes advantage of the open entrance door to a house when the owner is not home. The students were amazed to hear this. They politely pointed out that the businesses that develop materials that can be copied are rich and it really doesn't hurt them. Moreover, many people, such as students, are not able to afford the asking price. "We are not hurting anybody by doing this," my students insisted. "We need free software to further our knowledge and to keep up with the latest developments in the field of information technology so as to assist the development of our nations in the future." Given this argument, are these students being ethical?

- Studying aerial photographs of a company's plant.
- Taking plant tours.

## Gender Equality

The one area in which individualist and collectivist nations differ most significantly is that of gender equality. What is considered to be ethical and acceptable treatment of women in some nations is viewed as reprehensible in others. Laws that protect women against discrimination are commonplace in the United States and in other developed nations. However, in Japan and Saudi Arabia, where men are culturally favored over women, there is gender inequality in the important positions of business organizations (Mayer & Cava 1993). Korea, influenced by Confucian attitudes, perpetuates separate and better employment opportunities for men, even when women are more skilled and talented (De Mente 1991).

Even in countries that are progressively addressing women's equality in the workplace, there are still some lingering traces of discrimination. Davidson and Cooper (1993) note that in the United Kingdom women are protected by equal opportunity legislation. However, during employment interviews, women are often asked about plans for starting a family and about child care arrangements. (Still, men and women are generally afforded the same occupational opportunities). In 1977 Italy passed the Equal Treatment of Men and Women Act (ETA) which provides equal opportunities for both the sexes in the corporate sector. However, women in Italy still face discrimination and negative attitudes from men in the workplace.

## Environmental and Ecological Concerns

One of the most pressing issues that international management faces is the ecological impact of their operations, especially in regard to industrialization in less-developed countries. To protect the environment and the people from the unintended consequences of industrialization, most developed countries have established numerous regulations and enacted specific environmental legislation. However, many industries have avoided these regulations by setting up operations in countries where environmental laws are lax or nonexistent—indeed, this is one of the downsides of our global economy. And the range of environmental responsibility on the part of managers varies. Becker and Fritzsche (1987) found that French, German, and American managers had different attitudes about environmental pollution caused by industries. Managers from France and Germany believed that pollution would not harm the environment. American managers, interestingly, did not approve of actions that posed a threat to the environment.

## Social Responsibility

Corporate social responsibility, according to Sanyal (2001), manifests itself in many ways in underdeveloped nations, including:

- Charity contributions.
- Sponsoring (sports, museums, etc.).
- Establishing educational scholarships.
- Donating items, knowledge, and expertise.
- Providing free services to the special needs groups.

- Conserving and protecting the environment.
- Manufacturing ecologically friendly products.
- Investing in socially responsible forms.
- Creating working conditions and rules that adhere to the standards of developed countries.
- Producing safe products.
- Providing international assistance.
- Treating effluent and waste in an environmentally sound manner.

Corporate social responsibility is an organization's obligation to conduct business in such a way that safeguards the welfare of society as it pursues its own interests (Holt & Wigginton 2002). It originated in the United States in the nineteenth century, when business leaders pursued social interests long before the introduction of government regulations in this area. The steel magnate Andrew Carnegie (1835–1919), for example, suggested that the rich hold money in trust for the rest of the society to improve social welfare. Since that time, society has grown to expect organizations to undertake activities that are socially responsible and desirable.

Companies, of course, in being socially responsible must also reconcile this with modern economics and the view expressed by the economist Milton Friedman, that a company's only social responsibility is to make as much money as possible for its stockholders. Friedman argued that organizations that pursued any other additional course of action, such as providing social facilities or sponsoring a local charity, violated the profit maximization goal and proved a disadvantage to the organization in the face of competitors who did not engage in similar action (Hoffman & Moore 1990). This notion, referred to as the *classical view of social responsibility,* which would condone a manufacturing company generating a huge profit to its stakeholders while producing pollution, has led to another school of thought and the *socio-economic view* that recognizes that organizational objectives other than profit are valid for survival, including:

- Maximizing profits in the long term not short term.
- Being more than economic institutions.
- Giving back to a society that expects and encourages organizations to become involved—that is, treating society as a stakeholder.
- Taking a proactive approach.
- Recognizing the interrelationship between the economic and ecological environment.

The socio-economic view stresses that organizations engaging in socially desirable activities benefit through greater consumer recognition and strengthen their market position in the longer term (Collins & McLaughlin 1996). Another positive is that business ethics and corporate social responsibility are interrelated concepts that reinforce each other. Current research indicates that 90 percent of *Fortune* 500 firms have a corporate code of ethics (Sanyal 2001); and many multinational companies have already incorporated the socio-economic view of social responsibility into their codes of ethics, which is evident in Johnson & Johnson's:

*We are responsible to our employees, the men and women who work
with us throughout the world. Everyone must be considered as an individual. We must respect their dignity and recognize their merit. They
must have a sense of security in their jobs. Compensation must be fair
and adequate, and working conditions clean, orderly, and safe. We must
be mindful of ways to help our employees fulfill their family responsibilities. Employees must feel free to make suggestions and complaints.
There must be equal opportunity for employment, development and
advancement for those qualified. We must provide competent management, and their actions must be just and ethical.*

*We are responsible to the communities in which we will live and
work, and to the world community as well. We must be good citizens—
support good works and charities and bear our fair share of taxes. We
must encourage civic improvements and better health and education.
We must maintain in good order the property we are privileged to use,
protecting the environmental and natural resources.*

## Summary

In this chapter, the topics of business ethics and social responsibility were
discussed along with their implications for modern enterprises. International
organizations have an obligation to, among other things, preserve the ecological well-being of their host cultures and discharge their social responsibility
consistent with a socio-economic view. While there are no comprehensive
guidelines for the conduct of international organizations, some scholars have
recommended appropriate models of business conduct. DeGeorge (1993) has
suggested that multinational corporations take the following six steps to act with
integrity in their dealings:

- The firm should act in accord with its own self-imposed values that cannot be less than an ethical minimum, but may well exceed this. For example, a firm may neither give nor take bribes.

- In addition to satisfying the basic moral norms that are applicable everywhere, the firm should uphold other equally obvious moral rules.

- The firm should enter into business agreements by building on these rules.
Business agreements should be fair and benefit both sides.

- Because developing countries are poor in infrastructure, international
organizations have special obligations towards them.

- The firm should consider ethical dimensions of its actions, projects, and
plans before acting, not afterwards. This means that the ethical dimensions should be an integral part of strategic planning.

- Each person should be given his or her due. The firm should be open and
receptive to complaints from those affected and address their claims with
justice.

## Critical Discussion Questions

1. Why is the understanding of ethics across cultures important for international managers?

2. In what ways are ethics learned by the members of any given society?

3. How are ethics viewed by the consenquentialist theory?

4. What is the deontological perspective on ethics?

5. "What is ethically wrong in one culture may be acceptable in another culture." Critically discuss.

6. Is there any congruence between ethical behavior and legal behavior?

7. Why does modern society need business ethics? Provide examples.

8. Briefly discuss the major contemporary issues in international business ethics.

9. Why is socially responsible behavior important for international business?

10. Given increased competition, coupled with "corrupt" business practice in some parts of the world in today's business, does it pay to conduct one's business ethically?

# Applications

### Experiential

1. Research the extent that bribery is pervasive in developing countries and in what ways this unethical behavior potentially poses a major challenge to economic development in those countries. *Note*: You may want to begin by visiting the Web site of Transparency International at http://www.transparency.org, an organization that monitors corrupt business practices around the world.

2. Research the extent that multinational corporations operating in third world countries are responsible for unethical behavior and ecological degradation. List the unethical behaviors and environmental problems committed by such companies and study and discuss their impacts on the society and culture of host countries with your fellow students.

### Internet

Read the articles on global business ethics at the Web sites that follow. Each article advocates a particular approach to global business ethics and corporate responsibility. Once you have read the articles, summarize the key points of each article for subsequent discussion during tutorial or seminar time, and then answer these questions.

1. In your view, in what ways do these articles support or disagree with different ethical standards based on cultural differences around the world?

2. What is your position on "global business ethics" that could be applied uniformly to all corporations around the world? Provide justification for your view point.

http://www.sase.org/conf2003/papers/coutinho-bertrand.pdf
http://www.govst.edu/users/gcbpa/aboutcol/3rdworldconf/EthicalBiz.htm

# References

Agar, M. (1994). The intercultural frame. *International Journal of Intercultural Relations*, 18 (2), 221–237.

Amba-Rao, S.C. (1993). Multinational corporate social responsibility, ethics, interactions, and third world governments: An agenda for the 90s. *Journal of Business Ethics, 12, 553–572.*

Baker, B.N., Murphy, D.C., & Fisher, D. (1983). Factors affecting project success. In D.I. Cleland & D.R. King (Eds.), *Project Management Handbook* (pp. 669–685). New York: Van Nostrand.

Ball, D. & McCulloch, Jr., W. (1996). *International business: The challenge of global competition.* Chicago: Irwin.

Baumhart, R. (1968). *An honest profit: What businessmen say about ethics in business,* New York: Holt, Rinehart and Winston.

Becker, H. & Fritzsche, D. (1987). A Comparison of the ethical behavior of American, French, and German managers. *Columbia Journal of World Business, 22,* 87–95.

Becker, H. & Fritzsche, D. (1987). Business ethics: A cross-cultural comparison of manager's attitudes. *Journal of Business Ethics,* 6, 289–290.

Benson, G. (1992). *Business ethics in America,* Lexington, MA: Lexington.

Bourdeau, P. (1988). Viva la crise! For heterodoxy in social science. *Theory and Society, 17* (5), 773–787.

Buller, P.F., Kohls, J.J., & Anderson, K.S. (2000). Managing conflicts across cultures. *Organizational Dynamics, 28* (4), 52–66.

Caroll, S.J. & Gannon, J.M. (1997). *Ethical dimensions of international management.* Thousand Oaks, CA: Sage.

Carroll, R. (1988). *Cultural misunderstandings: The French-American experience.* Chicago: University of Chicago Press.

Cavanagh G.F., Dennis, J., Moberg, D.J., & Velasquez, M. (1981). The Ethics of organizational politics. *Academy of Management Review, 6* (3), 363–374.

Collins, R. & McLaughlin, Y. (1996). *Effective management* (2nd ed.). North Ryde, Australia: CCH Australia.

Crawford, J.W. (1974). *Advertising.* Boston: Allyn and Bacon.

Davidson, J. & Cooper, G. (1993). *European women in business and management.* London: Paul Chapman.

DeGeorge, R.T. (1986). *Business ethics* (2nd ed.). New York: Macmillan.

DeGeorge, R.T. (1993). *Competing with integrity in international business.* New York: Oxford University Press.

DeMente, B. (1981). *The Japanese way of doing business: The psychology of management in Japan*. Englewood Cliffs, NJ: Prentice-Hall.

DeMente, B. (1988). *Korean etiquette and ethics in business*. Lincolnwood, IL: NTC Business Books.

DeMente, B. (1990). *Chinese etiquette and ethics in business*. Lincolnwood, IL: NTC Business Books.

DeMente, B. (1991). *Japanese etiquette and ethics in business*. Lincolnwood, IL: NTC Business Books.

Dirksen, C.J. & Kroeger, A. (1973). *Advertising principles and problems*. (4th ed.). Homewood, IL: Irwin.

Donaldson, T. (1989). *The ethics of international business*. New York: Oxford University Press.

Eyles, Miltenyi, Davis Pty Ltd (1989). *English in the workplace: A shrewd economic investment* (Vol. 1). Canberra: Australian Government Printering Services.

Fatehi, K. (1996). *International management: A cross culture and functional perspective*. Upper Saddle River, NJ: Prentice Hall.

Flax, S. (1984). How to snoop on your competitor. *Fortune*, May 14, 28–33.

Fulop, L. & Linstead, S. (Eds.) (1999). *Management: A critical text*. South Yarra, Australia: Macmillan Education.

Grace, D. & Cohen, S. (1998). *Business ethics: Australian problems and cases* (2nd ed.). Oxford University Press.

Heidegger, M. (1962). *Being and time*. New York: Harper and Row.

Hellriegal, D. & Slocum, Jr., J.W. (1999). *Management* (8th ed.). Cincinnati, OH: International Thomson.

Hitt, W.D. (1996). *A global ethic: The leadership challenge,* Columbus, OH: Battelle.

Hodgetts, R.M. & Luthans, F. (2000). *International Management*. New York: McGraw-Hill.

Hoffman, M. & Moore, J. (1990). *Business Ethics: Readings and cases in corporate morality* (2nd ed.). New York: McGraw-Hill.

Holt, D.H. & Wigginton, K.W. (2002). *International management* (2nd ed.). Orlando, FL: Harcourt College.

Ivancevich, J., Olekans, M., & Matteson, M. (1997). *Organizational behavior and management*. Sydney: McGraw-Hill.

Jackson, T. (1993). *Organizational behavior in international management*. London: Butterworth Heinemann.

Jackson, T. (1995). *Cross-cultural management*. London: Butterworth Heinemann.

Jefkins, F. (1973). *Advertising made simple*. London: Howard and Wyndham.

Kant, I. (1964) *Groundwork of the metaphysics of morals.* H.P. Paton, trans. NY: Harper and Row.

Kohls, J. & Buller, P. (1994). Resolving cross-cultural ethics conflict: Exploring alternative strategies. *Journal of Business Ethics, 13,* 31–38.

Kumar, B.N. & Steinmann, H. (Eds.) (1998). *Ethics in international management.* Berlin; New York: De Gruyter.

Lefebvre, M. & Singh, J. (1992). The context and focus of Canadian code of ethics. *Journal of Business Ethics, 11,* 799–808.

Mahoney, D., Trigg, M., Griffin, R., & Pustay, M. (1998). *International business: A managerial perspective.* Melbourne: Addison Wesley Longman.

Mayer, D. & Cava, A. (1993). Ethics and the gender equality: Dilemma for U.S. multinationals. *Journal of Business Ethics, 12,* 701–708.

McDonald, G. & Zepp, R. (1988). Ethical perceptions of Hong Kong Chinese business managers. *Journal of Business Ethics, 7,* 835–845.

Mead, R. (1998). *International management: Cross-cultural dimensions.* Cambridge, MA: Blackwell.

Mill, J.S. (1957). *Utilitarianism.* New York: Bobbs-Merrill.

Mullins, L.J. (1996). *Management and organizational behavior* (4th ed.). London: Pitman.

Payne, D., Raiborn, C., & Askvik, J. (1997). A global code of business ethics. *Journal of Business Ethics* December, *16,* 1727–1735.

Perdomo, R. (1990). Corruption in business in present day Venezuela. *Journal of Business Ethics, 9,* 555–556.

Phatak, A.V. (1997). *International management: Concepts and cases.* Cincinnati, OH: South-Western College.

Robertson, D. & Schlegermilch, B. (1993). Corporate institutionalization of ethics in the U.S. and Great Britain. *Journal of Business Ethics, 12,* 301–312.

Rodrigues, C. (1996). *International management: A cultural approach.* St. Paul, MN: West.

Saee, J. (1993). Culture, multiculturalism and racism: An Australian perspective. *Journal of Home Economics of Australia, 25,* 99–109.

Saee, J. (1994). Fundamental challenges of social responsibility, ethics, consumerism and the law confronting the world of advertising. Paper presented at the Australia–New Zealand Academy of Management (ANZAM) conference, Auckland, New Zealand.

Sanyal, R. (2001). *International management: A strategic perspective.* Upper Saddle River, NJ: Prentice Hall.

Sartre, J.P. (1969). *Being and nothingness: An essay on phenomenological ontology.* H. Barnes, trans. London: Routledge.

Shaw, W. & Berry, V. (1989). *Moral issues in business* (4th ed.). Belmont, CA: Wadsworth.

Swinyard, W., Rinne, H., & Kau, A. (1990). The morality of software piracy: A cross-cultural ethics analysis. *Journal of Business Ethics, 9,* 655–664.

Taylor, P.W. (1975). *Principles of ethics: An introduction to ethics* (2nd ed.). Encion, CA: Dickenson.

Velasquez, M.G. (1992). *Business ethics: concepts and cases* (3rd ed.). Englewood Cliffs, NJ: Prentice Hall.

Vogel, D. (1992). The globalization of business ethics: Why America remains distinctive. *California Management Review, 35* (1), 30–49.

Weber, M. (1930) *The Protestant ethic and the spirit of capitalism.* London. Allen and Unwin.

Weir, D. & Schapiro, M. (1981). *Circle of poison,* San Francisco: Institute for Food and Development Policy.

Wellman, B. (1992). "Which types of ties and networks provide what kinds of social support?" *Advances in Group Processes, 17* (2), 28-45.

# Chapter 13

*International Human Resource Management*

---

## LEARNING OBJECTIVES

*After reading this chapter, you should be able to:*
- *Understand the critical role that human resource plays in an organization competing in the global economy.*
- *Describe different staff philosophies.*
- *Understand the key attributes of a successful manager operating in an international environment.*
- *Understand the issues and problems surrounding female participation in international assignments.*
- *Understand the importance of performance appraisal.*
- *Understand the role of management training for international postings.*
- *Describe the different managerial training programs.*
- *Describe a compensation program for a global organization.*

*The caliber of the people . . . the only source of competitive advantage.*

—Allan Halcrow, editor of Personnel Journal

## OVERVIEW

This chapter examines international human resource management with particular reference to staffing philosophy, performance appraisal, and management training, as well as compensation policy and their implications for global management. Globalization has given rise to the transfer and mobility of human resources (HR) from one country to another. Managers from one culture may manage the workforce of a host culture—or workers from one culture may find themselves in a new and different host culture, managed by members of that host culture. This has transformed many homogeneous workplaces around the world into highly multicultural organizations. Chiavenato (2001) has identified the notable transformations of human resource management that began before the modern process of globalization and taken new turns because of globalization:

- *The Industrial Age to the Information Age* saw workers focus less on muscular work (repetitive physical labor that doesn't add value) and more on mental creativity and innovative work. Specialization and multitasking have also increased due to the use of computers. In this way, information and knowledge have supplanted manufacturing as the source of most new jobs.

- *Restricted markets to globalization of markets and labor* call for management to develop a new global perspective in order to succeed in an international environment.

- *Bureaucracy to adhocracy.* Rigid organizational hierarchy is increasingly being replaced by flexible organizational structure—business units and profit centers that change rapidly.

- *Stability to change.* Previous managerial emphasis on permanence, tradition, and the past is giving way to creativity and innovation in the search for new solutions, new processes, and new products and services.

- *Command to orientation.* The traditional hierarchical notion of authority based on vertical imposition of orders and instructions is now being replaced with democratic leadership based on the organization's mission and vision.

- *Solitary to collective activity* has seen more and more teamwork replacing individual activity.

- *Followers of orders to entrepreneurs.* Rather than being conservative bureaucrats, workers are becoming increasingly innovative and creative.

- *Human resources to business partners.* In the past, workers were perceived as an organizational resource. Now, they manage the company's organizational resources.

- *Agents to leaders.* The old autocratic, authoritarian, people-controlling bosses are being replaced with democratic leaders and people promoters.

- *From financial to intellectual capital.* The focus on money as the most significant organizational resource is increasingly shifting to knowledge as the unlimited and fundamental input for business success.

In a contemporary competitive global economy, where the other factors of production-capital, technology, raw materials, and information are increasingly able to be duplicated, the caliber of the people in an organization still remains the only source of sustainable competitive advantage (Laabs 1996). Thus, firms operating overseas need to pay particular attention to human resources as being the most critical asset. Consequently, for international firms to manage their human resources, effective international human resource management as a corporate strategy has now become increasingly significant. This is a very complex challenge due to the differing political, economic, social, and cultural values found abroad and even domestically. These differences affect labor relations, industrial relations, and management practices and can be categorized into the following dimensions:

- *Cultural factors:* Power distance, individualism versus collectivism, masculinity versus femininity, uncertainty avoidance, and short- versus long-term orientation define a national culture that in turn affects overall management practices and labor relations. (See Chapter 2.)

- *Economic and idealogical factors:* Differences in economic factors translate into intercountry differences in HR practices. In a free enterprise economic system, there is a need for efficiency that favors HR policies that value labor productivity, efficient workers, and staff streamlining as dictated by market forces. In a socialist economy, HR practices tend to shift towards preventing unemployment, even at the expense of sacrificing economic efficiency.

- *Labor cost factors:* Higher labor costs may require a focus on efficiency and on HR practices including pay for performance aimed at improving employee performance.

- *Industrial relations factors:* Define the relationship between the worker, the union, and the employer, and vary dramatically from country to country. It is necessary for HR managers to see the differences between home-country arrangements in the degree of centralization, the role of unions, employer organizations, worker participation, content and scope of bargaining, and strikes and grievances.

Furthermore, the international human resource manager should keep in mind that there are differences in management styles and practices from country to country (see Chapter 2). Such differences can strain the relationships between headquarters and the subsidiary or render a manager less effective when working abroad. Therefore, the need to rightly select, train, and compensate international managers becomes of paramount importance (Dessler, et al. 1999).

With these in mind, the overall purpose of management of human resources globally is to enable the firm, the multinational enterprise, to be successful. This entails being (a) competitive throughout the world; (b) efficient; (c) locally responsive; (d) flexible and adaptable within the shortest of time period; and (e) capable of transferring knowledge and learning across their globally dispersed units (Schuler, et al. 1993).

For a firm to be successful, formal and informal control along with human resource management (HRM) policies must be congruent with the firm's strategy. Human resource management refers to the activities that an organization carries out to use its people—its human resources—

effectively. These activities include determining the firm's human resource strategy, staffing, performance evaluation, management development, compensation, and labor relations. Through its influence on the character, development, quality, and productivity of the firm's human resources, the HRM function can help the firm achieve its primary strategic goals of reducing the costs of value creation and adding value by better serving customer needs (Hill 2000). For this purpose, there is a need to have a strong corporate culture and an informal management network for transmitting information within the organization. The HRM function can help develop the proper employee selection, management development, performance appraisal, and compensation policies. To achieve this organizational strategic objective, management develops human resource planning that must be comprehensive in scope and, at the same time, responsive to the special nature of multinational corporations (MNCs)—and like organizations—and their competitive strategies. In addition, a comprehensive human resource plan ensures that such organizations have (1) the right people in place around the world; (2) staffing policies that capitalize on the worldwide expertise of expatriates, third country nationals (TCNs), and host country nationals (HCNs); (3) performance appraisals anchored in the competitive strategies of MNC headquarters and host units; (4) compensation that is strategically and culturally relevant; and (5) training and development initiatives that prepare individuals to operate effectively in their overseas locations and cooperate with other MNC units (Schuler, et al. 1993).

# STAFFING PHILOSOPHIES FOR INTERNATIONAL ENTERPRISES

Selecting the right employee with the right kind of qualifications for the right position at the right time—who could also fit into the corporate culture—is the ideal goal of international human resource managers. To achieve this, firms use a number of selection approaches depending on their staffing philosophies. In the following sections, four types of staffing policies in international business are discussed: the ethnocentric approach, the polycentric approach, the regiocentric approach, and the geocentric approach (Welch 1994).

## Ethnocentric Staffing Policy

The ethnocentric approach to staffing policy fills management posts in overseas subsidiaries with parent-country nationals. One consideration for adopting this approach is the desire for senior management to tightly maintain organizational coordination and control. The other advantages of appointing home country nationals include the following:

- Using expatriates is a relatively easy way to obtain personnel with detailed knowledge of company policies, procedures, and corporate culture.
- Given their length of service with the parent company, the expatriates possess a detailed knowledge of parent company management practices of related technology and product development.
- The need to maintain a foreign image in the foreign company.
- Parent company has a good deal of knowledge about expatriates' managerial competencies.

- Company loyalty is not an issue with expatriates, as they have partly been chosen for the job due to proven loyalty to the company (Rodrigues 1996; Phatak 1997).

Fatehi (1996) suggests that firms that select expatriates in preference to host nationals is partly due to such firms being highly centralized and reliant on low-cost production of commodity-type products for international markets. Where the political power of the host country is perceived as a threat, such firms also adopt this recruitment strategy so as not to become subordinate to the host country's regime. Another reason is the firm's lack of knowledge of the host culture or its nationals. In this case, management may even believe in the superiority of its own culture and its expatriates, a phenomenon that can be a great hindrance to successful international business operation strategically. Rodrigues (1996) identifies further disadvantages associated with this type of recruitment strategy:

- The unfamiliarity of expatriates with the whole host of issues, namely political, legal, and economic dimensions of the foreign country.
- Lack of adaptability to foreign culture by the expatriates who have to be repatriated at an enormous cost.
- Problems associated with intercultural communication occur, as the expatriates are not knowledgeable about the very complex culture and communication of the foreign country in which they operate.
- Highly expensive salary packages are required to attract qualified people for an international posting.
- Sometimes the best qualified people may not want the international posting.
- The expatriate may not be too productive in the early part of the international assignment due to the difficulty of adaptation to the local environment.

There is evidence to suggest that the lack of adaptability to foreign culture causes expatriates to fail in their international assignment, which can be an enormous cost to their employers if they have to be repatriated. Expatriate failure rates also represent a failure of the firm's selection policies to identify individuals who will not thrive abroad. Caudron (1991) has found that the cost of expatriate failure is high and it can be as high as three times the expatriate's annual domestic salary plus the cost of relocation. (Estimates of each failure run from $250,000 to $1,000,000.) Those who do stay can also be ineffective or only marginally effective. And failure is more common to U.S.-based multinationals than European or Japanese multinationals. And what induces such failures? Hill (2000) lists the following:

- Inability of spouse to adjust
- Manager's inability to adjust
- Other family problems
- Manager's personal or emotional immaturity
- Inability to cope with larger overseas responsibility
- Lack of technical competence

Research by Tung (1982) in this area found that spouse problems were the top reason for expatriate failure among European and U.S. overseas MNC employees. For their Japanese counterparts it is much less so. Family considerations, especially children's schooling, were also a top concern that hindered employees from taking overseas assignments or repatriating—or they worried that being away from home base would hurt their careers (Mead 1998). Though, the reasons for these failures were derived from company data, which gives the company's point of view over the expatriate's point of view—the picture emerges that MNCs also fail—in their procedures for selecting, training, and supporting their expatriates.

## Polycentric Staffing Policy

Polycentric staffing entails appointing host country nationals (HCNs) in middle- and lower-management ranks in overseas subsidiaries. Experienced international organizations such as Shell, Qantas, Dupont, TNT, and AT&T employ HCNs instead of transferring domestic staff (Wall Street Journal 1993). Many smaller firms setting up operations abroad hire HCNs because they do not possess enough managerial talent at home to send personnel abroad on a foreign assignment (Fetterolf 1990). There are other considerations behind the appointment of the HCNs by the international firms. There is the management belief that employing HCNs is beneficial to the company because they are familiar with the local environmental context and conditions such as local language, culture, customs, economics, business conditions, and, importantly, local legal requirements. Furthermore, there is an apparent economic advantage of hiring HCNs: It would be less expensive for the company to avoid the expenses associated with relocating expatriates and of paying their higher salaries. This recruitment policy is particularly appealing and effective when the firm wants to be seen as blending into the local environment for economic, political, and corporate image considerations—both within the host and home countries. Nevertheless, some drawbacks associated with this recruitment strategy are apparent:

- The difficulty of coordinating activities and goals between the subsidiary and the parent company.
- Loyalty may be to the host country, not to the company. It is conceivable to imagine that in conflicts between the company interest and the national interest, the HCN manager may favor national interest over the company's interest.
- HCNs may have difficulty in communicating with the home office and with other employees.
- Upon their appointment to the position, the HCN managers may then be unable and unwilling to move to another location.
- HCNs may lack perspective on the corporate culture of the home office
- In view of the foregoing, expensive training and development will be needed to address some of the identified problems, as outlined previously (Deresky 2000; Rodrigues 1996).

So what kind of staffing solution is better, expatriate or local? U.S. and European MNCs typically employ more local managers and far fewer expatriated staff in their overseas subsidiaries than Japanese MNCs. Tung (1982) found that the Japanese MNCs were more likely to staff senior levels in their foreign subsidiaries with Japanese. This is a cultural trait in the case of Japanese companies because managers who share the language and values of headquarters provide minimum risk (Mead 1998).

### Regiocentric Staffing Policy

Managers who adopt regiocentric staffing consider that the global market should be handled regionally. For example, all European markets should be coordinated through a headquarter in France or London. Thus, selection of staff is carried out within that region: France or London. This staffing policy is used when products are similar all over the world, but the marketing must be tailored to meet the needs of different cultures within a particular region (Fatehi 1996).

### Geocentric Staffing Policy

Geocentric staffing policy favors the appointment of a candidate for the position who possesses the best qualifications, regardless of his or her nationality, race, religion, color, and gender (Welch 1994). HR managers who implement this policy believe competence should be the prime criterion for selecting managerial staff (Rodrigues 1996). A good example of a company that pursues this staffing policy is Coca-Cola. Coke operates in more than 195 countries. Third-country nationals make up the majority of the international service employees and individuals of other nationalities are in charge of more of Coca-Cola's division offices than are North Americans (Personnel Journal 1994). While this staffing policy is laudable for its progressiveness and best practice, there are drawbacks, including increased training costs and relocation costs—and the requirements for detailed documentation requested by the host government for hiring a foreign national over one of its own nationals (Hill 2000).

## SELECTION CRITERIA FOR INTERNATIONAL MANAGERIAL POSITIONS

The factors that influence HR decisions are industry factors, strategic factors, technology, age and condition, headquarters availability, local national policies on staff, local availability, criteria for headquarters promotion, labor market factors, demand for management skills, location, communication, and culture. However, it should be kept in mind that all these factors are interlinked. For instance, cost and labor market factors are closely linked with questions of availability and promotions policy, which reflect strategic decisions and industry factors. The decision is complex, and there is no absolutely right or wrong answer for all situations (Mead 1998).

Firms willing to recruit new international managers need, first of all, to formulate selection criteria that are in line with the specific requirements for the international posting. It is generally argued that the personal and professional qualities needed as the essential selection criteria for a successful candidate should include: "A flexible personality, with broad intellectual horizons, attitudinal values of cultural empathy, general friendliness, patience and prudence, impeccable educational and professional (or technical) credentials—all topped off with immaculate health, creative resourcefulness, and respect of peers, if the family is endowed, all the better" (Heller 1980). Other desirable personal and professional characteristics include:

- *Technical ability.* By far the most critical skills for an international manager to possess are the relevant technical knowledge and competencies to be able to perform the job in the first place.

- *Managerial skills acquisition.* Again, this is a crucial knowledge, as this will be needed for an international manager in terms of being able to carry out a management position in an effective manner. The best indicator for this would be the candidates' past management track records and their achievements.

- *Cross-cultural sensitivity.* Candidates, in order to be successful overseas strategically, have to demonstrate that they have already developed high levels of cross cultural sensitivity involving high levels of tolerance and openness and understanding of peoples of other cultures in a nonjudgmental way which is deemed as a most critical indicator of international managerial competence.

- *Adaptability and flexibility.* This relates to the previous desirable characteristic, namely, cross-cultural sensitivity in that a person who already has demonstrable cross-cultural sensitivity may find it a lot easier to be adaptable to other cultures in a flexible manner than someone who lacks an international cultural dimension. Adaptability and flexibility embrace a number dimensions which an international manager needs to possess:

  - A high degree of ability to integrate with other people, with other cultures, and with other types of business operations;

  - Adaptability to change; being able to sense developments in the host country; recognizing differences, being able to evaluate them; and being able to qualitatively and quantitatively express the factors affecting the operations with which he or she is entrusted;

  - Ability to solve problems within different frameworks and from different perspectives;

  - Sensitivity to the finer points of differences in culture, politics, religion, and ethics, in addition to industrial differences (Phatak 1997); and

  - Flexibility in managing operations on a continuous basis, despite lack of assistance and gaps in information rationale.

- *Diplomatic skills.* Undoubtedly, it is desirable for international managers to have developed high level diplomatic and negotiating skills required in an international managerial position. Quite often, international managers have to liaise with the host government officials and politicians, particularly in the developing countries where the governments own and operate large public enterprises, so as to secure better business deals strategically.

- *Foreign language aptitude.* The ability and willingness of international managers to quickly learn the foreign language, as the fluency in a foreign language by the international managers partially contributes to their adaptation to the host culture as well as enabling the international managers to communicate with host nationals in their own language.

- *Positive attitude.* It should be a vital consideration for selecting candidates for an international assignment. The reason being that without candidates' inner desire for living and working overseas, nothing else will motivate them to genuinely want to be living overseas on an ongoing basis.

- *Emotional stability and maturity.* In much the same way as the positive attitude, emotional maturity is needed by candidates to be successful in their international assignments. A sense of emotional balance in one's life is critical in order to find harmony and stability in one's day-to-day living, no matter where one lives.

- *Adaptability of family.* The ability of an international manager to be effective in his or her international assignments to a considerable degree is contingent upon how happy the manager's spouse and children feel living in a foreign country. In many instances, where the manager's spouse or children find living overseas unsettling and an unhappy state of affairs due to cultural differences, as reflected in customs, language, food, and habits, etc. will take its toll on the performance of the manager working abroad (Voris 1975; Heller 1980; Phatak 1997; Saee 1998).

# FEMALE PARTICIPATION IN THE WORKFORCE

While the number and proportion of women managers working domestically has climbed in the past few years, the same cannot be said about sending women managers abroad. There are several erroneous assumptions about sending women managers overseas. One myth is that women are reluctant to transfer overseas or do not want to be international managers. Yet in one study, four out of five MBAs—women and men—would not refuse an international assignment at some time during their career. Similarly the belief that dual career marriages make it impossible to send female managers abroad is another mistaken assumption that limits women managers' access to positions abroad (Adler, 1987). More women in management are being transferred overseas by their employers—and husbands are now becoming "trailing spouses" who move with their wives. In 1994, the percentage of male-trailing spouses was 15.7 percent, up from 10.9 percent in 1993 (Ball & Wendell 1996).

Still, American companies are reluctant to select women for international positions. Solomon (1989) found that 80 percent of the companies sampled in his research saw disadvantages to sending women overseas. "Clients refuse to do business with female representatives," one company representative said. Another explained: "The desired expatriate is a

---

**EXAMPLE 13-1:** Nonadaptability of the Family: Challenges for a Firm

Several years ago a U.S. engineering company ran into trouble while working on a steel mill in Italy. The crisis stemmed neither from inexperienced Italian personnel nor from volatile Italian politics, but rather from the inability of an American executive's wife to adapt to Italy. Frustrated by the Italian language, her children's schooling, and the difficulty of shopping (she was used to American-style supermarkets and shopping malls), the executive's wife complained incessantly to other company wives who began to feel that they, too, suffered hardships and started complaining to their husbands. Morale became so bad that the company missed deadlines and, eventually, replaced almost every American on the project.

Source: Adapted from *Business Week* (1979, April 16). Gauging a Family's Suitability for a Stint Overseas. p.127

thirtyish married man with preschool-age children. This is to project our image as a conservative institution with good moral fiber.... Many of our potential female expatriates are single, and a swinging single is not the right image."

Another reason why women do not get promoted to managerial appointments abroad is that they are faced with the notion of *glass ceiling* in an organization's executive hierarchy above which females are rarely promoted and, for that reason, do not push so as not to harm how far they can get: an invisible yet real ceiling. Nevertheless, this reality is trending in the other direction as organizations in developed countries at least, given the effect of equal employment opportunity, government policies, and antidiscrimination legislation, do not want to face major legal and public relations difficulties (Ball & Wendall 1996).

Perhaps the most persistent inhibition to sending women managers abroad is the assumption that they would face too much foreign prejudice and that they could not succeed for that reason. The assumption here is that members of some societies are so unduly prejudiced against women managers that the latter could not do their jobs effectively. But the evidence belies the assumption. In one survey, nearly all the women managers (97 percent) reported that their international assignments were successful (Adler 1987).

Recent attention has been drawn to the connection between the strong participation of women in smaller businesses and the increased involvement of small business in international activities, resulting in a call for global mentor programs to encourage women to take their businesses into the international sphere (Dessler, et al. 1999).

# PERFORMANCE APPRAISAL

Recruitment and selection of qualified staff for overseas assignments are initial steps in international human resource management. The next task is the performance appraisal or evaluation. Its purpose has been identified by Mahoney, et al. (1998) and includes:

- Providing feedback to individuals as to how well they are doing.
- Providing a basis for rewarding top performers.
- Identifying areas in which additional training and development may be needed.
- Identifying problem areas that may call for a change in assignment.

Ideally, international performance evaluation should be carefully designed to avoid possible biases—and bias can exist. Host country managers can be biased towards their own cultural frames of reference and expectations. Their appraisals may be biased by distance and by their own lack of experience working abroad. Home office management is often not personally aware of what is going on in a foreign operation. For this reason, such managers do not take into account many less visible soft variables that are also important, for example, an expatriate's ability to develop cross-cultural awareness so as to work productively with local, host-culture managers and employees (Hill 2000).

Performance criteria also should be based on work goals. Notable is the fact that goals can be categorized in terms of hard goals, soft goals, and

contextual goals. Hard goals are objective, quantifiable, and can be measured such as return on investment (ROI), market share, and so on. Soft
goals tend to be relationship- or trait-based such as leadership style or
interpersonal skills. Contextual goals attempt to take into account factors
that result from the situation in which performance takes place. For
instance, MNCs routinely use arbitrary transfer pricing and other financial tools for transactions between subsidiaries in order to minimize
foreign-exchange risk exposure and tax expenditures (Dowling et al.
1999). Performance evaluation of subsidiary managers against hard goal
criteria is often supplemented by frequent visits by headquarters staff and
meetings with executives from the parent company. Soft criteria can be
used to complement hard goals and take into account areas that are difficult to quantify, such as leadership skills (Janssens 1994). However, an
appraisal system that uses hard, soft, and contextual criteria builds on the
strengths of each while minimizing their disadvantages.

Mendenhall and Oddou (1985) make additional recommendations for
improving the expatriate appraisal process:

- Stipulate the assignment's difficulty level. For example, being
  an expatriate manager in China is generally considered more
  difficult than working in England.

- Weigh the evaluation more toward the on-site manager's
  appraisal than toward the home-site manager's distant perceptions of the employee's performance.

- If, however (as is usually the case), the home-site manager does
  the actual written appraisal, have him or her use a former expatriate from the same overseas location to provide background
  advice during the appraisal process.

- Modify the normal performance criteria used for that particular
  position to fit the overseas position and characteristics of that
  particular locale. For example, the maintenance of positive
  labor relations might be more important in Chile, where labor
  instability is more common, than it would be in the United
  States; And

- Attempt to give the expatriate manager credit for relevant
  insights into the functioning of the operation and specifically
  the interdependencies of the domestic and foreign operations.
  In other words, don't just appraise the expatriate manager in
  terms of quantifiable criteria like profits or market share.

## MANAGEMENT TRAINING AND DEVELOPMENT

Selection is only a matching process. The crucial process for the newly
appointed manager is undergoing management training to perform in a
competent manner. Training is the process of altering employee behavior
and attitudes in a way that maximizes the probability of goal attainment
(Hodgetts & Luthans 2000). One priority should be cross-cultural training,
as this enables the newly appointed managers to get ready for challenges
arising from the foreign environment in which they will find themselves.
Studies have shown that up to 40 percent of expatriate managers end
their foreign assignments early because of poor performance or an inability to adjust to the local environment (Black 1988). Also, new overseas
managers entering a foreign environment experience culture shock (see
Chapter 6), a state of disorientation and anxiety about not knowing how

to behave in an unfamiliar culture (Oberg 1960). There are several recognized stages of this orientation–disorientation that such managers—or *sojourners* as we called them in Chapter 6 must go through. These are described in the following sections.

### Initial Contact/Honeymoon

During this phase, the sojourner fails to recognize new realities. The sojourner's own culturally influenced worldview persists; the sojourner sees one's own initial worldview in the second culture. The differences experienced by the sojourner may not be threatening but intriguing. In other words, sojourners feel a high degree of excitement and euphoria during this stage (Fogel, 1993; Gudykunst 1993).

### Initial Culture Shock

This stage is characterized by a sense of increasing confusion and loss. The foreigner experiences disorientation because of a lack of familiarity with everyday cues such as language, gestures, foods, and customs. Culture shock has often been described by individuals as lacking points of reference, social norms, and rules to guide their actions and understand others' behavior (Furham & Bechner 1989). Thus, during the initial period in a new culture, global managers often find that other people's behavior does not seem to make sense; and, even more disconcerting, that their own behavior does not produce expected results. They find that the environment makes new demands for which they have neither ready-made answers nor the ability to develop new, culturally appropriate responses. (See Example 13-2.)

### Superficial Adjustment

This stage is marked by the sojourner's attempt to find a solution to a difficult situation. The foreigner temporarily overcomes the negative effects of culture shock and has learned how to "survive" in the host culture. The sojourner can communicate basic needs in the host language and appears to be settled. Some sojourners still remain ineffective in their adjustment to the new environment—and blame others such as host nationals, the company, or their spouse. The following are typical comments you might hear:

- *Blaming the host national.* "These foreigners (who in fact are the natives) are stupid; anyone who had any intelligence would

---

**EXAMPLE 13-2:** The Queasy Stomach

On my third day in Israel, accompanied by a queasy stomach, I ventured forth into the corner market to buy something light and easy to digest. As yet unable to read Hebrew, I decided to pick up what looked like a small yogurt container that was sitting near the cheese. Not being one hundred percent sure it contained yogurt, I peered inside and to my delight, it held a thick, white, yogurt-looking substance. I purchased my "yogurt" and went home to eat—soap, liquid soap! How was I to know that soap came in packages resembling yogurt containers or that market items in Israel were not neatly divided into edible and inedible sections as I remembered them in the United States? My now "clean" stomach became a bit more fragile and my confidence waned.

Source: From *International Dimensions of Organizational Behavior*, 4th edition by Adler. © 2002. Reprinted with permission of South-Western, a division of Thomson Learning: www.thomsonrights.com. Fax: 800-730-2215.

never have laid out a city this way! Addresses seem to be scattered randomly down the streets."

- *Blaming the company.* "Why didn't the company tell me that the street numbers in Tokyo would not be sequential? How do they expect me to find our clients, let alone make the sales? The least they could have done is given me a map and a guide."
- *Blaming one's spouse.* "Here I have been traveling for the last two weeks, eating strange food, trying to get these foreigners to sign the biggest contract that the firm has never gotten, and I come home to hear you complaining that the kids can't take a bath because the plumber doesn't speak English. Some help you are!" (Adler 1997, 241)

In the final analysis, cultural differences begin to intrude and the sojourner experiences a loss of ties with his or her own culture.

### Depression/Isolation Stage

The sojourner experiences a growing loss of self-esteem because of awareness of deep cultural differences. The sojourner feels alienated from members of the host culture. Frequent misinterpretation of cultural cues and lack of ability to "fit in" occur because the sojourner feels a loss of control over his or her environment. His or her sense of identity and personality are threatened (Furnham & Bochner 1989; Harris & Moran 1991; Gudykunst 1993).

### Reintegration/Compensation Stage

The sojourner develops coping behavior to deal with self-esteem. Cultural differences continue to cause the sojourner to make negative judgments; however, the sojourner may develop strategies to help deal with anxiety, nervousness, frustration, and anger (Furnham & Bochner 1989; Harris & Moran 1991; Gudykunst 1993).

### Autonomy/Independence Stage

The sojourner accepts and sometimes even values differences between his or her own and the host culture during this stage. The sojourner feels more relaxed and demonstrates self-confidence. He or she is capable of interacting socially in the host culture. (For a detailed discussion, see Chapter 6.)

## OVERSEAS TRAINING PROGRAMS

Having observed the difficulties associated with adaptation, as experienced by a stranger such as the newly appointed manager, it seems that training would be very important to make the manager and spouse cope with the problem of adjusting to the foreign environment. Cross-cultural training, language training, and technical training can reduce expatriate failure. Bartlett and Ghoshal (1998) describe management training as having three aims: (1) to inculcate a common vision and shared values (called "cultural and spiritual training" such as in Matsushita, (organization cohesion" in Phillips, and "indoctrination" in Unilever); (2) to broaden management perspectives and capabilities; and (3) to develop contacts and shape management relationships. What types of cross-cultural training does an international firm need to develop to prepare the manager living and working in a foreign environment? Tung's (1982) research findings generated six types of recommended cross-cultural training programs:

1. *Environmental briefings* that include information on such things as geography, climate, housing, and schools.
2. *Cultural orientation* designed to familiarize the individual with cultural institutions and value systems of the host culture.
3. *Cultural assimilators* using programmed learning techniques that are geared to provide the participants with intercultural interactions.
4. *Language training* to facilitate communication with members of the host culture.
5. *Sensitivity training* designed to develop attitudinal flexibility.
6. *Field experience* designed to provide the participants with the real-life experience by sending them overseas, where the participants can actually undergo some of the emotional stress of living and working with people of culturally diverse backgrounds in a foreign country.

While overseas management training is deemed crucial for effective international business operations, when it comes to providing the actual training and development, the practices of most firms reflect more form than substance. Study in this area concluded that while there is recognition in international management circles that future prosperity in the global business environment depends on qualified employees who can operate effectively in foreign countries, few companies actually provided overseas management training and development for their employees (Dessler, et al. 1999). An international survey, for example, showed that only 32 percent of U.S. firms had formal training programs designed to prepare individuals for international assignments. This contrasted with 57 percent for Japanese firms and 69 percent for European companies that had formal training programs (Tung 1982).

# INTERNATIONAL COMPENSATION

The strategic purpose of any compensation system is to attract, motivate, reward, and retain competent staff, and a well-designed compensation system is essential to achieve this organizational goal (Sanyal 2001). The criteria that HR management needs to consider are differences in national salaries—and the best method of compensation for the expatriate managers—as well as the question of equity for its entire workforce. Establishing a compensation plan that is equitable, consistent, and does not overcompensate a manager is a challenging and complex task whether he or she is stationed at home or abroad. The method favored by the majority of American MNCs has been to pay a base salary equal to that paid to a domestic counterpart and then, in the belief that no one should be worse off for accepting foreign employment, to add a variety of allowances and bonuses (Ball & Wendell 1996). Another important reason for this compensation strategy is that it reduces the risk of perceived inequities and simplifies the job of keeping track of disparate country-by-country wage rates. On the other hand, it is also essential to compensate the manager for the high cost of living in some countries irrespective of whether they are developed or underdeveloped. Hill (2000) recommends the following policies for addressing problematic issues of compensation in terms of what to pay managers:

- Pay a similar base salary company-wide and then add on various allowances according to individual market conditions.

- Ask the local managers to conduct their own compensation surveys. Kraft conducts an annual study of total compensation in many countries. The survey covers all forms of compensation including cash, short-and long-term incentives, retirement plans, medical benefits, and perquisites.

- The most common approach to formulate expatriate pay is to equalize purchasing power across countries, a technique known as *the balance sheet approach*. The basic idea is that each expatriate should enjoy the same standard of living he or she would have had at home. Thus four main home country groups of expenses—income tax, housing, goods and services, and reserve—are the focus of attention. Therefore, base salary will normally be in the same range as the manager's home country salary to which is added an overseas or foreign service premium to compensate for cultural and physical adjustments.

Many multinationals also permit the top managers at corporate headquarters to participate in long-term incentive programs like stock option plans. However, compensation packages can be very complicated. There are also fluctuating currency exchange rates, differing inflation rates, and the taxation policies of the host country involved in the compensation equation (Ball & Wendell 1996). Some allowances that are added to the base salary in order to cover the differences between home and host countries include:

- Cost of living allowance for housing and consumer good differentials. This is a very controversial allowance. Critics argue that good international managers choose to experience the novel conditions of a foreign lifestyle, and that their families will eventually adjust their consumption patterns and tastes to the foreign environment. In view of this justification, cost of living is not needed or can at least be decreased over time (Rodrigues 1996).

- Tax equalization adjustment for host country taxes.

- Education of children, periodic family home leaves, language training, medical care, and so on.

- Differential for inflation, currency devaluation, and work-related legal fees.

- Expenses to comply with customary professional and social obligations.

- Hardship bonus for working abroad (Fatehi 1996).

- Moving and orientation allowances. Companies generally pay the total costs of transferring their staff overseas.

- Overseas premium. These are additional payments to expatriates and are generally established as a percentage of the base salary. They range from 10 to 25 percent.

- Contract termination payments. These payments are made as an inducement for employees to stay on their jobs and work out the periods of their overseas contracts.

There are also some perks given to executives as a means of minimizing taxes. Among the most common perks are:

- Cars, which higher up the organization ladder come with chauffeurs.
- Private pension plan.
- Life insurance.
- Health insurance.
- Company house or apartment.
- Directorship of a foreign subsidiary.
- Seminar holiday travel.
- Club membership.
- Hidden slush fund. Such funds are illegal, but some companies are said to have them. (Ball & Wendell 1996)

## Summary

Human resources play a critical role in sustaining a competitive edge for organizations in the modern global economy. It calls for recruiting, training, developing, compensating, and retaining highly competent and qualified people for management positions abroad. Staffing philosophy in an organization normally dictates from where new staff should be recruited. Some firms choose to adopt an ethnocentric policy, while others adopt differing staffing policies such as polycentric, regiocentric, and geocentric. Newly appointed staff should, as part of a sound HR management practice, be appraised on an ongoing basis to ensure that they are meeting the organizational objectives. Moreover, managerial training is needed to equip global managers with the right kind of knowledge and skills needed to succeed in an international environment. This includes both predeparture and postdeparture stages of their international posting. Finally, international staff and management should be provided with a reasonable level of compensation for carrying out their international assignments. A reasonable compensation package should include cost of living allowance and consumer good differentials as well as cover education of children, housing, leaves, hardship bonuses, moving and orientation allowance, and necessary perks to retain hires in their international postings.

## Critical Discussion Questions

1. In what ways does a multicultural staff employed in an international firm offer competitive advantages? Provide examples.

2. What are the specific benefits and drawbacks of employing an expatriate by a firm for an international assignment?

3. In what ways is a polycentric staffing policy more beneficial than an ethnocentric staffing policy for an international organization?

4. It is argued that while geocentric policy is the best staff selection method for an international assignment, however, it too has its limitations. Critically discuss.

5. For the newly appointed management staff to succeed in an international assignment, they would need to undergo management training. In your view, what specific types of managerial training will be needed for an international assignment and why?

6. In order to retain competent staff, international firms need to reward them well. In your considered view, what specific type of compensation package should a firm offer without necessarily breaching the equity issue inherent in a sound HR policy?

7. A modern organization should be all about "employing the best qualified person for the right position at the right time." Despite this, why have most organizations been reluctant to appoint highly competent female managers for overseas assignment? Is there any management prescriptive for remedying this worldwide phenomenon of prejudice against employing women in all spheres of society including higher echelons of modern organizations?

8. In what ways is international human resource management more complicated than domestic human resource management?

9. What have been some of the notable transformations of human resource management in recent decades?

10. In what ways does the equity-related issue complicate the task of hiring a highly competent staff for an international assignment?

## Applications

### Experiential

1. Conduct an interview with a manager of a MNC about the company's international human resource policy. Then compare and contrast your findings about the MNC with the knowledge of the staffing policy gained through this chapter.

2. Develop a set of guidelines for human resource policy incorporating equal employment opportunity issues; antidiscrimination issues and laws; equity issues; ethics; and incentive and reward systems that international firms could adopt when recruiting management staff for an international assignment.

### Internet

Below is a list of Web sites that provide useful information on different resources available to their membership including international human resource practitioners. First, familiarize yourself with the content of these sites. Then ask this question for each Web site: "In what ways can this site benefit international managers?"

**Paguro** (provides information and assistance to the expatriates and their families)

http://www.paguro.net/

**Society for Human Resource Management (SHRM)**

http://www.shrm.org/hrllnks/intl.htm

**Institute for International Human Resources, a division of the SHRM**

http://www.shrm.org/does/IIHR.html

**International Association for Human Resource Information Management**

http://www.ihrim.org/

**Institute of Personnel and Development**

http://www.ipd.co.uk/

**GMAC Global Relocation Services, Inc. (GMAC GRS)**

http://www.windhamint.com/

**United Nations Centre on Transnational Corporations and International Trade**

http://www.unicc.org/unctad/en/aboutorg/inbrief.htm

**Realtor.com** (provides information on costs of living in different parts of the world)

http://www.homefair.com/

# REFERENCES

(1994). Corporate coaches support global networks. *Personnel Journal, 73* (1), 58.

(1979). Gauging a family's suitability for a stint overseas, *Business Week*, April 16, 127.

Adler, N. (1987). Pacific basin managers: A giajin, not a woman. *Human Resource Management, 26* (2), 169–191.

Adler, N. (1997). *International dimensions of organizational behavior.* Cincinnati, OH: South-Western College.

Adler, N. & Ghadar, F. (1990). Strategic human resource management: A global perspective. In R. Pieper (Ed.), *Human resource management* in *international* comparison (pp. 235–260). Berlin: De Gruyter.

Ball, D. and Wendell, M. (1996). *International business: The challenge of global competition* (6th ed.). Boston: McGraw-Hill.

Bartlett, C.A. & Ghoshal, S. (1998). *Managing across borders: The transnational solution* (2nd ed.). London: Random House.

Black, J.S. (1988). Work role transitions: A study of American expatriate managers in Japan. *Journal of International Business Studies, 19,* 277–294.

Bochner, S.A. (1982). The social psychology of cross-cultural relations. In S. Bochner (ed.), *Cultures in contact: Studies in cross-cultural interactions.* Oxford: Pergamon.

Bonache, J. & Cervino, J. (1997). Global integration without expatriates. *Human Resource Management Journal, 7*, 89–100.

Brett, J. M. (2001). *Negotiating globally: How to negotiate deals, resolve disputes, and make decisions across cultural boundaries.* San Francisco, CA: Jossey-Bass.

Brislin, R. (1981). *Cross-cultural encounters.* Elmsford, NY: Pergamon.

Caudron, S. (1991). Training ensures overseas success. *Personnel Journal, 70* (12), 27–30.

Chiavenato, I. (2001). Advances and challenges in human resource management in the new millennium. *Public Personnel Management, 30* (1), 17–27.

Church, A.T. (1982). Sojourner adjustment. *Psychological Bulletin, 91*, 540–572.

Cooperrider, D. & Srivastva, S. (1987). Appreciative inquiry into organizational life. In R.W. Woodman & W.A. Pasmore (Eds.), *Research in organizational change and development* (Vol. 1, pp. 129–169). Greenwich, CT: JAI.

Deresky, H. (2000*). International management: Managing across borders and cultures.* (3rd ed.). New York: Harper Collins College.

Dessler, J., Griffiths, B., Lloyd-Walker, B., & Williams, A. (1999). *Human Resource Management.* Sydney: Prentice Hall.

Dowling, P.J., Welch, D.E., & Schuler, R.S. (1999*). International Human Resource Management* (3rd ed.). Cincinnati, OH: South-Western College.

Evans, P. & Lorange, P. (1989). The two logics behind human resource management. In P. Evans, Y. Doz, & A. Laurent (Eds.), *Human resource management* in *international firms* (pp. 169–190). New York: St. Martin's.

Fatehi, K. (1996). *International management: A cross cultural and functional perspective.* Upper Saddle River, NJ: Prentice Hall.

Fetterolf, C. (1990). Hiring local managers and employees overseas. *The International Executive,* May–June, .22–26

Fogel, A. (1993). *Developing through relationships.* Chicago: University of Chicago Press.

Furnham, A. & Bochner, S. (1989). *Culture shock: Psychological reactions to unfamiliar environments.* London: Routledge & Kegan Paul.

Goodman, M.B. (1995). *Working in a global environment.* New York: IEEE.

Gudykunst, W.B. (1993). Toward a theory of effective interpersonal and intergroup communication: An anxiety/uncertainty management (AUM) perspective. In R. Wiseman & I Koester, I. (Eds.), *Intercultural communication competence* (pp. 33–71). Newbury Park: Sage.

Harris, P. & Moran, R. (1991). *Managing cultural differences.* Houston, TX: Gulf.

Harris, P.R. & Moran, R.T. (2001). European leadership in globalization. In: M.H. Albrecht (Ed.), *International HRM: Managing diversity in the workplace* (pp. 41–54). Oxford: Blackwell.

Hedlund, G. (1986). The modern MNC: A heterarchy. *Human Resource Management, 25,* 9–35.

Heenan, D.A. & Perlmutter, H.V. (1979). *Multinational organization development.* Reading, MA: Addison-Wesley.

Heller, J.E. (1980). Criteria for selecting an international manager. *Personnel, 57,* 18–22

Hill, C.W.L. (2000). *International business: competing in the global marketplace* (3rd ed.). McGraw-Hill.

Hodgetts, R.M. & Luthans, F. (2000). *International management.* New York: McGraw-Hill.

Hoecklin, L. (1995). *Managing cultural differences: Strategies for competitive advantage.* Reading, MA: Addison-Wesley.

Hofstede, G. (1980). *Cultures Consequences.* London: Sage.

Janssens, M. (1994). Evaluating international manager's performance: Parent company standards as control mechanism. *International Journal of Human Resource Management, 5* (4), 853–873.

Janssens, M. & Brett, J.M. (1997). Meaningful participation in transnational teams. *European Journal of Work and Organizational Psychology, 6,* 153–168.

Janssens, M. & Brett, J.M. (2000). Competences and practices to stimulate meaningful participation in transnational teams. Paper presented in Showcase Symposium: "How can the innovative potential of cultural differences be realized?" at The Academy of Management Meeting, Toronto, August.

Janssens, M., Keunen, L., & Brett, J.M. (1998). Valuing cultural diversity. Unpublished report, p. 14.

Kim, W.C. & Mauborgne, R.A. (1993). Making global strategies work. *Sloan Management Review, 34* (3), 11–27.

Laabs, J.L. (1996). HR pioneers explore the road less traveled. *Personnel Journal,* February, 70–78.

Lazarus, R. (1991). *Emotion and adaptation.* New York: Oxford University Press.

Louw-Potgeiter, J. & Giles, H. (1987). Imposed identity and linguistic strategies. *Journal of Language and Social Psychology, 6,* 261–286.

Luthans, F., Marsnik, P.A., & Luthans, K.W. (2001). A contingency matrix approach to IHRM, In M.H. Albrecht (Ed.), *International HRM: Managing diversity in the workplace.* (pp. 83–102). Oxford: Blackwell.

Mahoney, D., Trigg, M., Griffin, R., & Pustay, M. (1998). *International business: A managerial perspective.* Melbourne: Addison Wesley Longman.

March, R.M. (1995). Asian literacy and Australia–Asia business relationships. Working paper, Department of Marketing, University of Western Sydney-Napean.

McPherson, K. (1983). Opinion-related information seeking. *Personality and Social Psychology Bulletin, 9,* 116–124.

Mead R. (1998) *International Management* (2nd ed.). Oxford: Blackwell.

Mendenhall, M. & Oddou, G. (1985). The dimensions of expatriate acculturation. *Academy of Management Review, 10, 39–47.*

Milliman, J.M., Von Glinow, M.A., & Nathan, M. (1991). Organizational life cycles and strategic international human resource management in multinational companies: Implications for congruence theory. Academy of *Management Review, 16,* 318–339.

Oberg, K. (1960). Cultural shock: Adjustments to new cultural environments. *Practical Anthropology, 7, 177–182.*

Phatak, A.V. (1997). *International management: Concepts and cases.* Cincinnati, OH: South-Western College.

Porter, M.E. (1986). Competition in global industries: A conceptual framework. In M. Porter (Ed.), *Competition in global industries* (pp. 15-60). Boston: Harvard Business School Press.

Rodrigues, C. (1996). *International management: A cultural approach.* St. Paul, MN: West.

Rosenzweig, P.M. & Singh, J.V. (1991). Organizational environments and the multinational enterprise. Academy of *Management* Review, *16:* 340–361.

Roth, K. (1995). Managing international interdependence: CEO characteristics in a resource-based framework. *Academy of Management Journal, 38,* 200–231.

Saee, J. (1998). Intercultural competence: Preparing enterprising managers for the global economy. *Journal of European Business Education, 7* (2), 15–37.

Saee, J. & Kaye, M. (1994). Intercultural communication competence in management training. Paper presented at the 44th Annual Conference of the International Communication Association Co-Host Australian and New Zealand Communication Association Conference on Communication and Diversity, Darling Harbour, July 11–15, Sydney, Australia.

Sanyal, R. (2001). *International management: A strategic perspective.* Upper Saddle River: NJ: Prentice Hall.

Schein, E.H. (1999). *Process consultation revisited: Building the helping relationship.* Reading, MA: Addison-Wesley.

Schneider, S. & Barsoux, J.L. (1997). *Managing across cultures.* London: Prentice Hall.

Schuler, R., Dowling, P., & De Cieri, H. (1993). An integrative framework of strategic international human resource management. *International Journal of Human Resource Management, 17, 717–764.*

Sels, L., Van den Brande, I., & Overlaet, B. (2000). Belgium. A culture of compromise. In D.M. Rousseau, & R. Schalk (Eds.), *Psychological contracts in employment: Cross-national perspectives* (pp. 47–66). Thousand Oaks, CA: Sage.

Solomon, J. (1989). Women, Minorities and Foreign Postings. *Wall Street Journal,* June 2, B1.

Taylor, S., Beechler, S., & Napier, N. (1996). Toward an integrative model of strategic international human resource management. *Academy of Management Review, 21,* 959–985.

Tung, R.L. (1982). Selection and training procedures of U.S., European, and the Japanese multinationals. *California Management Review, 25* (1), 51–71.

Tung, R.L. (1987). Expatriate Assignments: enhancing success and minimising failure. *Academy of Management Executive, 1* (2), 117–126.

Voris, W. (1975). Considerations in staffing for overseas management needs. *Personnel Journal, 0* (0), 00–00.

Welch, D. (1994) HRM: Implication of globalization. *Journal of General Management, 19* (4), 52–56.

Zachary, G.P. (1993). Like factory workers, professionals face loss of jobs to foreigners. *Wall Street Journal,* March 17, A1, A9.

# Chapter 14

*International Project Management*

It is not the strongest species that survive, or the most intelligent, but the ones most responsive to change. [Management of contemporary organizations is no exception to this rule.]

—Charles Darwin

## OVERVIEW

Many organizations more and more recognize that they can increase their flexibility and responsiveness in globally competitive market environments through the deployment of transnational project teams. Such teams consist of members coming from different countries and cultures, and their activities transcend national frontiers. The team members can represent different specializations within an organization, be located in different geographical areas, and still work jointly and in ad hoc project teams from inception to completion of projects. Indeed, such international project teams, where much of the boundary-spanning work in international business enterprise takes place, are important catalysts for individual and organizational development. This is especially true in the development of an organization's international outlook—as well as profits and other measures of success. Project teams also help the organization share information, knowledge, and resources across boundaries, transmit and recreate corporate culture, and provide examples of best practice (Heimer 1994; Iles & Paromjit 1997). The project management that takes place in such teams also provides an organization with another set of tools that originated with traditional, home office project management as it has confronted the following set of modern economic contingencies that emerged in the last century:

- The growing demand for complex, sophisticated, customized goods and services.
- The exponential expansion of human knowledge.
- Intense competition among firms for profit maximization and provision of quality service fostered by globalization of contemporary market economy.

This chapter will first introduce some background of modern project management and then relate it to the dynamics and factors of cross-cultural project management. These factors affect the performance of a project in an international setting, which, in turn, entail strategies and tactics that make the project successful. In other words, we will examine what brings about best practice in international project management.

## PROJECT MANAGEMENT: PURPOSE AND DEFINITION

The purpose of project management comes from the very definition of a project—a set of activities with a defined start and a defined end state and which pursues a defined goal and uses a defined set of resources (Slack, Chambers, & Johnston 2001). Project management, to achieve its goals and use its resources effectively, serves the following functions that fall under three categories:

1. *General project management processes:* Project integration, strategic planning, and resource allocation.
2. *Basic project management functions:* Scope management, quality management, time management, and cost management.
3. *Integrated project management functions:* Risk management, HR management, contract management, and communication management (Dinsmore 1993).

The objective of project management is to meet and exceed the expectations of the sponsors of the project. These expectations have been categorized by Kress (2001) as quality (producing desired outcome with minimum defects; cost (producing desired outcome for the anticipated cost); and schedule (producing desired outcome within the anticipated time frame). The factors underlying project management to achieve, as identified in Dinsmore (1993), require that project managers and project teams perform the following:

1. *Concentrate on interfacing.* This involves both defining frontiers and making efforts at bridge building between various areas that have interdependent relationships with the project in question.

2. *Organize the project team.* This calls for selecting qualified team members for the project as well as sound management practices to ensure a high level of motivation from the project team members through the appropriate incentive programs, coupled with the increased delegation of responsibility for the team members.

3. *Plan strategically and technically.* Use a top-down planning approach while breaking the project down into component parts using a work break-down structure or other project logic.

4. *Remember "Murphy's law."* "If anything can go wrong, it will." Thus, strategies, plans, and systems should be tested to ensure fail-safe implementation.

5. *Identify project stakeholders.* Identify who has a stake and influence regarding project outcome such as clients, users, managers, financiers, suppliers of technology, and higher management, and create systems for involving and satisfying their needs and expectations.

6. *Be prepared to manage conflicts.* Apply conflict management techniques—that is, negotiate when interests clash; promote collaboration when talents and capabilities are complementary; force the issue when important principals are at stake; and, finally, set off conflict if necessary to realize project goals.

7. *Expect the unexpected.* Reducing the unexpected keeps projects on track. In project environments, surprises can be minimized by participative planning; contingency allowances; use of expert opinion; and statistical comparisons with similar prior projects.

8. *Listen to intuition as part of project decision-making.* Intuition reflects the gut feeling formed by the experiences logged over the years.

9. *Apply behavioral skills.* This involves application of sound interpersonal skills on the part of project managers to influence their team members in a positive manner.

10. *Follow up and take remedial action.* Create a system for measuring progress, then estimate that progress against initial plans, and take remedial action.

## THE DISTINCTION BETWEEN LINE AND PROJECT MANAGEMENT

Jackson (1993) suggests that the competencies required of project managers are similar to those required of line managers. Both, for example, work to tight schedules and for specific objectives. However, line management practice is predicated on a "business as usual" approach. Project managers, on the other hand, have a "one off" finite deadline—but they are expected to:

- Convert business objectives to project objectives.
- Obtain value for money through planning and controlling both physical and human resources over a set period of time.
- Integrate complex effort and multi-professional growth of people, often across cultural divides.
- Communicate with all levels of management, upward and across.
- React to continual change.
- Accelerate innovation and change.
- Restructure new teams and develop attitudes and facilitate working relationship, often in a very short space of time.
- Work with and satisfy the needs of a client. (Jackson 1993, 318).

## KEY SUCCESS FACTORS OF PROJECT MANAGEMENT

To succeed in this, project managers, according to Weiss and Wysocki (1992), must possess five demonstrable attributes and qualifications:

- Background and experience relevant to the project.
- Leadership and strategic expertise.
- Technical expertise in the area of the project in order to make sound technical decisions.
- Interpersonal competence and the people skills to take on such roles as project champion, motivator, communicator, facilitator, and politician.
- Proven managerial competencies in relation to a track record of getting things done.

In addition to the personal qualifications of the project manager and his or her team members, Kerzner (1998) identified six critical success factors for successful projects that relate to the organization and its culture. Corporate understanding of project management is needed, along with executive commitment, organizational adaptability, sound project manager selection criteria, and a commitment to planning and control. To this list can be added yet another set of success factors drawn from Pinto and Slevin (1987) and Jackson (1993):

- *Project mission.* This involves determination of a clearly defined project's goals and mission by management with clear indications that the project is necessary and why.
- *Top management support.* No project is likely to succeed unless it enjoys the full support of the senior management within the organization—acquiring this support for the project is critical.
- *Project plan.* All the activities surrounding the project have to be meticulously planned for and the necessary resources required to carry out the project have to be fully allocated. There have to be ways of monitoring its progress in terms of the specific stage deadlines. Managers have to consider if the plan is workable; if the amount of time and money and people allocated are sufficient; if the funds are guaranteed; if the organization will carry

through the project; and if there is flexibility in the plans allowing for over-running the schedule.

- *Client consultation.* A detailed understanding of the client requirement is a must for a project manager. Regular meetings between the client and the project manager are deemed necessary at all stages of the project.

- *Competent project team.* Selection of competent staff, backed by training, is critical in order to ensure the success of the project.

- *Technical task.* Technical skills have to be matched with the right people in terms of qualifications and expertise.

- *Client acceptance.* Gaining acceptance from one's client for any given project is critical. A project manager needs to develop a strategy to sell the project to the client. Developing a good interpersonal relationship with the client is deemed necessary so that the project manager can negotiate with the client where appropriate.

- *Monitoring and feedback.* Obtaining feedback throughout the project from key individuals is necessary to ensure quality outcome for the project. This obviously involves establishing sound monitoring procedures to capture feedback on all aspects of the project.

- *Communication.* The concept of communication in project management refers to the spoken and written documentation, plans, and drawings used in the processes of an international project.

- *Troubleshooting mechanisms.* A system or set of procedures capable of tackling problems when they arise, tracing them back to the root cause, and resolving them. All team members should act as "lookouts" for the project; all team members should monitor the project; and when a problem is identified by a team member, action should be taken at once to remedy the problem.

Rosenau (1984) suggests that successful project management consists of satisfying the triple constraints of time, cost, and performance.

# BEST PRACTICE IN PROJECT MANAGEMENT

Best practice means adopting and benchmarking the managerial practices of successful organizations. Pfeffer (1994) suggests that utilization of best practice can lead to competitive advantage for a firm and its project management, whether domestically or for international project management. Best practice begins with the conceptualization and initiation stage and is furthered by yet another stage, competent planning. Both stages are described in the following sections.

## Conceptualization and Initiation

This stage involves identifying the business needs for setting of goals and specific objectives, and gaining support for the project from the key stakeholders by identifying and communicating the benefits of the project (Jackson 1993). It should also take into consideration the many managerial responsibilities—which can be quite diverse in the management of an international project—and which involve planning, organization, and control of a large number of complex factors, activities, and their interrelations.

Managing them simultaneously and giving them all equal attention is virtually impossible. Nevertheless, by adapting the Pareto rule of separating out the important few from the trivial many helps to focus attention on the key factors which are critical for achieving success (Morris 1996).

## Planning

Planning is broadly defined as determining what needs to be done, by whom and when, in order to accomplish one's assigned responsibility. It is a process involving the assessment of the environment for opportunities, threats, strengths, and weaknesses (Kerzner 1998). The components of planning normally include objective, program, schedule, budget, forecast, organization, policy, procedure, and standards. However, in an attempt to plan the work of a project management team, Johns (1999) has simplified the process of planning to include only five fundamental management tools, namely:

- *Project objectives.* These must be predetermined, clear, and measurable.
- *Work breakdown structure.* This enables personnel and clients to get a general overview of the project as a whole.
- *Project organization.* The organization of the project requires the accountability and ownership of tasks to be clearly defined and placed on key personnel.
- *Project schedule.* Scheduling of project accomplishments is a necessary tool for the success of the program. The schedule must be communicated in a simple and comprehensible form, so that all may easily acknowledge the direction toward which the project is heading.
- *Budget.* An effective method in which managers can control financing and task duration is through the determination of resource requirements used by each person in each task and the interdependence of each product onto others used in those individual tasks.

However, bear in mind that "the extent to and rigor with which these tools are used must be allowed to differ in a company, because the sizes and natures of projects differ, the natural styles and cultures of the people involved differ, and the business situations differ" (Johns 1999, 35).

Pinto and Slevin (1987) also consider the project plan as key because it involves scheduling of all the activities along with the resources required. They suggest that the plan be workable; the amount of time, people, and money allocated be sufficient; and that the organization be ready to carry through the plan and that funds are guaranteed.

## PROJECT MANAGEMENT: AN INTERNATIONAL PERSPECTIVE

International project management has virtually all of the same characteristics and opportunities that domestic project management has. However, additional constraints shape the objectives, goals, and strategies of cross-cultural project management. Factors such as political instability and risk, currency instability, competition, problems with the host government, nationalism, and so on can interfere with project management planning (Smith & Haar 1993). Such constraints require project management strategies that:

- Evaluate opportunities, threats, problems, and risks.
- Assess the strengths and weaknesses of its personnel to carry out the job.
- Define the scope of its global business involvement.
- Formulate its global corporate objectives.
- Develop specific corporate strategies in the organization as a whole (Phatak 1997).

The international project manager needs to develop a thorough understanding of the environmental factors that he or she will face. This entails knowledge of the following factors in a host country:

- Geography
- Finance
- Local politics
- National culture
- Local laws

For example in French-speaking African countries, local labor laws allow employees to take three days' leave of absence when a close relative dies. With the large, extended families that are common to this region, this can cause serious disruption to staff availability (Slack, Chambers, & Johnston 2001). Hence, developing an understanding of the host culture is crucial which obviously has a major impact on the way a project is conducted. (See also Chapters 2 and 4).

## Communication

We have already covered the issue of cross-cultural communication earlier in this book, especially in Chapter 4 and to some extent in Chapters 5 and 6. It, too, is a dimension that can positively or negatively affect project management. Lack of communication has been cited as the biggest reason for the failure of many change projects to meet their expectations (Pardu 1996). Successful communication needs to be focused, and the timing is of crucial importance. Used effectively it can reduce nonproductive effort, avoid duplication, and help eliminate mistakes (Beavers 1997). Time, cost, and performance vary considerably within the international areas. Time is a communication system, just like words and language. For example, Western culture views time as resource ("time is money"). Asian and Middle Eastern cultures view time quite differently as do many Mediterranean people. Consequently, concepts such as schedules and deadlines, which are essential to project management, are not held in the same regard and, therefore, are not followed as conscientiously as in Western cultures. Another communication factor to be considered is directness. In the United States one is direct and gets straight to the point. In other cultures, the direct route is avoided and even disliked. Arabs, some Europeans, and Asians do not go straight to a point (Smith & Haar 1993).

## Control Systems

Moder (1988, 324) sees controlling as "the process of making events conform to schedules by coordinating the action of all parts of the organization according to the plan established for attaining the objective." Control is essential to any project manager, especially for those who are dealing within an international context. The process of project control involves three sets of decisions. These include monitoring (or measuring), evaluating, and action. Through the use of an agreed metric toward the accomplishment of established objectives, actual project progress is compared to that of planned directions. Evaluating relates to the process of determining causes and their solutions to notable variations in performance within the project. The course of acting often involves a manager briefing appropriate individuals of progress in the project, taking corrective action in light of unfavorable situations, and exploiting opportunities to benefit from, and take advantage of it. These control processes are a necessity for any international project management, although, without the presence of project execution plans; procedures for analyzing, reporting and reviewing performance against baselines; and the disciplined process for considering, approving, and implementing change, the project will certainly lose control" (Johns 1999, 36).

Basic to any project management system, is a control subsystem, comprised of standards, comparisons, and corrective actions. Control and its associated problems in international projects are much more complex than in domestic ones as a result of differing political, cultural, economic, and legal environments. Geographic distance, language barriers, communication habits, culture, and differing frames of reference all influence the control subsystems (Phatak 1997). Also, criticism and how it is expressed can seriously affect managerial control; detailed reporting and tight control are not accepted in some cultures. For example, in Japanese culture, maintaining group cohesiveness is more important than reporting a problem and such problems are solved, if possible, at the group level before referring them to upper management (Clutterbuck 1989).

### Organizational Designs in Different Cultures

Authority, responsibility, and accountability vary by project, culture, and an organization's priorities and preferences. Security-sensitive projects tend to be the most centralized and tightly controlled.

In the cultural dimension, group decision-making works well in, say, Japan, but it is not prevalent in many other societies (Bass 1979). French companies show more autocratic behavior while large and experienced companies in the United States and most of Western Europe exhibit the highest level of management delegation (Berenbim 1989). Knowing these kinds of differences—Chapter 2 covers many of them—can be germane to project success because, among the many reasons for the failure of projects in the international environment, the most significant is the inability to get maximum performance out of people. Each culture has different expectations of the superior–subordinate relationships. Position, rank, authority, and respect are supported in many foreign countries by informal and formal codes of dress, behavior, attitudes, and the like. While delegation and participative management are practiced and supported in the Scandinavian countries, for example, this is not the case in many other countries. Clearly these organizational and operational patterns significantly affect project management (Smith & Haar 1993).

## ORGANIZATIONAL SUPPORT

Project management has provided a sound foundation for change management in recent decades. However, as Jones (1999) maintains, when companies experiment with project-based organization, what executive managers frequently find missing is instinctive knowledge pertaining to how to create an organizational management culture. The questions and challenges facing executives are how to:

- Create explicit senior management goals that support and encourage cross-functional project teams.
- Work with one another as a senior management team and how to mutually support cross-functional project teams.
- Establish clearly communicated priorities for work done by cross-functional project teams in relation to other work.

Many organizations will admit to having problems or issues that limit their use of project management for managing change (Clarke 1995; Kahn 1993). Yet by understanding these issues and working to eliminate them, it may be possible to improve the effectiveness of project management—and the main steps senior management must take in creating a project-based organizational culture are to:

- Write a clear policy stating the support of the project team's responsibility and authority to accomplish their missions, goals, and objectives.
- Continually repeat the messages that the project teams are empowered to act as long as their actions are in the best interest of the organization.

In a recent and ongoing survey of senior managers from international companies conducted at the Management Centre, Europe, cross-functional project teams were the primary way of conducting their business. These companies use management committees to review project teams' performance, priorities, and planning and control processes. Weak organizational support was exhibited by companies that do not have project management training or where upper management did not have lines of good communication between itself and its project teams—and a prerequisite for effective organizational support is the existence of a specific management forum in which the project teams can openly and regularly discuss problems they are encountering so that appropriate strategies could be developed to address these perceived problems at all levels (Jones 1999).

## Human Resource

Human resource in international project management is by its very nature far more complex and complicated than in the management of domestic projects. Motivation (discussed earlier in Chapter 9) varies widely by country and culture. With the kind of job security that exists in a so-called "free-market economy," American workers are motivated to work hard in order to earn money. To the French, however, quality of life is what matters most. In Japan, society and companies come first, and workers are motivated by permanent or life-time employment practices, bonuses, and fringe benefits based on the company's performance as a whole (Bello 1986). Another aspect in human resources is negotiations discussed in Chapter 10. Within an international context negotiations are made more difficult by differences in culture, trade customs, and legal parameters. Language barriers can complicate negotiations; interpreters can slow the pace of negotiations as much as facilitate them. Many projects that are technically, financially, and organizationally strong have failed as a result of cross-cultural factors because of the inability of managers and supervisors to comprehend and respond to the members of host culture societies—factors we have already learned in Chapter 2.

## Guidelines for International Project Managers

Kerzner (1998) identifies the following guidelines for foreign executives involved in initiation, planning, and implementation of projects:

- Be aware of the environment of the host country.
- Study the host company's developing plans and develop a long-range plan for future cooperation.
- Survey the financial institutions involved in the project and study the investment laws if applicable.
- Before undertaking a project, study its feasibility from the technical, economic, and operational point of view. Also study the contribution of the project to the development of the host country.
- Develop relationships with governmental and business leaders and develop a special relationship with a project's local "God Father."
- Choose the right project manager for managing and implementing the project and assign him or her to the project at an early stage.
- Communicate with the client and learn how to deal with the counterpart effectively.
- Study the different stages and phases of the project: preparation and initiation, implementation and operation.
- Study the decision-making process and the different organizations responsible for project implementation and operation.

## Project Personnel Management

Within an international project management team, a number of positions can be held by personnel from different countries and cultures. The project manager should explore the conditions and benefits, and then define clear standards that outline working conditions before recruiting personnel. International projects vary in working conditions, which relate uniquely to each individual work site involved, and the duration of the working week is also contingent upon the work nature and/or location of the project. Personnel, including the project manager, must meet certain criteria in ensuring that the most suitable individuals are employed for work overseas in different cultures:

- Technical and managerial skills and abilities
- Cultural empathy
- Adaptability and flexibility
- Diplomatic skills
- Family factors
- Emotional stability and maturity
- Motivation and aspirations

The availability of qualified and experienced local nationals will not necessarily obviate the need for expatriate managers. According to Robinson (1978), multinational corporations actually plan on recruiting and maintaining between 5 and 10 percent expatriates or third-country nationals in local subsidiary management. The reason behind this managerial strategy is the assumption that there are benefits such as providing multinational experience and intensifying corporate socialization process for all parties involved in the project. The international human resources dynamic of this is covered in Chapter 13.

## Client Consultation and Acceptance

As previously discussed, the client should be clearly identified—that is, the party who uses the completed project. Close consultation with the client is necessary for outside projects. Client acceptance is usually the bottom-line that should be backed up with perceived and tangible benefits—and this involves good communication. Hence, the following points are important to consider:

- Know the client and what he or she requires.
- Schedule regular meetings with the client.
- Ascertain whether the client is accepting or resisting.
- Develop a sound interpersonal relationship with the client so that you can negotiate with the client where necessary (Jackson 1993).

## Training and Education

Successful project management requires extensive and intensive training in techniques and methodologies of project operations (Smith & Haar 1993). This is especially necessary for international project management. The training strategy suggested by Kerzner (1998), includes:

- Training based on transcultural management in the context of the specifics of the job.
- Educational approach to training that enables the managers to analyze case studies.
- Training based on host national's perceptions.
- Training that sensitizes manager to awareness of his or her impact on host national work force.
- Training for the purpose of acquiring technical knowledge for performing the job.

The use of scheduling, costing, modeling, and programming techniques and methodologies should be much the same in large international projects. However, because of variation in education and availability of hardware and software, adjustment must be made in the project management systems.

## Breaking the Project into Bite-size Chunks

Breaking large projects down into subprojects or work packages is regarded as one of the most important tasks in the development of projects (Lewis 1996). It ensures greater ownership by all those "owning a piece" of the project, spreading responsibility and accountability across a greater number of people. It is easier to manage by delegating responsibilities to the project team (Clarke 1995).

## Product Perspective

The ultimate outcome of a project is an artifact with technological complexities and many years of operational life. Ensuring the consistency of the product configuration is key to being successful in international project management (Hameri 1997). In addition, it is the result of a distributed collaborative effort during the engineering phase as well as the production and assembly phases. Thus, the product perspective highlights the role of configuration management that essentially concerns the control of specification changes and the work/information/data flow during the engineering and manufacturing process (Stark 1992). The role of product data management will become even more important in project management areas. The reasons for this include:

- Increasing technological complexity of products.
- Longer project durations.
- Geographically distributed collaborators with the diversity of skills needed for international projects and the economic benefits of outsourcing.
- Increasing international investment.
- The need for expeditious and flexible performance.

## Risk Management

The risks exist from the political, economic, social, technological, and regulatory environments in which the project takes place (Smith & Haar 1993). Given the many differences, complexities, and uncertainties that distinguish international project management from domestic project management, a number of risk factors need to be considered for ensuring success in international project management. According to Kerzner (1998), it is important that risk management strategy is established early in a project and that risk is continually addressed throughout the project life cycle. These can include political, economic, social, and legal environments of the project.

## The Distinction between Project Strategy and Tactics

There is a major difference between strategy and tactics in project management. *Project strategy* defines, in a generalized rather than a specific way, how the organization is going to achieve its project objectives and to meet the related measures of performance. It accomplishes this in two distinct manners: (1) It defines the phases of the project. Phases break this project down into time based sections; (2) the project strategy sets milestones which are important events during the project's life at which specific reviews of time, cost, and quality are made (Slack, Chambers, & Johnston 2001). *Tactics* refer to client consultation, personnel recruitment and training, identification of tasks, gaining client acceptance, monitoring and feedback, communication, and troubleshooting. Projects are often typified by a weakness in either strategy or tactics, and this could, according to Slevin (1989), lead to different types of errors:

- Type 1: Failing to take an action when one should be taken;
- Type 2: Taking an action when one should not have been taken;
- Type 3: Taking the wrong action or solving the wrong problem; and

• Type 4: Solving the right problem but the solution is not used.
(Slevin 1989; Jackson 1993)

## Summary

In the rapidly changing and financially challenging international business environment, firms are adopting flexible strategies and structures such as project management method to speed improved quality products and services to their market segments and to provide quality customer service (Johns 1999). Project management across professional, national, and cultural frontiers is highly complex. The project manager's responsibility is to manage across these systems in order to meet specific business objectives within a finite timeline. The need to identify, distinguish, and respond effectively to a distinct set of managerial requirements, thus, becomes the foremost challenge facing international project managers. For firms to excel in international project management, they must implement appropriate strategies relating to the following critical factors: conceptualization and initiation; project planning; communication; organization; organizational support; human subsystems; breaking the project into bite-size chunks; client consultation and acceptance; education and training; and the product perspective.

## Critical Discussion Questions

1. What are the main reasons behind the rising organizational structure of international project management?

2. Describe the strategies and tactics needed for an international project management to succeed.

3. What are some of the challenges arising from international project management?

4. Critically analyze the statement: "Project management is about change management." Use outside sources.

5. Identify and discuss key success factors of international project management.

6. Outline best practices in international project management.

## Applications

### Experiential

1. Discuss issues and challenges facing an international project manager from Germany who is in charge of a culturally diverse project team with members from high context and low context cultures. Analyze this individually and discuss your findings with the other members of your class.

2. What are the issues and challenges of implementing best practices in international project management in which members of the project team are from individualist and collectivist cultures? Analyze this individually and discuss your findings with the other members of your class.

### Internet

Surf the Internet using a search engine such as Google and any databases that are available at your school, and identify some of the companies that have been involved in international project management as a result of mergers and strategic alliances. In so doing, try to identify issues, problems, and challenges that faced these companies due to their joint management of international project(s). Write a written report about these companies and discuss your findings with your instructor and classmates during class time.

# REFERENCES

Baker, B.N., Murphy, D.C., & Fisher, D. (1983). Factors affecting project success. In D.I. Cleland & D.R. King (Eds.), *Project Management Handbook* (pp. 669–685). New York: Van Nostrand.

Barham, K. & Oates, D. (1991). *Developing the international manager.* London: Business Books.

Bass, B.M. (1979). *Assessment of managers: An international comparison.* New York: Macmillan.

Beavers, D. (1997). Communication breakdown. *Supply Management, 2* (12), 34–35.

Bello, J.A. (1986). Behavioral problems of operational research implementation in developing countries. In U. G. Damachi & H.D. Seibel (Eds.), *Management problems.* New York: St. Martin's.

Berenbim, R.E. (1989). *Operating foreign subsidiaries: How independent can they be?* New York: Conference Board.

Burns, A.C. (1989). Executing the international project. In R.L Kimmons & J.H. Loweree (Eds.), *Project Management.* New York: Dekker.

Casse, P. (1979). *Training for the cross-cultural milieu.* Washington, DC: Sietar.

Clutterbuck, D. (1989).Breaking through the cultural barriers, *International Management,* December, 41–42.

Dinsmore, C.P. (Ed.) (1993). *The AMA Handbook of project management,* New York: American Management Association.

Fatehi, K. (1996). *International management: A cross cultural and functional perspective.* Upper Saddle River, NJ: Prentice Hall.

Hameri, A.P. (1997). Project management in a long-term and global one-of-a-kind projects, *International Journal of Project Management, 15,* 251–257.

Iles, P.H., & Paromjit, K. (1997) Managing diversity in transnational project teams. *Journal of Managerial Psychology; 12* (2), 95–117.

Irvine, D. & Ross-Baker, G. (1994). The impact of cross-functional teamwork on workforce integration. Paper submitted to the 9th Workshop on Strategic Human Resource Management, St. Gallen, Switzerland, March.

Jackson, S.E. (1992).Team composition in organizational settings: Issues in managing an increasingly diverse workforce. In S. Worchel, W. Wood, & J.A. Simpson (Eds.), *Group Process and Productivity* (pp. 138–176). Newbury Park, CA: Sage.

Jackson, T. (1993). *Organizational behavior in international management.* London: Butterworth Heinemann.

Johns, T.G. (1999). Managing the behavior of people working in teams: Applying the project management method. *International Journal of Project Management, 13* (1), 33–38.

Johns, T.G. (1999). On creating organizational support for the project management method. *International Journal of Project Management, 17* (1), 47–53.

Kahn, W.A. (1993). Facilitating and undermining organizational change: a case study. *Journal of Applied Behavioral Science, 29* (1), 32–55.

Kerzner, H. (1998). *Project management: A systems approach to planning, scheduling and controlling.* New York: John Wiley & Sons.

Kress, R.E. (2001). Quality project management: Key to success factor to exceeding buyer values. *Journal of Industrial Management, 36* (6), 22–40.

Lerpold, L. (1996). Multinational teams in strategic alliances: A case study of problems, their origins and their manifestations. Paper presented at the 11th Workshop On Strategic HRM, Brussels, Belgium, 13–15 March.

Lewis, R. (1996). Take the "big" out of big projects: Break them into manageable chunks. *Infoworld, 18* (20), 24.

Lewis, R.D. (1996). *When cultures collide: Managing successfully across cultures.* London, Nicholas Brealey.

Lim, D.S. & Mohamed, M.Z. (1999). Criteria of project success: An exploratory re–examination. *International Journal of Project Management, 17* (4), 243–248.

Meredith, J. & Mantel, S.J. (1985). *Project management: A managerial approach.* New York: John Wiley & Sons.

Moder, J.J. (1988). Network techniques in project management. In D.I. Cleland. & W.R. King (Eds.), *Project management handbook* (pp. 324–373). New York: Van Nostrand Reinhold.

Monye, S.O. (1997). *The international business blue print.* Oxford: Blackwell.

Morris, C. (1996). *Quantitative approaches in business studies* (4th ed.). Oakshot, LA: Pitman.

Oakland, J. (1989). *Total quality management.* London: Butterworth Heinemann.

Pardu, W. (1996). Managing change in a project environment. *CMA Magazine, 70* (4), 6.

Peters, T. (1994). *The Tom Peter Seminar.* New York: Random House.

Pfeffer, J. (1994). *Competitive advantage through people.* Boston: Harvard Business School Press.

Phatak, A.V. (1997). *International management: Concepts and cases.* Cincinnati, OH: South-Western College.

Pinto, J.K. & Slevin, D.P. (1987). Critical success factors in successful project implementation. *IEEE Transactions on Engineering Management, 3* (1), 22–27.

Robinson, R.D. (1978). *International business management: A guide to decision* (2nd ed.). Hinsdale, IL: Dryden.

Rosenau, M.D., Jr. (1984). *Project management for engineers.* New York: Van Norstrand Reinhold.

Saee, J. (2002). *Managerial excellence in project management.* Paper presented at the Academy of International Business, Southwestern Chapter 2002 conference. Vol. XIII, pp. 90-99.

Schroder, H.M. (1989). *Managerial competence: The key to excellence.,* Dubuque, IA: Kendall/Hunt.

Slack, N., Chambers, S., & Johnston, R. (2001). *Operations management* (3rd ed.). London: Pearson.

Slevin, D.P. (1989). *The whole manager.* New York: American Management Association.

Smith, L.A. & Haar, J. (1993). Managing international projects. In P.C. Dinsmore (Ed.), *The AMA Handbook of project management* (pp. 441–448). New York: American Management Association.

Snell, S.A., Davison, S.C., Hamrick, D.C., & Snow, C.C. (1993). Human Resource Challenges in the Development of Transnational Teams. Working paper, International Consortium for Executive Development Research, Lexington, MA.

Snow, C.C., Davison, S.C., Snell, S.A., & Hambrick, D.C. (1996). Use transnational teams to globalize your company. *Organizational Dynamics, 24* (4), 50–67.

Stallworthy, E. & Kharbanda, O. (1987). The project manager in the 1990s. *Industrial Management & Data Systems.*

Stark, J. (1992). *Engineering information management system: Beyond CAD/CAM to concurrent engineering.* New York: Van Nostrand Reinhold.

Timm, P. (1989). *Managerial communication: A finger on the pulse.* Englewood Cliffs, NJ: Prentice Hall.

Weiss, J.W. & Wysocki, R.K. (1992) *Five-phase project management: A practical planning and implementation guide.* Reading, MA: Addison-Wesley.

Wills, S. & Barham, K. (1994). Being an international manager. *European Management Journal, 12* (1), 49–58.

# Chapter 15

*Managerial Excellence in Global Management:*
*Cross-Cultural Dimensions*

    *Ideally, it seems... [international managers] should have the stamina of an Olympic runner, the mental agility of an Einstein, the conversational skill of a professor of languages, the detachment of a judge, the tact of a diplomat, and the perseverance of an Egyptian pyramid builder. [And] that's not all. If they are going to measure up to the demands of living and working in a foreign country, they should also have a feeling for the culture; their moral judgment should not be too rigid; they should be able to merge with the local environment with chameleon-like ease; and they should show no signs of prejudice.*

    *Thomas Aitken (1973)*

## OVERVIEW

With the globalization of business, the cultural diversity that organizations increasingly face in this new century is already apparent in their owners, managers, employees, clientele, and other stakeholders. Harnessing the creative human resources of this phenomenon to optimally benefit the strategic goals and missions of these organizations—and their global managers—is a formidable yet rewarding challenge. For this reason, and with the costs and benefits of cultural diversity articulated throughout this book, especially in Chapter 2, the key indicators of best practice and managerial excellence need to be assessed in the context of a global business environment.

## BEST PRACTICE AND CULTURAL DIVERSITY

Best practice in management—or managerial excellence—in a culturally diverse business organization means encouraging individuals to reach their full potential in pursuit of an organization's objectives (Jenner 1994; Thomas 1994). It means developing a corporate culture that fundamentally fosters and values cultural diversity. Corporate leaders and senior managers have a responsibility for institutionalising cultural diversity as the main ethos and guiding principles within their organization so that organizational processes, policies, and practices are seen to be reflecting cultural diversity in every conceivable way. The end result will be cultural synergy, a scenario "where multicultural teams can use their differences as a source of creativity to multiply productivity" (Weiss 1996, 18). Managerial excellence in this context entails building specific skills, creating policies, and implementing business practices that produce the best from every employee. This will require effective *intercultural* communication because everything an organization does and is dependent on for the way it functions is facilitated by communication (Thayer, 1990).

Managers typically spend around 70 to 80 percent of their time each day on communication processes in the workplace (Harris & Mann 1991; Putnis & Petelin 1996). This includes writing, talking, and listening. In fact, all business ultimately comes down to transactions, which depend almost entirely on how well managers understand each other. Communication underpins all managerial functions. Effective communication is essential for maintaining and enhancing organizational performance in a culturally diverse workplace both nationally and internationally. (For a detailed discussion on communication and intercultural communication competence, see Chapters 4 and 6.)

## MANAGEMENT OF CULTURAL DIVERSITY: A STUDY REVEALS THE CHALLENGE

A management study of Australian national and multinational organizations and their cultural diversity revealed the centrality of intercultural communication (Saee 1998b). Planning, workplace communication, recruitment and promotion, induction, training, supervision, industrial relations, management of change, customer service, financial management, and marketing within their organizations all require a level of managerial communication competence in this area based on the managers surveyed. Nevertheless, although cultural diversity was a significant feature of the workforce, the workplace, and the environmental context of these Australian organizations, cultural diversity was not an expressed feature in the core values of their respective "organizational cultures." The Australian managers who participated in this study showed limited understanding of what academics have started making a part of a manager's education, such as the cross-cultural relationships that Hofstede (1980; 1991) articulates, the theories of the psychological adaptation processes that sojourners undergo conceptualized by Oberg (1960), Bochner (1981; 1982), Brislin (1981), Harris and Moran (1991), Lysgaard (1955), Searle and Ward (1990), and Ward and Kennedy (1996) and of the uncertainty reduction theory advanced by Gudykunst (1977; 1983; 1984). Naturally, gaps exist in what managers know about intercultural communication, how to deal with cultural differences, communication difficulties, gender role conflicts, and religious differences even as they recognize these and more specific challenges (such as cultural stereotyping, divisiveness among staff where ethnic concentration in departments presented problems for management, and the like).

### A Model of Best Practice in Intercultural Communication Competence

Given the discrepancies in what managers knew about diversity management and what can now be learned from the wealth of academic literature, a model of best practice for intercultural communication competence has been developed (see Exhibit 15-1) that lines up key indicators for achieving intercultural communication competence (ICC) and where they are addressed in the academic literature—and in this text—in such a way that they can be applied to the management of cultural diversity in an organizational and global management context.

## APPLYING INTERCULTURAL COMMUNICATION COMPETENCE TO MANAGERIAL FUNCTIONS

It is important for managers who face cultural diversity in the workplace, whether nationally or globally, to recognize the key indicators (descriptors) of intercultural communication competence outlined in Exhibit 15-1 and to apply these indicators in their eleven primary managerial functions: planning, workplace communication, recruitment/promotion, induction, training, supervision, industrial relations, management of change, customer service, financial management, and marketing:

- *Planning*. Planning involves setting goals, assigning tasks, and coordinating activities (Mullins 1996).

- *Workplace communication*. Communication needs to be understood as a human interaction where the central concern is sharing meaning. As Timm (1980, 21) states, "Communication occurs any time someone attaches meaning to what is going on. Intentional communication efforts are successful to the degree that common meaning develops." Communication is the sharing of meanings and can be viewed in terms of interpersonal relationships (Penman, 1985).

- *Recruitment/Promotion*. Recruitment/promotion is defined as searching for, and obtaining, potential job candidates in sufficient numbers and quality for the organization to select the most appropriate people to fill its jobs (Goss 1994).

| Exhibit 15-1 | Best Practice Model of Intercultural Communication Competence |
|---|---|

| Indicator (Descriptor) | Sources in Literature |
|---|---|
| Understanding of cross-cultural dimensions: Collectivism vs. Individualism; Small vs. Large Power Distance; Femininity vs. Masculinity; Weak vs. Strong Uncertainty Avoidance; The Confucian Dynamism (also referred to as Long-Term Orientation vs. Short-Term Orientation) | Hofstede (1980; 1991); see also Chapter 2 |
| Understanding of cross-cultural, nonverbal communication | Basso (1990); Czinkota, et al. (1998); Morris (1994); Hall (1976); Harris & Moran (1991); Ricks (1993); Saee (1998); Samovar & Porter (1995); Saee (1998b); see also Chapter 5 |
| Understanding of psychological theories of adaptation processes | Bochner (1981;1982); Brislin (1981;1993); Harris & Moran (1991); Lysgaard (1955); Oberg (1960); Searle & Ward (1990); Ward & Kennedy (1996); Saee (1998a;1998b); see also Chapter 6 |
| Understanding of psychological theory of uncertainty reduction theory—for strangers | Gudykunst (1977; 1983; 1984); see also Chapter 6 |
| Understanding of psychological theory of uncertainty reduction theory—for members of the host culture | Saee (1998b) |
| Mindfulness | Bargh (1989); Langer (1989) |
| Adaptability | Duran (1992); Irwin (1996); Irwin & More (1994); Lustig & Koester (1993); Spitzberg & Cupach (1984); Wiemann & Bradac (1989); Wiseman & Koester (1993); Saee (1998); See also Chapter 6 |
| The ability to establish meaningful interpersonal relationships with member(s) of other cultures; the ability to enter into meaningful dialogue with other people; and the ability to deal with psychological stress within an intercultural context | Gudykunst, Wiseman & Hammer (1977); Saee (1998b) |
| Display of behavioral dimensions; e.g., respect; empathy; openness; nonjudgmentalness; tolerance of ambiguity; ability to perform role behaviors and interaction management. | Kealey (1995); Ruben & Kealey (1979); Saee (1998b); see also Chapter 6 |
| Trust | Saee (1998b) |
| Listening skills | Saee (1998b) |
| Equity/equal treatment of all individuals in intercultural context. | Saee (1998b) |
| Education | Saee (1998b) |
| Patience | Saee (1998b) |
| Competence in a second language | Saee (1998b) |
| Open-mindedness | Saee (1998b) |
| Understanding high-context and low-context cultures and their influences on intercultural communication | Hall (1976) |

- *Induction*. Induction is the process by which a new employee is taken into the organization and integrated as quickly and effectively as possible (Mukhi, Hampton, & Barnwell 1988).

- *Training*. Training is used by management as a strategy to improve current and future employees' performance by increasing, through learning and education, employees' abilities to perform, usually by increasing their skills and knowledge (Schuler, et al. 1992).

- *Supervision*. Supervision is about coordinating, directing, and guiding the efforts of members of the organization to achieve organizational goals (Robbins 1991).

- *Industrial relations*. Industrial relations is an area in which individual employees are increasingly expected, even required, to negotiate the change process. This includes, for example, participating in joint consultative committees and understanding and voting on enterprise agreements (O.M.A. et al. 1994).

- *Management of change*. A common assumption among management theorists is that conditions both outside and inside organizations are changing rapidly and profoundly (Ivancevich, Olekans, & Matteson 1997; Robbins 1991). Outside the organization, environmental conditions are generally becoming less stable. They are even becoming turbulent. Economic conditions, availability, cost of materials, money, technological and product innovation, and government regulation can change rapidly. Inside the organization, employees are changing by bringing higher educational levels, placing greater emphasis on human values, and questioning authority. The composition of the workforce itself is changing in terms of gender and ethnicity. Management, in response to these challenges, introduces change to better position the organization for dealing with issues arising from environmental challenges.

- *Customer service*. Customer service is widely considered to be one of the key areas in which organizations can have a positive and significant impact on customer satisfaction and retention.

- *Financial management*. Financial management-related activities include financial methods, budgets, and audits; financial methods include financial statements, ratio analyses, and break-even analysis. Commonly used financial statements are balance statements, income statements, cash flow, and sources and uses of funds statements. These statements are used by managers to control the organization's activities and by individuals outside the organization to evaluate its effectiveness (Stoner et al. 1994). Financial management is of great importance for the evaluation of organizational effectiveness, and in some organizations, financial management is seen as a catalyst for organizational innovation and entrepreneurial activities including diversification.

- *Marketing*. Marketing is a crucial managerial function within organizations designed to satisfy customer needs and wants through the development of appropriate products and services (Kotler 1997).

## A Model of Managerial Excellence in Global Management: Cross-Cultural Dimensions

A model of managerial excellence for management in a culturally diverse environment has been developed from an extensive survey of the academic literature (Hofstede 1980, 1984, 1991; Adler 1997; Harris & Moran 1991; Deluca & McDowell 1992; Morrison 1992; Rosen & Lovelace 1991; Saee 1998; Saee & Saunders 2000; Cox 1991; Cox & Smolinski 1994; Hayles 1982; O.M.A. & E.M.D. 1994; Karpin 1995; Trompenaars 1993; Trompenaars & Hampden-Turner 1997; Weiss 1996). This new model, shown in Exhibit 15-2, incorporates the indicators of intercultural communication competence for the eleven managerial functions surveyed in the previous section.

| Exhibit 15-2 | Best Practice in Managerial Functions Incorporating Intercultural Communication Competence |
|---|---|
| **Managerial functions** | **Competent managerial practice of each managerial function incorporating intercultural communication competence** |
| **Planning**—setting goals, assigning tasks, and coordinating activities. | • Capitalize on the full range of available resources including cultural diversity in the workplace.<br>• Acknowledge and institutionalize cultural diversity as part of the organization's mainstream processes.<br>• Actively elicit contributions from the culturally diverse workforce for developing, implementing, and evaluating organizational planning processes.<br>• Adjust organizational planning processes to accommodate cultural and linguistic characteristics of the culturally diverse workforce by translating summaries of business plans into major language groups of the workforce. |
| **Workplace communication**—all the means for giving instructions, delegating, sharing information, and so on involving oral, written, nonverbal, and electronic forms. | • Take care to establish and foster elements of trust and open communication with employees on a personal basis.<br>• Be sensitive and adaptable to the cultural and linguistic needs of multicultural employees when communicating with them. |
| **Recruitment/Promotion**—searching for and obtaining potential job candidates in sufficient numbers and quality so the organization can select the most appropriate people to fill its jobs. *Promotion* is defined in terms of recognizing and rewarding staff members who show consistently superior performance in their delegated tasks by higher positions with better pay and working conditions. | • Determine recruitment and promotion requirements for both the short and long term goals of the organization, with specific regard to language and cultural skills.<br>• Ensure that all management policies and practices are impartial/anti-discriminatory and transparent.<br>• Ensure that all interview processes are designed strictly to assess the applicant's qualifications and merit against specific documented job criteria only.<br>• Form interview panels for recruitment/promotion to include representatives of the culturally diverse workforce. |

| Exhibit 15-2 | Best Practice in Managerial Functions Incorporating Intercultural Communication Competence (Continued) |
|---|---|

| **Managerial functions** | **Competent managerial practice of each managerial function incorporating intercultural communication competence** |
|---|---|
| **Induction**—the process by which a new employee is taken into the organization and integrated as quickly and effectively as possible. | • Develop and deliver induction programs in such a way as to explain fully to all new employees, including multicultural employees, the acceptable standards of behavior in the organization and its corporate culture as well as workplace issues including equal employment opportunity principles and occupational health and safety requirements.<br><br>• Assess the effectiveness of existing communication processes for induction to suit the cultural and linguistic needs of the culturally diverse workforce.<br><br>• Conduct induction programs in the language chosen as a working language of a multinational company, and translate induction information into major community languages.<br><br>• Use bilingual staff at group information sessions to relate to multicultural employees with limited competence in the working language of a multinational company.<br><br>• Institute formal processes for feedback from employees including multicultural employees, to management. |
| **Training**—policies to improve current and future employees' performance by increasing, through learning and education, employees' abilities to perform, usually by increasing their skills and knowledge. | • Have a good understanding of and sensitivity to cross-cultural issues and principles and their likely impacts upon training processes.<br><br>• Incorporate flexibly these cross-cultural and linguistic considerations into overall training packages and strategies.<br><br>• Institute formal processes to gain feedback from employees on training effectiveness.<br><br>• Have a strategy and system in the formal processes of the organization for adjusting training programs to better suit culturally diverse employees in the light of employees' feedback.<br><br>• Determine pretraining requirements in spoken and written working language and numeracy of the multinational company.<br><br>• Focus on the development of mutual trust and building interpersonal relationships with culturally diverse employees as part of the aim of the training program. |
| **Supervision**—coordinating, directing, and guiding the efforts of members of the organization to achieve organizational goals. | • Have an understanding of and sensitivity to cross-cultural issues and principles.<br><br>• Demonstrate appropriate spoken and written working language of the multinational company and numeracy skills required to perform supervisory skills.<br><br>• Have a good theoretical and practical knowledge of supervision functions.<br><br>• Create and foster a friendly working environment for staff, where every employee's contribution is valued and recognized. |

| Exhibit 15-2 | Best Practice in Managerial Functions Incorporating Intercultural Communication Competence (Continued) |
|---|---|

| Managerial functions | Competent managerial practice of each managerial function incorporating intercultural communication competence |
|---|---|
| **Industrial relations**—involve managers and employees in discussing conditions of employment in the workplace. This includes, for example, participating on joint consultative committees and voting on enterprise agreements. | • Have an understanding of and sensitivity to cross-cultural issues and principles.<br>• Have a sound theoretical and practical knowledge of managerial functions as well as industrial issues, e.g., EEO and OHS.<br>• Identify and implement training requirements to maximize participation in the industrial relations processes, inclusive of the linguistic and cultural backgrounds of the workforce.<br>• Provide information to the culturally diverse workforce about the main aspects of industrial relations including awards and conditions of employment by translating summaries into community languages.<br>• Consult the culturally diverse workforce by a variety of means of communication particularly through interpersonal relationships. |
| **Change management**—used to develop and implement policies to deal with changing conditions inside and outside the organization. | • Consult widely with the culturally diverse workforce on all aspects of the proposed change so that employees are able to participate and take ownership of the issues involved in introducing the change.<br>• Have knowledge of cross-cultural dimensions and be well equipped with both theoretical and practical knowledge of management of change.<br>• Institute formal processes for feedback from employees on effects of the change. |
| **Customer service**—in a culturally diverse marketplace, the ability of organizations to respond to a greatly increased range of client expectations and demands. | • Identify internal and external resources such as the language and cultural background of the clients and employees (e.g., audit of existing staff language and cultural skills) available within the organization.<br>• Have a good knowledge of cross-cultural issues and principles so that managers can develop culturally sensitive customer services.<br>• Have a theoretical and practical knowledge of customer service.<br>• Commission market research to identify culturally diverse clientele.<br>• Develop formal policy for customer service based on data from market research.<br>• Institute customer service training for staff, especially in cross-cultural communication.<br>• Institute formal processes to evaluate customer service on a regular basis. |

| Exhibit 15-2 | Best Practice in Managerial Functions Incorporating Intercultural Communication Competence (Continued) |
|---|---|
| **Managerial functions** | **Competent managerial practice of each managerial function incorporating intercultural communication competence** |
| **Financial management—**related activities include financial methods, budgets, and audits. These statements are used by managers for controlling the organization's activities and by individuals outside the organization for evaluating its effectiveness. | • Institute formal processes to seek input from a culturally diverse workforce on the determination of and monitoring of financial performance within the organization so that employees are involved in making decisions for the organizational financial plan.<br>• Have a good knowledge of cross-cultural issues and principles relating to contributing to and reporting financial matters.<br>• Have both theoretical and practical knowledge of financial management. |
| **Marketing—**satisfying customer wants and needs through the development of appropriate products and services. | • Identify internal and external resources such as the language and cultural background of clients and employees, e.g., audit of existing staff language and cultural skills in the organization.<br>• Have a good knowledge of cross-cultural issues and principles so that culturally responsive products and services can be developed to meet market demands.<br>• Have both theoretical and practical knowledge of marketing.<br>• Commission market research to identify culturally diverse clientele, and adapt marketing strategies including delivery of marketing messages to better suit the marketing segments.<br>• Use their culturally diverse workforce with linguistic and cultural skills in marketing strategies. |

# A MODEL OF MANAGERIAL EXCELLENCE IN MANAGERIAL FUNCTIONS ACROSS CULTURAL FRONTIERS

To introduce the modalities of best practice in intercultural communication competence and global management within an organization, managers, and particularly senior management teams, need to foster a corporate culture that supports, celebrates, and values cultural diversity. Indeed, corporate culture should include cultural diversity. Once cultural diversity is incorporated as an essential part of the core ethos within an organization, management is then responsible to train the workforce on awareness of cross-cultural dimensions in a systematic and ongoing manner. Naturally, management would need to be trained in developing their own intercultural communication competence according to key attributes of the models illustrated in this chapter. Management policies and practices would also need to be modified in order to integrate all aspects of cross-cultural dimensions. Best practice in management of cultural diversity strategically entails creating and harnessing a corporate culture in a systematic manner that fundamentally values and empowers its culturally diverse workforce in all dimensions of its organizational *modus operandi*. To show how this is achieved, see the model of managerial excellence in global management in Figure 15-1. It shows the inextricable interrelationships between processes involving the intercultural communication competence of managers, a corporate culture sensitive to cultural diversity, and specific managerial functions to produce outcomes of best managerial practice in management of cultural diversity in any organization around the globe.

**Figure 15-1**  A Model of Managerial Excellence in Global Management

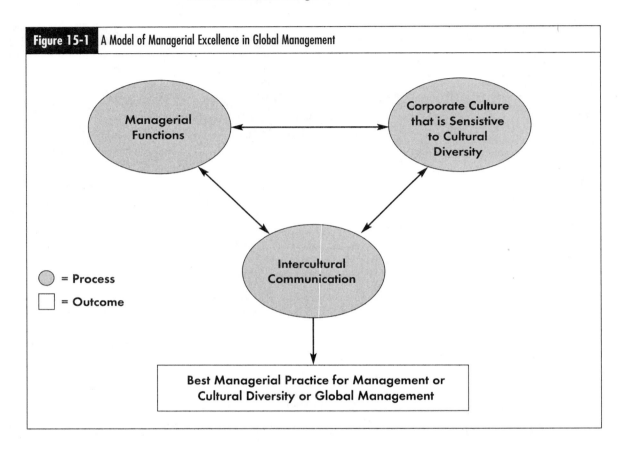

## Summary

Intercultural communication competence incorporating key indicators was set forth in this chapter along with a prescriptive list of readings and strategies. With an understanding of the various models proposed here, managerial excellence in global management can be assessed and obtained for organizations that must utilize their cultural diversity to achieve success. In other words, the organizational—or corporate culture—must mainstream cultural diversity as part of their overall strategic mission regardless of geographic location.

## Critical Discussion Questions

1. Describe key indicators of intercultural communication competence.

2. In what ways is intercultural communication competence important for international project managers?

3. List key indicators of managerial excellence in global management with particular reference to managerial functions.

# Applications

### Experiential

Undertake a study of a multicultural organization or multinational corporation in your home country in terms of management of cultural diversity, and upon completion of your study, compare and contrast your findings against best practices in diversity management as described in this chapter. Present your findings.

### Internet

Read the article on multicultural organizations that emphasize non-hierarchical, decentralized, and flat organizational designs from the following Web site. Then answer these questions.

1. What are the key points raised in this article?

2. In what ways does the article support and/or differ from the modality of managerial excellence in relation to the management of culturally diverse organizations that was developed in this chapter?

http://www.pmaij.com/99_4_4_white.html

# References

Adler, N. (1997). *International dimensions of organizational behavior* (3rd ed.). Cincinnati, OH: South-Western College.

Aitken, T. (1973) *The multinational man: The role of the manager abroad.* New York: Halstead Press.

Bargh, J. (1989). Conditional atomicity. In J. Uleman & J. Bargh (Eds.), *Unintended thought* (pp. 3–51). New York: Guilford.

Basso, K. (1990). To give up on words: Silence in Western Apache culture. In D. Carbaugh (Ed.), *Cultural communication and intercultural contact* (pp. 303–320). Hillsdale, NJ: Lawrence Erlbaum.

Bochner, S. (Ed.) (1981). *The mediating person: Bridges between cultures.* Cambridge, MA: Schenkman.

Bochner, S.A. (1982). The social psychology of cross-cultural relations. In S.A. Bochner (Ed.), *Cultures in contact: Studies in cross-cultural interactions.* Oxford: Pergamon.

Brislin, R. (1981). *Cross-cultural encounters.* Elmsford, NY: Pergamon.

Brislin, R. (1993). *Understanding cultures influence on behavior.* Fort Worth, TX: Harcourt Brace.

Cox, T. (1993). *Cultural diversity in organizations: Theory, research, and practice.* San Francisco: Berrett-Koehler.

Cox, T. & Blake, S. (1991). Managing cultural diversity: implications for organizational competitiveness. *Academy of Management Executive, 5* (3), 45–56.

Cox, T. & Smolinski, C. (1994). Managing diversity and glass ceiling initiatives as national economic imperatives. *Report prepared for the U.S. Department of Labors Class Ceiling Commission.* Washington, DC: U.S. Government Printing Office.

Czinkota, M.R. & Ronkainen, I.A. (1998). *International marketing* (5th ed.). Orlando, FL: Harcourt Brace.

Deluca, J.M. & McDowell, R.N. (1992). Managing diversity: A strategic grassroots approach. In S.E. Jackson (Ed.), *Diversity in the workplace: Human resources initiatives, Society for Industrial and Organizational Psychology—The Professional Practice Series.* New York: Guilford.

Dunford, W.D. (1992). *Organizational behavior.* Reading, MA: Addison-Wesley.

Duran, R.L. (1992). Communicative adaptability: A review of conceptualization and measurement. *Communication Quarterly, 40* (3), 253–268.

Goss, D. (1994). *Principles of human resource management.* New York: Routledge.

Gudykunst, W., Wiseman, R., & Hammer, M. (1977). Determinants of a sojourners attitudinal satisfaction. In R. Ruben (Ed.), *Communication Yearbook 1.* New Brunswick, NJ: Transaction.

Gudykunst, W.B. (1983). Uncertainty reduction and predictability of behavior in low- and high-context cultures: an exploratory study. *Communication Quarterly, 31,* 49–55.

Gudykunst, W.B. (1984). *Communicating with strangers.* New York: McGraw-Hill.

Hall, E.T. (1976). *Beyond culture.* New York: Anchor.

Harris, P. & Moran, R. (1991). *Managing cultural differences* (3rd ed.). Houston, TX: Gulf.

Hayles, R. (1982). Costs and benefits of integrating persons from diverse cultures in organizations. Paper presented at the 20th International Congress of Applied Psychology, Edinburgh, Scotland, July 25–31.

Hofstede, G. (1980). *Cultures consequences: International differences in work related values.* Beverly Hills, CA: Sage.

Hofstede, G. (1991). *Cultures and organizations: Software of the mind.* London: McGraw-Hill.

Irwin, H. (1996). *Communicating with Asia. Understanding people and customs.* Australia: Allen & Unwin.

Irwin, H. & More, E. (1994) *Managing corporate communication.* Sydney: Allen & Unwin.

Ivancevich, J., Olekans, M., & Matteson, M. (1997). *Organizational behavior and management.* Sydney: McGraw-Hill.

Jenner, L. (1994). Diversity management: What does it mean? *Human Resource Focus, 71* (1), 1, 11.

Karpin, D.S. (1995). *Enterprising nation: Report of the industry task force on leadership and management skills* (Vols. 1, 2 & 3). Canberra: Australian Government Printing Services.

Kealey, D. (1990) *Crosscultural effectiveness.* Quebec: CIDA.

Kotler, P. (1997). *Marketing management* (9th ed.). Upper Saddle River, NJ: Prentice Hall.

Langer, E.J. (1989). *Mindfulness.* Reading, MA: Addison-Wesley.

Lustig, M. & Koester, I. (1993). *Intercultural competence: Interpersonal communication across cultures.* New York: Harper Collins.

Lysgaard, S. (1955). Adjustment in a foreign society. *International Social Science, 7* (1), 45–51.

Morris, D. (1994). *Body language: A world guide to gestures.* London: Random House.

Morrison, A. (1992). New solutions to the same old glass ceiling. *Women in Management Review, 7* (4), 15–19.

Morrison, A.M. (1992). *The new leaders: Guidelines on leadership diversity in America.* San Francisco: Jossey-Bass.

Mukhi, S., Hampton, D., & Barnwell, N. (1988). *Australian Management.* Sydney: McGraw-Hill.

Mullins, L.J. (1996). *Management and organizational behavior* (4th ed.). London: Pitman.

Oberg, K. (1960). Cultural shock: adjustments to new cultural environments. *Practical Anthropology, 7,* 177–182.

Office of Multicultural Affairs and EMD Consultants (1994). *Best practice in managing a culturally diverse workplace: A manager's manual prepared for the Office of Multicultural Affairs.* Canberra: Australian Government Printing Services.

Penman, R. (1985). A rejoinder: Interpersonal communication competence in another frame. *Australian Journal of Communication, 8,* 33–35.

Phatak, A.V. (1997). *International management: Concepts and cases.* Cincinnati, OH: South-Western College.

Putnis, P. & Petelin, R. (1996). *Professional communication: Principles and applications.* Sydney: Prentice Hall.

Ricks, D.A. (1993). *Blunders in international business.* Cambridge, MA: Blackwell.

Robbins, S.P. (1991). *Management* (3rd ed.). Englewood Cliffs, NJ: Prentice Hall.

Rosen, B. & Lovelace, K. (1991). Piecing together the diversity puzzle, *HR Magazine, 36* (9), 78–84.

Ruben, B.D. & Kealey, D.J. (1979). Behavioral assessment of communication competency and the prediction of cross–cultural adaptation. *International Journal of Intercultural Relations, 3,* 15–47.

Saee, J. (1993). Culture, multiculturalism and racism: An Australian perspective. *Journal of Home Economics of Australia, 25,* 99–109.

Saee, J. (1998). Intercultural competence: Preparing enterprising managers for the global economy, *Journal of European Business Education, 7* (2), 15–37.

Saee, J. (1998). The nexus between management of cultural diversity and intercultural communication competence: A national study of major national and international organizations based on a multiple case study, Australia.

Saee, J. & Saunders, S. (2000). Intercultural communication competence and managerial functions within the Australian hospitality industry, *Australian Journal of Communication, 27* (1), 111–129.

Samovar, L.A. & Porter, R.E. (1995). *Communication between cultures.* Belmont, CA: Wadsworth.

Schuler, R.S., Dowling, P.J., Smart, J.P., & Huber, V.L. (1992). *Human resource management in Australia* (2nd ed.). Sydney: Harper.

Searle, W. & Ward, C. (1990). The prediction of psychological and sociocultural adjustment during cross-cultural transitions. *International Journal of Intercultural Relations, 14,* 449–464.

Spitzberg, B. & Cupach, W. (1984). *Interpersonal communication competence.* Beverly Hills, CA: Sage.

Spitzberg, B. & Cupach, W. (1989). *Handbook of interpersonal communication research.* New York: Springer.

Stoner, J.F., Yetton, P.W., & Johnston, K.D. (1994). *Management* (2nd ed.). Sydney: Prentice Hall.

Thayer, L. (1990). Corporate communication: Some thoughts on how to think about what needs thinking about. *Australian Journal of Communication, 17* (2), 28–36.

Thomas, R.R. (1994). From affirmative action to affirming diversity. in R.R. Thomas (Ed.), *Differences that work: Organizational excellence through diversity.* Boston: Harvard Business Review Book.

Timm, P. (1980). *Managerial communication: A finger on the pulse.* Englewood Cliffs, New Jersey: Prentice Hall.

Trompenaars, F. (1993). *Riding the waves of culture: Understanding cultural diversity in business.* London: Nicholas Brealey.

Trompenaars, F. & Hampden–Turner, C. (1997). *Riding the waves of culture: Understanding cultural diversity in business* (2nd ed.). New York: McGraw-Hill.

Ward, C. & Kennedy, A. (1996). Crossing cultures: The relationship between psychological and socio-cultural dimensions of cross-cultural adjustment. In J. Pandley, D. Sinha, & D.P.S. Bhawuk (Eds.), *Asian contributions to cross–cultural psychology*. New Delhi: Sage.

Weiss, J. (1996). *Organizational behavior and change: Managing diversity, cross–cultural dynamics, and ethics*. West Publishing Company, USA.

Wiseman, R. & Koester, I. (1993). *Intercultural communication competence*. Newbury Park, CA: Sage.

# Index

## A

Absolute Advantage
Theory of  6

Abundant factor  7

Acculturation  45

Achievement Motivation Theory
McClelland's  179

Acquired advantage  7

Activity, doing or being  30

Adaptability  117
of family  243

Adaptation  129

African cultures  32

Age of mercantilism  6

Agreement  196

Alliances  11

Allocation  12

Amae  146

Analogic code  126

Anglo theories  176
applying  176

Antecedent conditions  207

Anxiety  119

Asia  169

Asian Tiger, economies  20

Availability of information  10

## B

Barter system  3

Behavior  30

Behavioral dimensions  87

Behavioral Theory of Leadership  165

Being cultures  30

Best practice  274
a model of  275
managerial functions  278

Big picture  52

Bioinvasion  19

Bipolar opposites  123

Boycotts  19

Bribery  224

Buddhism
business implications  62
major concepts  61

Business ethics  219
defined  222
ethical dilemmas  224
ethical versus legal behavior  222
global markets  223
learned  220
moral philosophy and their relevance to  221
why needed  223

## C

Capital mobility  12

Catalysts for globalization  11

Categorization  121

Chicago School  12

Chinese value survey  36

Christianity  55
business implications  56
major concepts  55
religious groups  56
Eastern Orthodox  56
Indigenous Christians  56
Protestant  56
Roman Catholic  56

Clarifying  112